MW01029519

# *Unending Recovery*

## A FRESH LOOK AT THE ECONOMIC CRISIS, NEGLECTED ISSUES, REAL SOLUTIONS

*Nicholas Samuel PhD*

Copyright © 2014 **Authored By Nicholas Samuel PhD**
All rights reserved.
ISBN: 1495308952
ISBN 13: 9781495308956
Library of Congress Control Number: 2014901555
CreateSpace Independent Publishing Platform
North Charleston, South Carolina

I dedicate this book to my son
*Michael Migara Samuel*
whose interest and encouragement
inspired me to persevere.

# ACKNOWLEDGEMENTS

It is not possible to acknowledge everyone who contributed the life-time of learning that this book embodies. A debt of gratitude is owed to those insightful people who designed the mind-opening bachelor's program at the London School of Economics and Political Science and those wonderful professors in the graduate program at Michigan State University. An intellectual debt of gratitude must be noted to the iconic institutional economist, University Distinguished Professor, A. Allan Schmid of MSU, whose tidy mind has greatly benefitted my career as well as the thinking that fashioned vital parts of this book.

My thanks go to friend John Barnes of Surrey in England, short story writer and artist, who I believe must have had to wear his masochistic hat to tackle the several drafts that he persevered through. His initial feedback alerting me to the academic denseness in the text prompted a painstakingly comprehensive revamp, to make the text more readable to a general audience. I appreciate the initiative of John Barnes in exposing the writing in this book to a writer's guild in Britain for valuable feedback on its understandability. The criticism by a minority, that a serious subject was being treated in a "flippant" manner, was noted with satisfaction.

Thanks also to Dr. Frank de Silva, legal scholar, author, and police chief, for taking the time and trouble to comment on several early drafts.

I am also grateful to my former work colleagues, Trevor Berenger and Dr. Ian Dalziell, whose suggestions helped to improve the introductory chapters. Thanks go to my teacher, economist Dr. Annesley Fernando, for his useful comments on an early draft of two chapters and his emphasis on the need for a solution to the identified problem.

Because of my concern for lightened expression, I am grateful to my wife Marini for her feedback on the readability of selected excerpts suspected of academic density.

Thanks go to the helpful professionals at CreateSpace, especially the competent and patient editors, Lois and Laura. Their savvy fine-tuning contributed much to enhancing the final product.

I finally acknowledge my age of seventy-four, to which I owe a somewhat cynical disposition, and the determination to spread my wings and write less boring economics after a lifetime of staid writing for my bread and butter. My uneasy consciousness of Cassandra (from Greek mythology who uttered unheeded prophesies) tempers the devil-may-care attitude in this my last hurrah.

As I have chosen not to adopt many well-meaning suggestions, I absolve everyone but myself for the errors and shortcomings that remain in this book, which I hope are not too many.

S. Nicholas Samuel

*BSc(Economics)Honours London,U.K.; MSc(Agricultural Economics) Michigan, USA; PhD Michigan, USA*

# CONTENTS

Acknowledgements.................................................................................v

INTRODUCTION: VIEWFINDER .........................................1

    1.1 The Real Problem.....................................................................1

        Raise the Curtain ...............................................................1

        Plug a Gap ............................................................................3

    1.2 The Big Picture .......................................................................5

    1.3 The Carnival is Over ...............................................................7

    1.4 Nature and Scope.....................................................................8

THE FAMILIAR AND THE SIMILAR: INEXACT PARALLELS.....11

    2.1 Diagnostic Focus.....................................................................11

    2.2 Business Cycles........................................................................13

    2.3 Superficial Similarities............................................................16

        Familiar Bubbles.................................................................16

        Familiar Culprits.................................................................19

        Familiar Effects...................................................................23

    2.4 So Far in a Nutshell..................................................................24

UNUSUALLY BIG: NOT SO BEAUTIFUL..................................26

    3.1 A Grand Scale...........................................................................26

        The Back Story....................................................................26

        Villains and Victims ...........................................................30

3.2 Perilous Innovativeness ............................................................32

    Bad Government .............................................................................32

    Market Punishment .......................................................................35

3.3 International Contamination .....................................................40

3.4 Extraordinary Corruption .........................................................41

3.5 Conclusion: Destructive Expansiveness ...................................43

A GAME CHANGE: EXCESSIVE CORRUPTION ...........................45

4.1 A Difference of Kind .................................................................45

4.2 A Matter of Ethics ....................................................................48

    Absent Propriety............................................................................48

    Unpleasant Behavior .....................................................................49

    Complicit Players ..........................................................................52

    Unethical Public Policy .................................................................54

    Absent Repentance .......................................................................55

4.3 A Matter of Law........................................................................56

    Game Change ................................................................................56

    Game Players .................................................................................59

4.4 The Law in Action.....................................................................66

    Big is Noticeable ...........................................................................66

    Imperfect Justice...........................................................................67

    Spanking with a Feather ...............................................................70

4.5 Corruption: Summary and Conclusions ...................................72

INSTITUTIONAL FAILURE: THE BOTTOM OF THINGS.............75

5.1 The Apparent Reasons..............................................................75

    Unpicking to Unravel ...................................................................75

    Apparent Culprits..........................................................................77

    Market Charms .............................................................................79

5.2 The Real Reasons .....................................................................84

    Paradox of Freedom......................................................................84

    Fashioned Behavior.......................................................................90

5.3 Private versus Social ................................................................. 96

    The Fundamentals ................................................................. 96

    Good Inequality ..................................................................... 99

    Freedom versus License ...................................................... 101

5.4 Regulations for Congruence ....................................................107

    Understanding Regulation ..................................................107

    Understanding Deregulation ............................................. 110

5.5 Conclusions: Verities and Balderdash ................................... 114

FINANCIAL DEREGULATION: DON'T FENCE ME IN ................ 116

6.1 Regulation Autopsy .................................................................. 116

    Setting the Scene ................................................................. 116

    The Last Big Job ..................................................................120

    Assessing the Handiwork ...................................................127

6.2 The Real Culprits ......................................................................131

6.3 The Root Causes ...................................................................... 133

    The Cultural Element........................................................... 133

    The Pecuniary Element........................................................139

    The Constitutional Element ...............................................142

THE DISCREDITED PROFESSION: COWBOY ECONOMICS .....149

7.1 Rediscovering Economics ........................................................149

7.2 Vulnerable Economics..............................................................155

7.3 Reinvented Economics .............................................................158

7.4 Applied Economics....................................................................165

    A Lead into Temptation ......................................................165

    Quantification ......................................................................166

    Method of Analysis .............................................................171

7.5 Irrelevant Economics ...............................................................172

    New Ball Game......................................................................172

    Obsolete Economics.............................................................175

7.6 Whither Economics?.................................................................177

DEREGULATION FALLOUT: BOOST TO PSEUDO-MARKETS .180

8.1 Pseudo-Market Causes...................................................180

Unleashed Forces ........................................................180

A Larger Creation.......................................................181

A Different Creation ...................................................184

Back to the Future ......................................................190

8.2 The Pseudo-Market Condition ................................ 191

"Future Shock"............................................................ 191

Monopolization...........................................................192

Globalization ..............................................................195

Politicization...............................................................204

Corruption ..................................................................210

8.3 Pseudo-Market Dysfunction...................................214

8.4 Pseudo-Market Momentum ....................................219

Ingredients for Metamorphosis ................................219

Transformation Drivers............................................. 222

Transformation through Consolidation.................... 226

Transformation through Inertia ............................... 235

8.5 Pseudo-Market Re-regulation.................................238

Backtrack.................................................................... 238

Dead Duck..................................................................242

8.6 Conclusions and Implications.................................248

The Changing Big Picture .........................................248

Present Anxieties........................................................249

Unnerving Questions ................................................ 252

PSEUDO-MARKET FALLOUT: STYMIED RECOVERY .............254

9.1 "Butterfly Effect" ...................................................254

9.2 Obstacles to Recovery.............................................256

Market Hindrance......................................................256

Company Hindrance...................................................258

Momentum Hindrance ............................................. 268

Inequality Hindrance ............................................. 270

Perception Hindrance ............................................273

Policy Hindrance ..................................................... 278

9.3 The Mountain to Climb.......................................... 282

THE LONG HAUL: ON BORROWED TIME ..................... 286

10.1 The West or Bust.................................................. 286

10.2 Weakness in Unity ...............................................291

America's Condition ..............................................291

Europe's Condition .............................................. 297

The World's Condition........................................... 303

10.3 The Ordeal of Debt............................................. 307

10.4 Financial Intransigence .......................................311

10.5 Self Perpetuation ............................................... 313

The Doom Loop..................................................... 313

Japan Inc.: Sobering Example ...............................318

10.6 Conclusion: Dark Horizon ................................. 320

POLICY OPTIONS: LET US PRAY ................................323

11.1 Tired Tools..........................................................323

11.2 The Monetary Defense ...................................... 325

Unfamiliar Territory.............................................. 325

Monetary Munificence.......................................... 326

Living Dangerously .............................................. 334

11.3 The Austerity Path ..............................................339

The Personal-Debt Monomania.............................339

The Love of Austerity ........................................... 342

Austerity: Misplaced Affection.............................. 345

11.4 The Government Spending Path ......................... 351

The Love of Government Spending ........................ 351

Government Spending: Misplaced Affection........................355

11.5 Loggerheads and Conundrums.................................................359
11.6 Policy Caricature: Sink or Swim.........................................362
    Taking Stock...............................................................................362
    The Sink Scenarios.................................................................362
    The Swim Scenarios...............................................................365
    Conclusion on Both Scenarios..........................................366
11.7 The Devil and the Deep Blue Sea.......................................366
    Underwhelming Choices......................................................366
    Breaking the Mold...................................................................371
11.8 Conclusion: Policy Obsolescence.......................................373
FUTURE PROSPECTS: NIGHTMARES AND DREAMS.............378
12.1 The Heart of the Matter.........................................................378
12.2 The Ravage of Age...................................................................381
12.3 The Possible Nightmare.........................................................386
    A Dire Unanimity...................................................................386
    Facing Reality...........................................................................390
12.4 The (Not) Impossible Dream................................................392
    Hope Springs Eternal............................................................392
    The Free Market Star.............................................................393
    The Democracy Star...............................................................400
12.5 Conclusion: Conquer Pessimism.........................................404
SUMMARY AND CONCLUSIONS: REACHING FOR THE
STARS.....................................................................................................406
13.1 Something Different..................................................................406
13.2 Facets Fashioning Prediction...............................................410
    Big Picture Components.......................................................410
    Institutional Facet..................................................................411
    Market Facet.............................................................................414
    Business Facet..........................................................................417
    Economic Facet.......................................................................421
    Policy Facet..............................................................................423

13.3 A Prognostication ............................................................... 427

13.4 The Glimmer of Hope........................................................ 437

    The Needed Perception ........................................................ 437

    The Needed Action ............................................................... 439

REFERENCES............................................................................ 444

INDEX ........................................................................................ 450

AUTHOR INFORMATION....................................................... 457

# Chapter 1
## INTRODUCTION: VIEWFINDER

**The moving finger writes; and, having writ,**
**Moves on: nor all thy Piety or Wit**
**Shall lure it back to cancel half a line**
**Nor all the Tears wash out a Word of it.**
*The Rubaiyat* of Omar Khayyam (1048-1131)
Persian philosopher, mathematician, poet, astronomer
(Translated by Edward FitzGerald)

## 1.1 The Real Problem

*Raise the Curtain*

How much of the following can be believed?

Things are looking up, after going so badly wrong. Expectations are rosy because the United States is on a comeback trail, with recovery in the bag. A resurgent America is leading the ailing Western economies out of the woods of a blistering economic recession. With a durable turnaround firmly underway, it is only a matter of time before the American revival, when buttressed by Asian growth, will enable the European economy to rise from the ashes and pull its weight – thereby finally enabling a recovery that is sturdy and widely enjoyed throughout the West.

1

Further descent into a terrifying abyss has been averted in America and Europe by pragmatic policy-induced market buoyancy in stocks and housing – smart measures that lift hopes for recovery in the real economy. Prospects are brightened by tax increases and cutbacks in government expenditure for belt-tightening austerity, along with cheap and easy loans for businesses and consumers. Such a winning policy concoction has coaxed hopeful stirrings in the real economy; formerly listless businesses are now rising from the doldrums and unleashing investment for pepping up economies toward their former glory.

The unfortunate circumstances that brought Western economies to their knees were allegedly caused by bankers and others of their type, whose greedy dispositions are said to have gone from bad to worse. The good news is that these wrongdoers, having repented and reformed, are now doing the right thing. With financiers demanding balance-sheet discipline in increasingly "financialized" economies, how can things go wrong? The American economy is beginning to regain its swagger – a comforting development that suggests that the West's brightest days still lie ahead. All of this nourishes a hopeful future for everybody.

Is there really hope? While some may recognize a ring of truth in the above cheery statements, others may see a strawman. Those aware of the speciousness of the message would likely regard the promise of good times rolling again soon as overblown – even as a setup for a bad joke. Persons who can read the conflicting signs in telltale fundamentals would be able to see the difference between the uptrend of an ingrained recovery and stimulated upticks with shallow roots. The latter may only be delusive interludes because of fundamental imbalances and underlying market mutations that have moved the economy into unknown territory. If so, the condition behind the headlines would tend to instill more a sense of uneasy disquiet than blossoming optimism, as concern for the future takes hold among those who see plenty to fret about in the hidden reality behind the curtain of spin.

*Plug a Gap*

This book is written with the objective of better explaining something that does not seem to be going away fast enough; is deceiving many with false dawns; and can, at any time, take a turn for the worse. Getting to the bottom of things requires identifying the right questions in the first place and then framing them in broad terms to see the much-needed, and hitherto elusive, big picture; understanding a multifaceted phenomenon requires a multidimensional approach. While economics is the centerpiece of this narrative, a wide-angled view requires that the scope of the analysis be extended beyond the keystone of economics to the financial, the business, the psychological, and the political-legal. This enables a synthesized perspective that is unrestricted by artificial disciplinary boundaries.

This book ambitiously attempts to fulfill the unmet need for a comprehensive analysis of the global economic downturn, by providing an integrated perspective. The exercise is based on the belief that a panoptic analysis, that crosses disciplinary boundaries, offers the best chance of setting the record straight, and laying one's finger on what the future may have in store for us all.

This time round, Western economies are not just on the ropes. They seem to be down and at risk of being out for the count. The Keynesian "animal spirits," that should have enabled economies to get back on their feet by now, seem extinguished. Many less-than happy anniversaries of the collapse are in prospect as the current piece of theater ceases to follow a familiar script. Taking a good look behind the curtain reveals an economic condition in the West that has lost its shine and is, in fact, darkly uncanny.

Waxing lyrical about a recovery ignores its exclusive nature, its shallow roots, and the European albatross. It is understandable if the proclaimed recovery continues to feel like recession for the weary majority in America and Europe, for whom the fog of recession has yet to lift. A recovery that bypasses the majority, including much of the middle class who are the backbone of the economy, is an uninviting prospect, since it lacks both robustness and inclusiveness. A recovery that dispatches much of the middle class to join the ranks of the underclass would arguably be unworthy of its name.

Although this downturn is not anywhere as deep as that of the Great Depression, it is, in fact, much worse – and not just because it is more intractable. To offer the explanation of intractability is to beg the question. The prior question is whether the intractability is due to a problem that, although seemingly economic, is something much more than that. Of course, the symptoms are economic: investors are spooked by gloom; consumers are tightfisted; debt has soared to queasy levels; and confidence is sapped by threatening wild cards, both domestic and foreign. But the scale and nature of the recessionary downturn lacks an obvious parallel, giving it a cloak of mystery and making it hard to fathom. The applied economic medications have improved appearances to deceive the trusting but have not had much effect on the underlying malaise – raising the logical and sobering question of whether the treatment suits the ailment. This implies that the dosage could be wrong or that the medication has treated only the symptoms of a deeper and larger problem, one that lacks familiarity and defies diagnosis.

If the problem is misdiagnosis, this book might prove useful in suggesting where to look. More specifically, it will suggest places for policymakers to look where they have not looked before. The competitive capitalist free market has been the vehicle for delivering prosperity that is unprecedented in human history, and must necessarily be the vehicle for delivering future recovery. The central issue is whether the market mechanism that has worked like a charm in the past is up to the job of delivering recovery in the future. This includes the questions of how markets failed and brought about the crisis, why they failed, and what it will take to get them going again. A related matter is why conventional policies have repeatedly proven to be damp squibs, incapable of firing wilting real economies into genuine resurgence. Band-Aid solutions cannot be expected to do more than buy time if the underlying condition is insidiously cancerous. This means that if economies have not been living up to the expectations of policymakers, it is a more a reflection on the policymakers than the economy.

Several unanswered questions remain about the true nature of the current crisis and its future path. Questions that have been swept under the carpet will be retrieved for close examination. Proper answers will require an investigation of fundamentals that reaches deep enough to get to the bottom of things. Only deep-lying explanations can shine a light that is bright enough to penetrate the current murky condition of an "unending recovery." The answers to the following suite of ambitious questions will hopefully adequately fill the bill.

## 1.2 The Big Picture

It takes the right questions to get right answers. No less an eminence than the Greek philosopher Socrates has demonstrated the importance of asking the proper questions for enabling focus in search of truth. The three sets of questions to be presented are prompted by the worrying condition of a Western world hobbled by the weight of an economic burden that does not show convincing signs of lifting. Loitering questions are gathered and presented in the following three-part suite that sets the tone and scope for the rest of this book.

The following questions are not designed for comfort. While we see symptoms of an acute economic crisis and a drawn-out downturn featuring an ambivalent recovery, are we fooling ourselves that is all it is? If it is not a case of history repeating itself with a run-of-the-mill business cycle downswing, can old policy tools work in new misjudged conditions? Will doggedly trudging forward with tired policies, involving borrowing, printing and spending money to stimulate the slumped economy have what it takes to deliver real recovery, or are policymakers unwittingly prescribing palliatives that hamper the desired outcome? Will the pursuit of belt-tightening austerity through cutbacks in government expenditure and raised taxes really prevent the economy from going up the proverbial creek, or facilitate the process? If self-interest-based profit maximization is the driver of the free enterprise system, can bankers and others of their ilk be found at fault for doing what they are there to do? Why find fault with risk-preferring speculator sorts endowed with bullfighter nerves, when they perform the necessary role of bearing risks that the risk-averse fainthearted want to avoid?

The set of questions at the next level goes beyond being uncomfortable to being disturbing, and unravels as follows. If the allegedly greedy bankers were out of bounds, why were they permitted to be so, particularly in so-called democratic societies with supposedly civilized safeguards, including prudential regulation? If business leaders, who are expected to contribute to the public good, instead did bad things, can they be blamed for rational responses to distorted incentives? If political representatives had trouble understanding complex matters like financial deregulation, did they seek the expert advice of economists to preempt socially undesirable outcomes? If they indeed did so, did they get bum steers because the so-called experts, stuck in sub-disciplinary foxholes, were part of the problem?

Next, the questions go beyond being disturbing to being distressing, and are as follows. Why is there disconnect between how businesses are doing and economies are faring, with companies able to thrive within national economies that wilt? Is this peeling away of company profitability from economic recovery symptomatic of a mutation of the capitalist market system into something outside the bounds of economics as we know it? Are policymakers deluding themselves by thinking that the old order is still alive and kicking, when in fact it is dead or going? Are economists failing to get the results they want because of misplaced faith in stale policies that have passed their expiration dates? Does the stubborn economic problem reflect failure in the cherished institutions and foundations of Western civilization, due to the ideological blindness of Western societies and their leaders about plutocracy cross-dressed as democracy?

These far-ranging questions frame the overarching nature of the problem for a new take in a crowded field. The range of assembled issues alerts readers to a collage of perspectives. The merging of several fields of knowledge will better equip the analysis to eschew fantasy and get down to brass tacks. It would shine a brighter light on why the slogans "Global Financial Crisis" and the "Great Recession" might miss the point by the proverbial mile. To view the crisis as a severe business cycle downswing brought about by an acute financial crisis, may not be just narrow, but also shallow. Such a perspective conveniently blocks out unpleasant facts by stopping short of addressing the critically important deeper and broader questions asked earlier. Consequently, it denies the analysis the perceptual depth required to identify deeply ingrained systemic vulnerabilities. Misdiagnosis would derail prognosis.

## 1.3 The Carnival is Over

Darkness settled. Suddenly, in a spectacular flame out, the world's shining examples of free-market capitalism lost their sparkle. The almost-forgotten fairytale was denied its proverbial happy ending when the reality of unyielding market forces kicked in – more specifically, kicked most people in the teeth. The unreal world that promised a golden age of endless prosperity fell apart in grand fashion. The Great Moderation" (the official description label that Ben Bernanke, the former chairman of the Federal Reserve Board, gave to the fairytale condition of tranquil stability before the calm shattered), turned out to be "The Great Bubble" that blew the lid off Western economies when it burst and sent firms reeling, several biting the dust.

The carnival was over in the West. The moment of truth from the burst of this bubble pitched economies into recession, dealt the public a body blow, and revealed the alarming insolvency that meant goodbye to good times. Although the party took place in finance, the hangover continued everywhere in the economy. What started as a meltdown in the United States in 2007 has snowballed and morphed into a persistent, full-blown, global, economic mess of a wrenching nature. The grim reaper of economics has had a prolonged field day inflicting a smorgasbord of damage, including a brutal cull on supposedly reputed businesses and leaving several once-admired societies in reduced circumstances. The trials from the unforgiving elements of the crisis has put a strain on the link between body and soul for many, denied opportunity for much of the middle class, and left a bypassed majority disgruntled on the rack.

## 1.4 Nature and Scope

What's on offer? Although the dismal science of economics (the mother discipline with a glum Malthusian streak) does not readily lend itself to lightened expression and breezy fluency, an adventurous move in that direction will be attempted all the same – encouraged by its yawn-discouraging potential.

Because there is no sense in writing what others have before, this book seeks originality in more ways than one. For one thing, originality is sought by using old knowledge as a basis for developing new insights; the new insights come from using neglected information to fill gaps in the currently disjointed narrative on the economic crisis. For another, originality is sought by capturing synergistic upshots from juxtaposing ideas in arguments being haphazardly tossed about in the public domain. Moreover, the overall intention is to provide a wide-ranging narrative to ensure that nothing relevant is too remote to the topic in hand. Such comprehensiveness is considered unprecedented enough to qualify as something original.

While acknowledging some hesitancy in staking a claim to being avant-garde, this book seeks differentiation by occupying the lonesome middle ground that is a veritable "no man's land" between the journalistic and the academic (at the acknowledged risk of falling between two stools). This chance is taken with a view to benefitting from the strengths of both: readability from a friendly idiom and rigor from logical reasoning, respectively.

It is a non-academic book that nevertheless strives to retain the controlling scholarly influences of logicality, factuality, and objectivity. It seeks simplicity without being superficial and precision without being boxed-in by the boring but necessary stringencies of academia. Also, academic writing tends to focus on the trees, whereas the intention here is to reveal as much of the forest as possible. This means that the picture painted will require a big canvas and bold brushwork.

The central idea is to reduce the daylight between myth and reality. While common myths could reflect superficial perceptions, inertia in thinking can tend to draw inexact parallels that stop short of dovetailing underpinning *causes* that are hidden with economic *symptoms* that are evident. Better defining reality, by making the connection between symptoms and causes, is expected to show that the remedies needed for solving the current economic problem go beyond standard economics, which takes for granted the foundations on which the capitalist market system rests.

The scope is decidedly broad, but not too much at the cost of depth. The tall order is revealed in the suite of questions asked earlier that, when penetrative enough, would make a search for at least some of the answers worthwhile. It is hoped these answers will deliver a comprehensive perspective that encompasses several disciplinary areas but, emphatically, they do not have pretensions of being complete. The wide view adopted would avoid the compartmentalization of analysis by discipline, which is a typical deficiency in the current literature. Consequently, this book will integrate a range of aspects beyond the boundaries of standard economics. This unmet need is the primary motivation for writing it.

**

# *Chapter 2*

# THE FAMILIAR AND THE SIMILAR:

# INEXACT PARALLELS

## 2.1 Diagnostic Focus

A disciplinary perspective typically involves peeping through a hole in the fence for vista without panorama. Similarly, looking at the world economic problem from the narrow standpoint of just economics, or finance, or business, or the political-legal, or the psychological would lack the panorama needed to see the full big picture. Diagnosing the world economic problem in multidimensional terms is thought to be vital for the purpose of better joining the dots and gaining a fuller perspective of what is really an interwoven phenomenon. Regarding the current economic downturn simply – and conveniently – as a recession-related business cycle downswing precipitated by an acute financial crisis, could prove to be way off course. This book is devoted to showing that the seemingly overwhelming sense of déjà-vu is misplaced; this recession is no straightforward throwback. Although the symptoms are economic, the solution seems to need remedies that go well beyond economic orthodoxy. Surprisingly, many economists have tended to soar above the very matters that warrant their attention in this crisis; a truncated perspective has prevented many of them from spotting the precipice.

Psychologists accept that there is a human tendency to prefer the known to the unknown in what is termed a "comfort zone"–a state in which human beings have less risk from the unknown (White 2009). This implies an instinctive aversion to novelty. Persons who operate within the mental boundaries of a comfort zone are better able to cope with anxiety-causing situations and have less cause to be nervous. Consequently, it is understandable if people want to believe in the illusion of a common or garden-variety economic downturn (that is, a downturn like previous ones). A sense of déjà-vu is comforting when trepidation is outweighed by predictability. There would be comfort in the one-dimensional belief that the current downturn will recover within a relevant and finite time frame, implying an expectation that the West's brightest days still lie ahead. Such a belief places analysts, policymakers, investors, and consumers, in the comfort zone of known territory, providing consolation that the recession is reassuringly run-of-the-mill. There is less cause to be troubled because a traditional recession is the devil you know, and it is more easily dealt with by using policy tools that are also the devils you know.

Because of their nature, comfort zones preclude thinking outside the box; they could prevent policymakers from stepping out to look for solutions where they have not looked before. Comfort zones can be dangerously unreliable because they can have a loose connection with reality; according to psychologists, the sense of security provided by comfort zones is unfounded (White 2009). The relevant interpretation is that there is no security in familiarity when conditions are different, such as when a recession is freakish. This means that a comfort zone can make policymakers prone to blunders. More specifically, because of comfort zone temptations, there exists a real risk of drawing false comfort from the ostensible similarities between the current and previous downturns. It will be shown later that the parallels between the current and previous recessions are inexact and that policymakers, like high rollers, face high penalties for errors when taking elevated risks based on mistaken expectations.

The illusory domain of cloud-cuckoo-land becomes a place of refuge when the other place is scary. An unknown territory, the "other place," can, understandably, be a place of hand-wringing discomfort. An economic downturn of a radically different character would tend to push analysts, forecasters, and policymakers outside the mental boundaries of their comfort zones and into unknown territory. Hence, the unfolding analysis in this book is bound to instill some uneasiness in those seeking mental comfort from predictable outcomes.

Misunderstanding the crisis would get in the way of real solutions and lead to policies that make things worse, as seems to be happening. Casting around for policy solutions within the artificial confines of a comfort zone, in the belief that what exists is a run-of-the-mill downturn, does not bode well for adopting realistic solutions for a durable recovery that is sturdy and across-the-board. The comfort zone syndrome that prevents decision makers from thinking outside the box will likely cause them to be tethered to stale policy. Outmoded approaches tend to become the order of the day, with central bankers, for example, being prepared to bet the ranch on a traditional recession (that comes with an assured upswing). Accordingly, they seek comfort in the familiarity of rising stock and housing prices, though frothy they may be.

## 2.2 Business Cycles

For those who know, the specter of recession has a record of making unwelcome appearances due to the inevitable phenomenon of business cycles. Business cycles, which cause the economy to alternate between good times and bad, are nothing new; downswings have turned up like influenza to inflict periodic suffering at least since the beginning of free-market capitalism. Considered an extinct species during the pre-crisis Eldorado period of the "The Great Moderation," many see in this downturn the reincarnation of a business cycle downswing. If so, that is splendid news, as it will give the present suffering a comforting run-of-the-mill status. It soothingly means that a restorative upswing of the business cycle is just a matter of time.

While not completely understood – and even linked to sun spots in the past – business cycles can probably be attributed to a collision of random factors, with easy money for financial promiscuity being a central culprit. As analysts know, business cycles cause the economy to rise and fall with periods of economic contraction (busts – recessions with negative growth and high unemployment) followed by rather self-correcting periods of economic expansions (booms – prosperity with high growth and low unemployment). Going by past recessions, there is, like a person struck by influenza, a natural recuperative tendency in economies that are subject to traditional business cycle downswings.

Readers' stomachs may sink at the boring statistics that chronicle the occurrence of past recessionary downturns, but only if they ignore their enlightening benefit. Delving into the past reveals that since 1894 America has encountered thirty-two boom and bust cycles, according to the US National Bureau of Economic Research (2007). There is an average of seventeen months of contractions as the cycle swings down, followed by thirty-eight months of expansions as the cycle swings back up again. The downswings since the bitter experience of the Great Depression, besides the one that started in the United States in December 2007, were in 1949, 1954, 1974, 1981-82, and 1990-91. A downswing in the business cycle that is associated with six months of negative growth is generally accepted as defining a "recession." If a recession is a hole, The Great Depression of the 1930s was an abyss, in a class by itself and a once-in-a-blue-moon occurrence. At its nadir, the American gross domestic product (GDP) fell three times further than it did in 2007-08, the stock market fell 90 percent, unemployment reached 25 percent (about the level presently experienced in Greece and Spain), and half the country's twenty-four thousand banks failed.

As is generally known, business cycles of the past featured the predictability of sequential up-and-down movements –what went down tended to bounce back up. Therefore, if a business cycle swings down and stays down indefinitely, that would be rather odd, and even worrisome. The current downturn, triggered by the recession of 2007-08, is stuck in an "unending recovery." It has lasted over three times longer than the average and is expected to last very much longer. In the event that the supposed business cycle fails to swing back up in the near future, the question becomes whether it is a real business cycle at all. Trying to get to the bottom of this peculiarity – the possibility that the current downturn is associated with a business cycle downswing of indeterminate duration – is central to the analysis in this book.

Challenging commonplace beliefs is a rather foolhardy thing to do – unless one has pretty good grounds. The commonly held view is that the current downturn is severe in scale but unexceptional in type; although serious, it is regarded as a run-of-the-mill business cycle downswing that is bound to swing back up in response to usual policy measures. This view will be disputed in the following analysis. Some key features of the recession and its sluggish aftermath are historically familiar and some other ones are not. Therefore, it is easy to misread the situation. Cutting through the clutter will enable attention to be focused on the mix of unparalleled factors of an extraordinary nature that qualify the current economic downturn to be in a class by itself. The analysis will start by questioning the sanguine, if not lazy, view that this is a normal downturn when, in fact, it might not be so.

## 2.3 Superficial Similarities

*Familiar Bubbles*

By and large, this downturn does indeed have some features that bear a resemblance to previous recessions. These elements are obvious, and it is understandable that many should see shades of past downturns in current downbeat conditions. Bubbles arise when cheap and easy loans are used for purchasing existing assets like stocks and houses, rather than new assets, thereby inflating prices of existing assets to phony heights. The fun ended and things turned nasty with the burst of primary bubbles in housing and stocks. The pivotal housing bubble was the first to pop (with a bang), shattering illusions and sparking devastating reverberations, as its effects washed through the world economy.

As before, rising bubbles seemingly held the fascination for investors that Aladdin's cave has for children. Like on all previous occasions, the slump was preceded by eerily similar speculative bubbles that enabled happy-go-lucky investors to walk on air. Investors, imbued with a concoction comprising overconfidence (the result of by high-decibel bangs for the buck), spurious extrapolation, and preference for the usual, exhibited lax discretion in playing the market. Culturally driven by a belief in lucky strikes, investors displayed an antecedent mixture of gullible optimism and exuberant expectation. Although it was nice while it lasted, in retrospect the investment climate seems to have radiated the aura associated with Nigerian double-your-money scams.

Why did seasoned investors have little understanding of their portfolios and brainy people make calamitous mistakes? The short answer is they were hoodwinked by those whom they trusted. Unlike past embarrassments, on this occasion the embrace of risk by speculators was due more to ignorance (being fooled) than greed (foolishness), as explained in chapter 4. They were misled, not only by banks and ratings agencies, but also by finance economists, regulators, and relevant media. The chain reaction from such investor behavior drove the prices of assets to artificial levels because of overshoot. For those who know, artificial price levels are reached when the price paid for an asset by investors becomes too high in relation to its actual earning capacity. (Who would want to buy a factory at a price that exceeds its discounted earning capacity over its lifespan?) Amazingly, this elementary principle was ignored, not just by investors, but even by professionals who should have known better.

Because perkiness in prices is driven by human psychology, it is susceptible to hysterical behavior. Like before, the current slump was preceded by an investor party based on the belief that it was possible to "forever blow pretty bubbles in the air," quite forgetting the second part of the Tin Pan Alley song of 1918 that they also "fade and die." Although the party was in housing and stocks, the hangover was everywhere. Easy money and double-digit returns over several years encouraged speculation with abandon. Investors forgot that "if it's easy it must be fishy"; exhilarated by lavish returns they were oblivious to any fishy assault on their olfactory faculties. The investor belief in money for jam implicitly disavowed the Judeo-Christian ethic of "an honest penny" (associated with the travails of honest hard work), in favor of the "bread of idleness" (associated with money for old rope).

Investors were comforted by deceptively consoling theories from the special tribe of so-called finance economists, whose spurious rationalization of the situation obscured risk and fuelled a fanciful exuberance. Their theories peddled the illusion that markets were always right and investing was comparable to shooting fish in a barrel (see chapter 8 on "Cowboy Economics"). Reasoned calculation took a back seat when investor expectations blithely shifted from confidence to cockiness. Many investors borrowed in money markets to buy longer-dated, higher-yielding, securities the mere holding of which would rake in the lucre – or so they thought. Money from banks to investors went more into speculation than into normal business investment, such as factory construction and equipment purchase. Borrowing was the primary means of funding the speculation binge that characterized the times, facilitated by bankers at the ready to dish out loans to embellish their balance sheets.

In addition, as is common knowledge, consumers inclined to riotous living were able to flash the cash and have a ball. Money seemed to be no object as consumer private debt fostered a spending binge on conspicuous consumption, motivated by interpersonal social competition for "Putting on the Ritz": consumers who wanted to engage in their passion for fashion kicked up their heels and whooped it up; shopaholics had a field day and kept up with the Joneses with a vengeance; the deluded poor with expensive tastes were able to fleetingly experience the finer things in life in high-end shopping malls. Flexible friendships with credit cards were all the rage, with an average of over 1.5 credit cards for each man, woman and child in the United States. Influenced by the property gambling mania, that is part and parcel of Western culture, consumers wanting to live-it-up got ready money by treating their homes – whose values were artificially inflated – like ATMs. The additional borrowing took the place of income raises that had failed to come their way. The buoyancy from bubble-based paper wealth in stocks and housing enabled the hoi polloi to float on cloud nine; almost everybody in society never had it so good in recorded human history.

Many of those looking for someone to blame for the financial collapse finger central bankers. They were accused of ignoring flashing warning signs by being asleep at the wheel. The Federal Reserve Board stood by and did nothing of significance, blinkered by economic theories that were deceptively comforting. In the twenty-five years before the plunge of 2007, US stock prices increased over 1000 percent, company earnings by some 300 percent, economic (GDP) growth by less than 100 percent, and household incomes by less than 50 percent. These inconsistencies imply the existence of a stock market bubble, which was no doubt seen but not much noticed. Between 2002 and 2007, a fevered Dow Jones Stock Market Index rose by about a third and US house prices grew at the extraordinary rate of 11 percent a year. The artificial nature of the house price rises is brought into sharp relief when juxtaposed with average household incomes, which had hardly moved. The house price rises were clearly out of whack in relation to the incomes (i.e., valid purchasing power) needed to afford them.

*Familiar Culprits*

The culprits were dismayingly familiar. Another striking similarity between this economic downturn and previous ones was that most of the same financial miscreants were behind this one. As analysts know, the financial system lies at the heart of the market economy. Money flows are the lifeblood that the financial system is required to pump to places where it is most needed to keep everything in the economy working properly. Banks facilitate the money flow process by acting as intermediaries between savers who have capital to lend and borrowers who want to spend loan money on consumption and investment (including speculation). By facilitating the flow of money, banks play a supportive and systemic role in speeding things up and make things happen in the real economy. Banks thereby provide the financial plumbing for the operation of the real economy. As everyone now knows, this does not mean that things cannot turn grubby; the financial sector has amply demonstrated a knack for unleashing forces that can terrorize the real economy.

As any banker knows, banks are expected to be cautious when it comes to handling other people's money. Money is deposited in a bank in the expectation that it will be kept safe and available to the depositor when needed. It involves a bet that the bank will lend the money to people who will pay it back. Loosely, non-performing loans denote non-performing banks.

Despite such expectation, bankers are known to have a disposition for over-enthusiastic lending. Not much is new about banks, spurred by a spirit of acquisitiveness, lending as much as possible to make as much as possible. Getting people hooked on debt is something to be expected – simply the old Adam in them. Banking shenanigans predate the current crisis; economic history has many examples of bubbles inflated by easy money from banks. The process is enabled by lax monetary policies of complicit central bankers and governments. The government provided deposit insurance scheme, meant to head off liquidity runs by bailing out banks if things go wrong, has increased incentives for a grasping commercialism on the part of banks, by enabling them to shrug off risk. Such public backing for private markets makes it sensible for the banks to be cavalier in their lending; they know they can find protection against losses from lending mistakes by pinning risk on the public purse. Hence, the scheme is a form of protectionism that generates "economic rents" that are profits of a surplus or unearned nature with freebie connotations (see section 8.3).

It's easy; simply create money to make money! As analysts know, the commercial bank's main line of business, besides dealing with deposits and securities, is to sell the product of loans. Loans are regarded as assets, not liabilities; the more credit creation for loan giving the better. Artificial credit expansions (expansions not based on genuine saving) have been responsible for recessions for over 150 years, according to Spanish professor De Soto in his 2010 Hayek Memorial Lecture at the University of London. Fractional Reserve

Banking (FRB) effectively places a money printing press inside banks. FRB refers to the creation of money through book entries on the basis of limited actual money (deposits) banks have in their books or at the central bank. This is tantamount to a license to print money to give out as loans, leading to the inevitability of instability due to the chronic mismatch between assets that banks hold (long-term loans) and their liabilities (short-term deposits). It may be said that the recent type of banking profligacy commenced only as recently as the 1970s –and gone downhill since. Rashness inconsistent with their social responsibilities has caused banks that have gone broke to give a new meaning to the phrase "to break the bank" (although from the banks' standpoint it was a case of "break the government").

As economists know, historically central bankers have been specialists in rearguard action. They have played the limited role of savior, being lenders of last resort to bail out miscreant banks and to create liquidity in times of need. "There have been three great inventions since the beginning of time: fire, the wheel, and central banking" said Will Rogers (1879-1935), quoted in the undergrad's scripture, P.A. Samuelson's *Economics*. Central banks, especially the Federal Reserve Board, have grown over time to become big and burly with widened ambitions, providing succor to the economy by bailing out chunks of Wall Street, making upbeat public pronouncements to keep good news stories coming and the ball rolling, exercising oversight of the financial system, and accumulating a mountainous stockpile of bonds ($4.4 trillion in 2014).

It would seem that central banks have repositioned themselves to stand between the current state of economic torpidity (that is, somewhere between the living and the dead) and the second coming of a debacle (the market's time of judgment). As a result of its expanded role, central banking has come to have a lot in common with the game of chess: what others think they could do might be more important to central bankers than what they themselves might actually do. To manage expectations they engage in a war of nerves with psychological weaponry, their strategies including one-upmanship and mind games with investors and consumers. Doing nothing is far from being inactive. For this reason, they can be "damned if they do and damned if they don't."

It is small wonder, then, that central bankers' errors of both commission and omission made them accomplices in the plunge into the dumps. The central banks most responsible were the Federal Reserve Board, the Bank of England (BOE) and the European Central Bank (ECB). By taking a dangerously narrow view of their responsibilities they blinded themselves to looming imbalances that were the elephant in the room. They failed to take measures to curb the inflating asset bubbles and the first two actually encouraged the process (with dreaded inflation at bay, why spoil it for investors at play?). Central bankers fiddled while "Rome was burning" because implausible economic theories had blinded them to the early-warning smoke.

A stitch in time, in terms of prompt and adequate action then (responding to misbehaving fundamentals), would have saved a lot of trouble now (racing around printing money). All three central banks have acknowledged the error of their ways. They have admitted to being too narrowly focused on monetary matters of inflation and interest rates – a circumscribed perspective that prevented them from spotting the precipice. For instance, Sir Mervyn King, the former governor of the Bank of England has with characteristic understatement admitted that the bank was "too standoffish" in the past on matters of financial stability (Giles 2012). The European Central Bank was the narrowest of the three; it suffered from a bad attack of monetary myopia, being fixated on consumer prices alone (Richter and Whal 2011).

*Familiar Effects*

Easy money opened familiar doors – resulting in historically familiar kicks in the teeth for investors and consumers. As was previously explained, the availability of easy money enabled investors to bet the ranch and consumers to splash out. The wherewithal was there. The availability of credit at abnormally low interest rates, combined with sharp increases in paper wealth from the housing and stock market bubbles, enabled investors and consumers to have a ball.

As everybody knows, consumers who thought they had struck it rich suffered a body blow; bursting bubbles triggered a moment of truth – sudden realization that their pot of gold was a cruel mirage. There was dust and ashes when over one hundred million credit card accounts were closed in America, and a walk in the park for consumers suddenly changed to walking the plank. The consumption splurge of epic proportions had been enabled by a parabolic rise of debt that was based on illusory collateral; funny-money, camouflaged as real money, made householders feel loaded on empty. Their spending of home mortgage loan money resulted in a crushing setback from losing their nest eggs, dispatching many of them to the valley of tears to repent at leisure.

Like before, the recession was triggered when mundane reality kicked in and investor psychology changed because of the Buddhist effect: "enlightenment." Sudden realization that assets were overvalued jolted panic-stricken investors into realizing that they had a tiger by the tail. The desperate dumping of assets disturbed the status quo and triggered panic selling, causing stocks to fall out of bed at fire sale prices – the consequent downward price spirals signaling crashing markets. There was an automatic market correction of investment errors that had driven the prices of houses and shares to well above their discounted earning capacity. It was a case of easy-come-easy-go, as American house prices plummeted by a third and the stock market plunged over 38 percent from its peak in early 2007. There was inevitably bitter mortification and grief from fire and brimstone, as the average net worth of American households fell by 40 percent (from $126,000 in 2007 to $77,000 in 2010) and the average GDP per person fell by 5 percent (some $2,200).

Banks were hoist by their own petard, being unable to live up to community expectations of being "as safe as a bank." They suffered losses on happy-go-lucky real estate loans, misplaced insurance bets, arbitrage gambles gone wrong, and outright fraud that backfired. The devil-may-care business strategy implies that improvident banks were into *hara-kiri*; they created excessive credit, precipitated the recession, and disemboweled themselves in the process.

## 2.4 So Far in a Nutshell

The unmistakable mainstays of past crises were there again: bad politics, bad bank lending, bad central bank policy, and bad individual decisions. These provide ample grounds for lulling people who remembered ephemeral recessions into a false sense of security.

Western economies have been on the ropes in previous recessions, so some family resemblance to them must be acknowledged. As in previous recessions, there was over-investment by dint of a speculation binge as well as profligate spending by exuberant consumers. The ancillary ingredients were similar. There were cloud-cuckoo-land optimism, fairytale asset prices, and Pollyanna borrowings. The allegedly blameworthy were dismayingly familiar. Not much was new about bankers creating money to make money and using the candy of easy money to incentivize investors to blow price bubbles. The effects were the same as before. The current downturn is associated with the usual phenomenon of tumbling prices, triggered by the bursting of the usual bubbles in the pivotal housing and stock markets.

Consequently, the temptation of known territory places policy-makers, investors, analysts and others of their ilk in a comfort zone with of the devil they know. The happenings had enough family resemblance to previous recessionary downturns that those ensconced in their comfort zones could kid themselves into regarding the current downturn as reassuringly run-of-the-mill and, therefore, responsive to conventional, if not hackneyed, policy measures, when such measures might, in fact, be way off beam.

Because of the similar and the familiar, it is easy to misread the situation. Fragmented parallels can cause many to lose the thread of what is an interwoven phenomenon. Tying up loose ends will reveal the mix of unparalleled factors of an extraordinary nature that operate to place the current economic downturn in a class by itself.

The rest of this book explains why the economies in the West will not be going great guns any time soon in the absence of corrective surgery in places where policymakers have not thought to look. The next chapter will question the comfort zone based view that this downturn, although abnormal in scale, is normal in type. The two chapters after that cast further doubt on that sanguine perception.

**

# *Chapter 3*

# UNUSUALLY BIG: NOT SO BEAUTIFUL

## 3.1 A Grand Scale

*The Back Story*

In order to tell the fore story, it is first necessary to understand the back story. By and large, what seems superficially similar is eerily different. The "unending recovery," akin to eternal childhood, is an enigma. It has a hidden message crying out to be fathomed, even as claims of recovery wear thin for many. Protraction crystallizes discontent among those worn down by years of dissatisfaction. Some of it has spilled into the open, in Greece in particular and across Europe in general.

It is true that the current downturn has several features that are similar to those of previous recessions when things came unstuck, but the parallels are inexact. If there is a general sense of crisis gripping the West it would justified by the reality that this is no ordinary downturn associated with traditional sheepishness. At best, the so-called recovery is feeble and faltering, not vigorous and ironclad. In fact, the downswing is alarmingly deeper and dispiritingly longer than previous recessions, with fiendishly abnormal causes to boot (see later). To borrow the words of the English poet, Samuel Johnson (1779), the downturn has diminished "...the gaiety of nations and impoverished the public stock of harmless pleasure" for the majority to an extent not generally thought possible after the traumatic lessons of the Great Depression.

True, time was up for Western economies to suffer the ritual of a normal downswing of the business cycle, but not like this. Had this been a normal downswing, the business cycle would have inflicted its predictable suffering over a period of about two years, and been well into the smiley phase of a recuperative upswing by now. This means that, although it is high time for recovery, nothing worthy of the name is in sight, suggesting that the label is a misleading misnomer. The era of long expansions and mild recessions seem to have gone for good. While everyone would agree that things seem serious, what they may not know is that the condition is much worse than it is made to look.

For those in the know, the current downturn is neither fish nor fowl. It is in a class by itself, as economies keep bumping along off the rails with no bright prospects of a dash to pre-crisis prosperity. Long-term signs are pointing south. Across the rich world, yields on long-term government bonds, a barometer of investors' expectations, have fallen sharply. If we accept that the downturn is a recession-induced slump, it means that the business cycle has swung down wildly, causing the bottom to drop out of Western economies. Several strands of the disaster-sparking business practices of culpable financial institutions did not suddenly arise. They developed cumulatively over time to occasion a confluent combustion – one that has brought about an economic downturn of a dangerously different character with seriously misunderstood causes. The information presented in this book is expected to be compelling enough to show why such expansiveness and longevity combine for a calamitous condition that is as unusual as it is intractable within the current socioeconomic setup. But first, unpicking the dissimilar from the familiar is essential for unmasking the sorry state of affairs in Western economies.

What some economists claimed was a fairy godmother turned out to be the devil in disguise. Finance economists, once regarded as the past masters of financial wizardry were, funnily enough, proactive accomplices in the financial collapse. They believed that stock market trading was something that was cool, calm, and collected, rather than something that was irrationally exuberant and associated with intemperate features, such as impulsive stampedes and bandwagons from hell. This belief underpinned the theories that did much to separate investors from their wealth.

The economic theory holding sway was as speculative as the bubbles it helped create. Finance economists were blinkered by the "efficient market hypothesis" and other wonky conceptions. The "efficient market hypothesis" says that you cannot beat the market; the price of a financial asset reflected all the information available – and so provided optimal estimates of the true investment value of financial assets. This meant that financial markets always got prices right. That hit just the right note with rejoicing investors chasing the pot of gold at the end of the rainbow. Never mind that asset price rises were out of whack with telltale fundamentals on economic health like corporate earnings and GDP growth.

Belief in financial regulation, which waxed with the New Deal safeguards, waned with the newfangled theories of finance economists, who forgot the history of the idea. Cocksure finance economists ruling the roost assured impetuous investors that the extraordinary rises in asset prices were almost surefire investment propositions. This threw dust in the eyes of investors and snake oil on the speculation fire, causing eye-watering folly for investors and provoking the market into acting up. The economic rationalization of finance economists gave the green light for speculation with abandon and made a monkey out of investors because of their monkey-see-monkey-do approach to jumping on the investment bandwagon. It seemed there was no catch – until the burst bubbles cooked investors' goose, punishing them for their misplaced faith in economic voodooism. These aspects are more fully addressed in chapter 7 on "Cowboy Economics."

The economic collapse was no act of God, although anyone who believed that the disaster that came to pass was God's punishment for greed and wickedness can be forgiven for seeing agents of divine wrath (i.e., "fire" and "brimstone") in the bursting housing and stock market bubbles. Easy money opened the door to "the world, the flesh, and the devil," making divine punishment for the wicked (those guilty of the sin of profligacy), a reasonable expectation on the part of true believers. This is understandable, given that this time round the financial environment was exposed to unusual levels of exploitation not seen since the Great Depression. The stealthy erosion of the institutional fabric of laws, regulations, and business ethics introduced to protect the public following the follies of the Great Depression allowed such exploitation. As a result, bankers and others of their ilk were able to rake in hefty profits by shrugging off lines drawn in the sand that they considered bothersome.

Financial deregulation was not done in a fit of pique; it had been long in the making. In America, the government tore a plethora of strips off the fabric of protection over a period of several decades, to increasingly expose the public to banking practices that advantaged banks at the expense of just about everyone else. The fact that this action in finance left the overall economy badly shaken shows that policymakers were acting wildly, unmindful of the broader consequences of their actions (an aspect addressed in chapter 6). Let us note for now that there was a raft of legislative measures by the US Congress in the 1980s that expanded the types of loans that could be given and the discretion for setting interest rates. The legal rollback gradually watered down the need for banking transparency and encouraged secret liens (Simkovic 2011). (A *lien* refers to security offered by a debtor that the bank can take over in the event of default.) The opaque credit environment caused by covert liens permitted debtors – mainly, investment banks – to hide the extent of their leverage (using borrowed money for making banking profits), and make fools out of creditors.

*Villains and Victims*

For the first time since the Great Depression the good turned unusually bad. Banks have historically contributed much to the development of the economy by funding promising opportunities, but this time they turned nasty and did unusual damage. Banks chased high profit targets by living dangerously (that is, by practicing weak risk management). Banks failed to adequately distinguish between risk, which can be assessed, and uncertainty, which cannot. They encouraged investors to use ladles when they should have used bargepoles. Trusting investors were deceived into making risky investments requiring guts that most did not have – although it can be mischievously argued that investors who lacked such endowment needed to be more discerning by asking the right questions. Poor assessment of risk meant that investors were unwittingly shooting wildly; they could not have had much more success than dart-throwing monkeys when it came to picking winning assets.

Bankers, once the pin-up models of the business world, were behind the borrowing that reached extraordinary levels. By recklessly lending money on the flimsy basis of too little capital, banks bet on themselves and lost; in 2007-10 leveraged global banks notched up losses of some two trillion dollars. The elixir of leverage had become toxic in the downturn. Enough banks behaved like bazaar money lenders that the business strategy of the world's second oldest profession (money lending) came to bear some resemblance to that of the first. While the banks were "whited sepulchers" with a virtuous public façade, their actual behavior was contrary to the community image of respectable businesses. In the good old days banks acted according to the expected standards of their profession, guided by a culture that embodied the attributes of solidity, conservativeness, staidness, and social responsibility. This was no longer so. Banks were not above wanting growth at rates that were unbecomingly excessive for banks. They grew rapidly through mergers and takeovers, to reach proportions for ruling the roost as rarely before. They next turned to giving easy consumer loans as an undemanding means of maintaining their growth momentum, causing a tsunami of credit to wash through the economy and leave borrowers out of their depth.

For those who know, advanced economies rise or fall on the fluctuations in consumer spending, because it fuels about two-thirds of the economy (GDP) in advanced economies (70 percent of GDP in America). For most borrowers, playing the ace involved repaying home loans taken at high interest and replacing them with larger loans taken at lower interest, then spending most of the pile on cars, household appliances, clothing, and vacations. Other major sources of consumer finance were through home sales and home equity loans. A sobering statistic is that just before the recession struck in 2007, American household debt exceeded annual disposable income by 27 percent. In contrast, household debt was below such income by 23 percent back in 1990.

Investors lost their shirts; fortunes were lost when investors, unwittingly skating on thin ice, fell through to take a bath when markets plunged. The bursting bubbles left soaked investors staggering with losses that are unlikely to be fondly remembered. The stock market crash of 2008 made over $2 trillion in paper wealth disappear into thin air, providing a dismaying clue as to the amount of private debt that would have been held by those who came a cropper by borrowing to speculate. Stock prices plummeted by over 38 percent from their peak, while house prices fell by a third, leaving sixty-two million Americans with zero or negative net worth.

Speculators were true to type. There was not much unusual about daredevil speculators being caught with chaff, as this has been a standard embarrassment of every economic collapse. But this time there was a difference: the chaff heap was mountainous. Those who borrowed against artificially inflated paper wealth for speculative investment bore the brunt of the losses and suffering. When private debt rises faster than income and finances speculation on asset prices, asset prices skyrocket. The appearance of what seem like pots of gold encourages still more borrowing, giving rise to a vicious upward spiral (Keen 2012). American private debt peaked at 380 percent of GDP in 2008. It is small wonder that the banking system wrote off dud loans worth over $800 billion soon after the collapse.

As a result of the disappointing report card on banking performance, it is understandable if banks underwhelm as beacons of capitalist virtue. Arguably, the banking behavior ended once and for all any remaining image of bankers as the glamour boys and girls of the business world. Playing devil's advocate, it may be claimed that bankers are overly condemned because of a Western cultural prejudice that stems from banking falling outside the bounds of the Judeo-Christian ethic (to be explained in section 5.1); the Bible reports that moneychangers were turned out of the temple – suggestive of ungodliness in banking activities.

## 3.2 Perilous Innovativeness

*Bad Government*

Owning one's own home has been a basic human aspiration from time immemorial. It was not historically unusual for banks to encourage public borrowing for home ownership through mortgages. But this time they got carried away. It marked a new departure for policy because the scale was unprecedented to the point of being obscene. Predation was incentivized for a feeding frenzy, with high risk "subprime borrowers" being subject to vulturous lending arrangements. The US Housing and Community Development Act of 1992 amended the charter of mortgage twins Fannie Mae and Freddie Mac to enable the financing of "affordable housing" for low- to moderate-income families, with built-in targets. This caused the agencies to lend, lend, lend at full tilt. Many prospective home buyers were bluffed into taking out loans they just could not afford. Borrowers were sometimes required to initially pay low interest rates ("teasers rates"), that later rose steeply to more closely reflect the market realities of risk, causing monthly repayments to double and triple. But the lenders were not the only devils in the saga.

Borrowers were not necessarily angels. Deadbeat borrowers, awash with "subprime borrowings" beyond their wildest dreams, laughed all the way to the mortgaged mansions they could never afford. The so-called "liar loans" and "teaser rates" facilitated housing in the suburb of dreamland. Because loans were given with limited documentation and losers were not weeded out, borrowers could get loans by lying about their income ("liar loans"). There would likely also have been predatory borrowing by home buyers, who took advantage of the easy loans at initially low interest rates ("teaser rates"), with no intention of repaying when the required repayments later rose. Many borrowers who got it in the neck simply walked away from their homes. The kindest interpretation is that defaulting borrowers failed to properly assess their own ability to repay the loans taken, for the same reason that lenders failed to stand on ceremony by applying proper procedures.

There was ample cause for celebration because the bowl of cherries was thought to be big enough for both lenders and borrowers.

The implicit collusion from mutual predation enabled both borrowers and lenders to let themselves go with carnival abandon for nights out on the tiles. Mortgage lending and borrowing were considered as safe as houses because of the illusion that the only direction for house prices was up. From a lender's viewpoint, the situation was great for business. It gave the appearance of business strategy brilliance on the part of Fannie Mae and Freddie Mac, whose business performance boasted incredible sales growth, expert business management, and an outstanding altruistic service to the community through housing provision. Their apparent magic formula for business success had the effect of throwing out as irrelevant many of the principles taught in traditional MBA playbooks, or so it seemed at the time.

From the borrower's perspective, low-income mortgagors were able to move into upmarket homes. They could gain wealth from simply being there. And they had an asset they could borrow against for good times in the future.

The two agencies were able to easily meet their politically mandated targets for "affordable housing" through cavalier mortgage lending. They grew rapidly, their business expansion being artificially bolstered by an unfair competitive advantage in the marketplace from their quasi-government status. Central bankers, blinded by dogma like the "efficient market hypothesis," stood by and watched till the housing market crumbled about their ears.

Credible warnings were laughed at, when not ignored, by those wondering what the fuss was all about. The warnings came from foresighted analysts who saw the smoke from heated markets before anyone else did, and stuck their necks out risking ridicule by raising the alarm. The protestations of red flag wavers like Nouriel Roubini, a professor of economics at New York University (Sester and Roubini 2005; Roubini 2006), analysts Wiedemer and Janszen (2006), and Robert Shiller, a professor of economics at Yale University, were ahead of their time. They fell on deaf ears. These and several other analysts who saw a bad thing coming had to plough a lonely furrow in the face of hostility from financially heady onlookers, who ignored them or ridiculed them as queer fish and wet blankets.

The "almost anything goes" free rein given to the twin agencies by the enabling legislation was, contrary to appearances, a form of anti-social deregulation, no different from the deregulation of banks. It was not a case of prudential regulation, but of imprudent regulation. As in the case of the banks, measures that were ostensibly meant to help society did the opposite and inflicted terrible social harm. As explained in chapter 5, this was because the government failed to design regulatory guardrails for Fannie Mae and Freddie Mac that would have enabled them to formulate a business plan capable of reconciling *realistic* (i.e., market-based) company objectives with *genuine* (i.e., market-sustainable) community benefits. Therefore, the community suffering from the toxic operation of the agencies arose, not because of government intervention per se, but because of inappropriate intervention – a government policy that was laughably shortsighted and ill-considered. This was brought home to everyone, including the deluded policymakers who thought their political powers were superior to market forces, when the sacrosanct market forces that were treated with contempt exacted their price. There was the devil to pay.

*Market Punishment*

Failure to treat market sovereignty with respect caused scorned market forces to bring down the spuriously mortgaged house of cards, ending the period of happiness. The fun and games in contrived housing heaven ended when bad news from bad debts came in thick and fast. Reckless lending and greedy borrowing had led to a huge housing bubble, as evidenced by the mismatch between house prices that increased at 11 percent a year and household incomes that barely moved. The burst of the housing bubble showed that the win-win utopia was a cruel hoax. The crash was precipitated by increasing mortgage defaults that drove prices down by a third and resulted in over eleven million homeowners having negative equity in their homes.

The wild ride of a juggernaut had an undignified ending. Lehman Brothers, a sprawling global bank, was regarded as the epitome of successful business management. What makes its collapse so ignominious is that it was the largest bankruptcy in history, surpassing the Enron bankruptcy in 2002. If a venerated giant like Lehman Brothers could fail, any firm can disintegrate. The implosion of Lehman Brothers, despite its desperate attempt to divert attention from its self-inflicted wounds with loud-mouthed defiance, greatly expedited the process of financial collapse already underway, by adding to distrust and multiplying panic.

Lehman Brothers turned to dust because the housing market turned to bust. It was the heavy holding of toxic subprime mortgage-backed securities that caused the Goliath to collapse like a sack of meal in 2008; over ninety-six percent of its balance-sheet was borrowed. Lehman Brothers' chief folly was to acquire five mortgage lenders, two of which were wedded to the deadly practice of dishing out loans without full documentation (giving free rein to "liar loans" and "teaser rates"). During congressional hearings, Luigi Zingales, a professor at the University of Chicago, blamed Lehman Brothers' excessive use of leverage, short-term debt financing, lack of monitoring of markets, and lack of transparency, for its collapse. In sum, it was its outsized bets on real estate that brought the company down; that is, record subprime mortgage defaults by home-owners in dreamland, many of whom did not have a cat in hell's chance of meeting their repayments in the first place.

An offensive Frankenstein subprime mortgage product destroyed its creators in Frankenstein fashion. Securitization fuelled the catastrophic boom in American subprime mortgages. A subprime mortgage-based security is a noxious innovative product put together like Frankenstein's monster: it bundled income streams, such as credit-card debt and car-loan repayments, repackaging them as securities and then selling them on in "tranches" with varying levels of risk. There is nothing wrong with such slicing and dicing if done properly and in a balanced way. The problem was that these securities embodied dodgy mortgages – irresponsible mortgage loans to uncreditworthy house owners. This made the risks unknown and high for trusting investors. Hoodwinked investors, reassured by somnolent credit-ratings, blindly piled into the securities believing them to be virtually risk free. In the end, instead of the component risks compensating each other, they all moved in the same direction. The lopsided weight of the correlated risks upset the apple cart that was the financial system.

To rescue the situation, governments sacrificed principles at the altar of expediency, causing opportunism to hold sway. Caught off balance, desperate governments ideologically committed to capitalist free markets contravened cherished beliefs and took frantic intervention measures that bled them dry. Governments borrowed massively for the purpose of taking over some companies and bailing out others, creating extensive liquidity to stimulate consumer and business expenditures, besides living dangerously by giving blanket guarantees to depositors and creditors. There was cash for trash as governments took over worthless assets. Believers in small government presided over its expansion, to become practitioners of big government. For those with a strong ideological aversion to big government, embracing socialistic pragmatism to avert a meltdown seemed similar to the Incas embracing Christianity to escape the sword of the Spanish conquistador.

In America, the collapsing iconic enterprises that were saved by the bell of corporate welfare handouts included the financial giant Bear Stearns, the auto industry, Citigroup, American International Group (AIG), and Bank of America (which saved Merrill Lynch with a paradoxical death grip). The ugly twins, mortgage giants Freddie Mac and Fannie Mae, incredible as it might seem, ended up being nationalized.

It was catching, although the imitation was hardly flattering. The bailout policy style proved irresistible to copycat European governments that were also heavy on public charity to suddenly lightweight private businesses (although there should be no surprise that the socialistically inclined would socialize risk). European governments compensated domestic banks for losses from foreign misadventures, undertaken mainly in bogusly booming America. Banks such as the German Landesbanken, the Union Bank of Switzerland (UBS) and the Spanish Cajos were propped up with piles of public bailout money from their respective governments. Even staid financial icons of the British Empire, like the Royal Bank of Scotland and Lloyds of London, had their image sullied by being reduced to becoming humbled wards of the British government.

Let's face it; bailouts were anti-free market. Sir Mervyn King of Bank of England fame is reported to have said that if banks are too big to fail, they are too big to exist. But execution was discriminatory on a night of the long knives, although quite why is not clear. Perhaps it was intended to expunge the moral hazard from earlier bailouts. Be that as it may, the government's action to draw the curtain on Lehman Brothers smacked of ruthlessness, given that other no less sinful enterprises had been spared a similar fate. The failure to provide salutary rescue for Lehman Brothers (that is, to single out Lehman

Brothers for bankruptcy) was a puzzling policy inconsistency that gave Lehman Brothers an uncomplimentary prominence. It put the cat among the pigeons and caused financial markets to take fright, particularly in the highly leveraged and shadowy shadow banking sector. Panic-stricken investors scrambled for the exit in a desperate bid to escape the devastating shock waves from the transformation of icon into monster.

The awkward question arises as to what would have happened if all the other iconic mega-firms that were given the "kiss of life" through bailouts were instead given the "kiss of death" inflicted on Lehman Brothers. By propping up companies floored by the crisis, governments prevented the iron rod of market discipline from reigning; markets were prevented from imposing the punishment of pain and accountability on the blameworthy. Although swift bailouts served to staunch the bleeding, it made the suffering caused by bad business mismanagement to fall, not on managers and owners responsible for the bad decisions, but on the community that was the victim in the first place. Some grizzled observers may consider the decision to rescue errant companies, rather than the people who would suffer by their collapse, ripe with symbolism.

The lift provided by the bailouts enabled Wall Street firms to fly relatively unscathed over the turbulence in Main Street. The collapse caused havoc in Main Street when it inflicted a brutal cull that caused many seemingly reputed businesses to die like flies. The double whammy on the public was enabled by a behind-the-scenes connection between business and government that was considered liberty-safeguarding by some but venomous by others. It enabled miscreant enterprises to carry on without too much of a hiccup, while almost everybody else bore the brunt of the collapse.

If governments had played by the usual rules of free market capitalism and allowed these mega firms to meet Lehman's fate, the crash would have been very serious, perhaps triggering a systemic catastrophe, called "meltdown" in common parlance. The counterfactual outcome of how bad a meltdown there might have been without the emergency bailout measures is anybody's guess. The seriousness of the situation would have depended on whether the bailout money was instead shoveled into less glamorous stimulatory activities such as improving schools, providing more college aid, improving highways, restoring parks, giving mortgage relief, providing unemployment benefits, and increasing the number of police officers.

## 3.3 International Contamination

The unprecedented globalization of financial markets made the world an oyster for banks, causing the disastrous effects of the cataclysm in the West to travel swiftly. The fallout cascaded to wash through to far corners of the international economy, precipitating general havoc. America lit the fire, although conditions in Europe were favorable to mutual combustion. Serial crises tripped up America, and then Europe, with tertiary reverberations across the globe. Credit markets were able to grow more rapidly and become more widespread than before, because of the relatively recent phenomena of securitized financial products coupled with greater internationalization of financial institutions. Securitization bonds (unofficially bearing the less flatteringly label "toxic sludge") are recent products that took off in America only in the 1980s and in Europe in the 1990s and so could not have affected previous business cycle downswings as greatly.

Newly established internationalized banking channels operated as sewers to facilitate the transmission of offensive throughput. The years before the financial crisis saw banks sprawl across national borders for a ferocious growth of cross-border activities by banks that knitted together many markets and countries. The US mortgage lenders Fannie Mae and Freddie Mac were able to use the internationalized channels to spread their toxic waste, in the form of souped-up sub-prime mortgage-backed securities, in multi-million dollar bundles throughout the global financial system. Securitization bonds could be widely traded because of the involvement of multiple buyers including globalised banks, investment banks, insurance companies, and even hedge funds, whose business strategy had the effect of taking their worldwide multicultural clients to the cleaners. The widespread distribution of toxic bonds to international markets extended the expansiveness of the damage in an extraordinary manner, contributing to the unusual scale of this downturn and its current stubbornness.

In reflection of the expansiveness of the crisis, inter-bank trading was adversely affected like never before, insidiously undermining recovery. Apart from the physical-geographic aspect – the fact that toxic securitized bonds were virtually everywhere – the intangible, but real, psychological aspect exacerbated the condition. When financial institutions realized that the bonds they held were dangerous, they had an incentive to keep the extent of the vulnerability secret. They were able to do this because most of the toxic bonds were held in covert corners of their balance sheets. No one fully understood what the assets were worth or knew what horrors lurked in the dark corners of vaults. The glue of trust that held the system together was dissolved. Even though financial markets did not get Balkanized as feared, market functioning has been insidiously undermined to this day.

## 3.4 Extraordinary Corruption

Sharp practice was in vogue; as Hollywood is to movies, the finance sector was to malpractice. Playing down and dirty contributed to an economic crisis as never before. Business has always been plagued by corruption, but this time it was different: abusing

41

people's trust went from being the exception to the rule. Scandals came thick and fast, evidencing a degree of corrupt business behavior that was so predominating (i.e., widespread and endemic) that it qualified as a *culture* of corruption. Business culture refers to the way a company usually does things and corruption was the *du jour* of the business world. When market forces transformed finance sector success into scandal, a double whammy was revealed: firms had nicked customers, and done so for profits in worthless wooden nickels.

Many of those who engaged in corrupt practices continue to function as company executives with top banana status. It would take a leap of faith to believe that bananas that were once bent became assuredly straight. The lurking presence in the economic systems of America and Europe of those who contributed to the crises through unethical and illegal behavior, justifies a nagging concern: ailing economies may be vulnerable to continuing bad practice and, perhaps, even another collapse. It is not known to what extent the riot act has been read to the culprits and, if it has, the extent to which the warning has evinced sackcloth and ashes. Crossing the line once with impunity makes it easy to cross the line again, particularly when moral anguish and eating crow are not strong personality traits. This can make qualms about further destabilizing activity of the corrupt sort hard to banish.

The entire following chapter is dedicated to the unedifying aspect of grand corruption. Much of the analysis in the subsequent parts of this book depends on a proper understanding of the nature and scale of corruption, because of its broader and deeper implications for market functionality and economic recovery (to be explained). Let us note, for now, that rampant business corruption with a capital *C* contributed to the scale of the recession, and now contributes to its incorrigible aftermath.

## 3.5 Conclusion: Destructive Expansiveness

It was a humdinger of a recession; the world is hobbled by a deep-seated economic downturn that does not sufficiently lift. With key economies in Europe bumping along the bottom in a seemingly endless manner, there is no telling how long it will last. It will be later shown that a full-fledged American recovery is unlikely in the event of further European collapse. Several records for recessionary downturns have been broken, and the recessionary features of depth, expansiveness, and longevity combine to constitute a quantitative package of a mysterious nature. These unusual features serve to thoroughly distinguish this recession from its post-industrial antecedents.

Recriminating about the past provides a handle on the present. The widespread nature of the economic downturn came about due to the globalized contamination of financial institutions. The damage was spread around by globalized networks that produced over-expanded credit markets, the widespread distribution of toxic bonds, and the bursting of internationalized bubbles in housing and stocks. These have reverberated to rattle markets everywhere to this day and to smother the drivers of recovery: private borrowing, consumer spending, and business investment. The unusual difficulty experienced in getting off the rocks suggests that the conditions are unique and their longer term implications are disquieting. The bailouts repelled turmoil in crisis-racked businesses by causing the public to be menaced by debt. To the extent that bailouts have fostered an entitlement culture, there is a standing invitation to future crises in place. For this reason, those who thought bailouts were a bad idea then would consider them a worse idea now.

False trails from dubious economics led bankers and investors down a garden path to pixie land. Investors who had reached the heights of euphoria through speculative excess found they had a long way to fall. Widespread unethical and illegal behavior facilitated and fostered the scale of the recession and contributed to the excruci-ating aftermath of an "unending recovery." The fact that the policy prescriptions for resurgence are so divergent, despite all hunger-ing after the same non-negotiable end of stirring languid businesses into greater activity, indicates that the problem is complex. It defies understanding because it is one-of-a-kind for reasons to be explained in the rest of this book.

The recovery being experienced is a long way from making the Chinese envious; the drawn-out wimpy recovery shows that there has been a wretched deterioration in the prospects of key economies that play an influential role in determining the state of Western hap-piness. For this reason, the phenomenon easily qualifies as the "Great Recession" resulting from a "Great Financial Crisis"–descriptions that have been legitimized by the former chairman of the Federal Reserve Board, Ben Bernanke.

It is questionable, however, whether even these descriptions are apt, whether they go far enough in accurately describing the parlous state of Western economies. Such epithets do not recog-nize the impairment of underpinning sociopolitical institutions and the uncompetitive nature of market structures in economies. These underlying factors would, because of their concealed nature, make the downturn worse than it appears. The following chapters attempt to set the record straight on whether this freak recession is a land-mark event that marks the end of an era of opportunity and hope for the excluded majority in the West.

\*\*

# Chapter 4

## A GAME CHANGE: EXCESSIVE CORRUPTION

### 4.1 A Difference of Kind

Like the proverbial wolf, the recession was both big *and* bad. The reasons why the current downturn is big were addressed earlier. Such a quantitative difference, the scale of which was shown to put previous recessions in the shade, makes it different enough, but there is more: it is qualitatively different. Hence, apart from the expansiveness and protraction of the current recession that makes the wolf big, the recession is also of a different type that makes the wolf bad. Unscrupulous corporate behavior, besides contributing to the scale of the downturn and its ongoing frailty, painted the phenomenon in unseemly colors, the stigma of corruption giving the downturn a lower tone than usual. A basic rule of economics is broken when businesses prey on customers, instead of satisfying their needs. Given that probity is the mainstay of business success for all enterprises, particularly for those in the finance sector, the inelegant management choices made are hard to understand (but only if we assume that markets were not dysfunctional – see chapter 8 on "Pseudo-markets").

It is not as if corruption was unheard of. In 1864, President Abraham Lincoln expressed fears that corporations enthroned as a result of the civil war would engage in "an era of corruption" that "threatens the Republic," as reported by Wade Rowland in his *Greed, Inc* (Rowland 2012, 105). The 1932 hearings of the Pecora Commission that followed the Great Depression showed that the president's fears were amply warranted when it exposed a litany of untoward business practices associated with that disaster.

It is most unlikely that the scale of corruption leading up to the Great Depression was as widespread or blatant as it was in relation to the current crisis. The corruption associated with the current crisis assumed nightmarish proportions and caught off-guard even those realists who accept the inevitability of some corruption. In relation to the current crisis, it seems corruption was more the rule than the exception – the order of the day. Innovation in Wall Street was focused on circumventing regulations, and the US government's Financial Crisis Inquiry Commission report is painful for what it states about honesty: there was "an erosion of standards of...ethics that exacerbated the financial crisis" (FCIC, 2011). It was a less-than flattering assessment of business practices that characterized the time and came straight from the horse's mouth.

The scourge of corruption was caused by business strategies that were purposefully designed to be more under the counter than above board. Unethical and illegal behavior, both qualifying as corruption and having anti-social connotations, were rampant in the years preceding the recession. The search for ever-increasing profits caused most market players to be in it up to their necks. For others not so immersed, sailing close to the wind was more lucrative than being on the safe side. Fortunes were made by feathering one's nest, with the end justifying the means. Bank employees were central players in the corruption game. For many it would not be surprising that crooks love banks; after all, that is where the money is. Shown subsequently is that the banks were more ostensible than real culprits, and that bankers were to a large extent victims of the system. A breakdown of law and order in the world of business combined with competitive pressures, made corruption a matter more of necessity than choice.

Enron was a pocket-sized version of things to come; the shady business practices exposed by its disintegration in 2001 were a microcosm of the corruption bared some eight years later. Enron was accused of illegal deals, unethical accounting practices, and offshore accounts. The real reasons for its collapse were the attitudes and culture of the management, according to Robert Bryce (Bryce 2002). This "people factor" is most relevant for understanding the corrupt practices associated with the current crisis; there was a replay of Enron writ large. As a harbinger of the devil to pay, Enron was an audible warning shot across the bows; it demonstrated for all to see the price that would have to be paid on wider scale for business environments that are inappropriately deregulated. Chapter 6 explains why Enron's collapse was more than a hint at potential trouble, and why it was ignored at peril by myopic policymakers hell-bent on dismantling financial regulations.

Getting real about the current downturn has required facing unpleasant facts. What made the 2007-08 recession so ingloriously distinctive was an extensive business culture of dishonesty, evidenced by the *prima facie* lack of ethicality and legality characterizing it. Routinely swindling customers and allied corrupt behavior shifted risks away from firms and implied silent subscription to the market slogan *caveat emptor* (let the buyer beware). The fact that transgressions became everyday business practices testify to a failure of basic institutions for law and order in business. It strengthens doubts about whether the current crisis is merely an economic phenomenon and amenable to just economic solutions.

## 4.2 A Matter of Ethics

*Absent Propriety*

Hello? Has anyone heard of something called ethics?

For a business, the "Mr. Nice Guy" image has to be more than a flimsy façade because corporations are susceptible to shaming and ostracism. In competitive environments, business image counts; businesses seek at least the appearance of virtue and respectability. As with ethical companies like Unilever, close attention to social needs yields benefits to the company – meaning that ethical behavior is motivated by a self interest that is enlightened. Understandably, companies want people to have a good impression about their reliability, honesty, and concern for the environment. They may do certain things simply because they are the right thing to do, such as full disclosure about their (financial) product, for example. The requirements that businesses place upon themselves are meant to prevent harm to the community and enable them to exude the warmth of social responsibility. According to the British philosopher Bertrand Russell, ethics involve sacrifices for "cooperation with oneself." This means that business ethics are unwritten moral codes of conduct that place voluntary restraint on the business and govern civil interactions between the business and the public. Lord Moulton's definition that business ethics involve "obedience to the unenforceable" differentiates corruption due to unethical behavior (that sits outside the law) from corruption due to illegal behavior (that is indictable and liable to criminal prosecution).

Power requires responsibility on the lines of *noblesse oblige* (that means, with privilege comes responsibility for moral uprightness). Ethics are now more important than ever before because businesses are more powerful than ever before, especially the big banks. Size scares people. Big businesses tend to have pervasive influence with an upper hand over vast swaths of the general public, particularly those sitting below the salt. Not surprisingly, the very size of big businesses makes it difficult for them to avoid treading on community toes and, by implication, unwittingly impinging on individual human rights. It should be possible to take for granted that bankers and their fellow travelers would be mindful of their social responsibilities, would be cognizant of the principles that differentiate right from wrong, and would adopt business behaviors that conform to accepted standards of decency. In short, bankers are expected to have a mindset that is closer to that of "men of the cloth" than of "women in scarlet."

There was nothing new about the unethical business practices of those banks that were responsible for the financial crisis of 2007-08. The spur of avarice in banks and investors has been an embarrassing feature of past all recessions, as was previously stated. Excessive credit expansion by banks has been associated with bad decisions and concomitant recessions ever since the Industrial Revolution (that gave businesses features that were recognizably capitalist). But this time the scale and nature were significantly different for the reasons explained next.

### Unpleasant Behavior

This time round many banks did something that was, to say the least, a bit much and rather inappropriate. For one thing, the scale of money creation and lending was large to the point of bizarreness, certainly greater than since the Great Depression. For another, they went shady by rapidly expanding the shadow banking system – the banking outside the regulated system, where practices were reckless and contemptuous of niceties. Growth of the shadow banking system outstripped the lit-up counterpart for heightened vulnerability in the financial system.

The shadiness in shadow banking hid from investors the snakes in the grass. Shadow banking enabled banks to exploit loopholes in the regulator's Basel capital requirements and to smuggle in products for swindling investors. (Basel requirements refer to internationally applicable banking laws and regulations issued by the Basel Committee on Banking Supervision, first in 1988, then tightened in 2004 and more times since.) The Basel requirements were designed to ensure that banks had enough capital put aside to protect against risk, to them in particular and to the financial system in general – a tough leverage ratio that is a guardrail for risk taking. Moving assets on to off-balance sheet securitization vehicles in the shadow banking sector meant that shadow banking became shady banking. With the absence of reliable information about debtors' off-balance sheet debts and liabilities (including reliable information on the degree of exposure to toxic radiation from derivatives), it meant the wool could be pulled over investors' eyes.

Investors unwittingly flew blind because of a hazardous disconnect between the bearers of risk and the sources of risk. Risk was hid for profit; creditors were denied the ability to accurately assess the creditworthiness of debtors, and markets were denied the ability to appropriately price the riskiness of investments. An unethical practice that stood out a mile was the habit of many equity analysts in banks to heap praise on dud firms to induce investments in junk stocks. Hapless investors, prevented from knowing the score, were sold a bill of goods. Although making derivative bets against their own clients was legal for banks, it was not a nice thing to do; it was an unethical practice notable for its notoriety.

What took place went beyond aggressive lending to predatory lending. Since there was little or no regulatory policing of shadow banking, the greater scope for adventurism made shadow banking a road to greater riches than conventional banking. Not surprisingly, this enticement caused shadow banking to grow faster than its lit-up counterpart. As a result of the dangerous risks being taken in pursuit of handsome returns, systemic risks developed. Systemic risks are those that that spin-off beyond the particular offending bank to inflict harm on the rest of the financial system – making those engaged in the practice mischief-makers and socially *persona non grata*. Because the Basel requirements were set up to safeguard the overall community interest from possible abuses, deliberately circumventing such requirements did not make a favorable impression.

The bank is no ordinary business. The socially harmful effect of a lack of business ethics is magnified when the business is a bank, and it is magnified further when the bank is a big one. The big banks have a pervasive influence over society, made possible by their market power, political influence, economic ascendancy, and transnational status. Banks, unlike most other businesses, have a special social responsibility to ensure that the fabric of ethical conduct is safeguarded. This is because banks seek profits by using money that people have trustingly left with them for safe-keeping. The Basel capital requirements were prescribed on an international scale because the poor performance of one or a few banks in one country could adversely affect societies in other countries. Thumbing their nose at such international regulations, on top of the other questionable practices mentioned, gave the unethical conduct of errant banks a culpability that is historically notable.

Overall, it seems that the bad banks ruined the reputation of the good; innocent banks were unfairly tarred with the same brush and condemned for the serious mistakes of the villains. There are hundreds of smaller regional banks and a few big banks that could not be held responsible for the financial crisis, but the bad banks were bad on a scale that smeared the whole banking system with the taint of malfeasance.

*Complicit Players*

Breaking bread in unholy alliance transformed game-keepers into poachers. It would be giving the banks too much credit (no pun intended) to think they did all the damage by themselves. Unraveling the fabric of ethics on such a scale would not have been practical without the collusion of relevant stakeholders and ancillary agents. Acting in concert (albeit mostly in "nods and winks" fashion) was necessary for successful engagement in questionable practices on such a sweeping scale.

Directors and shareholders, who are supposed to safeguard the health of corporations, clearly failed in their role as gatekeepers; they failed to protect the interests of clients and customers. This responsibility allegedly took a back seat when they were hauling it in at the expense of clients and customers. Board directors responsible for corporate governance benefited from turning a blind eye to the dangerous risks taken by financial sector firms. This was because the board decided on the benefits for company management, and management decided on the rewards for board members – enabling a mutual back-scratching coziness that failed to do much for the cause of ethics. Shareholders were not much of a safeguard either; they were a happy bunch, automatically bribed into silence by the lavish returns they pocketed.

Where were the finance police? The short answer is that they were in bed with the policed. This unseemly spatial relationship occurred even though accountants, auditors and others, like ratings agencies, need to have a pristine reputation because their business involves selling their reputations. The auditors and accountants tasked with monitoring risk and overseeing corporate behavior were oblivious to considerations of conflicts of interest. They allegedly joined the party under the nose of regulatory officialdom that had gullibly fallen for implausible economic theories and the reporting of the fourth estate.

Not surprisingly, clubiness and opaqueness went together. Arguably, auditors failed in their jobs by not alerting investors to the triple-A ratings given to junk bonds by credit-ratings agencies. These auditors were paid high fees to do their jobs and, astonishingly, owed their jobs to the very companies they were auditing – a hand-in-glove situation that is flagrantly unethical by any measure because of rubber-stamping connotations. Another conspicuous example was the allegation that a well-known accounting firm "window dressed" the accounts of Lehman Brothers to deceive the world.

It was all very legal – only just unethical. The ineffectiveness of accountants and auditors in preventing shenanigans should come as no surprise because their signing off on dubious financial statements is protected by US law. Such legal protection means that a plaintiff cannot sue advisors, like accountants and lawyers, for fraud, unless the plaintiff was a direct client. This created the difficulty of bringing accountants to book for "salting the books" (it enabled accountants and auditors to turn a blind eye to questionable activities such as the fraudulently increased value of an invoice or account, when a beady eye was just the thing). By encouraging rubber-stamping, the legal umbrella can provide cover for careless and unethical conduct – vitiating the bounden duty of accountants and auditors to keep meticulous books. It opens the door for things to happen "accidentally on purpose" (to do things apparently by accident but in fact intentionally). In a nutshell this means that accountants and others of their ilk could get off the hook despite dubious books, because legal blocks prevented the aggrieved and the irate from calling them to account.

Winds of corruption spun a revolving door. The career path taken by some regulators led to the door of the regulated, where entry promised career boosts – and never mind that small matter of ethics. The prospect of financial sector jobs for the regulator

boys and girls made conditions conducive to solicitous conge-
niality between the regulators and the regulated – suggestive of
competitive sycophancy. This friendliness presumably explains
any lackadaisical inclination on the part of regulators toward the
enforcement of regulations (kindly and poetically called "regulatory capture" by economists). In practice this usually meant that
the targets of regulation had a good chance of avoiding regulations
with impunity as long as they did so beneath the radar (that is,
selectively and discreetly).

## Unethical Public Policy

Failure was rewarded; bailouts signaled that it was good to be bad.
The rescue money bought miscreants a free pass, while the victims
were left to pick up the pieces. Bailouts funneled money to the tune
of many billions from taxpayers to big business, and placed the latter
in the privileged position of "heads-I-win-tails-you-lose." From the
standpoint of some, this was liberty-safeguarding: it saved capitalism and the free market. For others, it was outrageous: the transfer of
funds from the innocent to the guilty rewarded the guilty despite the
harm they had inflicted upon the innocent. For those who shared in
the national anguish, bailouts were a demonstration of distributional
injustice.

The idea was not altogether diabolical; the saving grace was that
the blameworthy were given money in the expectation that the innocent would somehow be indirectly protected. According to the New
York based think tank, *ProPublica,* bailout payments to banks and
other financial institutions has made up some 41 percent of the total
outflow of US bailout money. In biblical beggar Lazarus manner, the
public dished out loaves to reward "rich man" wrongdoers hoping to
be saved in return through trickle-down crumbs from the rich man's
table.

The bailout money paid to firms that got it wrong has created a moral hazard. By rewarding firms that made bad decisions, it has reduced the incentive for firms to make good ones. All large-enough firms are encouraged to be careless about their decisions because they could find safety in the arms of the state if things misfired; governments could be expected to step in to save their bacon on account of their "too big to fail" status. To the extent that firms lost money in the collapse they had gained from corrupt practice, bailout money had the effect of compensating such firms for the loss of tainted money they did not deserve to have in the first place. Arguably, what transpires is a case of government-sanctioned money laundering, with good taxpayer money having the effect of legitimizing ill-gotten gains. One thing is clear when it comes to absent ethics: the bailouts take the cake.

*Absent Repentance*

Denial of wrongdoing might be seen by some as an absence of sackcloth and ashes. The limited evidence available does not indicate that any of those who practiced unethical behavior rushed to their priests for confessions. Why would anybody, when they are in a state of denial and do not recognize the error of their ways? Healing and reformed behavior are unlikely unless the miscreants come clean by contritely acknowledging wrongdoing, combined with a sincere intent not to travel down that path again. The fact is that sorrow and apology have been as scarce as hen's teeth. If one believes that reform cannot be expected in the absence of an acknowledgement of wrongdoing, hopes for improved ethical conduct are not bright if the example of the chairman of bankrupted Lehman Brothers, Richard Fuld, is in any way typical. When he appeared before the US Congress he did not, despite telling evidence, acknowledge any unethical behavior. He attributed everything to bad luck, bad judgments, and bad competitors who, among other things, allegedly spread malicious rumors. In particular, he did not make a point of acknowledging that there was anything wrong in receiving payments totaling $500 million over eight years while steering the company toward the largest bankruptcy in history.

The reality needs to be faced that the denial of wrongdoing is an impediment to atonement and reconciliation. A bigger worry is that the absence of repentance and reformation makes the future vulnerable to recurrent unethical conduct, perhaps even another financial collapse. It will be shown in chapter 8 that the absence of business ethics contributes to the existence of manipulative plutocratic pseudo-markets and their continuing advancement in the economy.

## 4.3 A Matter of Law

*Game Change*

Diehard speculators are investors on steroids, and there is nothing illegal or unprecedented about them causing recession-sparking price bubbles. Recessions will not be recessions without systemic miscalculations by starry-eyed optimists. Deluded investors, driven by a herd mentality and unabashedly seeking easy money by riding rising price bubbles, have been an emblematic embarrassment of all previous recessions. But there is nothing necessarily bad about the role of such speculators, which is integral to capitalist markets. In fine tradition, daredevil speculators perform the class act of bearing risks that timorous market participants want to elude by, for example, buying up risky stock that panicky sellers cannot off-load fast enough. Four years of double-digit returns had reduced the uncertainty associated with speculative behavior, causing it to thrive. The burst of the bubble, the moment of truth, was the penalty for investor misjudgment. But it was not misjudgment of the usual sort.

This time there was a game change. Investor *delusion* was a major cause of previous crashes, whereas investor *deception* was conspicuous in this one. Investor errors were due more to ignorance (being misinformed about risk) than to greed (knowingly taking on excessive risk). In other words, because bad investment decisions were based more on misinformation than on misjudgment, the embrace of excessive risk was due more to being fooled than to being foolish. According to Robert Muellor, the former director of the US Federal Bureau of Investigations (FBI), there was a "clear lack of integrity in the marketplace," including the "tricking" of home owners. He notes that while there have been bad business judgments in the past, today's financial crimes involve activities "that once would have been unthinkable" (Muellor 2009). Several players joined in the alleged "tricking" of investors, as will soon be apparent.

In-keeping with the spirit of the times, financial sector firms resorted to a smorgasbord of artful business practices that meant putting one over on customers was all in a day's work. The creative range of objectionable products and practices ensured that there was plenty to go around, with something bad available for everybody. Corruption was not due to the furtive activities of rogue individuals, but due to deep failings from a culture of rule-breaking and loop-hole seeking. That made playing fast and loose with the facts standard practice for many, as reported by the Financial Crisis Inquiry Commission (FCIC, 2011), as well as by Wall Street insiders Mike Mayo (Mayo, 2011) and William Harrington (*Market Watch*, 2012). Practices in the form of misinformation, withheld information, falsified documentation, and breaches of trust, enabled gushing profitability for perpetrators. The hedge fund managers demonstrated remarkable creativity in dreaming up ways to hide information on the lurking horrors in what their clients were buying.

Bum steers were a weak basis for market functionality; they prevented markets from working properly, contributing to the existence of pseudo markets (see chapter 8). What happened to the idea of open competitive markets, with all pertinent information in the public domain, and customers and competitors in command of such information for rational decision-making? Conspicuous by its absence was full and accurate market information, equally available to all market participants. The absence of such transparency meant there could not be market efficiency, including adequate assessment of investment risk – implying that hapless investors unwittingly flew blind.

Information manipulation cannot be good for market functionality. Since withholding or distorting crucial market information to deceive customers was usual business practice, the market failed for reasons of criminality – highlighting its pseudo nature. Deliberately misleading investors is fraud, while carelessly misleading them can be criminal negligence (an absence of duty of care)–both indictable offences, liable to criminal prosecution. A failure to carry out fiduciary duty is a special case reeking of swindle; it is a scam that involves the betrayal of trust to beneficiaries, and was responsible for cleaning out many firms and individuals.

Importantly, the market mechanism signally failed to impose the penalty of customer loss on businesses that deceived customers. The threat of customer loss for bad business practice is a crucial feature of functioning markets, a *sine qua non* of competitiveness – something that must automatically happen in a market worthy of the name. For this reason, markets featuring systemic and widespread criminality due to opaqueness and a breakdown of law and order have the status of dysfunctional markets ( that is, they are pseudo markets). This is one reason why the manipulative hand is dominant over the "invisible hand" in pseudo markets holding sway in key sectors of economies everywhere. This aspect touches on matters that are the central focus of this book, and will be more fully addressed in subsequent chapters.

*Game Players*

"Take the loot and run"; the lamentable spectacle of the now-defunct Lehman Brothers engaging in sneaky practice could have illustrative relevance. Lehman Brothers raised $10 billion from investors at a time when there were clear indications that its heavy holdings of subprime mortgage securities had placed the company in dire straits, if not already doomed it. It is a sacrosanct duty of investment banks to reliably price risks for both lenders of capital and borrowers of capital. Customer trust is the investment banks' bread and butter; customer confidence is what enables them to tap capital markets and conduct their business. For this reason, deceiving customers by hiding risk amounted to playing a confidence trick that tore the heart out of the investment bank's business mission. As long as Lehman Brothers' true condition remained hidden, it could count on the reputation of its bond indexes (which were the gold standard for investment managers around the world), to attract the investment that it did, but at the cost of defrauding investors. During Congressional hearings it transpired that, among other factors, there was a distinct lack of transparency (read, withholding of information to investors) at Lehman Brothers. Class action suits in New York and Australia allege that investors were duped by untrue statements and withheld information. It took five years (until 2012), for an Australian court to find Lehman Brothers guilty of misleading conduct in Australia.

It seems that for banks and other finance sector firms there was a no option but to be down and dirty in order to be up and running; for many it would have been a matter more of necessity than choice. Competitor illegality impels matching reprehensible behavior to stay the pace and stay in the game. This implies that fighting the tide of corrupt practice is futile if profitability and market share are to be protected. Lehman Brothers was alleged to have played fast and loose with the facts on investment risk. The question is whether all banks were at it; whether the business practices of every other big bank on Wall Street was much different from that of Lehman Brothers, given that they were all competing in the same market arena. The clear implication is that when a culture of corruption is omnipresent, it is natural for illegal and unethical practices to be business as usual.

Customers who were denied knowledge of lurking horrors could not bank on banks because, in the then-prevalent business environment, banks were, ironically, no longer "as safe as a bank." Tacit approval of the activities of banks (and those of the ancillary agencies riding on their coattails) by lackadaisical government regulators who should have known better, put investors off the scent and prevented them from smelling a rat. Because ill-gotten gains brought great riches for banks, there would have been much in-house mirth, as it were the *bankers* who were "laughing all the way to the bank."

Into the bargain comes the sordid tale of credit-ratings agencies whose business slogan would have suited the times had they been, "Chaff is wheat when we tell you so" or "Garbage is great." The behavior of credit-ratings agencies (the big three being Moody's, Standard & Poor's, and Fitch Ratings) betrays a comical interpretation of their mission, which would be hilarious if its effects had not been so serious. Credit-ratings agencies are alleged to have bamboozled investors into believing in toxic bonds by using the mantra of hyped ratings. Flattering subprime mortgage-based bonds with triple-A ratings made them irresistible to careless banks and hordes of trusting investors worldwide, who ended up holding the junk that befouled the international financial system. The financial crisis would not have caused as much havoc as it did if credit-ratings agencies, with an implied claim to a Midas touch, had been more discerning and not bestowed fool's gold (derivatives) with a twenty-four carat gold status (triple-A ratings). The Financial Crisis Inquiry Commission report to the US Congress and the president in January 2011 contained the following telling statement: "The three credit-ratings agencies were key enablers of the financial meltdown" (FCIC 2011).

Modeling frolics was good for business. The much-vaunted statistical models used by ratings agencies – their claim to fame – were the geese that laid for them the golden eggs of ratings. The ratings generated riches in the form of lucrative fees (till what everybody thought were eggs, were found to be lemons). The value of the ratings was in the credibility they infused into investment products being marketed. The supposedly infallible ratings from the modeling gilded the pill for coaxing investors. As most analysts know, generally speaking, models are black boxes that are the creatures of their creators and can be designed to give results that please. What comes out of these models when garbage goes in is common knowledge. For example, inputting continuing house price rises at 11 percent a year is unrealistic in the context of much slower (less than 0.5 percent) income rises. Even presuming that house prices will increase at all, just because they have risen in the past, is a trite extrapolation that is hardly scientific. The worthless junk placed in investor hands by inaccurate ratings made the modeling process guilty as charged.

Nouriel Roubini, a professor at New York University, saw it. The International Monetary Fund's (IMF's) chief economist, Raghuram Raj, saw it. Nobel Prize-winning economist Joseph Stiglitz, Australian professor Steve Keen, Yale University professor, Robert Shiller, analysts Robert Wiedemer, Eric Janszen and at least ten others, also saw it. What they all saw was a financial collapse coming a mile off. They went out on a limb to warn of the looming crisis, their message being that if things looked too good to be true, it was because they *were* too good to be true. Instead of receiving tributes for their prescience, Roubini was nicknamed "Dr. Doom" and Raj labeled "slightly Luddite" by the chairman of the Federal Reserve. All the skeptics were rebuffed as killjoy spoilers, ungrateful infidels guilty of looking a gift horse in the mouth. The best-selling book, aptly titled *America's Bubble Economy* by Wiedemer and Janszen (2006), that won the Kiplinger's award for one of the best business books of 2006, predicted the collapse. Furthermore, *The Economist* magazine placed information on the threatening housing bubble squarely in the public domain on June 16, 2005. An article titled "In Come the Waves" made the following uncanny prediction: "The worldwide rise in house prices is the biggest bubble in history."

The hard-to-miss contrary information in the public domain does not appear to have influenced the assessments of the ratings agencies. These pro-finance analysts, in cozy relationship with banks, were in dogged denial about the bubbles they were contributing to inflating; to all appearances, they stubbornly thrust their chin out and carried on regardless without discounting for authoritative and credible divergent information that was there to be seen. Because havoc was wrought by wrong ratings, any wry amusement from "I told you so" skeptics tempted to rub the noses of credit-raters in it, could readily be forgiven. The least these vindicated infidels deserved was the last laugh.

Analyst propaganda, which took the form of hymns of praise for financial statistical modeling, bestowed upon the modeling results a gospel status. An enthused media, waxing lyrical about the supposed infallibility of the models, added to the hype. Government supervisors, being taken for a ride by the troika comprising analysts, credit-ratings agencies, and the media, failed to question the results from the modeling. Their acquiescence imbued the fairytale output of the mysterious models with legitimacy in the eyes of investors. Shockingly, regulators fooled almost everybody into complacency by announcing that the financial system had become less risky because securitization had diversified the ownership of mortgage debt. Such powerful backing for the triple-A gold-laced packaging prevented investors from smelling the rat within. The merchants of investment products used dubious math to do a number on investors, as the bonds did not come with a caveat alerting investors to risks that required herculean daring. The din from the banging of the drum in favor of what was taking place deafened investors to the warning bell sounded by the guardian angel called "due diligence." Falling hook line and sinker for the hyperbole on modeling infallibility, most investors ignored the need for protection that comes from the precautionary investigation of targeted investments.

In the case of credit-ratings, it can be difficult to differentiate between the criminal and the mistaken (although for distressed victims both cats were gray in the night, being indistinguishable in terms of experienced pain). Unless the ratings agencies were incompetent, the wrong ratings could be associated with possible legal culpability ranging from outright fraud and criminal negligence to breach of contract. The fact that the credit-ratings agencies were paid by the very banks whose products they assessed, implies a symbiotic relationship, a possible conflict of interest, and an absence of *prima facie* ethicality. The allegation in the legal action being taken by the US Department of Justice against Standard & Poor's ratings agency is that it gave sound ratings to bad mortgages in order to keep clients in the banking industry happy. If the ratings agencies did not knowingly collude but instead based their advice on information provided by the banks or other sources without undertaking independent investigations, there could be still be culpability (that is, they could have failed in their duty of care to clients). Since the ratings agencies sold the product of credibility, they could be liable for breach of contract if the buyer subsequently found the purchase to be a dud and (here's the rub) the evidentiary requirements of the legal system can be met.

Ah ha! All this is forgetting that, as amazing as it may seem, credit-ratings agencies have the legal right to be wrong. A credit-ratings agency's right to present wrong views is based on the long-standing belief that its opinions are protected by the First Amendment of the US Constitution that safeguards freedom of expression. The ratings agencies claim the right to opine; their customers, not the law, should judge the validity of their opinions. Although the constitutional ground rules mean that prosecutors may have nothing on the credit-ratings agencies under the criminal law for this reason, they may, nevertheless, be able to pin something on them under civil law. This explains why the US Department of Justice has filed a case in a Los Angeles federal court against Standard & Poor's alleging poor statistical modeling *inter alia*, seeking to impose civil rather than criminal liability. Civil fraud is believed to sit outside the protection of the First Amendment.

Understanding the charge of civil fraud requires understanding the nature of the product being marketed by credit-ratings agencies. When an apple is purchased to satisfy a consumer need, it is really being purchased for the package of benefits that it offers comprising taste, color, size, and texture. The buyer wants and values these to satisfy the need. Similarly, the item being marketed by credit-ratings agencies is the intangible but real product of credibility. It provides customers a package of benefits comprising confidence (the bestowed rating), security (assurance in the investment contemplated), and convenience (not having to do your own research). Selling rotten apples makes a *prima facie* case for compensation, even when they have not been laced with poison. If what the ratings agencies sold was the product of credibility, which the buyer later found to be a dud, they could be liable for breach of contract or civil fraud. Irrespective of whether the credit-ratings agencies were responsible for something, the fact is indisputable that they played a noteworthy role in dissolving the glue of trust that held the financial system together.

Regarding contrary information on asset values in the public domain: did the credit-ratings agencies see, but not notice; or did they notice, but choose to disregard that which was inconvenient? The ample contrary information was unheeded by the ratings agencies at their professional peril. When predicting the future, there can never be certainty, only probability. Consequently, the ratings agencies should have, by having their finger on the pulse of the economy and their ear to the ground, discounted for the uncertainty occasioned by the authoritative contrary information in the public domain. But the questioning views in the public domain were ignored for whatever reason, and not allowed to influence the sacrosanct ratings. And this even though, as professionals, they were duty bound, both morally and legally, to take all available information into consideration when running their models. Under fire, their explanation was that they were expressing professional views in good faith that turned out to be terribly wrong; their actions were not criminal, just mistaken.

Whether such defense holds water in the light of what has been said earlier is an open question. The credit-ratings agencies had failed to act on troubling signs that others had decried. The jury is out on the following: did the credit-ratings agencies see the financial warnings but take no notice, or did they notice, but still fail to act?

If the naked truth has been revealed in the following statement, it would not be a sight for sore eyes. The few words attributed to Richard Gugliada, the former Managing Director of Standard & Poor's, speak volumes about the business strategy of credit-ratings agencies. Mr. Gugliada is reported by Bloomberg to have said, "I knew it was wrong at the time; it was that or skip the business" (Smith 2008). This is a gem of message, straight from the horse's mouth, and pregnant with meaning. It is interpreted to mean: straight business practice in a crooked business environment involves signing one's own death warrant. Enough said.

## 4.4 The Law in Action

*Big is Noticeable*

Who deserves first prize in the "stigma of infamy" stakes? So far the winner by a mile is Mr. Bernard Madoff, who masterfully rode the dark horse Ponzi, which triumphantly whizzed past the winning post, for the jackpot prize of $68.4 billion. This was the *cause célèbre* of the times; as scandals go, this one takes the cake (or victory cup). If we are looking for a single instance that casts light on both the scale of corruption and the uselessness of regulation in the licentious business climate that characterized the times, this case fills the bill nicely by providing poignancy from exemplification.

The shocking nature of business practices in a deregulated environment cannot be more starkly illustrated than by the case of Madoff Investment Securities of Wall Street. Madoff was the clever architect of a massive Ponzi scheme. It could not have succeeded for so many years unless high-flier investors kept falling for low-down trickery, fooled by a state of blissful ignorance about what was actually happening to their money. As is generally known, in Ponzi schemes, like pyramid schemes, existing investors are paid high returns, not from any legitimate business operation, but from funds contributed by new investors lured by the high returns being paid. Madoff was prosecuted only after the scheme came to its natural end. The rogue trader had been in the sights of the US Securities and Exchange Commission (SEC) officials, but obviously without sufficient firmness to stop him. Prosecutors estimate that Madoff made off with a cool $64.8 billion. He was convicted of fraud and sentenced to 150 years in jail. This makes the Ponzi scheme by Petters Group

Worldwide pale in comparison. The alleged fraud pulled in a measly $3.65 billion, and the relatively small fry, Tom Petters, received a fifty year sentence.

For those who know, business criminality of the sort described was a sign of the times; a business climate of industry self-regulation signaled "anything goes" for many. Deregulation fostered a business culture that caused license to be mistaken for freedom, as explained in the following chapter. The important point of the Madoff case was that the brazenly illegal scheme had to collapse under its own weight before anyone realized that the game was up. The business environment was sufficiently lax and easygoing for the fraud to go undetected despite Madoff coming under suspicion and being subjected to investigation. Given that the system had failed to bring the fraud to light despite its brazen proportions, the question is how many other less impudent frauds, by relatively smaller fry, went undetected. Another question is whether the Securities and Exchange Commission's (SEC's) closeness to industry had something to do with its allegedly slipshod approach toward fraudulent behavior. It seems it can all be blamed on the culture of regulatory laxity that reigned at the time.

*Imperfect Justice*

The wheels of justice are grinding only slowly, but this is unlikely to be due to foot-dragging truculence. For those in the know, the glacial pace is more likely due to the absence of many "open and shut" cases. Reports suggest that the cases are time-consuming to develop successfully because of their complex and obtuse nature. Additionally, it takes time for cases to work their way through a congested legal system, especially when the task of making charges stick is more difficult than usual.

Legal action rumbles on (the credit-ratings agencies face class action suits in courts as far afield as Los Angeles and Sydney), but the snail's pace and scale are clearly out of whack with the scale of the illegality. The slothful process is reflected in the fact that it took five years, until 2012, for an Australian court to find Lehman Brothers guilty of misleading customers. Five years after the recession some half a dozen former executives of Freddie Mac and Fannie Mae were still being investigated by the FBI for their role in the subprime crisis. Only relatively minor players have felt the heat of the court process. For example, insider-trader Raj Rajaratnam, former Goldman Sachs' ex-trader Fabrice Tourre (regarded as a minnow within the company), and Matthew Martoma, have received their just desserts. But prominent bigwigs of Wall Street are conspicuous by their continuing absence in the dock – small fish being demonstrably easier to catch than sharks. For these reasons, there would be some truth in the cliché "Justice delayed is justice denied"–a trite expression that could yet offer some explanation for any lingering bad aftertaste being endured by hoodwinked investors.

By and large, throwing the book at suspects is usually a wasted effort because white collars tend to protect "gentlemen criminals" (of both genders). Because most enforcement actions typically center on technical questions of disclosure, rather than simple fraud such as theft, the cases are prone to come apart at the seams. Business fraud and negligence are notoriously difficult to prove in courts of law because evidence tends to get lost in the shuffle. In the nature of business activities, any tracks left by suspects tend to be ambiguous, faint, or absent. Much business strategy formulation is shrouded in murk (or kept under the hat), putting much of it outside the scope of investigative scrutiny. In addition, the wide discretion inherent in business decisions, as well as their complexity and technicality, make it devilishly hard to get the goods on wrongdoers sufficient for meeting the evidentiary requirements of law courts. This gives rise to an unbridgeable gap between what is apparent and what can be proven. To use a prosecutor's cliché, "The absence of evidence does not mean evidence of absence"; the culprits know what they did and their victims find the bad experience hard to forget, yet not much can happen. When it comes to trying to establish a duty of care, finding what standard of due care should apply in business practices is still uncertain according to academic researchers Blumberg, Wirth, and Litsoukov (2011).

Legal action meant to settle the score can end before it begins. What is an open book to aggrieved victims would often be a closed book to jurors. Prosecutors simply give up because they see a court case as a wasted effort; they realize there is not a snowflake's chance in hell of winning because the complexity and subtlety of the evidence would leave juries, never very sophisticated, in a state of befuddlement. It is more a case of reality ahead of justice than of expediency ahead of justice. Joe Palazzolo, an ex-FBI official, was reported in *The Wall Street Journal* as saying that federal agents were frustrated by the difficulty of proving criminal intent; American officials are wary of bringing to trial criminal prosecutions where a jury might decide that the losses were due to bad judgment or market conditions, not deceit (Palazzolo 2011). For example, the US Department of Justice brought a case against two former executives at Bear Stearns, the failed investment bank, accusing them of misleading investors. The defendants got off scot free.

When push comes to shove, credit-ratings agencies are particularly slippery customers. Trying to pin something on them seems impossibly tricky because of the nature of their product, which is intangible. As is well known, credit-ratings agencies produced ratings that allegedly had no value or validity whatsoever. To accept the position that the agencies did nothing wrong, despite getting ratings so obviously wrong, assuredly makes a mockery of regulations designed to protect the rights of consumers and investors.

Consequently, all cannot be fair and square when just deserts are rarely forthcoming. Not much public satisfaction is likely to come out of the many investigations being undertaken, as investigation is a long way from indictment, indictment is a long way from prosecution, prosecution is a long way from conviction, and conviction is a long way from justice. This makes elusive the last link in the long chain of criminal justice; it also makes beating the rap more likely than not.

### Spanking with a Feather

While the wheels of justice grind slowly, it is unlikely they are "grinding exceeding small" (to quote the American poet Henry Longfellow, 1807-1882). In fact, there are gaps large enough to enable a flock of prospective jailbirds to fly through. When it comes to the crunch, "the hour of decision," even the handful in the net for alleged financial crimes can expect to get off lightly. Given the seriousness of the offence, observers can be forgiven for interpreting reluctant slaps on the wrist (fines rather than jail terms, many fines being token) as hearty slaps on the back (congratulations for having beaten the system).

For those who know, rough justice is the favored game in town. Few cases relating to the financial crisis have been brought against executives of large companies, and the ones that have come up have been of a civil rather than criminal nature. In many of the cases the government is said to have negotiated a settlement without fault that, among other things, excluded prosecution of executives. This means that predictable fines for wrongdoing can be regarded as just another cost of doing business – thereby encouraging a dawdling attitude to complying with regulations at best, and violations with measured irony at worst (see section 8.5 for much more on this). Because the absence of a requirement to admit guilt protects the image of miscreant companies and safeguards against their clients scattering, the fine payers are able to carry on with business as usual. In a *Newsweek* article, Peter Boyer and Peter Schweizer found Wall Street's apparent impunity puzzling and troubling, and they raised the question of whether Wall Street bankers were "too big to jail" (Boyer and Schweizer 2012).

Fines are only money for those in the money. While some may regard the payment of fines as being equivalent to corporations purchasing tickets to break the law, others may consider secret company-prosecutor deals as shakedowns that undermine businesses. Since 2009 the Securities and Exchange Commission (SEC) has filed over one hundred and fifty cases against mortgage originators and securities firms, most of which have been settled through monetary payments. In the JP Morgan Chase case, the bank was required to pay a fine of over $1 billion in connection with the "London whale" trading losses. The hedge fund SAC Capital Advisors pleaded guilty to insider trading and was required to pay a fine of $1.8 billion. In the Hongkong and Shanghai Banking Corporation (HSBC) money laundering scandal alleged offenders were not required to go up the river despite a suspicious whiff of criminality. Since corporate deals with prosecutors are mysterious, it is impossible to know the extent of any "sweetheart" element in the deals. This depends on the direction of the hidden coercive advantage: on which party has the upper hand behind the closed doors.

To question the propriety of who pays fines is to do more than quibble with the approach in vogue. Imposing fines, however hefty, does not mean that wrongdoers are walking around with empty wallets and handbags. Most of the fines have not been paid out of the pockets of the CEO's or other accused company officials but by their business owners – effectively, innocent shareholders. This probably enables offenders to come up smiling, if not smelling of roses, gladdened by the spanking with a feather.

## 4.5 Corruption: Summary and Conclusions

The recession was not only quantitatively different because of its expansiveness and protraction, but it was also qualitatively different due to corruption. The reported scandals were not of the fun sort and they tainted the recession in a historically unprecedented manner, making it a horse of a different color. Being able to repeatedly run a red light with impunity signals a breakdown in law and order. Therefore, this downturn is no run-of-the-mill phenomenon for the reason that it is different in terms of both its scale (large and long) *and* its type (affected by behavior of the corrupt sort). The size of the recession was fostered and nurtured by its type (the corruption).

Making a fast buck through corruption was in the nature of things, corruption becoming a way of life in the world of finance. Numerous bad eggs, also called economic agents, were entangled in corrupt business practices that were the order of the day; bankers, managers, accountants, share holders, company board members, and others riding the coat-tails of bankers, were involved in behavior that manifested a culture of corruption. Handsome returns were made, without being earned, by cloak-and-dagger business strategies such as rule bending, loophole seeking, and client hoodwinking. Credit-ratings agencies were caught napping or worse, with their assessments not being worth the paper they were written on. Deluded clients who were taken to the cleaners by miscreants made an unwitting contribution to the lifestyles of perpetrators that was beyond previous imagining.

The long arm of the law seems too short for the purpose of dealing with the messy condition of large-scale illegality. Injustice from impunity is a slam dunk, as miscreants win the game of hide-and-seek. All is not likely to be fair and square when widespread impunity camouflages widespread illegality. The cultivated public image of firms continues to shroud corruption as well as the lurking presence of those who have had a taste of it.

Lawyers were discouraged from chasing villains down "Mean Street," while what was legally permissible was ethically reprehensible. Only limited action has been taken to hold to account those who allegedly picked the pockets of others by creating dubious products such as junk derivatives and nonsensical ratings. There has been only limited satisfaction available to an out-of-pocket public because the formal process of justice tends to let most culprits off the hook. The public's weary resignation or apathy has taken much of the heat out of the situation. This contributes to a situation where most biters will not to be condignly bitten in return – implying that the drives for justice will, for most smarting investors, end with a resigned whimper.

For more paranoid minds there is constant unease that the less-than honest, believed to be everywhere hiding in plain sight, could turn up like bad pennies, their unwelcome reappearance ringing up the curtain for a replay of financial tragedy. The endemic corruption indicates a breakdown of sociopolitical institutions (regulations, rules, cultures), indicating a breakdown of law and order in the world of business. When lines in the sand got erased, competitive pressures made corruption a matter more of necessity than choice. This caused bad behavior in the financial heart to pervasively damage all corners of the economy. To the extent that there is a failure of sociopolitical institutions and these remain uncorrected, what is to prevent the miscreants embedded everywhere in the fabric of the economy from re-emerging to cross the line again? If there is habitual relapse into past bad behavior (recidivism, in legal parlance), such backsliding would subvert the operation of markets, and even trigger another collapse.

These bizarre reasons for the current malaise seem to define a new paradigm. There are preliminary grounds to question the extent to which this recession is just a mechanical malfunction, one that can be fixed by recourse to fiscal and monetary policies fashioned by worn and stereotypical templates. The qualitative features of the recession examined in this chapter, on top of the quantitative factors previously cited, justify placing the current economic downturn in a class by itself. This is because of a suspicion that the wolf of busted institutions might be bamboozling policymakers by wearing the deceptively reassuring sheep's clothing of economics. Sure, the apparent symptoms of the downturn are economic, but are the underlying causes so? The next chapter focuses on these underlying institutional factors that go to the heart of the matter.

**

# Chapter 5

## INSTITUTIONAL FAILURE: THE

## BOTTOM OF THINGS

### 5.1 The Apparent Reasons

*Unpicking to Unravel*

To gain insight into the root causes of the current economic downturn, the first thing called for is the tidying up of confused thinking. Confusion about valid reasons and real offenders has not been in short supply. Apart from unlikely groups such as clergy, children, and street criminals, virtually everyone has been blamed for the crisis. To all appearances, the blameworthy are greedy bankers, spendthrift consumers, useless economists, berserk mortgage brokers, unethical corporate executives, dubious ratings agencies, dishonest auditors, myopic central bankers, irresponsible borrowers, reckless lenders, gambler investors, compromised regulators, and sloppy politicians.

If blame cannot be pinned on anyone in particular, it means that no one is to blame – or that everybody is to blame. Does this make the downturn a case of hopeless social failure, condemning the public to sackcloth and ashes for its wickedness? To play devil's advocate by following this line of moralistic reasoning: the penance of the famine would be a deserved aftermath of the gluttony of the feast; it would be divine retribution for the motivation of greed. This means, the general community is receiving its just dessert; there is condign punishment for the sin of profligacy that must be redeemed through suffering by bearing the cross of current burdens in the purgatory of the downturn. If this specious argument fills the bill as an explanation of current social pain, this chapter would not need to be written; a postcard would cover it.

Rejecting this moralistic argument increases the chances that the truth will out, and the real causes and wrongdoers uncovered. Armageddon would be an injustice, rather than a purifying punishment, if the public were innocent. Who is really responsible? The only way to set the record straight is with some "whodunit" unpicking to separate scapegoats from culprits.

The object of the exercise is to get to the bottom of things with laconic assessment. This requires reaching deep enough to distinguish apparent causes from real causes, and superficial causes from root causes. Once this is done in this chapter, the following two chapters will enable differentiation between sheep and goats – specifically, the innocent and the guilty, corresponding to victims and villains. The symptoms of the current problem are classically economic: slothful growth, a lack of real jobs, and an overdose of public debt to queasy levels. Although the problem manifests obvious economic symptoms, the root causes will be shown to be somewhat more complex and less readily apparent.

Misdiagnosis impairs prognosis; failing to identify the real causes of the crisis would give rise to wrong remedies for its solution, and that this might be actually happening is shown in later chapters. By excluding the majority this recovery is, for most clued-up people, an apology for a recovery. The Roman philosopher Cicero said in the first century BC that the causes of events are more important than the events themselves. The identification of real causes will throw much needed light on why growth from the unfolding recovery has not been widely felt.

Surprising as it may seem, religion is at the bottom of things. It would be stale news for those who know that the free-market concept and the behavior of policymakers in relation to it cannot be properly understood without reference to the Judeo-Christian ethic (Abrahaminism). This ethic underpins the capitalist market ideology and it is the ground from which the beliefs in individualism and freedom of enterprise sprout. Getting rich through the travails of hard work enabled by the freedom of enterprise is, in terms of this ethos, not just a personal and social obligation, but also a religious one. The related notion of an honest penny is associated with honorable hard work in favor of the "bread of idleness." The fiscal policy of austerity, fashionable throughout the world today, reflects faith that the enforcement of painful budgetary discipline is the certain path to economic salvation. That discipline is a virtue is firmly embedded in the Judeo-Christian ethic.

*Apparent Culprits*

Confusion on the causes of this crisis is justified because sacred cows have had their sanctity doubted. Incredibly, the value of the free market (also more accurately referred to as "effectively competitive open market"), the revered mechanism that has been the beating heart for unprecedented human accomplishment, has been questioned by the rudely irreverent (unjustly, as it turns out). Ingrained in the consciousness of free market believers is the idea that competitive free market capitalism is a meritocracy that rewards the hard working and the talented. Instead, it has unjustly rewarded the unethical and the criminal, as shown in the previous chapter. Reported there is that the so-called free market has rewarded: not honesty, but deceit; not productivity, but manipulation; not hard work, but profligacy;

not responsibility, but recklessness. The subprime boom enabled the ordinary and the mediocre to relish lavish lifestyles from ill-gotten gains through shifty practice. In a perverse twist, the slickest became the fittest. The loss of the work ethic caused the market to lose both its verve and basis. The so-called free market was associated with the freedom to plunder; market operations had the perverse effect of reducing social wellbeing instead of increasing it, as they are supposed to do. These outcomes not only cast capitalism in a bad light but also denied capitalist free markets their raison d'être in terms of the Judeo-Christian ethic referred to earlier.

What's the difference between greed and profit maximization? Politicians, academics, journalists, analysts, and activists, have condemned the obvious profligacy in Wall Street, some of them perhaps remembering the (in)famous words of the obnoxious fictional character Gordon Gekko in the 1987 film *Wall Street* that "Greed is...good." The US House Committee on Financial Services, which has responsibility for overseeing Wall Street, blamed the lack of fiduciary duty of bankers for the financial crisis (not acknowledging any responsibility on its part). Academics Ross Garnaut and David Llewellyn-Smith have claimed that "regulatory capture" and a culture of greed aided and abetted the development of the crisis (Garnaut and Llewellyn-Smith 2009). In reflection of these views, a groundswell of heartfelt public discontent was evident in the raucous and incoherent behavior of the "Occupy Wall Street" protestors ("We are the 99 percent") who went to the barricades against the alleged greed of Wall Street capitalists. People with a similar axe to grind bewailed their perceived abandonment by making their presence felt in other parts of the world, with demonstrations taking place in the City of London (the Wall Street counterpart and the global home of finance), Hong Kong, Sydney, and other cities around the world.

Let's face it: capitalists tread on community toes. Ample evidence exists of the manner in which private business interests conflicted with, and took precedence over, overall public interests – inflicting suffering upon many communities around the world. In Europe, citizens of Greece, Spain, Britain, Italy, and Portugal suffer through budget cuts to appease impatient bond holders and bankers. In the United States, there are high levels of private indebtedness, negative equity in homes, home foreclosures, high unemployment, besides a general lack of opportunity undermining the American dream. In an amazingly prescient analysis about a decade and a half ago, the British philosopher John Gray predicted as follows: "The Utopia of a global free market has not incurred a human cost in the way communism did. Yet over time it may come to rival it in the suffering that it inflicts" (Gray 1998).

## Market Charms

There is injustice in obliviousness; for those who know, capitalist free markets stand unfairly condemned. The alternative to a freely competitive market system, even an imperfect one, is a bureaucratized nightmare, a recipe for inefficiency, typically delivering poverty. There are several convincing examples of capitalist free markets engendering rates of economic growth that far surpassed the growth rates of the bureaucratic alternative they replaced. Take two conspicuous ones: China and India.

China opened up and pulled ahead. The Chinese open market experience has beaten even fanciful expectations. The Chinese economic miracle of the last thirty years can be proffered as an outstanding example from recent history of the success of the capitalist open market system. The opening up of China's market released pent-up energies that caused growth rates to soar. When the Chinese dragon took wing, jaw-dropping rates of double-digit growth replaced decades of Maoist stagnation. Admittedly, several facets of the Chinese economy remain under the not-so-invisible hand of government. What is more, the headlong economic growth at breakneck speed has broken necks in terms of human rights violations (the bulldozing of villages in the path of new highways and mass relocations being staples of Chinese development). But none of this detracts from the central message that economic growth surges are associated with reduced government intervention.

The contrasting Indian example reinforces the above point. After several semi-Socialist decades of futile central planning, an open market India emerged from the rut to be a potential rival to China. Then the stifling hand of a mindless bureaucracy re-emerged to choke off a promising start – putting the kibosh on its growth rate (the loss of vigor halving it from its peak, to a little over 5 percent). India is haunted by the bureaucratic legacy of its dismal Socialist past, the heel of a stifling bureaucracy being difficult to shake off despite being recognized as the villain of the piece. Indolent paper pushing, that gives procedural headaches for Indian businesses and forces them to take refuge in foreign countries like Dubai and Singapore, nevertheless puts naan and curry on the dinner tables of Indian bureaucrats. The implied tangled mass of bureaucratic red tape has tied the Indian elephant in knots for a disappointingly ponderous performance. Because overbearing government smothers investment, it is most unlikely that the lumbering Indian elephant would be able to match the performance of the slick Chinese dragon any time soon.

If these examples of capitalism's success are not convincing enough, the developmental gap between drab East Germany and vibrant West Germany in the past, and between poverty-stricken North Korea and high-tech South Korea today (where the northern half starves while the southern half thrives), should be enough to place an element of doubt in the minds of even diehard Socialists. In Cuba, a nanny state has produced an infantilized society, while Venezuelan socialism with its hallmark empty store shelves, has plucked food out of the mouths of the poor.

Generally, free markets have engendered unprecedented prosperity. This is not to deny that "necessity was the mother of invention" from time immemorial, long before capitalistic free markets emerged with the Industrial Revolution. Technological and social advances materialized under different socioeconomic systems from the discovery of fire and later gunpowder, to the invention of the wheel, the plough, the cannon, the windmill, and countless others. Be that as it may, the available evidence shows that the shift to freer environments led to bursts of progress. The freer environment of the Renaissance, despite the feudalism of kings and princesses, was associated with the invention of the printing press in 1439 for knowledge dissemination – enabling the flowering of the arts and sciences. Some two hundred years later, the ditching of the "mercantile system" (or "mercantilism"), a labyrinthine tangle of business regulations, gave rise to capitalist free markets and enabled the Industrial Revolution.

Since then the record of capitalist open markets has not been all bad; in fact, it is nothing to be ashamed of and is arguably spectacular. It has brought forth tremendous advances in science and technology. It has eradicated poverty on a grand scale (more people have been pulled from abject poverty in Asia than during any other period in human history). It has provided welfare safety nets in the form of health services and support for the needy. It has enabled amazing innovations in medicine. It has revolutionized communication and transportation. All this and more have occurred because the free enterprise system, when working properly, is capable of encouraging individual initiative, motivating enterprise, rewarding individual effort, and engendering social prosperity.

The releasing of commercial zeal through the vents of opportunity offered by the capitalist market system has been the secret to wealth creation. No other system in history has been able to foster human ingenuity and creativity on such a scale, and generate so much development for unprecedented prosperity and social wellbeing. It is the profit motive that has put a television in the home, a car in the garage, and a mobile phone in the hand. There is sound researched evidence that the capitalist free-market mechanism has been able to deliver a level of human prosperity unimaginable to previous generations. According to the British economist and world scholar, Angus Maddison, economic growth surged some seventy times more in the last two hundred years since the Industrial Revolution, than it did in the nearly two thousand years before then (Maddison 2010). Given such a record, it is small wonder that the free market capitalist system has attracted an increasing number of countries that crave prosperity and want to come into their own, into its dynamic orbit.

It is plainly evident that properly functioning capitalist free markets can increase social benefits more effectively and efficiently than can centralized planning by government. On the bases of countless empirical examples, there is no question that profit-driven open competitive markets, where the means of production are *privately* owned, provide the most efficient means of gaining *social* benefits. As any economist knows, this occurs through the efficient allocation of scarce community resources among competing uses by price signals from the freely operating market forces of demand and supply. This is the concept of the "invisible hand" of the market enunciated by the "father of *laissez faire* economics," Adam Smith, in his magnum opus, *The Wealth of Nations*(1776). According to Kenneth Boulding, a worthy disciple of Adam Smith, "*The Wealth of Nations* was a scripture, where economics took shape as a total body of ideas" (Boulding 1973, 232). In terms of the timeless resonance of Adam Smith's theory, the motive of competitive self-interest acts as an "invisible hand" in the market, guiding decisions and resources for maximum efficiency and social benefit. This contrasts with the hand of government splashing out subsidies to white elephants enterprises, as in China and other socialist-type economies. In free markets, price signals channel resources to where they can be most profitably used, because needs-driven consumer and business demand ensures the production of goods and services that promise maximum social satisfaction. No central planning mechanism can match the performance of the free-market mechanism, as the cited Chinese and Indian experiences illustrate. The notion of the "invisible hand" reflects the self-regulating and deterministic mindset of Adam Smith's age, which did not, however, give the green light to unfettered markets that enable "anything goes" mayhem of the type reported in the previous chapter.

Asking whether an open competitive market system will work to deliver recovery is like asking if the Pope is a Catholic. The reported evidence shows that if competitive capitalist open markets cannot do it, nothing can. Karl Marx in his *Das Capital* saw no future for capitalism, but was unable to come up with a blueprint of an alternative. In his *Das Capital*, Marx saw capitalism as containing within it the seeds of its own destruction, but what transpired since the end of the Cold War was the dismantling and abandonment of Communist economies everywhere – the free market being the winner of the ideological clash. The victory has provided support for the belief, if proof were needed, that the advent of a classless utopia cannot be administered and is a pipe dream. The surviving non-market economies, like backward Cuba and dirt-poor North Korea, hardly qualify to be cheered as models of success worthy of emulation.

There seems no basis for a clash of visions with regard to what is required for economic recovery in the West. Few in the West have reason to quarrel with a properly functioning capitalist open competitive market mechanism; belief in it is the universal common ground behind the bitter tensions in policy and ideology. History has shown that the capitalist market system is as good as they come.

This is because the capitalist free market system is the natural order of things. One has only to consider the territorial, acquisitive, and possessive nature of all in the animal kingdom to believe this. History has shown that these utilitarian animal character traits can be harnessed for human prosperity; the motive of human greed, that is inherent and incorrigible, can be a force for good when it finds market expression through virtuous vents exuding entrepreneurial drive, initiative, and dynamism. Shown later is that this happens when community-designed institutional frameworks transform the wild impetus of greed into the respectable motivation of profit maximization – thereby taming the beast of greed for socially desirable outcomes. Such a line of thinking is unlikely to surprise those who thought that that was what democratic civilization was all about in the first place. The fact that the point needed to be made suggests that somehow, somewhere along the way, Western civilization has tragically lost the plot. Examination of this is central to what comes next.

## 5.2 The Real Reasons

*Paradox of Freedom*

Did the free market fail? The answer to this deceptively straightforward question lies beneath the surface, because market performance depends on less visible factors that underpin the market. These underpinnings are: the *institutions* governing business behavior (mainly laws, regulations, rules, and business ethics needed for the orderly functioning of markets, just like traffic rules are needed for the orderly functioning of transportation); and market *structures*, which determine the competitive pressures required for market dynamism and efficient economic performance. These underlying factors are usually accepted as given and taken for granted by economists and policymakers. Such underpinning factors, despite being indispensable for the proper working of the free-market mechanism, typically fall outside the scope of standard economic analyses. Economists tend to soar above them for the reasons to be explained in chapter 7 on "Cowboy Economics."

Here is a possible surprise for free market devotees: paradoxically, restraint is essential for freedom; only with proper restraints can competitive markets be free to properly function. As to what constitutes "proper" will become clear as this explanation proceeds. Measures to give road users more freedom by abolishing traffic rules would lead to chaos, cause traffic jams and even gridlock (the antithesis of freedom). On the other hand, the traffic *regulations* in place, which restrict how fast one can travel and where one can park, enable orderliness for the *freedom* of road use by all.

This analogy draws attention to an apparent paradox that competitive free markets cannot operate freely unless they can operate within an institutional framework made up of a hierarchy of laws, regulations, rules, and cultures that restrain them. Sellers of goods and services are restrained to the extent that they must have a proper legal title before they can sell anything. Therefore, no one has the freedom to sell a used car without being able to establish lawful ownership of it. Likewise, parties to a contract are restrained to the extent that they have to adhere to certain formats and requirements for contracts to be legally enforceable. Laws restrain businesses by stopping managers from intimidating consumers into purchasing and harassing competitors into exiting (thuggery not being acceptable as a business strategy in civilized societies). The institutional framework governing businesses was redesigned to outlaw the use of child and slave labor, measures that had the effect of limiting hiring options for business. Despite their restraining nature, they could not be said to be anti-free market if the values underlying them are accepted.

In fact, laws of this sort, though restricting business choice, could be said to strengthen the market by making it to work in a way that better conforms to community values. The market is improved. Government action that regulates corporate governance reduces executive freedoms in some areas but, paradoxically, strengthens the operation of the free market system in general. It would do this by making managers more accountable to shareholders, the people who ultimately keep businesses in business. Policing insider trading on stock markets increases the market's freedom to trade efficiently. This is because market participants can trade with confidence only if they believe in fair opportunity – specifically, that some traders do not have the inside track from insider information. An unfair advantage for some subverts the system for all.

Hence, institutional frameworks draw the line to enable market players to fall in line for the good of the market system. This prevents reprehensible market behavior, like marching in customers at the point of a gun or in other non-criminal ways standing over and strong-arming suppliers, competitors, and clients. The point is that nowhere are properly functioning free markets free to produce and sell anything (e.g., bombs), or behave in any manner that they want (e.g., cheat). There is an inescapable institutional framework that governs business behavior in all markets, particularly in so-called free ones. A proper legal structure is the keystone, the central supporting element, of institutional frameworks governing business behavior and market conduct. According to Hannah Arendt, the German-born American political philosopher (1906-1975), "No civilization...would have ever been possible without a framework of stability, to provide the wherein for the flux of change. Foremost among the stabilizing factors...are the legal systems that regulate our life in the world and our daily affairs with each other" (Dingle 2008).

The extension of the argument is not exactly rocket science: different institutional frameworks give rise to different business practices for different market outcomes, without necessarily curtailing the freedom of markets to operate. Such redesigned markets can in fact work better for all concerned. For example, if the community decides through its representatives in government that only properly qualified persons should be accredited to operate as mortgage brokers, all those not qualified will no longer be free to operate their business and consumers will be denied access to their cut-price services. This means that mortgage brokerage businesses are still free to operate, but only within the now redesigned institutional framework. This notion had a major implication for financial deregulation: such deregulatory measures pushed outwards the perimeter of the institutional framework governing bank behavior. This provided an enlarged ambit of discretion for banks, thereby enabling them to change their behavior for the worse and give rise to market outcomes that left much to be desired. Because of inordinate expansion, competitive pressures can routinely induce and foster unethical and illegal practices of the type reported in the preceding chapter – making corruption a matter more of necessity than choice (explained later).

For many it would presumably be hard to swallow the oddity that policing delivers freedom. Paradoxically, freedom of enterprise requires a government policing role: the restraining influence of proper laws, regulations, and rules so that it *can* be free. As former Oxford professor and president of the Royal Economic Society of Britain, Sir Hubert Henderson, is reported to have said in relation to the paradox of free markets, "A considerable departure from *laissez-faire* is necessary in order to realize the theoretical results of *laissez-faire*" (James 1981, 110). By implication, competitive free markets must paradoxically be set up through government intervention; proactive and ongoing government intervention enables freedom of enterprise without threats of thuggery, hoodwinking, misinformation, and other forms of inappropriate business behavior. Importantly, these practices are stumbling blocks to market functionality because they undermine the market's ability to smoothly operate. According to British political philosopher, Professor John Gray, "Free markets were based on the theory that market freedoms are natural and that political restraints on markets are artificial. The truth is that free markets are creatures of state power..." (Gray 1998).

The hard way of learning the lesson that appropriate regulatory laws paradoxically bestow freedom on markets comes from receiving a jail sentence. One recalcitrant student was Raj Rajaratnam, the rupee-rags-to-billion-dollar-riches Wall Street operator of the hedge fund Galleon. For this Sri Lanka-born immigrant, who enjoyed the largesse of market freedom for several years, his American dream has become a penitentiary nightmare of eleven long years from 2011. This infamy happened because he stretched the rules governing free stock markets, to include the liberty of trading on the basis of hot tips from insider friends, the fair-weather ones giving the high-flyer a low blow by turning on him and spilling the beans.

At the risk of stating the blindingly obvious, profit-maximizing business choices can never be made in a vacuum. In a properly functioning free market business decisions must necessarily be made within an institutional framework as defined by the elements of law, regulatory architecture and business rules for business ethics. The ethics involve, in Lord Moulton's words, "obedience to the unenforceable." The elements are interrelated, as the nature of the law-based regulations provides guidance for the development of industry ethical rules; regulations based on laws signify a spirit that sets the tone for business cultures. Therefore, laws beget regulations, regulations beget industry rules (including ethical rules), industry rules fashion industry cultures, and industry cultures determine business behaviors. In other words, business cultures, industry rules, regulations, and laws, lean on each other in a hierarchical fashion. As this makes industry culture a corollary of relevant industry laws, it follows that it was the laxity in regulatory laws that gave the green light to the corrupt practices reported in the preceding chapter.

It is impossible, and is in any case, reprehensible, to attempt to regulate too many facets of business behavior. This means, business must be left to its own devices but within the space defined by institutional frameworks. Properly designed, this institutional framework is the infrastructure that defines the scope of business activities considered appropriate, and can be expected to exclude objectionable practices such as swindling, stealing, cheating, and hoodwinking, all of which were rife before the crisis, as reported in the preceding chapter. This implies that proper laws would anchor industry regulations for fortification of the ground rules that guide business behavior and corporate governance. Leaving businesses to define their own ground rules on the basis of industry self-regulation is a recipe for a free-for-all that gives rise to the sort of wretched tales of woe reported in chapters 3 and 4. What happened to customers, clients, and the community in general helps to drive home the point that proper regulations enable firms to be friends of freedom instead of agents of oppression.

The need for a "carrot and stick" partnership for market functionality was alluded to by the free market devotee and Nobel Laureate economist, Milton Friedman, a philosophical big fish of the Chicago School, whose thinking underpinned the sort of economics that made a substantial contribution to the current crisis. Friedman is said to have famously proclaimed that the single *social* (author's emphasis) responsibility of business is to increase profits, but only so long as it "stays within the rules of the game" (Keltner and Piff 2012)—the "rules" necessarily being embodied in the institutional framework governing the operation of businesses. This statement rests on the conventional assumption that private profitability promotes the social good, something that students learn in elementary economics courses. That must surely come with the implied caveat that the "rules" must not be recipes for antisocial hanky-panky. In "carrot and stick" terms this means that you can have your carrot of profits, but you will get the stick if you breach the institutional framework that governs your conduct.

Even the father of free market capitalism, Adam Smith, did not subscribe to naïve market fundamentalisms as do his ill-informed contemporary disciples. He condemned the abusive market power of mega monopolists of his day like the British East India Company, calling them "nuisances in every respect," because they impeded the efficiency of markets to the detriment of society. He believed they should be kept on a tight leash to ensure the social good. It seems a good bet that what Adam Smith said in the eighteenth century applies today to the multinational Leviathans that pass for firms (see chapter 8 for development of this point).

## Fashioned Behavior

To say that bankers were greedy begs the question: what caused and enabled their supposed greedy behavior in the first place? The concept of greed is nonsensical in economics. Those who blame business greed for the current economic problem are on weak intellectual grounds for the several reasons implied in the earlier analysis. At what point along the "business-motivation continuum" does profit maximization become greed? Are the accusers claiming that Wall Street bankers, who had a good reputation since the Great Depression, spontaneously underwent a behavioral change that caused them to suddenly become greedy and precipitate the

2007-08 recession? On the other hand, if the bankers and their business comrades in the financial sector were greedy all along, who was remiss in not setting up effective regulatory safeguards to protect society from the harm inflicted by such greed? (We are getting warmer in the search for real culprits.) If bankers were a law unto themselves through "regulatory capture," why were there no monitoring institutional mechanisms in place to preempt, arrest, or remove such anti-social behavior? In all events, businesses are expected to maximize profits for their owners, and that would make it unreasonable to expect bankers not to make rational choices to that end within the ambit of the institutional framework governing their behavior. Bankers cannot be found at fault for doing what they are there to do: maximize profits within "the rules of the game" as defined by institutional frameworks.

It is intellectually mischievous to condemn business greed while advocating business profit maximization. The concept of greed does not make sense except in the context of a relevant institutional framework. Consequently, profit maximization stops being profit maximization and becomes greed only when profits are made through the violation of regulations and industry ethical standards that are embodied in properly designed institutional frameworks governing business behavior. If the choices made by economic agents turn out to be harmful to society, it would only be because they were being governed by distorted incentives from cockeyed institutional frameworks. Such institutional frameworks would result from deficient regulatory architecture and poor ethical standards giving rise to socially unfriendly business cultures, as was indeed the case. It is imperative to assume that the players in the capitalist economic system (bankers, managers, accountants, company board members, financial analysts, credit raters, etc.), make rational maximizing choices based on self-interest within the ambit of the institutional frameworks governing

91

their operations. If bankers exhibited greedy behavior, such greed was enabled by institutional frameworks that had been made so permeable by lax regulation, that they enabled the greed that was always there to seep through and inflict the damage reported.

Let's get logical. While it was possible for bankers and other financial sector players to appear greedy, whether they were actually so is a different matter for the reasons explained earlier. It does not seem reasonable, and would indeed be nonsensical, to expect managers who are out there competing against each other in the fishbowl of public scrutiny, to act against the interests of their shareholders and forgo opportunities for business profits (including payoffs for them) when such practices are permissible under governing institutional frameworks. This is particularly the case when so-called greedy practices are the order of the day and engaged in as normal business practice by competitors. It is unreasonable, even preposterous, to expect some competing bankers to hold back from maximizing profits of their own volition, without assurances that their competitors will do likewise. In any case, the notion of self-regulation is just not practical on an individual bank basis for this simple reason: each competing bank could not know how much and when to withhold action, without colluding with competitors, and thereafter hoping there would be no cheating (that is, stealing a march on restrained competitors through free riding).

Firms' outfoxing one another with questionable practices was integral to competitive behavior in the then-prevalent climate. This is confirmed by no less a personage than Nomi Prins, former managing director of investment bank Goldman Sachs, who spoke volumes when he reportedly said that banks had to resort to dubious behavior to retain and increase their market share: "...it was a drive for survival and dominant market share in a limited banking space" (Smith 2010). The logical inference is that firms jockeyed for position to gain a competitive edge in their search for a share of the spoils. The pressure to outdo competitors happened in conditions where lax institutional frameworks due to deregulation had made room for practices of a corrupt sort to take place as normal behavior – causing "survival of the fittest" to mutate into "survival of the slickest."

Operating by the old book no longer made sense, because what was stated there had been nullified by deregulation. It should not come as too much of a surprise that a spiraling breakdown of law and ethics was triggered by competitive pressure – more accurately, by a cutthroat free-for-all, which fuelled a competitor preempting race to the bottom, where was found the gutter. If captains of industry were found in the gutter, it was because deregulation caused and allowed them to be there. Since institutional frameworks governing business behavior had been debilitated by deregulation, competitive pressure made corruption a matter more of necessity than choice; market players had little choice but to be in the gutter, because that is to where the action had descended. They had to be in it to win it; getting down and dirty in the gutter became a winning business strategy for staying in the game.

When the permissiveness of deregulation merged with the pressures of oligopolistic gamesmanship, the opportunity for profit coincided with an opening for dishonesty. To think that businesses foolishly engineered their own demise is to fail to recognize that competitive pressures gave them no choice, as confirmed by the words of Goldman Sachs' managing director referred to earlier. Because of deregulation, institutional frameworks governing banking behavior had fallen short by ceasing to provide an adequate line in the sand.

The business of business is, of course, business. Grasping market opportunities is the name of the game in the competitive world of "dog eat dog," where it is a case of every firm for itself. When there is oligopolistic gamesmanship, which is almost certainly what existed, it is a case of firms jockeying for the share of the spoils (which economists call "rents," as more fully explained in chapter 8). Weak institutional frameworks threw up new opportunities for the now less hampered businesses to proactively grasp in order to steal a march on competitors and stay ahead of the pack. More to the point, in the case of banks there was now no regulation against what was previously prohibited. This was the case when, following deregulation, bankers got access to the previously forbidden fruit of depositor savings in commercial banks for previously unthinkable purposes (like playing the market). Such laxity enabled banks to formulate strategic business practices in the best interests of shareholders in an arena that had been made larger through deregulation. The deregulated institutional framework signaled that it is now okay to go for it; certain business strategies that were previously forbidden but now available can seem idiotic to forgo, especially when oligopolistic competitors circled for a share of the spoils. Self-regulation on the basis of unclear rules would not be much of a foundation for business uprightness when oligopolistic gamesmanship involves elbowing for advantage.

It would be unreasonable to expect bankers not to be true to the life-giving cause of profit maximization, particularly when competitive winds are howling in fiercely contested markets (more accurately, in conditions of oligopolistic gamesmanship for division of the spoils). Bankers under this type of competitive pressure (which requires playing a second-guessing game for outsmarting competitors through one-upmanship), cannot be blamed for going on the loose and taking liberties that were newly permissible in the now deregulated environment (when the cat's away, the mice will play). Bankers cannot be expected to toe the line when there is no line to toe – the line having been erased by deregulation. If bankers stick at nothing, it is because there is nothing there to stop them.

Consequently, Wall Street bashing is not only simplistic but also shifts the focus away from the real culprits, and the real culprits can blame Wall Street to divert blame away from themselves. In any case, not only American banks were responsible for the financial crisis, as Europe had its share of allegedly profligate villains. "Demonizing the bankers as if they and they alone created the financial meltdown is both inaccurate and short sighted," Citigroup chair Richard Parsons is reported to have said (Sheer 2010).

Bankers, as the public's favorite bogeyman, at the receiving end of curses, have borne an unfair share of damnation. Although their record is not spotless, doing the maximum for their shareholders is what bank executives are there to do, and to this extent, credit should be given where credit is due (pardon the pun). Deregulation shifted the focus of banks from customer relationships to shareholder value, and there is a legal requirement to do so because of the famous case of *Dodge v. Ford* (1919). The Michigan Supreme Court ruled that business (The Ford Motor Company, in this case) should promote shareholder interests – not public interests; the business of business must be business, not social service. The next chapter shows that there is justification for believing that bankers have taken too much of a fall for the faults of others. It is obviously not good to shoot the wounded, even when they seem the enemy.

In conclusion, believers in incentive theories of human behavior must accept that the motive of profit maximization is an essential requisite, the *sine qua non*, of the free market system; when there are competitive pressures, profit maximizing behavior is necessary for survival. If the profit-maximizing behavior of bankers and others of their ilk inflicted community harm, it must be accepted that deficient institutional frameworks that governed their behavior did not just give them the opportunity, it gave them no alternative. It gave them no choice because competitive pressures made it imperative for firms to match competitors' strategies, however dubious, so as to stay the pace and stay in the game. This means a firm would need to at least match its competitors' efforts through countervailing measures to steer clear of losing market status or having to eventually pack it in. If banks are bad, it is because they *can* be and *need* to be. Hence, the deficient make-up of the institutional framework governing banking behavior leaps into the spotlight as the real reason for the string of alleged banking scandals.

## 5.3 Private versus Social

*The Fundamentals*

Conspicuous by its absence is the much-vaunted harmony between private business interests and overall community interests (brought home in the previous chapter). American congressman Charles E. Wilson famously said in 1953, "What is good for the country is good for General Motors, and vice versa." More recently, Simon Johnson and James Kwak in their book *13 Bankers* are reported by Lessig to have stated that "...it was part of the worldview of the Washington elite that what was good for Wall Street was good for America" (Lessig 2011, 82). The assumption underpinning these views is that social good automatically flows from company profits, thereby providing the raison d'être for capitalist free markets. Instead, in this recession, there was conflict between private profitability and social prosperity, as neatly encapsulated in Mark Williams' observation in 2010 that "Wall Street hijacked Main Street." The invalidity of the generally accepted cardinal assumption that business profitability enables social prosperity has come to mean that company profits can be as antithetical to public wellbeing as affluence is to poverty.

Why in the current crisis did private business activity do bad things to the country by turning harmony between business and public interests into conflict? The answer has been provided in the preceding analysis. To repeat it for emphasis: it is because deficient regulatory architecture caused weaknesses in institutional frameworks governing business behavior, thereby giving rise to the corollary of weak industry ethical standards and concomitant anti-social business cultures. But we are not yet at the bottom of things, as the foregoing answer simply begs the question. The question remains: why was there conflict between business and community interests?

It takes getting down to brass tacks to explain why matters fell short. Explaining the gap between what should have happened (harmony between business and social interests) and what did happen (conflict), requires specifying the ideal (the normative) in order to expose the failings of the actual (the positivistic). More specifically, understanding the conflict between the business interest and the community interest requires examining the fundamentals determining how the market system did actually work, compared to how it ought to have worked. Understanding this disparity would enable one to put one's finger on the answer to the question: why on earth this crisis?

The answer requires going back to square one, to enter the holy of holies of democratic thought. In the preceding analysis it was shown that quantitative and qualitative factors caused and characterized the recession. They were associated with many different types of institutional failure, from those that enabled the excesses of banks, to those that enabled auditors to have conflicts of interest. To get to the root of institutional failure requires delving into political science to identify the sacrosanct principles determining how Western democracies (the location of culprit economies) should have ideally performed.

How do we explain the gap between the actual and ideal? The personage being relied upon to explain the ideal is the Enlightenment thinker, Englishman John Locke, called the "Father of Classical Liberalism." His notion of "life, health, liberty and possessions" in the eighteenth century shaped Western democracies in general and the American Declaration of Independence in particular. The basic notion in Locke's political theory is that of a "social contract," whereby governments have a contract with society. This means that governments must rule with the consent of society and exist to serve its interests – implying that having a vote must also mean having a voice. Reflecting this view, George Washington said that the only keepers of the American Constitution are the people. Hence, governments should be both the creatures and agents of the community, existing for the public good. According to eighteenth century British philosopher Edmund Burke, the legislature has "...to follow, not force, the public inclination." Laws embodying the will of the people can then be seen as providing the basis for business regulations that systematize the collective understanding of fairness and justice for all (including for businesses).

How does everybody get a square deal? This is achieved by designing institutional frameworks that are capable of reconciling business and public interests. Governments must proactively intervene to ensure freedom of enterprise, while at the same time drawing the line to prevent business action from reducing social wellbeing; the institutional framework acts as a ring of steel to ensure freedom of enterprise without social harm. The logical upshot: business moguls and ordinary people can become best friends; firms get placed on the same side as the public as was assumed by Congressman Charles E. Wilson. The crucial implication from what was stated earlier (*a la* Locke at al.) is that it is the responsibility of a properly representative *government* to design institutional frameworks that can reconcile increased business profitability and increased community prosperity. Laws and regulations would give the public a fair shake only when grass roots can hold sway over the design of such institutional frameworks. This is recently confirmed by American political scientist, Francis Fukuyama, who states that neither free markets nor democracy can flourish without proper political institutions from a competent state (Fukuyama 2014).

That is what it takes for capitalist free markets to work; free markets cannot work unless they work for all, and they can work for all only if there is a collective commitment for collective benefits through properly designed institutional frameworks governing business conduct. This is the hallmark of a properly functioning capitalist free market system. It should be clear that capitalism extends beyond market operations, to encompass the collage of values, beliefs and priorities of people in control, which in a true democracy must be the general community. It enables wealth accumulation to take place within the defined rules of the game, so that anybody can become rich without resorting to thievery.

*Good Inequality*

Inequality can be nice. Inequality, like greed, can be good for free-market capitalism, depending on whether or not markets are functioning on the basis of institutional frameworks designed in the interests of the community (in terms of the thinking of John Locke and others mentioned earlier). Designing institutional frameworks that reconcile business and community interests in the market automatically determines a level of inequality in income and wealth that is necessary for growth and acceptable to society. The former makes inequality imperative, while the latter makes it virtuous. This implies that inequality gets imbued with the quality of goodness in conditions of properly functioning markets.

There is no equity in equality because efficiency considerations require that people be paid for what they accomplish i.e., that productivity be rewarded. This means that the free market system can work only if the efficient and the smart are rewarded more than the lazy and the ordinary. The carrot of high and unequal reward is essential for engendering the dynamism of entrepreneurship. What is an acceptable level of inequality is ultimately a matter of political value judgment, depending on a balance of social considerations (technically, on a social welfare function based on Locke's notion of a social contract, as reflected in community-based institutional frameworks).

It must be squarely faced that farcical institutional frameworks that make markets dysfunctional can throw up an inequality sans its acceptable properties – implying that markets must be effectively open and competitive for inequality to be acceptable and salutary. Something is rotten in the state of the economy when unrighteous inequality can rear its head through institutional frameworks that are riddled with holes. This happens when there is denial to the majority of sufficiently large trickle-down crumbs from the loaves on the rich man's table. In America and most European countries, the economy is stagnant for the majority but growing for the minority; income rises from growth accrue to the already rich, leaving the majority in the lurch. In America, while corporate profits have reached an all-time high, increasing by over 17 percent a year, the majority tastes few of the fruit: in the five years since the collapse, GDP went up 8 percent while the income of 90 percent of households went nowhere. In Europe, although growth in Spain, for example, is hovering around 2.3 percent and Spain is consequently regarded as the star of the eurozone, most Spaniards are left behind as reflected in an overall unemployment rate of US Great Depression proportions (some 25 percent) and a sky-high youth unemployment rate (exceeding 50 percent)–enabling the anti-establishment Podemos party to rapidly gain ground. When the inequality of income of individuals is caused by the absence of properly designed institutional frameworks for properly functioning markets, its denouncement is not out of jealousy, but out of a concern for genuine recovery. How inequality hinders economic recovery is explained in chapter 9.

A skewed recovery, when income soars at the top but is stagnant for everyone else, makes recovery a minority interest with a winner-takes-all connotation – and can be regarded as a blot on the economic landscape when it shrinks the crucial middle class. The facts are that while real wages for the top one percent are escalating in the America and Europe, middle class real wages are falling, and this is due to falling productivity and the displacement of skills due to automation. Several authors of divergent persuasions are remarkably agreed that the type of inequality that currently exists in the United States is unfair, inefficient, and anti-recovery in nature. On one side of the fence is, for example, Nobel prize-winning economist, Joseph Stiglitz with his *The Price of Inequality* (Stiglitz 2013), while on the other side is, for example, politician and analyst David Stockman with his *The Great Deformation* (Stockman 2013).

*Freedom versus License*
If the person holding a gun has a responsibility to use it wisely, then indiscriminate deregulation would be like shooting wildly and asking for trouble. The change to the institutional framework governing business behavior that is brought about by deregulation must be related to the altered market outcomes that automatically result from such a change. Deregulation that does not pick and choose and not tied to accurately predicted outcomes amounts to buying a "pig in a poke," (that is, have effects that produce an unpleasant surprise of the type reported in chapter 8 on "Deregulation Fallout").

Deregulation gave rise to socially undesirable outcomes because license was mistaken for freedom. Of particular relevance to what has transpired in this economic recession is that deregulation took place that was unrelated to socially desirable outcomes. This resulted from faith being placed by policymakers in a condition beyond freedom:

license. License refers to the freedom of the wild ass, better known as the "law of the jungle."

License is not freedom; an ass that runs wild drains freedom of its meaning. When civilized laws are silenced, licentious behavior becomes the norm, as illustrated by the business chicanery reported in the previous chapter. There can be no such thing called "freedom" when ill-defined or fractured institutional frameworks give rise to the condition of license that enables businesses to run roughshod over competitors, clients, and the public. When the condition of license exists, it means there is a jungle out there. When the law of the jungle prevails in the business world because of license, the resulting behavior of business leaders would be like that of hunter-gatherers at best and that of animals at worst. Specifically, firms in a licentious business environment would be guided by ruling principles that prescribe ruthless self-interest as the key to business success. The following behaviors or tactics will be associated with businesses operating in conditions where the law of the jungle prevails: *'dog eat dog'*, *'might makes right'*, *'anything goes'*, *'every one for himself or herself'*, *'at each other's throat'*, *'kill or be killed'*, *'eat or be eaten'*, and *'survival of the slickest'*. These vivid descriptions, inconsistent with the orderliness and dignity associated with civilized free markets, lead to the following conclusion: the information in chapter 4 describes conditions suggestive of a jungle where the ass ran wild; a place where unbridled self-interest caused licentious business behavior to be rampant because of a breakdown in law and order attributable to deficient institutional frameworks.

To regard unchecked business conditions as free market conditions is to mistake geese for swans. Open competitive markets governed by community-designed laws must be recognized as being different from unfettered markets characterized by business behaviors that reflect a pathological neo-liberalism. Businesses have shown they can run

riot without the restraining influence of proper institutional frameworks. Such licentious-prone business conditions enabled plenty of
bangs for the buck from business practices that were fast and loose,
the breakdown of law and order in business enabling Wall Street to
become easy street. The free rein given to the agencies Fannie Mae
and Freddie Mac were a form of anti-social deregulation, no different in concept from the deregulation of the banks. The government
failed to design an institutional framework governing the operations
of Fannie Mae and Freddie Mac that reconciled valid (market-based)
company objectives with authentic (market-sustainable) community
benefits. Hence, the community-suffering from the operation of the
agencies arose, not because of government intervention per se, but
because of the wrong type of government intervention; government
legislation that was shortsighted and ill-considered made the institutional framework governing their operations defective and deficient. According to the eighteenth century French philosopher Denis
Diderot, "Morals are in all countries the result of legislation and government; they are not African, or Asian, or European; they are good
or bad" (Dingle 2008).

Industry deregulation brought about market degeneration. It
would be a mistake to regard the deteriorated market condition
caused by deregulation – the one that existed prior to the collapse –
as a competitive open market, because the so-called market was out
of whack; its anti-social performance was the opposite of what was
expected of it (for the reasons stated by John Locke et al.). In such
conditions, the market lapses into being an imposter and has only
the semblance, not the substance, of a free market. Markets were
less free because, apart from the element of greater monopolization
due to deregulation, the information needed for the market to function competitively was absent due the business repertoire of withheld information, misleading information, falsified documentation,

and breaches of trust, as described in the previous chapter. In other words, because of a lack of transparency the market did not have the information necessary for competitive forces to properly operate and deliver efficient outcomes – implying the absence of open competitive markets or, conversely, the prevalence of dysfunctional pseudo-markets (explained in chapter 8).

The current economic condition cannot be attributed to a failed competitive free market. It could not have failed because it was not even there. What failed in 2007-08 was a stealthy, licentious-prone, oligopolistic or monopolistic, business condition that was masquerading as a freely competitive open market and mislabeled as such. Open competitive markets in key sectors of the economy had by then undergone a metamorphosis, particularly in the financial heart, and mutated into something different from what a proper free market is supposed to be – that is, into "pseudo-markets."

Industry self-regulation: is it illusion or humbuggery? (Take your pick.) Subscribing to the doctrine of industry self-regulation can be seen as simple-minded illusion at best or the humbuggery of vested interests at worst. The financial meltdown proved that the victorious belief, that financial markets were capable of self-regulation (i.e., self-policing), was a figment of the imagination of believers in indiscriminate deregulation (conversely, of those who were oblivious to the notion of institutional frameworks). It became a dangerous assumption when it was used to fashion national policy-making by people who could not see the difference between license and freedom. In any case, it was a tremendous rationalization because it suited the self-interest of both the informed (the humbugs perpetrating an anti-social hoax) and the ill-informed (the deluded disciples of market fundamentalism).

For many, if not most, fans of financial deregulation, industry self-regulation is a belief system based on spurious science and ingrained ideology. The Financial Crisis Inquiry Commission report to Congress and the president hit the nail on the head when it reported that there was "widely accepted *faith* (the author's emphasis) in the self correcting nature of the market and the ability of financial institutions to effectively police themselves" (FCIC 2011). The spurious science behind the "faith" in industry self-regulation can be traced to a type of economics called "finance economics," which wrongly theorized that banks could be left to regulate themselves because the mathematical models that were being used for financial decision-making tamed risk (risk being the font of profits for banks, to state the obvious). This field of economics failed to recognize a straightforward truth: modeling risk does not mean managing risk. Explained in chapter 7 on "Cowboy Economics" is that the mathematical models used to predict risk in the future were based on information from the past – false assumptions giving false confidence for a false belief in industry self-regulation. The confidence came from ideological underpinnings based on cultural values in general (to be explained in section 6.3) and market fundamentalism in particular. Market fundamentalism takes the form of an overpowering belief that unregulated markets can enable economic prosperity better than regulated ones do (and never mind the matter of institutional frameworks). Market fundamentalism in its purest form means that unfettered markets can do no wrong and that, therefore, everything about the market is sweet and nice including, presumably, business players like bank managers and credit raters.

Not to put too fine a point on it, industry self-regulation is an article of faith not much different from a belief in fairies. In the light of what has been laboriously pieced together in the foregoing analysis, accepting industry self-regulation requires a quantum leap of faith. Apart from being a false belief, it is unscientific and emblazoned with ideology. The belief indicates a detachment from reality that, like an expectation that pigs fly, beggars belief. It is like expecting orderly driving despite saying: "There is no speed limit on this highway, but everyone please drive carefully; there will be a range of prizes depending on the order of arrival at the other end, with the best prize for the first arrival, the second best prize for the second arrival, and so on." As explained by American philosopher Eric Hoffer (1902-83), "When we believe ourselves in possession of the only truth, we are likely to be indifferent to common everyday truths" (Dingle 2008). For these reasons, industry self-regulation (self-policing) seems a non-starter as far as industry governance goes.

The "leave-it-to-the-market" belief underpinning financial deregulation stands discredited by the economic devastation that speaks for itself. The belief flies in the face of reality. Blowing the lid off the financial sector can be expected to have enabled many to see the light from the flash, and so put an end to any manic belief in self-regulation. If more evidence is needed, there is the Libor scandal. For those who know, banks rigged an interest rate used to peg contracts worth trillions, and it is the largest single scam in banking history to date. Libor is a hideous child of banking industry self-regulation; one look at Libor should scotch any illusion of beauty in industry self-regulation. It appears, however, that even such incontrovertible evidence has not succeeded in shooting down in flames everyone's belief in industry self-regulation. Many refuse to be convinced despite the hard-to-miss smoking ruins of devastated economies that serve the purpose of a proverbial smoking gun. Why spoil the fantasy with facts? Diehard believers in industry self-regulation continue to be blind to the poignancy of the collapse and deaf to the hoots of derision around them.

The distinct message from the foregoing analysis is simply this: it is mistaken to think that agents engaged in the competitive rough and tumble of open markets can regulate themselves without public intervention through legislative action. Such action is needed if only to preempt cut-throat free riding, with an attendant free-for-all race to the bottom as firms jostle for advantage. The botched attempt to tame the beast of regulation poked corruption into existence. What comes about in the end is a market that is not like a market should be; it is a simulacrum of a market that lacks the substance of functional markets because of anti-competitive and anti-social traits (see chapter 8).

Markets can, not only go bad, but also go mad; insufficiently regulated markets, driven by human frailties, can go bananas (i.e., get pathological). In fact, markets have exhibited all three forms of schizophrenia: "glad mad" (exuberance), "bad mad" (corruption), and "sad mad" (depression). Without community-designed institutional frameworks made up of civilized laws, sane regulations, and ethical decency, unfettered markets driven by profit maximizing self-interest can go berserk and deliver mayhem and havoc, as they have shown they are capable of doing. Impaired core elements can make a problem that starts in one area to contaminate other areas. This was the case when banks went ape and caused other firms like credit-ratings agencies, mortgage brokers, and real estate agents to run amok. Only through the adoption of grass-roots-based institutional frameworks would it be possible to contain the potential excesses of the free market system and bring about the critical accord between the pursuit of profit and the wellbeing of society.

## 5.4 Regulations for Congruence

*Understanding Regulation*

To experience is to believe. It took a calamity to prove that proper regulations can indeed deliver harmony between business interests and overall community interests. Following the cataclysmic plunge of the Great Depression when markets also broke down, Western governments redesigned markets to enable the reconciliation of business and community interest. Businesses came to operate in a manner that better served community interests as well as their own. This was done through institutional changes that established the New Deal in America and the Welfare State in Europe. Welfare measures, although targeting the disadvantaged in society, had the incidental effect of providing hidden subsidies to business in several ways – for a happy happenstance. Handily, productivity gains to businesses flowed from several sources: a better educated workforce due to state subsidized education; a healthier workforce due to public health care measures; and a more flexible workforce because of unemployment relief and government training programs (both of which cushioned dismissals). By enabling congruence between the interests of business and the interests of society, these institutional changes succeeded in delivering a period of shared prosperity in the West – until the current debacle, that is.

There is a now a greater reliance on regulation, rather than on money, for improving social conditions. For cash-strapped governments, gaping deficits and onerous debt have discouraged welfare spending measures and increased dependence on regulations to achieve policy goals. An entitlement culture had blossomed to transform welfare safety nets (insurance against hardship) into safety cushions (comfortable living), and cause institutional thrombosis to afflict overburdened welfare systems in most countries. As a result, welfare has become less affordable to governments and less attractive to business. During the West's high-growth past, businesses were inclined to support, or at least tolerate, welfare measures for the reasons mentioned. But cheap foreign labor from globalization and less need for low-skilled labor due to increased mechanization have reduced to business the incidental benefits from welfare measures. These developments have meant that, as governments tighten their belts, regulation rather than money has the greater role to play in achieving governments' social-policy goals than before.

"Thou shalt not" regulations can be shields rather than swords. Regulations are commandments that define relative rights for the protection of conflicting interests. They determine how some people's rights relate to those of others in the distribution of rights throughout the community, benefitting some and disadvantaging others. Changing regulations redistributes rights and establishes a new relativity in relation to the rights of different groups in the community. What financial deregulation has done is to redefine relative rights between those who were previously protected by the regulations (the public) and those who now have greater freedom of enterprise (the banks). It transferred rights away from the general community to the financial industry, which consequently strengthened the rights of the financial industry at the expense of the general community.

That is not necessarily bad; freer markets that deregulation enables could generate greater business activity and thereby engender greater benefits in terms of both business profits and community prosperity. Applying the principles of Institutional Economics propounded by iconic economist Alan Schmid (1994), one of the tidiest minds this author has had the privilege of learning from, the redistribution of property rights could be said to have had two implications. Firstly, it shifted the coercive advantage away from the general community to the financial industry, giving the financial industry the upper hand. Secondly, it redistributed income away from the general community to the beneficiaries of the deregulation. In the five straight years leading to the 2007-08 collapse in America, when there were record corporate earnings and banking profitability (ROE) exceeded twenty percent a year, ninety percent of income gain went to one percent of the population and the household income of the majority barely moved.

*Understanding Deregulation*

Deregulation based on slash-and-burn dogmatism gave enlightened deregulation a bad name. The evidence adduced in chapter 4 of unethical and illegal activities suggest an insufficiency; they reveal that institutional frameworks governing business behavior embodied squishy regulations, causing law and order to break down in business. That enabled corrupt business practices to become more the rule than the exception.

In principle, the less regulation the better; no self-respecting manager would want to be followed around by regulators breathing down his or her neck. What is needed is a minimum of regulations. The deregulation policies of, for example, American president, Ronald Reagan, and British Prime Minister, Margaret Thatcher, unchained economies for freer enterprise, capital movements, and trade – thereby ushering in a global economic boom. The deregulation of the airline industry by the Carter administration was a boon to travelers.

Is rolling back regulations good or bad? The quick answer is that it is a mixed blessing because "regulations ain't regulations." There is no inconsistency between the two positions mentioned, as the apparent contradiction can be easily reconciled. Stripping away regulation that suppresses business opportunities for community benefit must be differentiated from deregulation that changes business behavior in a way that is harmful to the operation of the market, and consequently denies the community market-generated benefits. The point is that deregulatory dismantling is not necessarily bad; what is bad is the roll-back that takes place without regard for how it affects the general community. In undertaking deregulation, it is essential, as someone said, to "begin with the end in mind" in order to avoid getting ones wires crossed. Hence, there is no basis for ritually condemning or praising deregulation.

Just as missing the correct turn at the crossroads could get one lost, missing regulatory inflection points can cause deregulation policy to lose its way. What is detrimental to the economy and detracts from human happiness, is deregulation that dismantles regulations beyond a certain inflection point. The trick is to identify a critical inflection point, the tipping point that separates beneficial deregulation from harmful deregulation. Hence, inflection points serve to separate deregulation medicine from deregulation poison.

Deregulation can be therapeutic when it gets rid of ball-and-chain hindrances to free market operations. Clearly, economies that are hobbled by investment-stifling regulation will lose out on opportunities for growth. Some types of regulation are without doubt an encumbrance to the freedom of enterprise and choke-up markets. The economy is well rid of creaking laws (including taxation laws) that shackle business initiative and corroding regulations that stymie business creativity. In general, too much of the wrong sorts of laws and regulations will, of course, hamper efficient market performance.

Before the critical inflection point is reached, deregulation would release the creative energies of business for good because market operations are improved; markets can work better because they are made more open and competitive. Up to such a point, deregulation has the capacity to improve the performance of the free market, with business initiatives enabling increased profitability as well as community prosperity, for shared benefits. Disposable regulations are usually those of an economic nature that seek to control prices, profits, competitiveness, and firms' entries and exits. For example, the deregulation of the airlines in America, Europe, and others, enabled greater efficiencies and benefits to the community in terms of cheaper tickets and convenient scheduling. The deregulation of several industries in Australia and New Zealand did wonders for their competitiveness.

Other deregulation can be downright harmful; it is where angels fear to tread. This refers to thinking nothing of going beyond the critical inflection point where the scales are tipped against net benefits from deregulation; going past this critical point is associated with bad news from the resulting ill effects of deregulation on the state of happiness of the community. Unsurprisingly, the deregulation measures in this category are those that damage market functionality and are evidently of a financial nature. They were shown to weaken prudential regulation, regulation of corporate governance, and securities regulation. They include regulations that determine company requirements for reporting, audit, and accounting – the dilution of which, by making propriety optional, have proven to be a recipe for skullduggery. Because net benefits can go either way, taking a meat axe to the business regulatory architecture without concern for market functionality is understandably chancy.

All that glitters is not gold. Unselective deregulation exposes illusion in public policy formulation caused by a woeful lack of hard-headed economic rationality in the decision-making process. Because of the success of *economic* deregulation in the past, policymakers were lulled into a false sense of security on *financial* deregulation, when they are as different as chalk from cheese. Policymakers wrongly believed that what was sauce for the economic goose was sauce for the finance gander: that financial deregulation was able to deliver as much of a magic carpet to prosperity as economic deregulation could. What they did not realize was that, while economic deregulation can be made to grease the market mechanism to enable its smoother functioning, financial deregulation has a propensity to throw a wrench in the works. The confusion caused an iron fist to be taken to something that needed to be handled with kid gloves. This is as good an example of an inexact parallel as one can get for the reason that the assumed similarities are as deceptive as they are spurious.

The gung-ho approach to deregulation was bound to have surprising effects, mostly unpleasant if you were a member of the excluded majority. Giving free rein to banks led to a loss of economic and political control, a laxity that turned out to be damaging to market freedom; rooting out regulations to achieve freer markets has had the opposite effect of limiting market freedom. Indiscriminate financial deregulation can destroy a functioning free market in the name of freedom and substitute in its place licentious-prone business conditions that inhibit the ability of markets to freely function. Specifically, business stealth denies markets the information needed for their proper functioning. When combined with other damaging features, such licentious-prone business dispositions give rise to anti-competitive and anti-social plutocratic pseudo-market conditions in the financial heart and elsewhere, as explained in chapter 8.

Consequently, indiscriminate deregulation, like shooting wildly, borrows trouble. Careful policy aim based on savvy planning is needed for deregulation to deliver net overall benefits. Deregulation without adequate research findings is an unknown quantity, scientific investigation being a "must have" for knowing the score. This refers to assessing the economic benefits and costs of proposed deregulation measures, to safeguard against deregulation springing a nasty surprise. More specifically, in order to have some second sight, economic research is required to determine the critical infection point at which the interests of business become harmful to the interests of the general community. Deregulation can then be weighed in the balance, so that its merits and demerits may be pondered for a fastidious and judicious approach to decision-making that maximizes overall social benefit through business success. It follows that undertaking deregulation trusting in the enchantment of ideology, instead of relying on robust research-based information, amounts to, in biblical terms, making bricks without straw. This should make it clear that deregulation calls for informed, research-based, policy-making that is grounded on cool assessment and not for gung-ho, ideology-driven, action involving shooting from the hip.

## 5.5 Conclusions: Verities and Balderdash

The intellectual tool of a conceptual framework has proven handy for showing that getting to the bottom of things involves getting down to brass tacks to expose fundamental realities – and thereby shed light on where the deregulation policy formulation process went off the rails. Getting a handle on the basics has exposed root causes, provided an understanding of bankers' practices, absolved certain groups from culprit status, and offered clues for identifying the real villains of the piece. The bankers and other financial sector firms are shown to be more ostensible than real culprits. A full exposure of the real culprits must await the analysis in the following two chapters.

Effort was made to drive home the point that it is crucial to distinguish between freedom and license and avoid the blunder of mistaking license for freedom – a misconception that has given rise to policy-making on the hoof and the unleashing of a wild ass on the public. For corrupt firms, making hay was made possible by the ample sun shining through a regulatory architecture that was riddled with holes – an activity that was shown to be unfriendly to the public. The introduction of business license through indiscriminate deregulation destroyed the decorum needed for free markets to effectively function. Properly functioning open markets require the policing role of the state to prevent businesses from going haywire. Lax institutional frameworks will inevitably give rise to licentious-prone business behavior. What can you expect from a pig but a grunt?

The notion of industry self-regulation was shown to be enough to make a dead cat laugh. Industry self-regulation is exposed, not only as being ludicrous, but also as a dangerous myth that is out of whack on both theoretical and practical grounds. Subscribing to this belief caused policymakers to play fast and loose with financial deregulation, and generally make a hash of things. The law of the jungle was allowed to prevail over the laws of civilization because of a fundamental misunderstanding of what it takes for free markets to be free. Only when governed by community-designed institutional frameworks can markets be expected to systemically reconcile increased business profitability with greater community prosperity. Consequently, those who still believe that they have a monopoly on the truth when it comes to industry self-regulation, arguably fall in the same league as those who believe that the earth is flat and inhabited by goblins, unicorns and leprechauns. For those still wondering why belief in industry self-regulation persists: it's the culture, stupid.

Because deregulation is a double-edged sword, a bull-in-a-china-shop approach to using the instrument of deregulation has been shown to be inadvisable, to put it mildly. Credible research, rather than ideology, was shown to be the sounder basis for watershed policy formulation; going off half-cocked on the ground that the answers are already known from ideology has proven to be a shaky basis for path-breaking policymaking. Sound research into deregulation would have opened the black box for differentiating between apples and oranges – and so enabled identification of the type of deregulation that benefited all. The rest of this book is devoted to throwing light on the harrowing significance of such obvious wisdom.

\*\*

# Chapter 6

## FINANCIAL DEREGULATION: DON'T FENCE ME IN

### 6.1 Regulation Autopsy

*Setting the Scene*

Financial deregulation did not happen at a stroke. The financial deregulation saga is a chapter of accidents – although at the time that it happened it was hailed as a story of triumph over the "big bad wolf" that was government. Financial deregulation mutated from being a bad idea to being a self-inflicted wound. The captains of finance and their political allies destroyed an American regulatory system that had made American banking responsible and respectable since at least the New Deal times of the 1930s. This is confirmed by the evidence that Western banks basked in the honor of ranking near the bottom of the international league table on corruption for at least fifty years, until the financial collapse of 2007-08.

A curate's egg best describes the deregulation performance of the Reagan administration; it was both good and bad. The Reagan administration was driven to move forward with ever more deregulation, in search of the elusive holy grail of an unfettered business environment. Naturally, it had set its sights on both economic and financial deregulation, cutting its teeth on the former (which was successfully accomplished) and doing the spadework on the latter (which was left to its successors as an unfinished work in progress).

On the plus side was the Reagan administration's boom-generating removal of regulatory obstacles to economic performance, which freed up trade and capital movements. This set the stage for prosperity. It enabled the administration to taste blood and whet its appetite for further deregulation. On the minus side were its reforms of a financial nature, which have had sorry, long-term, consequences. This set the stage for ruin. The President's Commission report of 1982 called for greater deregulation of mortgage banking and an increased role for capital markets in the secondary market for mortgages. The Administration fell for the "warped fallacy" that doing away with protective compartmentalization was good (Acharya et al. 2011). The Reagan administration set its seal on an important chapter of the financial deregulation saga, by putting in place the Garn-St. Germain Depository Institutions Act in 1982. This set the scene for future disaster by easing regulation of savings and loans and paving the way for the subprime mortgage-induced collapse in 2007-08. These views are supported by David Stockman, US politician, businessman, banker, and budget director in the Reagan administration. In his hard-hitting 719-page tome, *The Great Deformation*, he writes that it was only a matter of time before virtually the entire industry collapsed into insolvency (Stockman 2013, 178).

It was not exactly a movie, but it nevertheless had a sad ending. The Reagan administration, with the deregulatory bee in its bonnet, set the stage for the main act in the deregulation drama that was to follow. Although the Reagan administration's financial deregulatory bark was worse than its bite, the Reagan administration laid the foundation for a policy mindset conducive to extreme financial deregulation. In other words, although the Reagan administration missed the boat on its declared objective of further deregulating the financial sector, hanging fire did not prevent the setting-up of a fertile stage for its future fruition. In fact, the Reagan administration can be credited with preparing the ground for the subsequent opening of financial deregulatory floodgates.

The Reagan administration's unfulfilled wish was finally acted out in grand fashion when the Clinton administration unabashedly danced to the bankers' tune (which should have been *Don't Fence Me In*). When the Clinton administration came on the scene it did not miss a beat in becoming the leading light. It took a leaf out of the Reagan administration's metaphorical '*Deregulation Made Easy*' handbook and proceeded in its dubious wisdom to stage-manage the successful delivery of the goods, for completion of the job.

In the interim, the regulated tail relentlessly wagged the regulating dog. Bankers (with analysts, journalists, bureaucrats, and politicians in tow) made the climate increasingly favorable to financial deregulation. They were all cheerleaders, loudly singing in chorus the siren song in hyped praise of deregulation, deafening the general public to the pitfalls in the cause. But financial deregulation forces did not sneak in on an altogether clueless community. It is just that not enough of them cried foul loudly enough to be heard above the descant of the deregulatory trumpets that had been blowing noisily for many years. Figuratively, the running battle evokes an image of hidebound gun-toting deregulator types, trigger-finger itching for more financial deregulation, steadfastly returning down the deregulation path to their happy hunting grounds with an obsessive will, and using their blazing guns to shoot holes in the New Deal regulatory architecture in holier-than-thou fashion, oblivious to the perils of the mission. What was lacking in foresight was made up for in determination. The heady optimism about the financial deregulatory mantra rubbed off onto most decision-makers, as anti-regulation winds of change howled wildly, not just in America, but also in Europe.

The changes in the wind put the wind up political doubting-Thomases on deregulation, maverick heroes who held their own by daring to march to a different tune to that blowing from deregulatory trumpets. The savvy refusal of such politicians to drift along with the overwhelming majority on deregulatory measures can probably be attributed to the fact that they knew a thing or two from the disastrous experience of the Great Depression, and perhaps from Enron. They certainly knew something that the majority did not. History needs to record the courage of their convictions, and attendant refusal to bow down in the house of Rimmon – their ability to walk tall by refusing to sacrifice principle at the altar of conformity. They were given a hard time for knowing better than most and daring to pick holes in proposed financial deregulatory measures, even accused of being the enemies of liberty by more fire-breathing elements.

Exaggerated expectations of prosperity from financial deregulation, combined with the vulnerability of the alleged infidels to smear campaigns by vested interests, caused hot heads to prevail over those seeking cool assessment. It is small wonder that the latter species, those wanting to preserve financial regulatory safeguards, came off second best, being hunted to near extinction by a majority drawing the long bow on the fantasized merits of financial deregulation. In the end, regulation backers were drops in an ocean of acquiescence. To take just one of several examples: only eight (of one hundred) valiant US senators refused to play ball and vote for a key deregulatory bill to repeal the iconic Glass-Steagall Act of New Deal fame – with the disagreeing majority who voted for financial deregulation conjuring images of turkeys voting for Thanksgiving.

The regulatory environment became loose and lax because only bad (i.e., lame duck) regulators qualified as good regulators. Deregulation plans were not allowed to gather dust, as steps kept being taken to cut the ground from under the New Deal regulatory architecture through less formal de facto measures. This included the ad hoc watering down and undermining of New Deal regulations through the appointment of industry-friendly monitors and regulators. In an uncanny exercise of insider influence, the banks were often able to handpick their favorites to regulate them, in what became a race to the weakest regulator. This genial regulatory regime understandably provided a slack environment for banking, a state of affairs politely described by economists as "regulatory capture" (but more aptly called "regulatory farce"). In any case, because political support for banks tied the hands of regulators, even the most diligent of regulators would not have been overly enthusiastic about enforcement, not being game to buck the deregulatory trend. Naturally, the new environment spawned a culture that made regulators toothless, unable to apply what remaining regulations were left.

*The Last Big Job*

At last in1999 there was victory – albeit of the pyrrhic sort. After seventeen years, the holy grail of financial deregulation was finally reached, and a not-so-funny thing happened (in terms of lobbyist largesse) on the way to getting there. Hands-down victory was delivered once deregulation apostles gathered enough critical force for the final act that gave the green light to the zenith of deregulation. Deregulation believers broke new ground, with the victory taking the form of patchy, informal, de facto deregulation being replaced by solid, formal, de jure deregulation – thereby transforming the suboptimal to the optimal. The prevailing heady mood was not conducive to a moment of regret – gung-ho financial deregulation was the only game in town. The deregulators' overplayed hand knocked the socks off an admiring public.

The proclaimed "wave" of deregulation pronounced by the deregulation devotee, Senator Phil Gramm, and reported by Robert

Scheer (2010), was no hyperbole. If anything, it was an understatement. The die was cast when deregulation took the form of an earth-shaking root-and-branch demolition of an icon, namely, the hallowed Glass-Steagall Act of New Deal fame. It then made a splash with a two-wave tsunami in the form of two pieces of legislation, both with the word *"modernization"* in their titles: the Financial Services Modernization Act of 1999, which repealed the Glass Steagall Act (also known as the Gramm-Leach-Bliley Act) and the Commodities Futures Modernization Act of 2000, which gave free rein to derivatives (labeled "financial weapons of mass destruction" by Warren Buffet, business magnate and philanthropist). The word "modernization" in the titles of these pieces of legislation was presumably put in for its reassuring connotations, given that the tsunami that swooshed in to wipe out most of the New Deal safeguards was comprised of these Acts. They were the centerpiece of the Clinton Administration's deregulatory pride; adopting the package involved going the whole hog to give bankers everything but the kitchen sink – thereby making most of their wilder dreams come true.

The Clinton administration changed gears to run a red light and get in there by passing the two "modernization" Acts deftly joined at the hip. This worked like gangbusters for financial deregulation, judging by the fairytale business success of banks since. The titles of the deregulatory "modernization" Acts were facades that concealed a less-than uplifting meaning. In fact, the titles were misnomers, as instead of being "modern" they were retrograde, making them a spooky blast from the pre-New Deal past. But laying the unwelcome truth on the line was understandably not in the interest of bankers and their fans.

The Clinton administration nailed its colors to the mast of deregulation by passing this legislation. It was seemingly oblivious to their potential for the venomous disturbance of market fundamentals, their ability to set off shockwaves capable of reverberating around the world, and their incidental boost to the perilous plutocratic pseudo-market condition (that is explained in chapter 8). At the time, deregulation was regarded as a big deal, a smash hit that was a feather in the cap of the Clinton administration, with strong support from across the political spectrum for what was validly believed to be a history-making accomplishment. Although at the start the Clinton administration was not reputed to be in the same financial deregulatory league as the Reagan administration, in the end it put the Reagan administration to shame with the overdose of salts it unstintingly gave the cause of financial laxity. As a result, there was general contentment; everything in the garden was rosy (or so it seemed until the hurricane came in 2007-08).

"Where ignorance is bliss 'tis folly to be wise," wrote poet Thomas Gray in 1742. This insightful quotation applies to the two "modernization" Acts that romped home to usher in havoc with shoddy financial deregulation. Taken together these ill-considered "Acts," reeking of misconception, were wolves in sheep's clothing. The sheep aspect was that they were portrayed as progressive pragmatic measures that would provide greater banking efficiency and give an impetus to economic progress. The wolf aspect was that the political pragmatism argument served as a camouflage for ideological bias, while the banking efficiency argument served as camouflage for banking licentiousness (reported in chapter 4). The profound double-whammy in the wolf aspect was choreographed to give ideology-based decisions the appearance of respectability by using the flimsy fig leaf of economic rationality. The "modernization" Acts could qualify as period pieces, because they encapsulated times when there was blind service to dogma combined with a spirit of decadence.

That which was dying was killed off, but its passing still made both a symbolic and real difference. The Glass-Steagall Act of 1933, the embodiment of regulatory wisdom acquired from the Great Depression, was finally killed when the Clinton administration, in its contrary wisdom, pressed the button for its execution in 1999. Deregulation prospects were bolstered following lobbying by the CEO's of the (jaunty) Travelers Group and (staid) Citicorp to repeal the Glass-Steagall Act, so that they could strike it rich with the largest ($70 billion) corporate merger in history. It was a marriage of convenience for a mismatched odd couple that was more deadly than funny. Unsurprisingly, the marriage proposal received blessings from family in the banking industry and government, importantly from patriarch Robert Rubin, President Clinton's Treasury Secretary, the "Father of Deregulation"–making it a marriage made in the Treasury or perhaps Las Vegas, but certainly not in heaven. The repeal of Glass-Steagall was supported by the Federal Reserve chairman, Alan Greenspan (a fan of industry self-regulation) and backed by a range of policymakers and analysts trumpeting their zeal for deregulation. Starry-eyed analysts drew a longbow with exaggerated claims, while relevant media beat the deregulation drum in ostentatious support, all designed to cheer the public into falling for the spurious message that financial deregulation was the best thing since sliced bread.

It is true that getting rid of the Glass-Steagall Act was not as important as it would have been had it not been watered down over the years. The dumping of Glass-Steagall is best regarded as the formal culmination of an insidious ad hoc deregulatory process that had increasingly riddled the fabric of banking regulations with holes since the 1960s. Although in its last days Glass-Steagall was but a shadow of its former self, it was nevertheless the cornerstone of the New Deal regulatory edifice for over the six decades of its existence. Consequently, the Glass-Steagall Act was no pettifogging dead letter as some self-interested deregulators would have you believe. On the contrary, it was quite something, a crucial piece of New Deal legislation that regulated the financial services industry and gave the business of American banking worldwide respectability for several decades (despite its gradual undermining since the 1960s). Although it had passed its testosterone-charged heyday, its dismantling still left a gaping hole in the banking regulatory fabric. As will be shown in chapters 8 and 9, by enabling banks to go viral and engendering tremendous knock-on effects, the repeal of the Glass-Steagall Act was a defining moment in the history of capitalism. It is a stretch to assert that what was discarded was already dead, as some self-interested deregulation culprits have claimed. Such a claim is quite illogical. If Glass-Steagall was already a corpse, why was there such clamor for it to be killed?

Let us not speak ill of the dead. The Glass-Steagall Act, although enfeebled by loopholes at the time of its death, had played a valiant though diminishing role in protecting Main Street from Wall Street. Its repeal was right up the banks' street (i.e., Wall Street), as it opened the door to previously forbidden fruit. It was originally designed to safeguard against the very banking sins that made the current downturn possible. Bankers closed ranks to work the oracle of deregulation through persistent and aggressive lobbying, to get their hands on depositors' funds. The key to Glass-Steagall's effectiveness was the wall that it erected between commercial banks which were entrusted with depositors' funds and the largely unregulated Wall Street investment banks, like Goldman Sachs. The demolition of this wall meant "open sesame" with connotations of an Aladdin's lamp being placed in the hands of bankers; most of the limits on risk that Glass-Steagall had placed on banks could now be rubbed away in "Ali Baba" fashion. Commercial banks could now enter a previously no-go area and get their hands on the previously forbidden fruit of depositors' savings for a new-found laxity toward activities that previously required straight-laced propriety. In other words, depositors' funds could now be used to speculate in stock or commodities markets – something that has proven to be as irresistible to banks as a flame is to a moth (with similar dire consequences). Even less happily, this new temptation was introduced in circumstances of deposit insurance, which encourages banks to take risks they know the public can be made to pay for if things went wrong (i.e., when loans went bad).

The supposed panacea for economic ills was really a prescription for economic ruin. The financial deregulatory measures in the "modernization" Acts were clearly not up to scratch. By failing to identify critical infection points previously referred to, they showed up policymakers as failing to get their act together. "All you need is ignorance and confidence and the success is sure," said Mark Twain. Failure was mistaken for success, chickens were counted before they were hatched, and the promised utopia turned out to be a fool's paradise. The measures that were the "apple of the eye" (a cherished achievement) of the Clinton administration, turned out to be the "apple of Sodom" (fruit that looks delicious on the tree, but dissolves in smoke and dust when bitten), and later, an "apple of discord" (a source of strife between banks and society). Financial deregulation swept away a tidy, ordered, system that had served everyone well for decades. Deregulators knocked the public dead and brought the house down, but not in the manner they expected.

The politicians who had failed to learn from mistakes of the past were condemned to repeat them. Politicians, caught in the cobweb of deregulatory euphoria, forgot the compelling lessons of the Great Depression and Enron. They broke the golden rule that required them to hedge their bets in case the promised bonanza from deregulation turned out to be fool's gold. All the way along the line, at every point in the deregulatory process, the Great Depression and Enron disasters had a message of caution for those who might have bothered to stop and look. The alarm bells of the previous disastrous experiences, parallels in every particular, failed to ring true for deregulating politicians; a cacophony of deregulatory trumpets meant that past calamities could not ring a warning bell that was loud enough to be heard. Aiding and abetting in the wild goose chase for free-market heaven were analysts, advisors, and lobbyists. Bitten by the financial deregulation bug, they were generous in giving politicians enough rope to ensure their misfortune. Seasoned deregulatory warriors were lured into serious miscalculation when they swallowed hook, line, and sinker the fairytale about the pot of gold at the end of the financial deregulatory rainbow, and trustingly leaped into the dark.

That thing called "regulation" was almost forgotten because it was so out of fashion. Supporters of regulation had the hopeless job of swimming against the tide from the deregulation tsunami. Friends in high places closed ranks to facilitate the dismantling of regulation by making common cause with banks, adopting a hostile stance toward regulation, and steamrolling opposition on the right side of history. A hand-in-glove troika, speaking the same language on the evils of financial regulation, was nonchalantly running the show, dedicating the apparatus of government to their supposed hallowed cause. The troika comprised politicians living and breathing financial deregulation, industry lobbyists with pockets stuffed with campaign cash, and ex-financial professionals now employed in the executive branch of government (viewed suspiciously by some as double agents). It might help to have one's own in positions one wishes to influence.

Due to the hard line taken by bankers' friends at court, measures were opposed that would have brought more transparency to the market for new financial instruments. In particular, there was a lack of transparency with regard to a new class of financial products, namely derivatives, which grew rapidly to play an unedifying role in the financial market collapse, as was explained in chapter 3. Mortgage-backed securities were exempted from supervision by the Securities and Exchange Commission (SEC). Consequently, there was no strong incentive for banks to pass up the chance for fraud, to be cautious about risk, or to publicly disclose the prices and values of their instruments. An anecdote reported by Lawrence Lessig demonstrates the unfriendly attitude to regulation: when the SEC chairman Arthur Levitt tried to introduce tougher conflict-of-interest rules for the accounting industry, the Senate Banking chair, Senator Phil Gramm of deregulation fame, threatened to cut the SEC's budget (Lessig 2011, 73). The SEC chairman had clearly failed to notice that the woolly but emphatic platitudes on the benefits of financial freedom by opinion leaders had caused the word "regulation" to become a dirty unmentionable.

*Assessing the Handiwork*

Financial deregulators went charging in expecting utopia, only to find a Pandora's box. Deregulation was a victim of its own success in the sense that deregulation killed the free market with kindness by giving it an overdose of freedom to the point of license. The condition called the free market has now more or less failed in the financial and other sectors, as evidenced by the systemic conflict between business and community interests. The fact that over ninety percent of households in America hardly derived an income benefit from the pre-recession boom – at a time of record corporate earnings and banking profits of over twenty percent a year – provides empirical evidence that the strategic congruence between private profitability and social prosperity was conspicuous by its absence. This is believed to have happened because of the boost to dysfunctional plutocratic pseudo-markets, as will be explained in chapter 8.

The hard-to-miss evidence of the nosedive into recession proves that the policy pendulum swung too far in the deregulatory direction. It swung well beyond the critical inflection point, gratifying the professional needs of lobbyists and giving excessive rein to financial firms. There is unequivocal recognition that "widespread failures in financial regulation and supervision devastated stability" in the report to Congress and the president by the Financial Crisis Inquiry Commission (FCIC 2011). Willy-nilly deregulation, driven by a deeply ingrained superstitious belief in the false idol of industry self-regulation, resulted in the baby being thrown out with the bath-water. True, as memories of the Great Depression receded, deregulation increasingly became the in thing. But it is unlikely that fading memories alone would have been enough to bring it about. It also took blind service to dogma mixed with inducements of campaign money from powerful lobbyists, for successive US administrations and Congresses, pushed by banks at every turn, to strip away key safeguards and cause yawning gaps in financial oversight in critical areas.

Deregulators wanted to set the economic world on fire, but not in the manner that it turned out. They made a hash of things as the lobbyist's pecuniary hand came to replace Adam Smith's "invisible hand" – setting the stage for the more forceful manipulative hand of plutocratic pseudo-markets to outmaneuver the "invisible hand" (see chapter 8). Financial deregulation continues to impose a hidden spin-off cost in form of damage to the market mechanism, a condition of worsening decay that is later shown to hamper durable economic resurgence (see chapter 9). Assuming that at least some of those who voted for the dismantling of financial regulation did the unthinkable and bothered to read the bills, properly doing their homework might have brought home to them the peril in the bill. They were being mesmerized by corporate mercenaries into giving free rein to titanic firms ready to do almost anything to make a quick mega-buck (in which regard they did not disappoint).

Policymakers unmindful of their actions and caught on the hop, did not stop to count the cost, their sketchy grasp of the situation resulting in a tragically flawed calculus. They were in denial about the chance that their measures may not hold water; they showed no consciousness of the adverse domino effect of the change being initiated; they failed to realize they were playing with fire by not differentiating between economic and financial deregulation; and they were oblivious to the high penalty for error of their actions. They fell for "Dead Sea fruit" (that is, fruit that looks delicious on the tree, but crumbles to the touch). The legs that slapdash deregulators thought they could stand on turned out to be brittle prosthetics.

Financial deregulators, once home and dry, arguably handed the keys to the kingdom to bankers, even as they gave a poisoned chalice to the public. There was remarkable sang-froid about giving near carte blanche to powerful and aggressive banks on a roll. Deregulators seemed not to realize they were tempting fate and that their actions were so profound as to end up drawing the shades on effectively competitive open markets that embody entrepreneurial spirit, and not just in banking (see chapter 9). Regardless of whether deregulation-obsessed policymakers were driven by a naive belief in industry self-regulation or other less innocent motives, there is no doubt they have made their mark and become legends in their own lifetimes.

The actions of the deregulators have ushered in forces that have left them a lasting legacy; it promises to stand the test of time and be more unforgettable than any marble monument. This refers the monstrous edifice of a pseudo-market condition reeking of plutocracy that gives financial deregulation a resonance beyond its immediate effect, and is later shown to be a sort of expanding wild frontier in the world economy. As more fully explained in chapters 8 and 9, the boost to plutocratic pseudo-markets is the unintended but foreseeable upshot of a causal chain of events precipitated by deregulation, and they have become a burgeoning force to be reckoned with. Free choice and community benefits associated with open competitive market conditions are pathetically sparse in plutocratic pseudo-market conditions. This is because their key general feature is that an anti-social manipulative hand holds sway over the pro-social "invisible hand." Policymakers, who sowed the wind with deregulation, reaped the whirlwind: the big boost they gave to the rise of oligopolistic or monopolistic markets with plutocrats in charge. Such a legacy does not easily lend itself to mythologizing.

Deregulators did not just over-promise and under-deliver; they delivered the opposite of what they promised, for a good demonstration of what a proper fiasco should look like. They have the following results to show for their efforts: more poverty instead of greater prosperity; plutocratic pseudo-markets instead of freer open markets; less competitiveness and plodding instead of more competitiveness and dynamism; a condition where might is right instead of where entrepreneurship is right; and a condition favoring survival of the slickest, instead of survival of the fittest. By working wonders for the opposite of what they intended, it seems many policymakers have become their own worst enemies in bruising fashion (although some diehard Rip-Van-Winkle elements still display symptoms of a lack of realization).

As is well known, deregulation generated a heady climate of confidence that influenced the level of wild risk-taking leading to the financial collapse of 2007-08. Banks were the lucky winners of the much-sought-after prize, namely, the golden calf of kindly regulation that enabled a coach and horses to be driven through the protective institutional framework governing bank behavior. Financial deregulation showed all the hallmarks of a blithe overconfidence based on the cockeyed idea that unfettered markets are a pathway to economic nirvana, whereas the actual destination has turned out to be anything but a state of bliss for the excluded majority. The deregulation process had fallen prey to the politics of self-delusion. This behavior, if shown by an individual instead of a government, would likely be regarded as psychopathic.

## 6.2 The Real Culprits

The buck stops where? Responsibility for the crippled financial market must be left at the politicians' door. A less temperate and wider view is that politicians have blood on their hands from knifing the free market goddess. Although it is true that bankers and their fans were behind the deregulation fiasco, the ultimate responsibility for it must fall squarely on those politicians in the thick of things, whose blind commitment to the dubious cause made it all possible. Bankers are red herrings when it comes to identifying the real culprits; politicians, not bankers, must get top billing as the villains of the piece in terms of the preceding analysis (the others being lesser performers and bit players). It beggars belief that politicians should blame bankers for not playing by the very rules that they were responsible for clumsily discarding. It seems that just as a bad worker blames his tools, a bad deregulator blames bankers. Passing the buck for their failures misled the innocent public into looking for culprits in the wrong places (inside banks), even as the public's favorite bogeyman (the banker) became the scapegoat for politicians.

Deregulating politicians, finding they had nowhere to hide, took cover behind the metaphorical skirts of bankers. Avoiding blame is a skill prized by politicians the world over. Behavior that involves ducking and weaving to appear blameless and dodge responsibility for carrying the can on the deregulatory fiasco is explained by the fact that making a clean breast of things would require deregulating politicians to admit to a monumental blunder – a pill too big and bitter to swallow. Some may have thought better of their deregulatory *faux pas* and put it on by playing possum of sorts. There is, of course, nothing new here about drawing a veil over one's errors, refusing to face the music, or refusing to eat humble pie by eating one's words. To wash one's hands off a hanging matter is not an original idea for shirking responsibility since Pontius Pilate thought of it first. A more recent case in point was the washing of hands by the chairman of the US House Committee on Financial Services (which has responsibility for overseeing Wall Street), who blamed the crisis on the lack of fiduciary duty on the part of bankers – not acknowledging any responsibility on the part of his committee. He expected bankers to toe a line that his committee had a hand in erasing.

The flight of fantasy extended to advisors who misinformed politicians on the real effects of financial deregulation – the ones who gave politicians the rope with which to hang themselves. Robert Rubin, treasury secretary in the Clinton administration, the "Father of Deregulation," came from the financial industry that he deregulated (he was co-chair of Goldman Sachs, which is said to have led the fight for deregulation). When his deregulatory task was done, he went with hefty compensation (over $15 million a year) to the financial firm that supped from the deregulation cup and was party to the financial meltdown (Citigroup). Besides the implied alleged issue of conflict of interest, the irony is that, in a fitting metaphor, the deregulation that the company wanted and that Rubin helped engineer, backfired in the financial crisis to bring them both down. Denial delivers bliss by providing an easy way out from having to stew in your own juice. Notwithstanding their state of blissful denial or willful denial (the latter requiring intellectual acrobatics), deregulators' actions in contributing to the edifice of monstrous plutocratic pseudo-markets have spoken louder than words (shown in chapter 8).

The financial crisis seriously undermined the credibility of politicians promising better times. Financial deregulation put public safeguards into private hands and gave more freedom, not to the market, but to bankers who had a pervasive influence over the market.

This was done through a redistribution of property rights. Reflecting the successful play by the banks for a transfer to themselves of more rights, deregulating politicians took away a bundle of rights from the community and gave it to the banks. As a result, politicians have made systemic the conflict between business and public interests. Because the public was left with the short end of the stick, the coercive advantage has shifted in favor of firms, while income growth has moved away from the majority of households; a few firms filled their boots, while the public got clogs. Narrow financial interests reign over wider public interests. Worse, the banks' gain has been the economy's loss because banking practices are shown to pervasively hinder economic resurgence (see chapter 9).

On financial deregulation, a tide of mediocrity engulfed politics, and not only in America. It is arguable that getting to know the perils of slipshod financial deregulation does not require the Wisdom of Solomon; all it takes is an elementary lesson in history (*a la* The Great Depression and Enron). For this reason, the baffling question arises as to why those responsible for public wellbeing did the opposite of what was expected of them and, instead, inflicted public harm. Given the safe assumption that not all deregulators are bonkers, the answer to the question as to why deregulating politicians handed the public a poisoned chalice instead of a bowl of cherries, can be found in three mutually reinforcing elements: the cultural, the pecuniary, and the constitutional. These are root causes and are examined next.

## 6.3 The Root Causes

*The Cultural Element*

Some people are as perplexed by the belief in industry self-regulation, as others are devoted to it. The policy of industry self-regulation (underpinned by a deregulatory mindset) is no laughing matter. It has shown itself to be capable of degrading open markets by substituting licentious-prone business conditions in their place. Those impolite skeptics falling about with guffaws at the policy-driving belief in industry self-regulation, as well as those more polite ones laughing up their sleeves for the same reason, stand condemned. They deserve a telling off for their ignorance of the utterly serious and well-intentioned frame of mind behind the caring act of liberation that financial deregulation was supposed to be. This is why so many find it hard to understand why the supposed smart act of financial deregulation has failed to deliver the expected state of public gladness. The culpable have to come to terms with the mental challenge thrown up by calamitous events that have unmasked financial deregulation as a false idol, one that its many disciples in all Western countries have inadvertently worshipped at their peril.

Impasse can be nice. The United States is founded on a dislike of government power, as evidenced by the constitutional checks and balances among the three branches of government (the Executive, the Legislative, and the Judicial); the Founders were ever suspicious of a strong central authority. Such an arrangement has always ensured weak government, although, in recent years, the condition has advanced a step further and mutated into deadlock. While weak government is traditionally desired, even stalemate has its fans; there are many for whom government gridlock can be somewhere between satisfying and joyous. A condition where the branches of government are in a state of paralysis, when not much gets done, is great news for entrenched interests wedded to the status quo – those from left to right on public gravy trains, who like to keep things just as they are.

Government can be regarded as the enemy of liberty. The stereotypical American belief is that government intervention threatens life, liberty, and property, occasioning an inverse relationship between government and freedom – more government means less freedom, and vice versa. The belief that smaller government is better government is a core American value, one carved in stone; it is an article of faith that has an odor of sanctity about it. The notion has its basis in the thoughts of fiery philosopher, Thomas Paine, an immigrant from England, who stirred the hearts of people in a fledgling United States. He wrote in 1776, "Government even in its best state is but a necessary evil; in its worst state an intolerable one" (James 1981, 91). Echoing this view, President Ronald Reagan is reported to have said that government was not the solution but the problem; his rallying cry was, "get government off our back." There are many who regard government programs of any sort as a step on the road to serfdom, if not totalitarianism, although it is never easy to know when expressed fears of government plots threatening liberty are coded arguments by apologists for plutocracy.

Directly relevant to the matter at hand, namely the topic of financial deregulation, is the view of American founding father, Thomas Jefferson. He is quoted as saying, "A wise and frugal government, which shall restrain men from injuring one another, which shall leave them otherwise free to regulate their own pursuit of industry..." The "men" relevant to financial deregulation, it turned out, were bankers who, because of greater self-regulation, were able to undertake their "own pursuits of industry" and bring about the profligacy and corrupt practices reported in chapters 3 and 4. There is no doubt that such a narrow and perverse interpretation violates Thomas Jefferson's noble ideal of free enterprise; he would have had at heart the liberty of the community at large. The "freedom of industry" Jefferson referred could not have meant the freedom of firms to plunder the community on the lines of what so brazenly happened.

Less regulation is desirable because it means less government. Since opposition to government is embedded in core American values, deregulatory measures can have an air of virtue about them. Although older forms of anti-government ideology in America, like an unwillingness to tolerate deficits, are similar to European conservative values, many others are as American as apple pie. Many see a nanny's apron strings in government programs, and there is deep suspicion that government programs tend to redistribute income from hardworking taxpayers to freeloading moochers, some allegedly driving "welfare Cadillacs." Increased government spending for community welfare is a lightning rod for cynicism by those who see it as bad form, even as encouraging social parasitism by giving pork to society's leeches guilty of the sins of scrounging, shirking and slacking in shameless violation of the Judeo-Christian ethic.

It is understandable that lovers of democracy would resent an Orwellian Big Brother. After all, no citizens in their right mind who value liberty would want a sinister force, like a government bureaucrat, taking their money and following them around to supervise their lives. It is hard to dispute that size does matter when it comes to government; there are undoubted perils in big government. Too much government intervention crowds out private sector activity, prevents the grasping of opportunities, discourages individual initiative, and hampers the forward march of the economy. Economic regulation can be anathematic, the *bête noire* that throttles businesses through government command and control; less government can animate industries anaesthetized by regulation. What happened to the defunct Soviet Union illustrates that economies can get crushed by excessive government.

For many, the "Acts" of deregulation were expressions of patriotism. The small government cultural value is expressed post collapse by Republican senator Thomas Coburn (2012). In *The Debt Bomb* he takes the position that larger government, by curbing liberties, has the effect of dismantling the US Constitution. The logical inference for deregulation from the "big government" argument is that deregulation measures demonstrate allegiance to country; by lessening government they would do nothing less than strengthen the operation of the American Constitution. Because the ideological aversion to government is a key component of US exceptionalism, industry regulation cuts across the American cultural grain. In practical terms, adopting policies that minimize government intervention (e.g., financial deregulation) is consequently second nature for many across the American political spectrum.

Such an attitude is conducive to regulations being shunned as offensive, and regulators being despised as intrusive enemies of liberty. Working to reduce the reach of government, such as through a do-or-die approach to deregulation, can then become a patriotic holier-than-thou mission, a laudable cause that can make policymakers jump at the chance of winning brownie points, especially from business. Little wonder that believers in small government, ideologically averse to government intervention, were swept off their feet by the enchantment of financial deregulation, enabling financial sector lobbyists to easily strike the right note and make the measures a shoo-in. By implication, sticking to one's guns on belt-tightening austerity becomes perfectly logical for those subscribing to the hallowed belief in small government. When influenced by such thinking, policymakers would not have much compunction about shooting from the hip when the target was government spending or, more to the point, government regulation.

Once bitten, never shy. Going down the small-government "pathway" has repeatedly led to a large-government "highway"–giving rise to outcomes that are bizarrely contrary to what is espoused and intended. Ironically, the "small government" argument has led to large government, making small-government believers become big-government practitioners. Government is still America's largest job sector, directly employing some twenty-two million workers from garbage collectors to solicitors at the Federal, State, and local levels.

That is the least of it. As is common knowledge among economists, US government handouts to industry is an entrenched bad habit from year one. It has funneled billions of dollars to grain and cotton farmers (which arguably qualify as boondoggles), as well as to the oil, mining, and ethanol industries. Farm subsidies harvest $20 billion a year from the pockets of taxpayers. Surprisingly, free market believers keep accepting, year after year, the unhelpful market distortions that result from these handouts. Distortions are also associated with the deposit insurance scheme, which effectively subsidizes risk-taking by banks. An educative example that stands out is as follows: that because of World Trade Organization (WTO) requirements, the American government pays a penalty of over $140 million a year to compensate farmers in Brazil for subsidies given to American cotton growers – implying, besides the market distortion, a double-blow for taxpayers.

The high level of public debt in the West can be attributed to the downturn caused, not by bigger government, but by smaller government. Shrinking the government's role through the withdrawal of regulatory control gave banks and other businesses wide latitude to run amok–and that includes the lax regulatory supervision of government-sponsored agencies Freddie Mac and Fannie Mae. Specifically, large-scale government intervention through the provision of publicly-owned rescue money labeled "bailouts," and even socialistic nationalization, were needed because of business profligacy enabled by less regulation of the banks and mortgage agencies. The retreat to *smaller* (insufficient) government left room for bad things to happen, including the undermining of sacrosanct markets signals – something that should be inviolate for free market believers. Some significant component of the public debt in the United States, at least $6 trillion, is due to downturn-related factors: bailout money, higher expenditures on social services (including a bloated food stamp program), and reduced revenue inflow.

This view is diametrically opposite to the interpretation of the condition referred to earlier (that large government is responsible for current ills). Such divergence alludes to a policy impasse that does not bode well for a solution to this crisis – an aspect that is central to the issues addressed in chapter 11on "Policy Options."

*The Pecuniary Element*

What about the supposed root of all evil? It was not only culture that was behind the financial deregulation; money seems to have also played a role – for a persuasive confluence of culture and money. It is understandable that money struck responsive chords. Because of a cultural mindset predisposed to deregulation, monetary inducement was projected into fertile conditions that likely caused lobbyists to be accommodated without compunction. The rosy conditions meant that it would not have made sense for bankers to pass up the opportunity to consolidate their hold on the financial system.

Correlation, famously, is not causation – not necessarily, anyway. Although there is no direct link, there is a broad positive correlation, a happy happenstance, between campaign contributions and policy formulation on deregulation. Humans are extremely suggestible, according to social psychologist Robert Cialdini. In his classic work *Influence: the Psychology of Persuasion* (2006), Cialdini notes that a gift as minor as a can of soda increases receptivity to a "salesman's pitch."

Campaign contributions are, of course, no cans of soda. There is no need to wonder about the persuasive powers of cold hard cash, especially when it comes in bundles. A meeting of minds on deregulation was a coincidence, either induced or fortuitous, that handily benefited both politicians and bankers. In the ten years to 2008, the financial industry spent $2.7 billion in lobbying for deregulation and contributed more than $1 billion to political campaigns, according to the Financial Crisis Inquiry Commission (FCIC 2011). At the time of the deregulatory measures, a lot of loaves and fishes coincidentally transferred from Wall Street into the larder of President Clinton's Democratic Party, as recorded by Robert Scheer (2010). A similar happy happenstance is reported by Paul Krugman in relation to Senator Phil Gramm (Krugman 2012, 84), who was a leading light in the movement devoted to the unholy cause of snuffing out critical financial regulations.

On balance it appears that campaign contributions did more to reinforce than change beliefs. On the basis of what was stated earlier, it seems a safe presumption that most deregulating politicians were unaware they had latched onto a loser. For this reason, it would not be accurate to say that the bankers had many politicians over a barrel. By implication, since it took two to tango (a dance appropriately requiring a contrapuntal ability to seduce one's dancing partner) there is every reason to believe that the mutuality of interest caused the deregulatory moves to be eagerly spontaneous expressions by both partners. More specifically, deregulation is not likely to have typically caused political principle to be sacrificed for expediency; there was already a strong cultural aversion to regulation by those who benefitted from the money indirectly given for its dismantling. It is difficult to know the relative role of money and ideology in the deregulation saga. The problem is similar to that of knowing which of the two blades of a pair of scissors cuts the paper (to paraphrase the description of market forces by the iconic Alfred Marshall).

It would seem that, for most politicians, deregulation was not a put-up job, or part of some sinister objective or clandestine agenda. The disastrous consequences of deregulation have not done justice to the bona fide intentions of the ardent majority who voted for it in all innocence. They would have genuinely believed that the financial deregulation path was a road to riches and would have had no idea that going down that road meant riding for a fall. As Lawrence Lessig stated, many of the key figures believed in deregulation as an ideal and were motivated by principles more than anything else (Lessig 2011, 74). No doubt deregulation was a labor of love for many, being undertaken in good faith by those who thought nothing of giving it a go (nothing ventured, nothing gained), not realizing that it was a Pandora's box of obstinate trouble. Going by what Lessig stated, most deregulators would not have blown it had they known it. This meant that bankers and their devotees bluffed their way past gatekeepers who were community guardians. For many deregulators, the worst that can be said is that relentless deregulation propaganda by vested interests brainwashed them about what was at stake and made them take leave of their senses. Even though deregulating politicians may have laid all their cards on the table, the problem was that they had been dealt a losing hand by advisers they trusted. In the circumstances, the cap of seediness would better fit the manipulators than the manipulated.

In the end, the bare-bones impression is inescapable that the heady concoction of ideology, misinformation, and money caused many of those who voted for financial deregulation to swallow the "its-good-for-the-economy" bait and shoot themselves in the foot. There seems good reason for believing that this had the effect of blurring the vision of politicians, making them easy meat for banks and denying them awareness of the Belshazzar-style writing on the wall about the fate that awaited open competitive market sectors. The sad triumph for those acting in good faith on financial deregulation was not only because of the economic collapse and the attendant suffering, but also because of the increasing damage to open competitive markets in the wake of the tremendous boost given to the spreading plutocratic pseudo-market condition. That is shown in chapter 9 to have the ominous capacity to stymie economic growth and also entrench and worsen this economic downturn.

## The Constitutional Element

Representatives in all democracies need campaign money. In both the Westminster parliamentary system of government and the American presidential system, the needs are the same. On the one side are politicians searching for cash for their election war chests; on the other side are interest groups loaded with cash who want a special favor or two from politicians. Lobbing, involving as it does beating a path to the politician's door (it is bad form for the opposite to happen), is not in itself corrupt. It has the benefit of enabling minority voices to be heard, such as those of charitable organizations. Nevertheless, the practice is conducive to wheeling and dealing and vulnerable to the bending of politicians' ears in an anti-social manner by pressure-wielding big business.

It is never about the money, yet it can be all about the money. Lobbyists are everywhere in Western democracies; all elected politicians are at the mercy of vested interests for support, whether from labor union leaders (derided by critics as blue-collar thugs) or corporate magnates (derided by critics as white-collar thugs). Even though palms may not be directly greased, the policymaking process can still be defiled by the viciously viscous lubricant. Generally, the ever-present fear of having the rug pulled from under them tends to keep money-seeking politicians in line, irrespective of the system. The need for campaign money makes upholding double standards inescapable in all types of representative democracies. Hence, the need for money tends to clip the wings of politicians, cramp their style, and require them to sing for at least a part of their supper. Byzantine deals and cozy arrangements are not out of the question, and obligation to business can manifest as stonewalling or innuendo on particular issues. Dependence on vested interests places politicians on the horns of a dilemma when business and public interests are in conflict, a particular quandary for them in the plutocratic pseudo-market conditions described in chapter 8. Although all this does not necessarily give rise to cravenly sycophantic behavior by dependant politicians, the fact remains that their ability to work without fear and favor is compromised by the need to keep one eye on the purse strings. This has the knock-on effect of greasing the process for the emergence of plutocratic forces. In the end it could give rise to anti-social coalitions between political and business interests that throw up the socially unfriendly conflation of political, market, and capital power.

Irrespective of the political system, businesses work governments behind the scenes, the corridors of power being a world of shadows resonating with the undercurrents of mysterious lobbyist activity. Dodgy payoffs must be secretive in order to be effective; to be seen to boss elected politicians around is considered bad form and not a smart thing to do. What may be regarded as bona fide cooperation by politicians could be gamesmanship for big business, as happened with financial deregulation. In any case, because many of the more powerful companies are transnational titans with much influence over the domestic economy, politicians understandably shy away from potentially bruising David-versus-Goliath type confrontations with global giants capable of making trouble.

Resorting to American-style lobbying in the Westminster parliamentary system would usually be seen as an exercise in stupidity. In the parliamentary system, open flirtation between individual members and special interests is frowned upon though it happens to some significant but unknown extent (dealing needing to be secretive to be effective). A lobbyist foolish enough to offer money directly to a member's individual campaign and a member foolish enough to accept it would likely be the subject of scandal or worse. In Australia, all it took for a state leader to be brought down in 2014 was the *faux pas* of not acknowledging the gift of a bottle of wine. In any case, giving money to a member of parliament is not likely to achieve much unless the person being lobbied was of Cabinet rank, or had influence at that level (because the legislative process is centrally controlled at the Cabinet level of the Executive Branch). This means, for lobbying to be successful, the lobbyist interest must become a party interest, making exertions in relation to individual representatives usually a waste of time. For example, in Australia (which follows the Westminster parliamentary system), mining industry lobbyists can become office bearers of the right-wing Liberal Party (APP 2012), while trade union officials have ready access to their many cabinet-level ex-colleagues on the other side. The Canadian government shows signs of having fallen for mining industry charms. In Britain, Prime Minister David Cameron and senior ministers wine and dine business leaders who donate money to the party, but deny that access buys influence (Mason 2012). Company directorships for senior members of the government are commonplace.

In the Westminster system, to be seen to be open to lobbyist influence still has an element of shamefulness about it. The system requires lobbyists to be discreetly influential, and for politicians not to flaunt their espousal of business causes. Stealth is preferable to openness when it comes to dealing with lobbyists, and when it gets out in the open, the wheeling and dealing can be euphemistically called "industry consultation." A World Bank study concluded that influence was more easily bought in the American presidential system than in the Westminster parliamentary system (Lederman, Loayza, and Sores 2001). This finding is hardly startling for those aware of the marked differences in the legislative processes between the two systems, and the legal limits on campaign contributions under the Westminster parliamentary system.

In America, on the other hand, there is nothing shameful about dealing with lobbyists. Lobbying is normal, integral, and inevitable – making corruption normal, integral, and inevitable. In stark contrast to the Westminster parliamentary system, the American legislative process is wide open to influence by the paid agents of special interests, whose rights are protected under the "free speech" provisions of the US Constitution (the First Amendment). The corridors of power are crammed with lobbyists who outnumber politicians many times over, and whose job it is to run rings around politicians in a world of shadows. Spending on lobbying has more than doubled in the last fifteen years from the already high base associated with financial deregulation – conjuring the image of an underground tunnel between Wall Street and Capitol Hill. As is generally known, in the US any member of Congress can introduce a bill that is first referred to a committee or sub-committee. As a result, unlike under the Westminster parliamentary system, any member of Congress is open to influence – and that could extend to fellow committee members won over to the cause.

Arguably, campaign contributions are to politicians what spinach is to Popeye. Vested interests have lobbying down to a fine art, and expect to be made a fuss of because of their possible whip hand over political careers. This tends to ensconce lobbyists in the drivers' seats. Such vulnerability makes politicians fair game to big business, and this might have the former on an often invisible string to be pulled as the occasion demands. Adding to the pressure on politicians of direct lobbying, are Political Action Committees (PACs), where affluence buys influence. They are mutually reinforcing in keeping politicians in line without a formal *quid pro quo*. This phenomenon of business money for political influence has been made rife by the US Supreme Court landmark decision in *Citizens United v. Federal Election Commission* of 2010. This law has enabled corporations to give unlimited amounts of money to political candidates through PACs. Naturally, the absence of limits on campaign finance encourages excessive patronage and gives powerful vested interests a weight beyond their numbers. This tilts the balance away from one-person-one-vote (democracy) to one-dollar-one-vote (plutocracy), and makes the shadowy influences of plutocracy part and parcel of the processes of democracy. In his *Republic Lost,* Lawrence Lessig labels the corruption in the US Congress "dependence corruption" (Lessig 2011, 230). Such dependence means that there exists an invisible sword of Damocles that insidiously operates to keep politician in line at all times. Lessig's portrayal of the relationship between politics and money reveals how corruption corrodes the political apparatus – causing what seems to prevail in the American system to be based on a leaf taken from Machiavelli's *The Prince*, rather than from Aristotle's *Ethics.*

In the United States, the form of corruption practiced is unique because of its compatibility with the appearance of respectability. The flow of money to politicians is indirect and behind the scenes, enabling a sophisticated form of corruption of the camouflaged sort. Anything to do with money happens at arms' length, and that enables influence-peddling to take place as if money was not involved. Corruption is not of the crude *quid pro quo* type commonly practiced in other, mainly non-Western, countries, where politicians' outstretched palms are openly crossed with silver. In such foreign situations where there is a thriving environment of graft, and public officials from top to bottom are openly on the take, there is no need for corruption to be furtive to be effective.

In the United States, backstairs corruption gets dignified by the harsh punishment meted out for corruption of the foreign (i.e., direct or open) sort. For example, jail terms were imposed on Republican Congressman Randy D. Cunningham in 2005 (eight years) and Democratic Congressman William J. Jefferson in 2009 (thirteen years). Arguably, the boom was lowered on these politicians because they lowered the tone of American corruption. It appears the problem for them was that they did favors of a specific nature and got their just desserts for not meeting proper corruption standards. This suggests that lining pockets must have class to be accepted in the American system; taking money must be sophisticated, hypocritical, and devious enough to be harmonious with a cultivated image of honesty.

Despite an arguable touch of elegance in American corruption, there cannot be much that is quaint about a swamping corruption that gives rise to bloopers like financial deregulation. There are no prizes for guessing that corruption can put grit into the machinery needed to produce institutional frameworks that are friendly to both business and community interests (as explained in chapter 5). Therefore, the need to keep on the right side of campaign benefactors could compromise policy positions, giving rise to institutional frameworks of the sort that enables conflict between business and public interests, as happened with financial deregulation. A successful election of the funded candidate means that the business that funded the candidate now has a friend in the right place, a person who would continue to look after its interests without any direct agreement on specific matters. The corruption takes the form of positions being shaped to favor a particular industry by public pronouncements, or by dropping support for a particular measure that the industry does not like, but without a formal *quid pro quo*. This brings to mind the caveats inserted to win over opponents when measures were introduced to re-regulate banks through the blizzard of regulations called the Dodd-Frank bill (see section 8.5).

All this serves to further explain the financial deregulation washout. It explains why banks are likely to possess more clout than people in influencing the political process, the public being reduced to second-fiddle status. Blurring the line between corporations and individuals through PACs has had the effect of further blurring the line between corporations and government. Add to this the power of lobbyists, and the balance gets tilted away from democracy and toward plutocracy (i.e., the control of government by the wealthy). This means there is usurpation of power by the wealthy from the community at large that blunts democratic forces and toughens plutocratic forces. When the operational strategies of businesses systematically extend into political strategy, and playing the political game becomes part and parcel of what businesses do, companies gain influence over social outcomes in the manner of the merchants of Venice of old. This means, the arrogation of power from politicians to themselves gives business leaders a numerically disproportionate say in who gains and who loses in society (i.e., they are able to overly influence the definition of a social welfare function, as was the case with financial deregulation).

**

# Chapter 7

## THE DISCREDITED PROFESSION:
## COWBOY ECONOMICS

### 7.1 Rediscovering Economics

This chapter shines a light on the dark role played by so-called finance economists and others of their ilk in contributing to the collapse, and now perpetuating the downturn. To set the scene we make believe that we have entered the happy "what if" world of hunky-dory economics. We imagine that in this world, the current downturn does not happen because economists do what they are supposed to do. Recessions are rare, and when they do happen they are moderate; they are shallow and short. In this pretend world, preemptive measures can be taken because economists routinely alert policymakers to impending danger by closely monitoring key indicators of economic health such as corporate earnings, productivity increases, and GDP growth, while ensuring that markets are sufficiently functional through openness, competitiveness, and contestability. In these make-believe circumstances, the pantheons of economic wisdom are fully clothed emperors holding sway over the economic policy formulation process.

We come back down to earth and ask whether economics can still be regarded as economics if its only concern is increasing the monopolistic profits of banks and other firms, without explicit regard for social welfare? It may be hard for some economists to believe that economics is really a social science for improving society's lot via private profit maximization – at least, that is what it is supposed to be. "The main motive of economic study is to help social improvement" said Arthur C. Pigou (the successor to the "father of standard economics," Alfred Marshall), in his classic work *Economics of Welfare* of 1932 (James 1981, 66). This means that private profitability is expected to define its relationship with the economy through social prosperity.

For those who know, the Enlightenment begot economics. Although a weakling from the time of birth, economics has usefully contributed to rational thinking, rigorous analyses, and more informed policy formulation ever since. By the end of the eighteenth century economics had emerged as an identifiable subject in its own right. The Age of Enlightenment provided its ideas for the Industrial Revolution through economics, known then as "political economy" (referred to hereafter as "traditional political economy"). As any political scientist knows, the essence of the philosophy of the Enlightenment is that humans, because they are human, are universally rational. Adam Smith's concept of the "invisible hand" previously referred to, is based on the fundamental assumption that economic agents will act in an economically rational manner to maximize benefits to themselves within the rules of the game.

As most economists know, in the beginning there was "political economy." In search of light, philosophers enunciating the principles of economics in the eighteenth century considered society as an integrated totality, and called the incipient field of economics "political economy." The trans-disciplinary ambit of traditional political economy encompassed contemporary subjects such as social theory, law, government, political and economic history, and the history of political and economic thought. Its panoptic perspective imparted a "feast of reason" (to quote the eighteenth century British poet, Alexander Pope). Traditional political economy, through its multi-disciplinary dimension, breaks down boundaries to provide economics with the big picture through context – a significant lacuna in the pathetic type of economics that was behind the current crisis.

The subfield of finance economics has lost the safety that comes from context and perspective. The multidisciplinary dimension, which was integral to traditional political economy, was lost as economics became increasingly narrower and shallower to the point of becoming socially dangerous in finance economics (as its contribution to the current crisis palpably demonstrates). Economics shed the broad perspective that characterized traditional political economy, when the context-giving subjects dropped off the syllabus. It then became just "economics" with the publication of Alfred Marshall's seminal 1890 textbook *Principles of Economics*. Alfred Marshall earned the title "father of standard economics," by polishing and tidying economic theory. He was keen to ensure that the symbols of mathematics were subservient to the logic of words. This is another matter of significance for explaining the failure of finance economics in the current economic crisis (explained later). Marshall's subordination of mathematics to words is evident in the relegation of mathematical expression to footnotes in his magnum opus.

Even deregulators can command respect. Adam Smith, believe it or not, was a deregulator – and a lovable one at that. This may seem like vindicating manna from heaven for the deregulatory tribe of finance economists and other birds of a similar feather. But hold on; there is no reason for glee. It is not surprising that Adam Smith was a deregulator, as his thinking underpinned the dismantling of the maze of obstructive government regulations put in place by the economic system of "mercantilism" and its replacement with capitalism. The market restrictions that Adam Smith identified were those of the disposable variety, in the category of regulation on the airline industry (successfully removed by the Carter administration and other countries around the world), as well as restrictions on trade and capital flows (successfully done away with by the Reagan and Thatcher administrations). The mercantile system relied on government intervention for wealth creation, and no self-respecting economist would want to be labeled a mercantilist. Because it was pervasive in hampering individual initiative in relation to industry and trade, it qualified for removal by clearly falling in the safe zone before the critical inflection point previously referred to (see section 5.4). This meant that deregulation, through the dismantling of mercantilism, was generally able to, over the long haul, engender both business profitability and social prosperity (until now, that is).

As is common knowledge among economists, proper economics trains the mind to think straight. In order to appreciate what went wrong in economics, it is necessary to appreciate that standard economic theory, despite its limitations, anchors a useful framework for logical thinking. It has, over the years, tidied minds and provided countless analysts with generalizations for orderly policy formulation. It provides the principles that are indispensable for the purpose of defining problems, analyzing issues, and interpreting results. The theory comprises a body of principles that are generalized tendencies, the more important ones having the status of economic laws (like the laws of demand and supply). These laws are deductions of pure theory and assert what happens when certain conditions are met. Economic theory is, therefore, a branch of logic that constructs systems of hypothetical propositions of a qualitative nature. Pure theory is an abstraction from particular real-world conditions. In this respect economics is no different from any other science. Also, as in all sciences, pure economic theory preceded the applied; before any science can be applied, obviously a body of theory must first be built up.

Economists came to the fore. Traditionally, generalists knowledgeable in the classics and arts were regarded as being best able to analyze and process information for the purpose of problem-solving in decision-making. For example, formerly generalists occupied permanent positions in the upper echelons of the much-admired British civil service, as well as in the public services of former British colonies like Canada, Australia, New Zealand, and India. Subsequently, economists came to increasingly occupy positions previously reserved for generalists, especially since the Second World War. Although today economists are seen by many as a dreary bunch, there was a time when it was so prestigious to be an economist that even pen-pushing clerks gave themselves the mantle. "Nowadays, in most of the world's capitals, nearly every official fancies himself as an economist..." wrote R.L. Morris in the *Economic Journal* over six decades ago (Morris 1954). As a result, it came to pass that the world was increasingly fashioned by the economist's image of it (depending on the type of economist wielding influence).

Since this economic crisis erupted, there have been many examples of pots calling kettles black. Some ongoing criticism of standard economics is surprisingly ill-informed and includes cheap shots that reflect a paucity of understanding, to put it mildly. Some critics, with probably no practical experience in the real world of economic policy formulation and with little or no knowledge of the institutional aspect of economics, consider themselves expert enough to condemn standard economic theory. As a result, the body of knowledge called the "science of economics," built up by great minds over two hundred years, is discredited because of its abuse by those who contributed to the current crisis.

For those who know, assumptions are both necessary and inevitable. The critics appear to forget that the conditionality of theory is true of all scientific laws. According to Milton Friedman, writing in his *Essays in Positive Economics,* "Truly important and significant hypotheses will be found to have 'assumptions' that are wildly inaccurate descriptive representations of reality and, in general, the more significant the theory, the more unrealistic the assumptions in this sense" (Friedman 1953, 8-9). Critics do not seem to realize that it is not required for assumptions (e.g., profit maximization) to be correct, but for the economy to behave "as if" they were correct. Critics do not seem to appreciate that in this respect there is no basic difference in method between economics and other sciences. The divergence of economic norms from real-world conditions does not automatically qualify the theory for the garbage bin; theory can still perform the function of providing a point of reference for policy guidance. Keynes is reported to have said, "The attempt to combine theoretical and practical enquiries tends to confirm the popular confusion as to the nature of many economic truths. What are laid down as theorems of pure science is constantly interpreted as if they were maxims for practical guidance" (James 1981, 56). Neither does economic theory become pointless for policy guidance just because finding mathematical equilibrium is an illusory hope. Chasing the rainbow of equilibrium appears to be a mug's game, a questionable endeavor best left to game-playing mathematicians who consider themselves economists.

Visible results show economics to good advantage. It may surprise some critics of economics to know that standard economic theory has actually worked in practice, its significant limitations notwithstanding. Over the years, economic theory has provided credible guidance for policy formulation in relation to industry competitiveness and more efficient resource use in America, Britain, New Zealand, and Australia, among many other countries. For instance, the current competitiveness of Australian agriculture is attributable to reforms based on detailed economic analyses painstakingly undertaken over several years under the direction of minister John Kerin of the boldly reformist Hawke government (in which deregulatory process this author was privileged to play a leadership role). Similar deregulatory reforms targeted other sectors of the economy and knocked industries into shape by exposing them to the forces of international competition. The successful results are there for all to see; the evidence speaks for itself. Hence, despite its limitations, economics has repeatedly given a good account of itself when not abused.

## 7.2 Vulnerable Economics

The very nature of economics makes it vulnerable to witchcraft. The dreaming recorded earlier revealed how economics could have ideally worked. But to understand why it did not, it is necessary to understand its innate qualities as well as well as its inherent frailties that have made it susceptible to uninformed criticism, abuse, and subversion – vulnerability being in the nature of the beast.

There is strength in weakness; assumptions that have enveloped economics in protective armor are, paradoxically, also its weakness. But standard economics, as generally practiced over the ages, has always been the happy prisoner of its assumptions. Economics, since its beginning, has been generally subject to the *ceteris paribus* assumption (the assumption that other things remain the same, or are held constant) which, although defining an area of analysis that is taboo for many, is later shown to ironically harbor the solution to the current problem (see section 11.8). The subsequent analyses will lay bare relevant underpinnings cloaked in *ceteris paribus*, to show how they divorce economic policy formulation from an effective solution to this crisis (that may not, however, qualify as a silver bullet). The underpinning factors usually assumed away, and hence not questioned, include sociopolitical institutions such as industry regulation, business corruption, and the income distribution. These are useful assumptions for the reason that they enable the greater universality of economic laws. What is more, they are prudent assumptions, because they enable economists to steer clear of upsetting apple carts; they enable economists to avoid donning green tights (i.e., playing Robin Hood roles), or antagonizing the establishment in other subjective value-driven ways. This is especially so in relation to the distribution of income which, despite what finance economists might say, reflects the distribution of the power in society.

The optimum in economics is always conditional. When economists make recommendations that something is optimal, what is optimal is optimal only if "other things" remain the same, such as, for instance, the regulatory framework or income distribution or, for that matter, institutionalized business corruption. Because underpinning socioeconomic institutional factors are therefore not generally questioned, matters such as legal and ethical guidelines (embodied in the institutional frameworks referred to in chapter 5), tend to automatically fall outside the scope of typical economic analyses. For this reason, what is proffered as objective analysis is in fact surreptitiously value-loaded, implying that it supports the *current* regulatory framework, distribution of income, state of corruption, inter alia. While economics has long deluded policymakers by being deceptively value-free, it played it safe by doing so. It must be acknowledged that economics' assumptions have been accepted by many eminent minds over the years and, therefore, embody the collective wisdom of time – although this has not deterred some Johnny-come-latelies from rashly criticizing great economists of the past.

Not rocking the boat implies circumspection. By accepting existing sociopolitical institutions (e.g., banking regulations) and market structures (e.g., plutocratic pseudo-markets) as givens, standard economics is able to discreetly steer clear of bleeding-heart types of political activism. As economists who work in the policy arena must know full well, economic advisors who push private causes soon lose their credibility as objective analysts – and could end up being shown the door. Obviously, taking sides based on value judgments is not consistent with professional objectivity from impartiality, dispassion, and nonpartisanship. Pushing social causes is not usually regarded as being within the professional province of proper policy economists; technically speaking, it is not the role of economists to define what is known in the profession as a "social welfare function." Professional protocol usually requires policy economists to leave social value judgments to politicians. For instance, it is for representative politicians to decide who in the community should gain and by how much, when it comes to deciding critical infection points for deregulatory measures. Nevertheless, economists can legitimately provide information on the implications of alternative solutions, identifying gainers and losers. Politicians can then make their policy value judgments (i.e., define the "social welfare function") in the light of the fuller information made available by economists.

Understandably, vested interests tend to like the status quo. By accepting underpinning conditions as given, standard economics ensures conservatism – to the delight of vested interests. Making the assumption that laws, regulations, income distribution, tax benefits, and sundry gravy trains remain unchanged (and hence outside the scope of analyses), places economics in a situation where it automatically supports the status quo (i.e., vested interests). In other words, through *ceteris paribus* assumptions economics entrenches the status quo for the benefit of vested interests. This makes it a perfect Trojan horse for the business world. It is not surprising that economics became the secular religion of Western society and triumphant finance economists the darlings of business moguls.

Economists were into big stuff leading up to the current crisis. Finance economists, flying high, were welcomed as priests of the new secular religion, with a hobnobbing seat at the policy table of powerful business moguls, whose hearts they had won. Naturally they sang in unison with the big noises in corporations with whom they rubbed shoulders. The advice of highly regarded finance economists was, for their paymasters, the cat's meow. They were seen as the font of economic wisdom, the whiz kids of capitalism, the golden boys and girls of a golden age whose mission it was to blaze a pecuniary trail. Their output was "caviar to the general," or so it was regarded at the time. The finance economists ruling the roost were cocks-of-the-walk in the economics profession, often drowning out mainstream economists. They rode high atop the bubbles they helped to create in the frothy conditions before the slump that they had a not-so-invisible hand in whipping up.

The expectations of economists by their paymasters were as inflated as the bubbles being created. Finance economists and their fellow travelers came to be overrated in the business world. They, like Moses, were expected to smite the rock and bring forth water. Consequently, increasing demands came to be placed upon finance economists and others of their ilk by powerful paymasters who saw economists as valued instruments of wealth creation, and compensated them accordingly. It is understandable if the lucrative nature of the job meant that economists had to deliver to expectations to be worth their salt.

## 7.3 Reinvented Economics

Economists were not quite like Moses; neither was economics a magic formula. Investors and business paymasters, particularly bankers, placed a lot of faith in the superiority of economists and in the infallibility of their models. Unintentionally courting trouble, rejoicing investors and paymasters came to expect more from finance economists than it was within the capability of the imperfect science of economics to deliver. Judging by their actions (examined later), finance economists and their fellow travelers were in no mood to disappoint anybody – and were evidently prepared to smite the rock as hard as it took. They were not discouraged by the bar being set too high, they were unbowed by the inherent limitations of economics, and they were disinclined to discard the bogus mantle of science that hid the inadequacies of their models. They had the temerity to overextend economic theory into murky corners of analyses for which it was ill-equipped. The economy was booming and economists needed to punch above their weight if they were to be worth their salt. The flourishing conditions were conducive to heresy because, in the words of American philosopher Eric Hoffer (1902-83), "A heresy can spring only from a system that is in full vigor" (Dingle 2008). Finance economists flung caution (which comes from adopting truly scientific methods), to the wind and succumbed to the temptation of overreaching themselves.

An economics reinvented by finance economists delivered results that were as spurious as the bubbles that they had helped to blow. The manner in which economic principles are applied to explain issues and estimate phenomena will, of course, affect the relevance and credibility of the conclusions reached. This implies the need for a process of inquiry that is scientific in its approach and the specification of mathematical models based on a theory that is valid. Finance economists and their type overreached themselves by pursuing illusory goals because of their failure to recognize the limitations inherent in economics and the real nature of the market conditions being modeled. They were hell-bent on modeling a market that had largely ceased to exist. For one thing, economics is blind to dysfunctional markets and corrupt business environments for the reason that these are embodied in the *ceteris paribus* assumption and consequently outside the scope of typical analyses. For another, economics, as an imperfect science of generalized tendencies, is limited in its ability to deliver the exactitude required in dynamic financial markets that are more uncertain than risky. This is because they are corrupted to the point of not being proper markets, and hence subject to operational subterfuge – an aspect addressed in the explanation that follows and more fully in the chapter that follows.

Finance economists hit the right note with views that caused investors and bankers to rationalize the activity of chasing rainbows; by modeling frothy conditions, finance economists gilded the pill for coaxing investors and putting a smile of satisfaction on the lips of their paymasters. History shows that it amounted to living dangerously on borrowed time that was good while it lasted – that is, until the bursting bubbles gave the game away by exposing the snakeoil nature of the economists' output. What was spun as a mantra for profit was really a recipe for ruin. Investors and bankers caught with chaff because of the advice of finance economists found, in a moment of truth, that their tower of strength (the economists' models), had rested on a foundation of quicksand. Finance economists and their believers, being mutually oblivious to reality, acted out the biblical warning that when the blind leads the blind, they would both fall in the ditch.

Perhaps unwittingly, smoke and mirrors were part and parcel of the game. The methodology of applied economics leaves the door open to processes that are at odds with reality – making barking up the wrong tree a constant possibility. The fact is that mathematical models can never be more than simplified representations of reality, with the best of models depending heavily on the prior beliefs of the analyst. This leaves room for self-deception by analysts, for the inclusion of fudge factors, and for models to be based on the pizzazz of hyped-up theories. As reportedly stated in 1885 by no less a person than the "father of standard economics," Alfred Marshall, "The most reckless and treacherous of all theorists is the one who professes to let facts and figures speak for themselves, who keeps in the background the part he played, perhaps unconsciously, in selecting and grouping them..."(James 1981 p.57).

For finance economists, some standard theories were inconvenient truths; newfangled theories carried the day. To justify one fanciful theory the finance economists subscribed to the convenient view that asset prices are only valid in relation to other asset prices, thereby rationalizing bubble-creation and fuelling cumulative momentum in markets. In terms of the "efficient market hypothesis" that was driving decision-making at the time, you cannot beat the market; the price of a financial asset reflects all the information available – and so provides optimal estimates of the true investment value of financial assets. This meant that financial markets always got prices right. On the contrary, Keynes recognized that many of our positive activities depend on spontaneous optimism, rather than on mathematical expectations. Events have proven Keynes right.

Other concepts, such as the "market discipline hypothesis" used by finance economists, also made light of orthodox theory and peddled fantasies; they ignored market realities, especially the dysfunctional state of markets (referred to as the plutocratic pseudo-market condition in chapter 8). In terms of their notion, buyers and sellers would generally get prices right, because wrong prices would send one or the other up the creek. This view implies that it would be self-defeating for businesses to withhold information, distort information, or engage in other means of swindling and hoodwinking customers thorough overpricing and undervaluing. It is believed that such behavior would drive their customers to their competitors, the threat of customer loss having the disciplinary effect of keeping such potentially miscreant businesses in line. This is clearly balderdash; widespread and systematic fraud was rampant and was an ingloriously distinguishing feature of the crisis (as was shown in chapter 4).

Assumptions, although the underbelly of quantitative models, nevertheless serve to make things practical; they enable the problem to be considered with disturbing features removed. Although assumptions make analyses more manageable, the credibility of the results from the models unavoidably depends on the validity of the assumptions. The computer will tell you the logical consequences of your assumptions, but it will not tell you if your assumptions are valid. A model that rests on unrealistic assumptions will obviously deliver dubious results, especially when shoddy data are forced into a procrustean bed of theory or model specification. Put kindly, methodologies of this type will be weak in their predictive powers, especially when they predict the opposite of what actually happens in the future.

For those in the know, finance economists subscribed to assumptions about market conditions that belonged in the realm of fantasy; Pollyanna assumptions can deliver a convenient solution, by preventing reality from spoiling the party in the land of the pixies. There exists the ever-present danger in all mathematical modeling that attempting to make the analysis manageable through assumptions would throw-up fanciful results. The models used diverged from reality because the market had moved on; the assumptions made about the market were outdated. It will be shown in the following chapter that the market had mutated into something not like what a market is supposed to be. Market forces had become distorted, dysfunctional, and dishonest with the rise of plutocratic pseudo-markets, particularly in the financial heart of the economy. Market performance was now open to manipulation to an unprecedented extent, making questionable the data used as well as the modeling of markets that had become ersatz.

A healthy skepticism toward the whole modeling process is justified by seemingly unacknowledged developments in the marketplace.

For one thing, unprecedented industry consolidation had increased monopolistic powers for more forceful market power plays and less market predictability. For another, amplified globalization enabled a higher level of inter-country market manipulation, resulting in greater opaqueness because of transnational vastness and jurisdictional ambiguities. Moreover, the increased plutocratic influence of businesses had enhanced their ability to derive unearned benefits from legal changes and inflexibilities that protected gravy trains. Weak regulation had enabled dubious, and naturally hidden, business practices to become commonplace in the bargain. How can a market that is corrupt, stealthy, secretive, and routinely manipulated be plausibly modeled?

Because the modeled markets were dysfunctional, the condition called into question key assumptions made by the finance economists. Finance economists blithely assumed that despite the distorted, stealthy, and manipulated market conditions, each investor had perfect foresight (no seer required). The finance economists assumed that markets were cool and rational rather than wildly exuberant, enabling the future to be known to investors and their expectations fulfilled (no religious vow required). The finance economists assumed that sellers will not defraud customers, not because sellers are paragons of virtue, but because if they did so, they would lose customers to their more honest competitors. In making this assumption the finance economists ignored the hard-to-miss audacious and widespread corruption all around them, and the resultant difficulty of finding a competitor who qualified as honest. Since generally businesses were using a common playbook for their cheating game, customers being taken for a ride cannot be blamed for being unconscious of their victimhood. In any case, with corruption being normal business practice, to whom could customers turn even if they did find out the truth? The finance economists heroically assume stable expectations when financial market models are constructed, even though expectations cannot be assumed to be stable when the economy suffers markets that are dysfunctional, and therefore more uncertain than risky. At the base of it all is the spunky assumption that free-markets exist in relevant sectors like finance, when what really exist are dysfunctional plutocratic pseudo-markets.

It is therefore a reasonable presumption that the smile on the face of investors and financial sector paymasters would have quickly disappeared once they realized the snakeoil nature of the output from the models. Because the models used by finance economists predicted the *diametric opposite* of what happened, pop-eyed gasps of astonishment would have been mild reactions. Risk arises from the potential change in the value of an asset in the future; it reflects how much the trader stands to lose. But the mathematical models used to predict risk in the future were based on information from the past – bad data combining with dubious theory and false market assumptions to give useless results. Dubious data were crunched for results that were expected to substitute for expert judgment. For this reason, even the sound advice of Andrew Lang (1844-1912) would not have helped finance economists. He said that statistics should be used like a drunkard uses a lamp post – for support, not illumination. In this case the lamp post itself was unreliable because markets were dysfunctional. The market had moved on and mutated into a plutocratic pseudo-market. Unsurprisingly, finance economists and others of their ilk, undone by their own mathematical devices, ended up biting the hands that fed them.

The theories and related assumptions of finance economists, believed to be beyond compare in making sense of the then-prevalent conditions, carried the day. Such theories had incidental effects: they provided a smokescreen for wealth creation by financial sector firms; they enabled the consolidation of economic and political power by banks in plutocratic pseudo-markets; and they had the effect of drawing a veil over the decaying market conditions leading to the collapse, causing almost everyone to be caught off guard.

## 7.4 Applied Economics

*A Lead into Temptation*

A fuller understanding of the failure of finance economics requires a probe into the frailties of applied economics. The field of applied economics opened the door to an economics not like what economics is supposed to be, and facilitated the shambles in both economics and economies. Two factors facilitated the abuse of economics. One was that applied economics enabled economic theory to be nudged away from its social science moorings, severing ties between private and social interests, and making the label "economics" a misnomer when applied to finance economics. Because that sort of economics was no longer a valid social science, economics was robbed of its soul, and so denied its essence. The new economics, by its narrowness and shallowness, effectively became a critique of traditional political economy, rather than being a branch of it. This heterodoxy placed foxes in charge of the henhouse.

As most practical economists know, the other factor enabling the abuse of applied economics was the change in the scientific method from deductive to inductive: the enunciation of general principles from what you observe in a particular situation, like a stock market. As will be explained more fully later, this means that seeing is believing if you also notice – and that would require insight from context. This method of inductive reasoning left the door of opportunity ajar for excessive mathematization that caused rising prices to be seen but bubbles not noticed. More generally, the dignity of intellectualism in the science of economics came to be overridden by a narrow vocationalism, on the mistaken presumption that information was knowledge. Ironically, this alienated supposed social scientists from their raison d'être: to deliver social benefits through private profits (rather than foster profits that impoverished society).

*Quantification*

Techniques meant for good were misused for ill. As applied economists know, mathematical models are used to reveal relevant characteristics of data, so that quantitative information may be better summarized and evaluated. Methods such as programming, statistics, and simulation came to be used for illuminating problems in economics and improving practical solutions. Widely used is the econometric technique in the experimental-statistical area of methodology, which has a specialized relevance to applied economics. All these techniques enable quantification to give form to the vagueness of ideas. By providing numerical magnitudes, the use of quantitative methods was supposed to improve the quality of conclusions in applied economics – and so improve the usefulness of economics for problem-solving in decision-making. Why, then, did finance economics do the opposite?

Ignoring the pointed finger of scorn enabled mechanistic mathematical methods to override reasoned thinking. Quantification that was underground, became acceptable (although not altogether respectable), and then took over. Nineteenth-century political economists did not think that bare-bones mathematical methods could be applied to human behavior, arguing that men and women were not subject to the laws of mathematics (Arrow 1951). In particular, in 1879 political economist Thomas Leslie bemoaned mathematical methods, stating that the very attempt shows an entire misconception of the nature of economic problems (James 1981, 72). Yet the works of Henry Moore in the early part of the twentieth century, despite being derided by some economists, led to increasing quantification in economics. After the Second World War, the quantification of economics gradually emerged from the academic underground, to become fashionable after the 1960s. Wasilly Leontief's Input-Output analysis in the 1950s was a major boost to quantification, although he later condemned the excessive mathematization of economics (to be reported shortly). Quantification took off when advances in statistical techniques coincided with the advent of computerization. The abstruseness of mathematical models shifted economics to an esoteric plateau and enabled economics to become distanced from social relevance. Finance economists and their professional comrades used mathematical models to blind their clients to dubious science and to blind themselves to the interests of society – and that despite the supposed raison d'être of economics being the improvement of social welfare.

Excessive mathematization explains the spectacular failure of the finance economists' methods to manage risk, and explains a fair amount of the recklessness of banks leading up to the crisis (and perhaps since). Algebraic mathematisation is an approach to economic analysis whereby symbols replace words and functions replace sentences. Alfred Marshall was a mathematician, yet he emphasized the importance of words over symbols. In his great work, *Principles of Economics* (1890), he purposefully relegated mathematical expression to footnotes. In fact, he is on record as stating that because mathematisation can capture only part of economic activity, to rely on mathematics is a "waste of time" as it can be "positively misleading"(as quoted by A.C. Pigou, *Memorials of AlfredMarshall,*422, and reported in James 1981). His views have proven to be spot-on in explaining the pathetic performance of the mathematical modeling behind the crisis. Because models are an abstraction from the real world, the modeling that took place moved the inexact science of economics further into inexactitude – to the point of irrelevance due to market dysfunction. And this happened despite appearances to the contrary that fooled so many. In a broader sense, the fiasco that was the finance economists' modeling vindicated fears that mechanical approaches undertaken in the name of economics would deny the importance of context comprising wider and deeper factors, as well as downplay the role of human judgment in decision-making.

Mathematical models: are they tools, toys, or weapons? Mathematical tools, toys to those chasing the rainbow of equilibrium, became dangerous anti-social weapons for financial sector gamesmanship. Quantitative models can take on lives of their own and their methodology can become an end in itself, with emphasis more on outward trappings and superficial objectives, than on getting socially relevant results. A focus on quantitative formulation can take precedence over the soundness of economic theory, mathematical sophistication being achieved at the cost of intellectual acumen. Models can come to control their creators because of the inclination on the part of the creators to dismiss information that does not conform to expectations, or fit the specification of the model. The results from mathematical methods that are automatic tend to substitute for logical thought that is judgmental – and so give a false aura of exactness, objectivity, and certainty, sufficient to make bankers and investors bet the farm on them.

It took a cataclysmic financial collapse to prove that "modeling risk" can never mean "managing risk." Finance economists were blind to the reality that taming risk with mathematical models required a leap of faith. This can be attributed to at least three simple reasons. First, the models used were necessarily abstractions from reality (and therefore never able to capture enough of the real world, particularly one in a state of flux). Second, modeling depended on dubious data from pseudo-market sources (where market performance depends to a significant but unknown extent on hidden manipulations, including information management). Third, modeling relied on data from past market conditions that were decreasingly relevant to future market conditions (because of the evolution of the market toward increasingly dysfunctional pseudo-market conditions, particularly in banking). Poor data would surely afflict the ability of the best of models to reveal the truth. For these reasons, financial risk models were unable to cope with inflection points, unusual events and, importantly, changed market conditions. It is not adequately recognized that the results from quantitative models are optimum only if several conditions are simultaneously met and these include the legality and ethicality of business conduct. Mathematical modeling has enabled the emphasis to shift from solving community problems for increased social wellbeing, to increasing private profitability at the expense of social wellbeing. In the circumstances, for finance economists and others of their ilk, mathematical models arguably became tools for digging their own professional graves.

There was style over substance; the beauty of mathematical formulation enabled the finance economists and their fellow travelers to be wrong in an elegant manner. It has been known for decades that econometrics can quickly degenerate into "econome-tricks." As a PhD student from Michigan State University this author was privileged to be present to listen, captivated, to Wasilly Leontief, the "father of Input-Output Analysis," unleashing a fusillade at the mathematical menace to economics in his address to the American Economic Association in 1970. He predicted the rise of dubious economics, not unlike finance economics, when he said as follows: "Unfortunately uncritical enthusiasm for mathematical formulation leads often to conceal the ephemeral substantive content of the argument behind the formidable front of algebraic signs. In no other field of empirical inquiry has so massive and sophisticated a statistical machinery been used with such indifferent results." This statement sheds further light on why finance economists and fellow travelers have failed to give a good account of themselves, to put it politely.

What is sauce for the physical science goose is not sauce for the social science gander. While the physical sciences like engineering, physics, and chemistry, lend themselves to mathematical methods, the social science of economics does not, certainly not to the same extent. Unlike when applied in the physical sciences, mathematics, when applied in economics, it is open to error or abuse due to economics not lending itself to fixed functional forms or having equally precise data. The problem in the physical sciences is the mathematical one of solving for a unique value, whereas in applied economics it is one of computing best estimates within identified margins of error. Economics, which is an imperfect science of tendencies, is not amenable to the application of automatic methods except in limited conditions. Mathematics cannot make up for the inherent insufficiency in economics. In fact, its adoption in economics did the opposite: it increased inexactitude in an already inexact science. Consequently, the application of mathematical methods to economics can open the door to a darker and dangerous economics, as indeed happened. The models used by finance economists were black boxes that were capable of camouflaging tenuous data and wild assumptions, and successfully delude the hapless faithful into believing that "garbage in" meant "gospel out."

The burgeoning mathematisation was at the cost of intellectual context from pluralism. An increasing mathematization caused economics to evolve away from the panorama of a multidisciplinary social science dimension, resulting in an intellectual perspective that was narrower and a perceptual depth that was shallower. The output of quantitative models, that should have been incidental to the process of logical reasoning and judgment on risk management, instead became the sole or main basis for risk assessment – implying that the handmaiden was allowed to take charge as the mistress. Economics shed its broad multidisciplinary characteristics when it evolved away from traditional political economy, and then lost its way when it morphed into finance economics that had moved in from the fringes.

To the dismay of most mainstream economists, the abuse of quantification caused economics to break away from its moorings in the social sciences – and drift away into disrepute. Economics became detached from wider considerations of social welfare because of the attempt to make the stochastic economic goose imitate the deterministic physical-science swan. The gap from this detachment was large enough to enable the new tribe of cowboy-finance economists and their fellow travelers to make good. This they did by galloping to the forefront of the profession from a murky intellectual backwater, sporting borrowed plumes and brandishing mathematical weapons. Although in the end they were undone by their own devices, it was not before their tools became anti-social weapons for finance sector gamesmanship, and contributed to causing incalculable damage to both economics and economies.

## Method of Analysis

When economic theory came to be applied for problem-solving, the methodology opened the door to skullduggery. Economics went from being used for the purpose of giving light (i.e., knowledge for its own sake), to being used for giving fruit (i.e., for providing benefits beyond knowledge), to use a distinction made by A.C. Pigou in his classic *Economics of Welfare* in 1932. This explains the nature of the black-box models used by finance economists and others of their ilk, which were judged by their capability to deliver fruit in terms of investor returns and banking profits.

Applied economics involved a change in the method of analysis; the method of economics changed from being primarily deductive to being primarily inductive. This development made economics vulnerable to exploitation by finance economists and birds of the same feather. The method of pure economics is deductive, meaning that it infers (deduces) things from the world around us; it involves reasoning from the general to the specific. In more technical terms, particular propositions are inferred from universal premises. Therefore, its propositions are of an *a priori* nature.

By contrast, applied economics is inductive, meaning that it goes from a particular set of facts to drawing broad conclusions. Theories come from evidence; generalizations are made on the basis that what is true in a particular observable case is generally true in other similar cases. This shift in methodology probably explains the discredited "efficient market hypothesis" of finance economists, which rationalized and encouraged the devastating bubble-creation activity (that was described in chapter 3). The overall message is simply this: to be correct, any theory must have explanatory power and stand up to practical use. The failure of finance economics to meet these conditions, as evidenced by their failure to envision the downturn, cooked their goose.

## 7.5 Irrelevant Economics

*New Ball Game*

Has economics become a square peg? It would be stretching the point to claim that economic principles designed for analyzing open competitive markets, would assuredly throw up credible results when applied to conditions where markets are neither open nor competitive (that is, when markets are of the dysfunctional and pseudo sort – examined in the following chapter). As explained more fully there, plutocratic pseudo-market conditions are characterized by four anti-free-market features: monopolistic market power, manipulation of global markets, control over political processes, and licentious-prone business practices. In such conditions, company performance would not be solely, or even mainly, determined by factors such as productivity, business efficiency, product innovation, and strategic marketing, but at least partially by non-market and non-operational factors, much of it behind the scenes. This means the performance of businesses is at least partially the outcome of hidden factors: cutting deals of the sweetheart sort, nod-and-wink political understandings, unethical customer and competitor exploitation, hidden illegal practices, and international market manipulation, among other esoteric factors. Under these conditions firms do not accept their business environment as fixed and given (that is, as something exogenous), but as something to be routinely manipulated as an extension of business strategy by using the potent plutocratic strong-arm and stand-over capabilities at their disposal.

In the circumstances, using mathematics to model plutocratic pseudo-markets is a whole new ball game. Can economic principles explaining functional markets be used to model dysfunctional markets? No credible mathematical modeling of the market can be undertaken without a theory of plutocratic pseudo-markets and reliable data for analysis. The plutocratic pseudo-market phenomenon is an incompletely defined condition because of its mysterious, and even unacknowledged, nature. An economic theory of wheeling and dealing has yet to be enunciated. Without a theory of plutocratic pseudo-markets for their interpretation, the data from plutocratic pseudo-markets by themselves, even if accurate, will not mean much at all. "Facts by themselves are silent," said Alfred Marshall. The problem is compounded when the facts are treacherous.

Companies using information-manipulation as a business strategy are not likely to let analysts know where the bodies are buried. Because truth lies at the bottom of a well when dysfunctional market conditions are prevalent, it beggars belief that information gathered from such markets will generally be of a type that reliably puts analysts in the picture. On the contrary, it is reasonable to assume that analysts will be out of the loop when there is business advantage to be gained through withheld or inaccurate information. When information is power, truthful information on business operations is not likely to be readily shared. This means that getting the lowdown would require data collectors to strike it lucky. Banks that are making hefty gains from practices such as own account trading, money laundering, rate-rigging, are not likely to let information gatherers in on the secret. When a firm has some secret understanding with a sympathetic politician whose lips are sealed, keeping a lid on things becomes a recipe for success. It would also be a case of "mum's the word" when a multinational firm has a hidden agenda for inter-market manipulation from which it hopes to make profits through acquisition, rather than through business operations. It is an expected feature of wheeling and dealing that one plays one's the cards close to one's chest – causing the information-provision to be more cagey than forthright. In such circumstances, secrecy and manipulation are the passwords to success, especially when firms are big enough to move the market. As mentioned earlier, putting a spin on things and being economical with the truth were not alien to Wall Street, as alleged by former Wall Street insider Mike Mayo (Mayo 2011) and former senior analyst at Moody's, William Harrington (*Market Watch* 2012). Manipulation thrives on a culture of secrecy; planted rumors and sly innuendo are bound to make the task of quantifying and modeling markets steeped in hanky-panky a rather frustrating affair.

Market modeling can be somewhat of a charade when markets are ersatz. Nailing down market information would be difficult; data would be under a cloud when law and order have broken down and market variables are at any time open to unknowable manipulation by a range of players, including executives, lobbyists, politicians, and analysts. Consequently, models become dangerous instruments when their bases are bereft of credible theory and their functioning depends on, in Mark Twain's words, "lies, damned lies, and statistics."

It is small wonder that economists, who once received warm accolades, now get the cold shoulder.

*Obsolete Economics*

To purists, an element of voodoo in the science of economics is like a pinch of cow dung in the pail of milk, but for economics to have been adulterated to the extent that it has been, it would have taken more like a clump. It is true that in today's pragmatic world, many people would judge the worth of economics by more than the rigor of its philosophic logic. Many expect economics to justify its existence by improving decision-making for problem-solving in business and government. Economics has come to be judged by what it can contribute toward greater prosperity via private enterprise – as evidenced by the shift of economic departments in universities from social science schools to business schools. Seen in this light, applied economics had a contribution to make, if only it had not broken away from its social science roots and been corrupted through faulty theorizing and quantitative game playing.

When pseudo-market conditions prevail, a new sort of economics is needed. Pseudo-markets entrench disequilibrium and make it a normal condition. In such a condition, quantitative modeling would need to accommodate pseudo-market practices that are administered and negotiated, and therefore non-random. The analysis that works is more likely to be deterministic (with a single value) than stochastic (estimates within a range of probability). If so, attempts to measure and discern systematic relationships would fail if statistical methods that assume randomness are used. The non-random conditions will require new methodologies and appropriate formulations that recognize the pseudo-market nature of the condition being analyzed.

If economists recklessly promise more than they can deliver, their output is likely to be of a specious nature that, when unmasked, would lay bare the spurious eminence of such economists and shatter their heroic reputation. The report card on finance economists and others of the same inclination shows a failing grade. Economists, who could have helped to evade or mitigate the calamity currently engulfing the world, not only failed to do so, but actually contributed to the process; they were a part of the problem, when they should have been a part of its prevention. The scientific nature of the discipline was undermined by hyped-up theories based on Pollyanna assumptions that made light of broader and deeper aspects of economic thought.

Understandably, economists, who once warmed the cockles of many hearts, are now frozen out of the public's confidence; they used to be regarded as useful, but now regarded as unsound. The smart-alecky doings of a few economists caused the professional reputation of all economists to be tarnished. Specifically, the finance economists and their fellow travelers have, by their fanciful economics, sullied the reputation of innocent mainstream economists (it being a case of "give a dog a bad name"); because mud sticks, the doings of finance economists and others of their ilk have caused mainstream economists to be sold short. Reputed economists who saw through the finance economists and their fellow travelers, and should, therefore, be at the forefront of policy formulation, have been prevented from doing their stuff; many are reduced to voices crying in the wilderness. In fact, there is evidence that the winning solutions of these unheeded advocates of reform are tending to be losing propositions because of widely shared public skepticism about the usefulness of economics (see chapter 11). As the baby appears to have been thrown out with the bathwater, the world is probably be poorer as a result, and not just metaphorically.

In sum, much of Adam Smith's legacy, as well as the economic principles that Alfred Marshall formalized, have come to grief in plutocratic pseudo-market conditions. Trying to mathematically model the market and risk in such unfathomable and misunderstood conditions must logically require more hope than expectation. Applying free-market principles to licentious-prone business conditions where, in addition, political influence, monopolistic market power, and transnational manipulation hold sway, would likely cause attempts at standard economic analyses that are professionally honest to collapse in an indeterminate heap.

## 7.6 Whither Economics?

For traditionalists, restoring the position of economics will require going back to the future. Economics is discredited because it is undermined by excessive vocationalism at the cost of intellectualism – causing it to fall into disrepair. A return to traditional political economy will cleanse economics and restore its intellectual eminence by providing an "apparatus of the mind" (to borrow words attributed to Keynes in a more general context). A broader approach can be expected to improve the balance between the intellectual and the vocational in the discipline of economics. This requires introducing context into economics by broadening the economics syllabus – thereby equipping economics with the perspective that comes from pluralism. To quote W. Roscher (1817-94), isolating economics from its broader context is like bleaching a plant by denying it sunlight (James 1981, 58). A rounded education in economics would require grounding in subjects giving broader and deeper insight – with teachers who know what they are doing because of acumen from context. In particular, the teachers should be able to retrieve *ceteris paribus* from under the rug and subject it to overt examination and explicit analysis. This means the study of economics will encompass subjects like economic history, government, social theory, and the history of economic and political thought. "It has long been agreed that the economist is not trained who is not numerate; but neither is he trained if he is not historiate" said E.H. Phelps Brown writing in the *Economic Journal* of March 1972 (Brown 1972, 9). The infusion of intellectual context through pluralism would safeguard against economic theory degenerating into an old wives' tale, as well as reestablish the lost nexus between private profitability and social welfare in the application of economic principles.

Although resistance to renewing the economics profession has been experienced in the past, the question arises whether it may more easily be overcome in the future, given the sobering evidence from the failed handiwork of finance economists and others of their ilk, which speaks for itself. Would extant finance economists and their fellow travelers experience conversion similar to that of Saul on the road to Damascus and, like Saul, acknowledge the error of their ways, be heartily sorry for their misdoings, and atone for their past by taking up traditional political economy? Logic suggests that finance economists, too far into the vocational side of things, should be in hot water for predicting the exact opposite of what happened. Although they clearly failed to cut the mustard, the stark reality is that the financial disaster is a long way from being their Waterloo.

In the case of finance economists and others of their ilk, physicians cannot be expected to heal themselves; their belief that markets are self-correcting does not seem to apply to them correcting themselves. Although there are exceptions, there is no strong evidence that finance economists and others of their ilk have generally changed their tune to one that accords with a prodigal son's lamentation of repentance. The signs are that an expectation of epiphany is overly optimistic and that, consequently, expecting finance economists and their sort to turn over a new leaf is a lost cause.

For volte-face to happen, finance economists and others of their ilk will need to emerge from their sub-disciplinary foxholes and take up a syllabus closer to traditional political economy. A change of heart seems too much to expect from those oblivious to the fact that their number is up. There are no signs that they are prepared to accept that financial markets are a long way from being open, transparent, competitive, entrepreneurial, and contestable. Such faith is based on several assumptions, among them: that there is no significant difference between free market competition and oligopolistic gamesmanship; that dysfunctional pseudo-markets can be plausibly modeled; and that data from these manipulated markets can be used for credible quantitative analyses for decision-making, even about the future. Those who hold their breath waiting for transformation are bound to die of suffocation. In the meantime, unreformed finance economists and their types, who insist on being called "economists," would be in roughly the same situation as a bald man, as bald as a coot, who insists on being called "Curly."

All things considered, the prognosis for the economics profession is unsurprisingly pessimistic. The influence of finance economists does not auger well for social ills because the doctor is as sick as the patient. Vocationalism trumps intellectualism; dubious mathematical modeling in the name of economics has priority over desperately-needed blue-sky research on intellectual fundamentals. This is an urgent necessity because of the threat to economies from the emergence of plutocratic pseudo-markets. So long as miscreant finance economists and their professional comrades continue to peddle their discredited wares and persist in calling themselves economists, the economics profession faces an uphill task to restore its credibility and dispel reputational disgrace. For those who love economics as a social science, it is the end of a dream.

**

# *Chapter 8*

# DEREGULATION FALLOUT: BOOST TO PSEUDO-MARKETS

## 8.1 Pseudo-Market Causes

*Unleashed Forces*

Financial deregulation let the genie out of the bottle. The damaging action of such deregulation has meant that the problem that broke free is greater than the one that was replaced – and is difficult to undo. The forces were unleashed by lax banking controls, causing shareholder value rather than customer needs to fashion business strategy. The excitement from the casino connotations of investment banking has come to override the boring business of old-fashioned commercial banking, to be ensconced on top. This includes the arena of shadow banking, a suspect shady place operating largely outside the ambit of regulatory scrutiny.

The *size* (structure) and the *nature* (behavior) of banks have changed to transform financial plumbers into masters of the economic universe. Examined next are three broad aspects: first, how deregulation boosted plutocratic pseudo-market conditions through knock-on effects; second, how the momentum inherent in such conditions keeps thinning the ranks of industry to enhance the plutocratic influence of remaining firms; third and most important of all, why plutocratic pseudo-market conditions are a hindrance to durable economic recovery in the real economy where the majority live and opportunities are needed.

*A Larger Creation*

Financial deregulators sold the public a pup that has grown up and turned unsociable. It is a matter of record that banks first got big before they then went bad. A structural change boosted by deregulation, preceded and facilitated a behavioral change that has, in addition, spread the condition to several sectors of the real economy.

Deregulation spawned a rash of financial acquisitions and mergers. This triggered a paroxysmal structural transformation in the industry that took off like a wildfire and ended up toughening the economic-*cum*-political muscle of bankers and others of their ilk. Swallowing the juiciest targets through acquisitions was one way of undertaking corporate cannibalism by banks on a roll. Smothering a weaker company with the kiss of death manifested a merger mania. There was no reluctance in holding one's horses when it came to drumming out competitors; profitable but less sturdy banks were sitting ducks, prey to predatory takeover offers that were, in godfather Corleone terms, "too good to refuse." At the risk of dizziness from detail, in the thirty-five years to 2006, just before the financial crisis took hold, the number of independent banks in America had fallen by half to 6500, implying a doubling in structural concentration. Between 1960 and 2005, the assets of the ten largest banks tripled from about 20 percent of banking industry assets to 60 percent (Janicki and Prescott 2006), and this has since quadrupled to some 80 percent. Banking assets swelled to around 200 percent of GDP in Western economies before the collapse, being over 100 percent of GDP in America and over 400 percent of GDP in Britain.

Reflecting Wall Street resurgence since the collapse, American banking titans are once again dominant in global finance, with JP Morgan Chase, Goldman Sachs, and Citigroup riding high and accounting for about a third of the revenue of global investment banking. As will be explained shortly, a relatively few banks, mostly American, are increasingly coming to rule the roost in global finance with worrying implications for a genuine recovery (that is, one that is robust, overarching, and sustained).

It may be claimed that the economies of banks are bigger than that of many countries (after a fashion). The combined annual profit of the big five American banks (JPMorgan Chase, Bank of America, Citigroup, Wells Fargo, and Goldman Sachs) exceeds the size of economies (nominal GDP) of each of over eighty countries, while the annual profit of JP Morgan alone ($ 21.8 billion in 2014) exceeds the GDP of each of over thirty countries, including Jamaica, Moldova, Iceland, and Malta. The five largest US banks account for more than half the country's banking assets. The British Hongkong and Shanghai Banking Corporation's (HSBC's) $18.7 billion annual profit in 2014 puts it in the same league as America's Big Five.

Sheer size delivers market advantages for sitting pretty. Fewer and larger banks mean greater market domination through increased monopolization (that is, oligopolies acting in concert). When banks get larger and fewer, each one gains control of a greater share of the market (structural concentration increases). Although the playing field has never been level, bank enlargement had the effect of tilting the imbalance even further in favor of national champions, gilding the lily by adding to their already ample market power. This raises doubts about whether there is a competitive free market to speak of. The mutual exclusiveness between bigness and competition is a threatening feature of plutocratic pseudo-market conditions where banks operate, as shown in the analysis that follows.

Bigger is better, but only for banks. Three mutually reinforcing factors have coalesced to motivate the emergence of banks of gigantic proportions. First, deregulation provided the opportunity for banking organizations to become larger in order to encompass both commercial and investment banking, opening the door to additional casino-type business strategy options. Second, bigger size means more political-cum-market brawn, raw muscle rather than business efficiency providing the easier means to profitability (explained later). Third, the bigger the bank, the bigger is the implicit government subsidy to the bank because of its "too big to fail" status. If larger size is associated with a greater assurance of bailouts if things go bad, banks that were previously "too big to fail" would now be *much* too big to fail"–making bankers' elation a worry for taxpayers.

Bigness seems to deliver more might than efficiency. It is true that businesses are naturally inclined to seek greater efficiencies, and efficiency likes scale; a larger scale of operation is theoretically capable of reducing costs and increasing profits because of size economies. Evidence suggests, however, that banks have become such lumbering giants that they may in fact be operationally inefficient due to size *dis*economies – that is, they have a plodding disposition from being bloated and unwieldy. Synergies can be undone by bureaucracy that snarls things up and the practical difficulties of running a tight ship when that ship is enormous. That big can be bad for business was found to be the case by Citigroup, which has been downsizing to improve performance. When the executives of the big banks publicly plead ignorance to what is going on, it suggests that banks may have become too big and complex to be efficiently managed. Citigroup, for example, is in 101 countries and its employees exceed two hundred thousand. How can top executives take matters in hand when the right hand does not know what the left hand is doing? This implies not just a lack of communication, but also a lack of control. The happenings at HSBC, JP Morgan Chase, Barclay's Bank, Standard Charters, and Switzerland's UBS reported later, suggest that banks have become cumbersome. Running a tight ship with a firm hand is not very practical in colossal firms that have a myriad of functions requiring elaborate bureaucracies that sprawl across several international markets featuring a complexity of jurisdictions.

This gives rise to the specter of operational inefficiency, a conveniently indiscernible affliction which mega-firms are typically quick to deny they have. Inefficiency in private enterprise is a contradiction in terms. It denies a crucial merit of the capitalist free market system as claimed in standard economic textbooks: that private enterprise is inherently competent, its efficiency automatically arising from the operation of an "invisible hand" that is compulsively driven by competitive pressures. Raised eyebrows seem justified about the validity of the fundamental principle that market economies ipso facto give rise to private sector efficiency. Argued later is that the love of bigness seems to be more for non-operational reasons, such as political clout, than for operational reasons, like efficiency.

*A Different Creation*

The prevailing impression that "might is right" in banking, can be presumed to make a substantial contribution to the dark mood of distrust that seems to have taken hold in the community in relation to the financial sector. The larger bank size enables greater behavioral latitude for an almost "anything goes" disposition, the regulatory presence notwithstanding (explained later). Banking muscle comes from the mammoth size of banks as well as the opaque nature of their operations. Murkiness is enabled by the wide range of complicated interactive banking functions that span the globe.

The big banks that have emerged following deregulation conduct their complex operations within corporate structures that bestride a variety of ambiguous business environments. This affords them a mysteriously complicated mix of investment banking businesses in several markets, which automatically gives them opaqueness for shrugging off public scrutiny – thereby enabling banks to spread their wings and soar above mundane matters, such as preemptive regulatory control. The staggering complexity of regulation is an enforcement nightmare, especially when it comes to untangling monies made from legitimate activities from those made from questionable practices, like own-account trading (see later). There are no prizes for guessing that such a situation enables bankers to run rings around regulators, making the regulatory supervision of banks less than smooth sailing in murky waters. In addition, there is the elusive business of shadow banking, which because of its very nature smacks of complexity and secrecy and takes place within and outside banks, often in a shady underground, mostly outside the ambit of regulatory oversight.

When all these strands come together in synergistic confluence, it is natural that the now better fortified banks will be much more difficult to deal with than before deregulation. The information presented later shows that even a hint of a threat to banks' cherished autonomy will not be taken lying down. There is no denying that banks made a bad impression when they came out swinging at re-regulatory measures designed to avert the next financial crisis. And that was despite their less-than charming role in the previous one. Provoking a fight when the relationship with the community was scarred was an ill-advised move that bankers could ill-afford (but only if niceties mattered).

Most analysts know that own-account trading is as tantalizing to banks as cookie jars are to children. It is understandable that banks cannot help being enticed by the allure of forbidden fruit, namely, engaging in casino-type activities for their own profit through own-account trading (that is notable for making profits fizz). The temptation to have a hand in the cookie jar of own-account trading is increased by the availability of cheap and easy money, in a situation where government insurance protects retail deposits. Now there is added incentive to engage in such esoteric activities because banks' revenue from staples (bonds, commodities, currencies, and derivatives) has fallen by more than a third since the collapse. In addition, non-banking credit sources (e.g., insurance firms, seen by bankers as would-be bankers who did not make the cut) are giving the banks a run for their money.

The melding of cheap money and government insurance is suggestive of unwitting government encouragement for an element of Las Vegas in every big bank. Despite a continuing attempt to prevent own-account trading with devices such as the "Volker Rule"– a "thou shalt not" regulation – in America and the establishment of two regulatory agencies in Britain, the practical job of policing to prevent banks from taking their own positions for lucrative payoff is difficult when such activities can be obscured by several factors. These include the intricacy of functions, the mist of transnational vastness, and the muddiness of shadow banking. A good guess is that US banks are either ignoring attempts to prevent them from trading for their own profit, or are thinking up clever ways of evading any measures introduced. In Europe, the overlapping of client trading and own-account trading has made the regulation of own-account trading a "mission impossible" in practice.

Each revealed act of banking misconduct lets a cat out of the bag and reinforces the mood of cynicism that has taken hold in the community. That the cats are of the big sort is revealed in several cases, among them: the JP Morgan Chase "London whale" trading losses; the Barclay's Bank Libor scandal allegations; and the HSBC and Standard Charted money laundering allegations (where banks were accused of being willing conduits for dodgy money). These examples suggest that the lessons of the financial crisis have not been sufficiently learned, if at all. Since negative facts are hard to establish, these dubious practices may only be the tip of an iceberg that has been accidently exposed – that is, mistakenly revealed symptoms of a problem that is widespread and lurking. The collapse of MF Global, an iconic Wall Street brokerage firm, is a post-crisis example of what could still happen to banks. Its collapse was precipitated by gambles on financial futures that cost its customers $1.6 billion.

The Libor scandal is a hideous child of banking self-regulation. By being the most remarkable of abuses, it takes the first prize for brazenness (so far). Among the banking sins referred to earlier, it was a cardinal one that rubbed salt into the wound of the global financial crisis. The Libor scandal revealed the fake nature of Libor (the interbank lending rate), which can be regarded as a crown jewel of the City of London (the world's main international banking hub), because it makes a major contribution to the City's preeminence in global finance. The Libor interbank lending rate underpins worldwide banking transactions; it is a key money market rate that is used as a benchmark for all financial transactions around the world. Despite the partially successful attempts by banking vested interests to downplay its significance, the Libor scandal has the dubious distinction of being the biggest financial scam in world economic history that has come to light. It involved the alleged rigging of prices for every financial product on earth, including business loans, household mortgages, and credit card debt. Fines for Libor abuse have been paid by Barclays Bank, Union Bank of Switzerland (UBS), and the Royal Bank of Scotland. Soon after Barclay's Bank was alleged to have manipulated Libor interest rates, Sir Mervyn King, the governor of the Bank of England, reportedly said, "From excessive levels of compensation, to shoddy treatment of customers, to deceitful manipulation of its most important interest rates...we can see we need a real change in the culture of that industry" (Giles 2012). These few lines encapsulate the problem in a nutshell and, being from the horse's mouth, give them the seal of credibility.

In fact, it is likely that Libor is only one of several banking sins deserving cardinal status. The movements of several financial benchmarks have allegedly been influenced by fiddling – teeny-weeny fixes capable of raking in hefty piles of ill-gotten gains from fleeced societies everywhere around the world. While Libor-rigging was the most grotesque so far, and its damaging fallout continues, in a dismaying sequel, Libor's equivalent in the world of interest rate swaps, ISDAfix, has also come under question. This is an obscure benchmark in a $300 trillion market that is used by governments and corporations. In addition, the validity of commodities pricing from crude oil to wheat to gold have been the subject of skepticism, if not investigation. A US Senate committee alleges a possible conflict of interest on the part of Goldman Sachs, JP Morgan Chase, and Morgan Stanley because of "massive involvement" with physical commodities markets. Furthermore, there is a strong smell of a large rat in currency pricing, which has a turnover of over $4 trillion a day, and where the tiniest of fiddles can shovel in the tidiest of sums – something capable of putting the Libor scandal in the shade. Playing the stock, commodities, and foreign exchange markets must be regarded as a temptation that is a collateral consequence of a monetary policy that plays fast and loose with cheap and easy money.

From taking a broad view, it seems there is no convincing evidence that the big banks have reformed and stopped repeating past banking sins. There is more reason to believe that they have *not* changed, than they *have* changed, going by the litany of questionable practices that have come to light. The big banks still seem to emphasize rewards for short-term behavior. They still tend to be opaque in their disclosures (one striking example is the big secret with regard to their exposure to the eurozone financial crisis). There is no evidence that their accounting practices have adequately changed. They still seem to be gambling billions on complex derivatives and other instruments, whose risks they do not properly understand. Their dispositions still seem to be tilted more toward betting than hedging. They have not assuredly eschewed the fixing of prices, in particular the fiddling of benchmark rates, when they think they can get away with it. And there are no convincing signs that bankers are overly shy about accepting high executive bonuses, now ineffectively capped in Europe. For example, The Royal Bank of Scotland paid out over $700 million in bonuses in 2013 despite being a ward of the British government, and making a loss of $13.7 billion to boot. Why give up hidebound ways when one has a thick-enough skin?

These home-truths should have a disheartening influence on those longing to hug a banker; now is not the time. The foregoing information seems to contain a mix of ingredients capable of shaking the faith of even those diehards with persevering belief in banking righteousness. The Rubicon seems to have been crossed into an expansive territory of banking invulnerability; deregulation appears to have made governments cross a point of no return in relation to their ability to forestall a frightening range of inappropriate banking practices. But this does not exhaust the social perils from banking capabilities. Governments are less able to prevent the influencing of the state of happiness of their societies (specifically, their socioeconomic policies) by immensely powerful banks. This is because the increased financialization of the world economy has enabled financiers of the "gnomes of Zurich" sort to get too close for the comfort of national governments, as will be shown shortly.

*Back to the Future*

Following financial deregulation, banks have travelled back to a pre-New Deal future that has an aura that somewhat resembles the poorly policed "Wild West" of the past. The bad call that was financial deregulation wrote the bankers a blank check, or so it seems, judging by their intemperate behaviors in the past and questionable practices in the present. The economy is only as strong as its weakest link which, paradoxically, is the powerful financial sector.

Bankers used deregulation to turn the tables on politicians. They seized the day to put their deregulation victory to good purpose, by enhancing their capacity to lord it over their economic-policymaking political patrons. Deregulating politicians were hoist by their own petards by being forced to cede power and dignity to their own creation – implying an element of Frankensteinism. Deregulating politicians are victims of their own success to the extent that the bestowed pole position has enabled bankers and others of their ilk to entrench themselves as oppositional plutocrats. Far from being little tin gods, financiers are the new nobility, whose fiefdoms are based, not on the medieval power of land protected by armies of peasants wielding bows and arrows, but on the modern power of money, protected by an army of dependent politicians exercising political power.

The shoe is on the other foot, since the servant has become the master. Deregulation of the financial sector has enabled bankers to hold a whip hand over the economy, which finds itself in a "tail wags dog" situation. In this topsy-turvy world, banks have gone from being servile service providers to the economy, to ruling the roost in the economy – thereby gaining a controlling influence as never before, in a world financialized as never before. As a result, the banker's traditional finger in the economic pie is now more like a fist.

The risks flowing from the banking synergy referred to above has engendered a cheerless consensus. There is dire unanimity among experts that the evils of banking synergy (from mammoth size and operational latitude) create conditions conducive to all hell breaking loose in the real economy again, as happened before, only worse. Reported in section 12.2 is a meeting of knowledgeable minds on the likelihood, if not inevitability, of a repeat of turbulence in financial markets precipitated by the noxious synergy in the banking sector. Bracing for the replay has justification because the perceived chances of this happening are much magnified when the synergistic condition (previously described) has its basis in the plutocratic pseudo-market condition (examined next).

## 8.2 The Pseudo-Market Condition

*"Future Shock"*

The inadvertent fallout from erroneous deregulatory measures pushed the envelope to make deregulation come to grief in markets that were transformed from being effectively competitive Dr. Jekylls to being pseudo-market Mr. Hydes. Financial deregulation turned the idea of business freedom on its head, reversing the benefits that were supposed to flow. It helped put the kibosh on effectively competitive open market conditions, by accelerating the rise of plutocratic pseudo-market conditions in their place – thereby boosting a growing market dualism. Pseudo-markets are broken markets that are, in other words, phony markets. They are wolves masquerading in the sheep's clothing of open competitive markets. A freely competitive pseudo-market is a contradiction in terms for the reasons to be explained shortly.

As implied, deregulation did not initiate the pseudo-market process. Growing larger for competitive advantage has been a natural progression for firms at least since the dawn of capitalism. For example, between 1899 and 1904, over twenty-five hundred company mergers radically transformed the market structure of the US economy. Deregulation opened a new chapter by giving the historically ongoing process of company enlargement an inadvertent but tremendous kick in the pants. This irreverent impetus delivered a "future shock" (a phrase coined by Alvin Toffler in 1965), a condition caused by the premature arrival of the future. To paraphrase Toffler, there was too much change in too short a period of time, in this case precipitated by dogmatic slash-and-burn deregulation. In this sense, deregulation hastened a process of deterioration already underway in open competitive markets and, conversely, expedited the emergence of plutocratic pseudo-markets. In other words, deregulation upped the ante by greatly accelerating a natural evolutionary process in capitalist markets.

The large firms of yesteryear are scraggy poor relations compared to today's brawny mega-firms. They were big and fearsome to be sure, but pale in comparison with today's portly titans that are, because of the pseudo-market traits to be identified, a threat to competitive markets on an international scale, and even to Western democracy. Technology and culture have made today's pseudo-market firms a far cry from firms of even sixty years ago; they are different in terms of both degree and kind. The four menacing ingredients of plutocratic pseudo-markets are: monopolization, globalization, politicization, and corruption. Each one of the fearsome foursome is a nail in the coffin of entrepreneurs in open competitive markets. Take each in turn.

*Monopolization*

Massive firms with the individual capability to influence the industry and market, if not the economy, and wearing the "too big to fail" mantle, are part of the furniture in plutocratic pseudo-market conditions. The firms in pseudo-markets are technically oligopolies, each large enough to have their behavior affect, without control, both the industry (competitor behavior) and the market (prices). They tend toward monopolization when they act in concert with or without collusion, as happens when they match each others' practices. This happened with regard to the widespread corruption reported in chapter 4. This condition of oligopolies acting in concert, as they usually do, is referred to simply as "monopolization" from now on.

When a few giant firms enjoy bazooka-wielding freedom, their gains could come at the expense of all other firms, clients, and the public at large. At the least, a natural head start from monopolistic market power enables easy profits from high prices to consumers and low prices to suppliers, resulting in the inefficient use of a country's resources. We have seen a sharp increase in the structural concentration of banks; weaker rivals of banks have been swallowed up when they have not been sent packing, resulting in banks becoming fewer and bigger. The enlarged banks in thinner ranks savor still-larger market shares, and have the drop on others not similarly blessed – thereby undermining the much-vaunted feature of competitiveness in capitalist markets. It was reported in chapter 4 that record profits were made by businesses that were seedy, inept, and rigged, and that many employees suspected of misbehavior got off scot free. For businesses that treated their clients so badly, banks keep doing remarkably well. Theory suggests that monopolization might have something to do with aggrieved clients having nowhere else to turn.

Enhanced market power from enlarged market share gives pseudo-market firms a natural upper hand, and loads the dice against relatively weaker players, many with cap-in-hand. Business on the level becomes difficult when the playing field has sizable mounds. Market leadership has its basis in competition-inhibiting monopolistic market power that makes less endowed firms fair game; it enables the more powerful firms to ride high, if not rough-shod, over relatively weaker competitors, clients, employees, as well as over weaker firms in all other industries that the market leaders have dealings with.

The duality of power in the market is typically associated with meek surrender on one side of the fence; protecting weaker firms from powerful industry leaders is just not practical. The inability to quarantine weaker firms from market leaders means that for weaker competitors, raw deals rather than square deals become the order of the day. As a result, firms operating in open competitive market conditions live on borrowed time; the reigning status of massive firms in an industry endows them with prerogatives over less sturdy rivals and clients, ensuring an automatic competitive advantage that equips them to play for keeps. For instance, if you are a small vendor you are at the mercy of large, monopsonistic, buyers like Walmart in America, Tesco in Britain, Aldi in Germany, or Woolworths in Australia and New Zealand. Standing up to these monopsonistic titans for a better deal risks being sent to Coventry, if not to the wall. There is ample researched evidence showing that the power of monopsonistic buyers tends to get the better of weaker players. Such demonstrative behavior can usually intimidate weaker market players to the point of discouraging investment and growth of affected firms in the channel, like processors and suppliers (Samuel and Ratnatunga 1993). Also, pseudo-markets enable global supply chains to shackle competition, making conditions fertile for price manipulation that can disadvantage price-taking firms in open competitive sectors. Understandably, the overshadowing presence of pseudo-market firms causes firms in open competitive sectors to just trundle along the edge with a minimalist mindset.

When there are hard-boiled elements in one small but crucial sector of the economy, it is to be expected that firms in all other sectors will tend to get pinned down and lose their sway. Such interactive power plays would be greater when they happen in the finance industry, where gigantic firms can usefully brandish their bazookas to bear down upon market participants, not just in their own sector, but almost everywhere. This probably explains much of the dominance of the financial sector in the real economy. It also leads to a vital conclusion with wider ramifications: the structure of the industry enables market leaders to turn a profit, not necessarily by getting more efficient, but by putting the screws on less sturdy rivals and clients. As to why this is a factor hindering economic recovery is explained in chapter 9.

*Globalization*

For Western societies, globalization has evolved to become more a threat than a triumph, associated more with peril than prosperity. Despite its amply demonstrated ability to generate global wealth, globalization is no longer all it was cracked up to be. This is because plutocratic pseudo-market conditions enable multinational firms to command the world stage and cause anti-competitive and anti-recovery effects (for reasons to be explained later).

After a temporary slowdown, globalization is back with a vengeance. It is true that free-spirited globalization has become a thing of the past. The tendency toward regional rather than multilateral trading arrangements has put a dampener on globalization, and complicated life for multinationals whose supply chains cross multiple borders. But globalization has not been stopped in its tracks; far from it. A spate of cross-border acquisitions and mergers has caused industry consolidation to advance globalization. Explained later is that the current gloomy outlook has spurred the process because money is cheap, balance sheets are strong, and mergers can conceal corporate embarrassments in troubled times.

For multinational firms, apart from the evident profits from their open international operations, there are stealthy gains to be had from hidden practices that insidiously undermine competitive conditions in the marketplace. Such practices can take place with impunity for several reasons that include: differences in business environments among countries; attendant opaqueness from jurisdictional ambiguity; and the use of electronic communication to advantage. These factors have caused the element of lawlessness that was always prevalent in international business practice, to surge in recent times. The enhanced streak of business licentiousness from globalization, by heightening market manipulation on an international scale, has given rise to competition-eroding effects like never before.

What is important about the internationalization of functions, strategies, and profits is not that it happens but its scale, context, and source. Multinationals have mastered the intricacies of inter-country manipulation for unearned gains (surplus profits called "economic rents" by economists and explained shortly). Practices such as "transfer pricing" are as old as multinational companies, particularly those engaged in the production of goods and services. Transfer pricing is a multinational business strategy that uses mis-invoicing to evade taxes through tax arbitrage and dodge duties through the undervaluing of goods. Invoice-manipulation comes in handy for skirting capital controls, as well as for exploiting exchange rate and other differences that apply to different branches of the one company operating within different national jurisdictions. When it comes to profits, where they are made can often be only a matter of definition: make high profits in low tax countries and low profits in high tax countries – creating opportunities for creative accounting and a strong motivation for foreign takeovers by US companies. (This tax loophole was supposedly closed in 2014.) These developments have enabled manipulative practices to happen in circumstances where international operations, never transparent, are now far less visible and more mysterious than ever before. This has fostered a happy-go-lucky disposition on the part of firms inclined to routine inter-country manipulation of the sort that undermines the viability of competitive open markets.

The big banks are recent players that grace the world economy with their near omnipresence. As companies outgrew the domestic markets that begot them, and spread their wings by moving on to do business internationally, the large banks followed them to their foreign destinations, to help finance the investments and other business activities of multinationals. Consequently, global manipulation extended to banks. Their influence on the real economy can be large, insidious, systemic, and pervasive. The practices can affect, not just the bank engaging in the practice, but whole economies of nations worldwide because of the globalization of finance. It was previously shown that the toxic bond mischief perpetrated by American mortgage twins Freddie Mac and Fannie Mae had disastrous repercussions, not just domestically, but also internationally (as do Libor fixing, alleged foreign currency manipulation, and the rest of it).

Globalization reduces the influence of national governments over their financial sectors in particular, and their economies in general. The transnational nature of massive banks and other multinational firms, whose operations sprawl across countries, means they can avoid dancing to tunes played by national governments; they can circumvent or downplay the less acceptable parts of domestic policies of particular nations. They can transfer assets and activities from a less congenial business environment in one country, to a more congenial business environment in another country – causing one country's tough measure to become another country's golden opportunity. Such artful maneuvering, involving the shifting and shuffling of activities and assets to exploit differences in economic environments, is normal business practice for multinational corporations. Hence, trying to control globalized companies through domestic policies is like trying to squeeze a balloon; squeezing in one place results in expansion in another – implying that national policy cannot fix problems that are global, especially in banking, where there is an escape hatch called shadow banking. Globalism overrides localism.

Understandably, when globalized economic forces are dominant, national economic policies can be rendered impotent – with the loss of iconic industry touching a patriotic nerve to make matters worse. The British have seen more than twice as many of their companies subject to foreign takeovers as have any of Europe's other leading economies. The fate that global market forces have dealt British manufacturing firms is arguably a harbinger of what is to come in the West generally. Britain has long lost its edge as a manufacturing hub for motor vehicles according to John Barnes, who notes that once there were twenty-five automobile manufacturers in Britain, but now there are none (Barnes 2013). Barnes reports the disappearance of well-known international brand names in automobile manufacturing, like Austin, Morris, Singer, Standard, Riley, Humber, Triumph, Rover, and Hillman, which were household names in the countries of the British Empire. "The last one to go was MG, which was sold to the Chinese who promised to continue manufacturing in Dagenham, retaining a workforce of many thousands. But later the Chinese had other ideas: they sacked the entire workforce, dismantled the plant, and shipped it over to China" (Barnes 2013). There was a more recent manifestation of this broken promise syndrome when America's Kraft took over British chocolate icon Cadbury and left a bitter aftertaste when it shifted some part of British production to Poland. The British oil, gas, railway and aircraft industries are shadows of their former selves, says John Barnes (2013).

The plight of two other victims of globalization illustrates the perils of globalization. Although America is the largest manufacturer on earth, and pockets of US manufacturing are undergoing a renaissance, the fact if that one in six factory jobs have disappeared since

2000 and are not coming back. Italy is experiencing a whopping shrinkage (by over 25 percent) in its industrial base due to the downturn and has the third largest stock of government debt in the world. The only way for Italy to protect its previously vaunted appliance industry, for example, is to shift production to lower-cost countries in order to be able to cope with competition from foreign firms, like the giant Chinese firm Haier. A similar dilemma confronts Italy's reputed fabric and motor vehicle industries.

In the West generally, domestic production is falling afoul of globalization, as comparative advantage in manufacturing continues to erode and the prospects for real recovery recede. The deindustrialization caused by globalization has created rustbelts, boarded-up buildings, hardscrabble neighborhoods, and increased daytime television watching. The implication is that all is not well in the world of work; by inducing post-industrial decline, globalization forces have gobbled up Western jobs, destroying old jobs much faster than new ones can be created, and causing permanently higher levels of unemployment and underemployment. Millions of manufacturing jobs have disappeared as the West's share of global manufacturing shrinks, and machines deny workers the ability to offer employers something they want.

Such job losses are excluded from policy concern due to rejection of the "'Luddite Fallacy" (that mechanization causes unemployment in the overall economy). The prevailing theory, deeply ingrained in the policy psyche, is that the displacement of labor in one area due to technological advancement will lead to more profits, more investment, and the expansion of employment opportunities overall – a historical truth. To think otherwise is to be a Luddite (originally notorious for breaking labor-displacing textile machinery in England circa 1800). This makes a person with a Luddite disposition an enemy of progress. Although true in the past, the question is whether the theory has been rendered obsolete by globalization. If so, it means the unprecedented developments from globalization have caused the "Luddite Fallacy" to be fallacious. The reality is that mid-level skilled workers like machinists and trades people have been left in the lurch by globalization, their positions gone for good and skills made permanently redundant. The luckier ones are being pushed into lower quality service jobs like stacking shelves, sales, cleaning, waiting at tables, and other forms of drudgery. Even accepting that labor-displacement through technological progress does, in terms of the "Luddite Fallacy," result in greater capital formation, investment, and an overall increase in employment, most of this seems to leak out to non-Western *nouveau-riche* countries, where middle class wealth swells due to the foreign direct investments of Western multinationals.

It can be predicted with a fair degree of confidence that the new ball game due to globalization promises a Spartan future for Western nations, as expanding plutocratic pseudo-market conditions crowd out open competitive markets, degrade Western economies, and impede recovery (explained in chapter 9). This cheerless scenario includes the phenomenon of a steady efflux of investment capital from the West, as footloose businesses continue to uproot themselves and head abroad on a permanent quest for greener pastures in China, India, Indonesia, and Brazil, among others. For example, despite Chinese wages being higher than most others in Asia, they are still less than a quarter that in America. Consequently, when there is globalization, increased company profitability does not necessarily translate into increased social prosperity in the home country. The pseudo-market condition peels the performance of transnational companies from the performance of domestic economies, thereby enabling pseudo-market companies to go great guns within Western economies that are going nowhere.

The peeling away of company profitability from national prosperity reveals a new type of export: economic recovery. Western multinationals have sunk some $2 trillion in Asia. Business profits of Western companies operating in pseudo-markets can be high from profitable foreign operations where costs and taxes are low – meaning that increases in company profits in the West come from exporting economic recovery to the East. Over half of the income earned, and most of the jobs created, are outside the country in which the relevant Western multinationals are headquartered. It is easier to whisk money away and tuck it in obscure places when company operations straddle countries with lax regulatory regimes. The differences in business environments enable international manipulation by multinationals using loopholes to devise ingenious ways of shifting earnings abroad, one commonly used tax avoidance technique on the menu being the flavorsome "double Irish with a Dutch sandwich," based on a secret recipe known only to some insiders (e.g. tax accountants).

Western politicians appear to be kidding themselves when they smile on globalised plutocratic pseudo-market firms and give them sweeteners in the belief that they will deliver recovery and benefit the long-suffering majority in the community. Inducements to such titans are unlikely to spill over into gleaming automobiles, overseas vacations, or upgraded televisions for ordinary folk in the West. Companies make profits in the West, but the cars, televisions and vacations are purchased by *nouveau-riche* consumers in foreign countries, the well-off local minority, and shareholders (many of them foreigners). So far there is no strong evidence that plutocrats in pseudo-markets, not renowned for their sentimentality, take the worries of the general public in their home countries to heart.

The grim panorama of compatibility between hefty company profits and social disadvantage can hardly be missed in the official numbers. While corporate profits have reached an all-time high in the United States, increasing by over 17 percent a year, the majority tastes few of the fruit. In the five years since the collapse, GDP went up 8 percent even as median income went down 4 percent. Wages as a percent of the economy have dipped to an all time low, with fewer Americans working than at any time in the past three decades. It is understandable that the fruits of their labor have fallen considering that middle-income jobs are being replaced by low-wage jobs, causing some of the middle class to sink into the quagmire of the underclass. Machines are doing to many types of middle class jobs (e.g., airport check-in clerks) what computers did to typists. Since the crisis, real median family income growth in America is lower by 8 percent, and the net worth of 90 percent of the population has dropped by a fourth (the median household real net worth has fallen from $135,000 to $82,000 over five years since the collapse). Also, the number of food stamp recipients has more than doubled (although about half of this is due to demographic change and the simplification of procedures for qualifying). Despite the cheapness of money, American house prices are still below their pre-crisis peak by 1.8 percent (as against an increase by 9.7 percent in Britain). The grim toll means that the loss of the American dream is worryingly durable for many Americans, as economic opportunities become scarce and upward social and economic mobility stalls. The exclusive nature of the recovery would justify doubts among many about the reality of the cherished American dream.

The grim panorama extends to Britain, as reflected in its internal inconsistencies. Bumper banking profits of over $30 billion for the four biggest banks (HSBC, Barclays, Lloyds, and Standard Charted) took place at a time when consumer confidence was sagging at a nineteen year low, and lackluster productivity was falling still further. Looking behind the curtain of spin reveals the shrinking of real earnings per person by over $7,000 since the crisis.

These are chilling straws in the wind. They foreshadow that global market forces are capable of ravaging the West's industrial base, and condemning the majority of those living in once-admired economies

to a permanently lower level of living. Greece's condition is a caution-
ary preview, if not a dire foreboding, of what a more general collapse
in the West would look like. Despite being propped up by huge loans
that amount to 175 percent of its GDP, Greece's economy has shrunk to
levels of more than eight years ago. The overall unemployment rate is
a blistering 25 percent (of US Great Depression proportions) while a
stubborn youth unemployment rate exceeds a sky-high 55 percent. If
Greece's elaborate financial support system is hypothetically scrapped,
the current adversity would qualify to be mourned as a "paradise lost."
Such a possibility would be ripe with symbolism, as what then gets
portrayed is the anachronism of twenty-first century poverty slap-
bang in the cradle of Western civilization.

Those who are comforted by the thought that Greece is an outlier
(one that is at the "worst case" end of the spectrum of future possi-
bilities for the West) and not a harbinger, should consider the plight of
Spain. Spain is not very much better off, with an unemployment rate of
US Great Depression proportions and youth unemployment exceeding 50 percent. Italy's fix provides more foretaste of future possibili-
ties: its real GDP per person has shrunk to a level of 17 years ago.

Luddites could still have the last laugh because of more bad economics. This refers to the dogged attachment to a theory on labor
displacement and mechanization that is probably obsolete because it
fails to factor in the skullduggery from globalization – in particular,
that globalization makes the pseudo-market condition a ubiquitous
spook. The faith placed by governments in the capacity of transnational firms to deliver economic recovery in the West seems to be
misplaced for reasons that will become clearer as this narrative proceeds and truth unravels. It will be explained in chapter 11 why those
setting a lot of store by orthodox economic policies are likely to feel
betrayed when dysfunctional plutocratic pseudo-market conditions
thwart their success. Conventional policy measures meant to pull the

majority out of recession will be shown to fall short in such bogus market conditions.

The foregoing thoughts about the unfriendly effects of globalization in the West would have missed their point if they are interpreted as stating a case for "beggar thy neighbor" protectionism. True, the twin forces of technological innovation and economic liberalization have combined to drive ever greater volumes of products, capital, and people across national borders to produce the globalization effects of openness, and the concomitant undermining of effectively competitive open markets. But erecting barriers to create gated economies is not the answer. Protectionism, although having the effect of putting a dampener on globalization, would result in self-inflicted wounds from self-defeating outcomes. Such self-harm would be the logical result of the denial of opportunities from comparative advantage, according to which well known theory benefits are maximized when countries specialize in what they are relatively better at producing. Therefore, building protectionist walls would be the wrong remedy for the ills of globalization, when the real problem is the ascendency of anti-competitive pseudo-market conditions. These hamper economic progress for the numerous reasons to be pinpointed in the following chapter.

*Politicization*

If it is bad news that political influence improves business performance at public expense, it is worse news that such influence is also a roadblock to recovery. As firms get larger, they get fewer in number. As a result, business power gets concentrated in fewer hands whose forte is political arm-twisting. The greater homogenization of interest coupled with the command over more resources, sets the stage for greater business influence over the political process by pseudo-market firms. This opens the door to plutocracy, which is an institutionalized condition beyond the informality of old-fashioned cronyism.

The harnessing of pseudo-market strengths enables ordinary business leaders to grow into the previously elusive role of plutocrats. As plutocratic pseudo-markets move to center stage in Western economies, politicians can be expected to fall into the groove of opaque relationships with big business, with pliant politicians serving as proxies for forces to which they are beholden. Such enhanced plutocratic influence will presumably be associated with the draining away of the influence of entrepreneurial firms operating in open competitive market conditions.

An undertow of plutocracy insidiously influences current economic policy formulation, a lot of it coming from financial forces in increasingly finacialized economies. The perilous chumminess between politicians and business tycoons had its beginnings way back, as evident in US President Rutherford B. Hayes' statement circa 1877 that the American government was "...of corporations, by corporations, and for corporations," as reported in *Greed, Inc.* (Rowland 2012, 105). It seems a safe bet that plutocratic influence has billowed since then to match the massiveness of modern corporations that have grown to become transnational titans. This makes the problem that President Hayes confronted small beer compared to what exists today.

For business moguls in pseudo-markets, exerting influence over political processes is integral to business strategy, because politicians can be helpful in driving their pigs to market. Reciprocally, politicians can be dazzled by the glitzy possessions of plutocrats, like bankrolling wallets or handbags. A cultivated political stance that pleases a plutocrat can make big money, enough to swing an election, flow the politician's way. Plutocrats would not be plutocrats if they did not throw their weight (and money) around when they think their interests are jeopardized. Large firms, particularly the big banks, can improve their performance, not necessarily through increased efficiency, productivity, innovation, technology, and marketing, but by swaying political decisions in their favor (e.g., financial deregulation). Backstairs influence implies underhand intrigue in court for possible unworthy (i.e., anti-social) conduct.

It makes eminent good sense for political strategy to become a normal extension of business strategy when the smell of opportunity is stronger within the offices of politicians than out there in the marketplace. A manager could find that the payoff to the business is greater from putting pressure on politicians, than from the same amount being spent on research and development, for example. Lawrence Lessig reports instances where business lobbying in America yields a return of well over 100 percent (Lessig 2011, 117). That would make the payoff from most alternative forms of investment to lobbying seem chickenfeed. This amply explains why spending on lobbying in America has more than tripled since the glory days of deregulation in the 1990s.

Governments have come to be regarded, not as agents of society, but as hostile forces to be controlled in the business interest; pseudo-market conditions are conducive to making politicians handmaidens of business tycoons. Such a situation is in marked contrast to information in standard economic textbooks, namely, that firms adapt their strategies to suit external (i.e., exogenous) political and economic environmental conditions, which for them are fixed and given. The textbook principles are exposed as myths in circumstances where, for firms operating in pseudo-market conditions, environmental manipulation is business as usual – implying that company operations routinely go beyond the nuts and bolts of business and into the realm of politics. In section 6.4 it was shown that corporate influence over the political process in America is normal and inevitable, because it is integral to the constitutional process. The influence of the mining industry over the political processes of Australia and Canada are other hard-to-miss examples. The financial deregulation windfall to banks was a sort of mega-freebie from government. "Regulatory control" is a specific manifestation of company influence over public process for private benefit. The fact that bailout money went to companies rather than to the general public is ripe with symbolism in this context. Plutocracy kneecaps democracy.

Hidden links provide strength from unity; the unnoticed intertwining of banking functions strengthens banks' political influence. The financial system is interconnected on account of products such as derivatives that cause banks to be tangled up in complicated dealings with other financial institutions. This means that although banks may be physically separate, all financial institutions are functionally interdependent. Such interdependence gives them a still higher level of actual concentration than the already high level of apparent concentration. To the extent that the finance sector's collective hand is thereby strengthened, so would, presumably, its persuasive powers in its dealings with politicians.

The financial sector has become more than ever a controlling political force, not only in America, but also in Europe, and to a lesser extent in many countries around the world. In America, politicians depend on corporate money, and this is the case to some extent in all Western democracies. The American Dodd-Frank bill, that was designed to rein in the banks, was watered down at the cost of crushing complexity to placate bankers showing a fist of opposition. In Europe, faceless financiers call the shots when it comes to determining the terms of loans given to debt-impoverished countries. It seems generally accepted that beggars cannot be choosers, even when it comes to deciding the destinies of a sovereign nations. Because indebtedness empowers creditors over debtors, the gnomes-of-Zurich types, backed by pseudo-market-based power, are able to influence the public policies of sovereign nations according to private balance sheet imperatives. As explained in the following chapter, the process of economic recovery is hindered by plutocratic pseudo-market firms, especially in banking, that tether economies to contrarian forces.

The power of business over politicians is there to be seen beyond finance. Corporate lobbying is politically embedded in the political processes of Western democracies, including America, Europe, Canada, and Australia. The payoff from lobbying, at well over 100 percent as previously reported, makes political arm-twisting a more profitable business strategy than most other alternatives. The power of business moguls over politicians was embarrassingly demonstrated at the World Economic Forum in Davos some years back. For fans of plutocratic theater, Davos is a rich performance that goes beyond a basic gabfest to address problems of humanity from budgets to blindness. At that previous get-together, instead of seeking to control business behavior in the interest of their societies, leaders of countries obsequiously sought business favors – showing everybody who was boss. The buttering-up exposed the surrender of sovereignty by in hock national politicians to big business. The forum is designed to generate ideas for remaking the world, but seemingly only through the plutocratic influences represented there. If the generated ideas are carried through they can be expected to disproportionately benefit and entrench the recovery-inhibiting pseudo-market condition at the expense of under-represented open competitive sectors – for growth benefits that are more exclusive and international, than widespread and domestic. Austerity cutbacks, for example, will adversely affect competitive firms focused on domestic markets more than they would multinational pseudo-market firms that are better equipped for sales in foreign markets. For this reason, a forum searching for recovery could be guilty of fostering forces that hamper it. This impression is substantiated by ongoing developments. An example that shocks is a draft plan said to have been prepared by European Commission officials. The plan proposed that multinational firms should be legally empowered to sue governments for anything judged to "discriminate" against free trade, but was deafeningly silent on the government's countervailing right to sue firms for anti-social (e.g., monopolistic) practices. On the face of it, it seems that these measures have the potential to seriously jeopardize the sovereign right of countries to adopt policies for the public good. It would be a one-way street: firms can challenge government policies, but governments are denied comparable rights to hold corporations socially accountable. Even if the draft plan never sees the light of day in final form, the very exercise is a telling indication of the brazenly anti-social mindset of the authors. Besides showing a blatant lack of regard for wider social considerations, it probably illuminates the dangers to society from backstairs plutocratic influences over economic policy formulation processes.

From a worldwide perspective, anti-democratic plutocratic pseudo-market firms are, paradoxically, most numerous in the democratic West. According to the latest *Fortune* "Global 500" list, three-fourths of the world's largest companies are from the West, with the rest being mostly from China, Japan, and South Korea. This has come to mean that in Western countries, democracy and plutocracy, instead of being strange bedfellows are, astonishingly, friendly bedfellows (*a la* the craven spectacle in Davos just mentioned). This does not mean, however, that the West is more plutocracy-ridden than, say, China.

Although plutocratic influences may be stronger in non-Western countries than in the West, it is less of an issue for them. Because they have an attachment to state capitalism, reflective of a weaker democratic tradition than in the West, plutocratic influences would be much less distasteful, and even considered normal. It is a Chinese tradition for business tycoons and politicians to be friendly bedfellows, cozy under the red blanket of party membership. This means, the state-owned enterprise is king. The Chinese government subsidizes a sprawling portfolio of investments, and is unable to stem the flow of cheap and easy money to state-owned enterprises because of the plutocratic pressures emanating from them. As a result, brash outfits strut the Chinese economic stage inebriated by a cocktail of economic and political power. Even so-called private enterprises, like the Chinese conglomerate Fosun and insurance giant Anbang, have powerful connections with the Chinese political elite, relations being cultivated by the giving of top business positions to the relatives of party bigwigs. State owned or sponsored enterprises would tend to be particularly harmful to Western capitalism when they subscribe to a philosophy that makes it acceptable to violate intellectual property rights by stealing someone else's idea and copying someone else's product. State capitalism cannot, unlike in the West, be regarded as violating any cherished Chinese democratic norm. It is consistent with the Chinese Confucianism-based cultural value of collectivism, but is repugnant to the Western Judeo-Christian-based cultural value of individualism.

Stealth can be good for business. The benefits to business from its influence over the political process are likely to be greater when the exertion happens behind the scenes; corporate influence over politicians is more effective when hidden than when publicized. It was explained in chapter 6 how corporate lobbying is embedded in the political processes of Western democracies. The public policies of elected governments get insidiously adapted to better suit business interests without full disclosure of the extent of the clandestine pressures experienced. Consequently, in a world where plutocratic pseudo-market conditions hold increasing sway, company performance can be expected to be more and more covertly influenced by political machinations of an unknowable and unpredictable nature.

## Corruption

Because dysfunctional markets have been shown to be licentious-prone, the attendant seedy air can be conducive to thriving business corruption. Corruption was shown to be associated with secrecy, misinformation, and withheld information, denying markets the transparency needed to operate effectively and efficiently. This enables monkey business to be normal business in plutocratic pseudo-market firms, given their traits of monopolization, globalization and politicization. It is logical that the strengths from their pseudo-market standing offer firms new opportunities for corruption. For example, under the deregulation-enabled licentious-prone business conditions in the financial sector described in chapter 4, the game changed to enable profitability through duplicity. This is particularly so when larger firms make the running and set low standards for other players in the fields they dominate. The ubiquity of illegal and unethical conduct signals the existence of a business culture of corruption. Because corruption must be secretive to be effective, its existence is likely to be mostly invisible (except, perhaps, in retrospect – *a la* the post-crisis disclosures), and its effects never measureable through modeling.

When it is usual business practice for crucial market information to be withheld or distorted in order to deceive customers, as happened before the crisis, it means that the market fails for reasons of criminality. Such markets cannot be regarded as properly functioning open competitive markets. When markets fail to impose the penalty of customer loss on firms that hoodwink customers, there is unmistakable proof of market dysfunction. Keeping firms in line through the threat of customer loss is a crucial feature of functioning markets, a *sine qua non* of competitiveness; customer loss is a penalty that corrupt firms must automatically pay in a market worthy of the name. For this reason, markets featuring widespread corruption are, ipso facto, dysfunctional markets; i.e., they are pseudo-markets.

Business licentiousness rubs salt into the economic wound that is the plutocratic pseudo-market condition. Since culprits do not exhibit reptilian tails, policymakers continue to turn a blind eye to the existence of those who have previously tasted the forbidden fruit of ill-gotten gains. As a result, countless many, invisibly embedded in the fabric of the economy, continue to enjoy impunity from their illegal and unethical practices. This obliviousness enables the villains to continue in the driver's seat, or at least have some sort of navigator role. The covert presence in the economic systems of America and Europe of those who contributed to the crises through unethical and illegal behavior is a lurking threat that makes the economy vulnerable to recidivism, and even another collapse. Nothing convincing has taken place to prevent what happened before from happening again.

Mistaking license for freedom is a misconception for corruption. When the institutional framework governing business operations are excessively weakened by indiscriminate deregulation, conditions are favorable for business strategies to include the practice of routinely pulling a fast one on customers and clients. As explained in section 5.2, business decisions need to be governed by community-designed institutional frameworks defined by laws, regulations, industry rules, and company culture. These are hierarchically interrelated, since the nature of the law-based regulations sets the tone and scope for the development of industry-specific ethical rules, which in turn fashion business cultures. Therefore, when laws weaken the regulatory regime, they weaken the signals for industry ethical rules, and that could result in the corollary of a culture of corruption in the industry of the sort reported in chapter 4. Take Libor: it purported to track the price of loans between banks, but was manipulated in the absence of effective policing. Widespread and systemic corruption is, therefore, the logical result of a breakdown in sociopolitical institutional safeguards for law and order in the world of business.

When licentious-prone business practices are prevalent in plutocratic pseudo-market conditions, information-management becomes a strategy for business success. This means that when unethical and illegal practices become a normal part of business operations, business success becomes dependent more on secrecy than on transparency. As reported in chapter 4, bankers, aided by gatekeepers (accountants, board members, auditors, shareholders, and ratings agencies), were alleged to have routinely engaged in practices of a dubious nature, which goings-on they did not expressly publicize as an available service. Businesses in the shadow banking system have a reputation for hiding from investors the lurking horrors in investment products.

The micro business climate is conducive to corruption of the fraudulent sort. As business people who are true to themselves must know, the pressure to meet targets is a pressure for fraud. This is helped by factors like the use of contractors and the exposure of Western firms to third-world business practices, where bribes are called commissions and the outstretched palm is a normal posture. The following telling example illustrates the point: the oil firms BP, Royal Dutch Shell, and Statoil were raided by the European Commission in an investigation of alleged market-rigging which, if it happened, would be symptomatic of impaired markets. Such behavior epitomizes market dysfunction because it would not have been possible under effectively competitive open market conditions. Typically, while open competitive markets are associated with transparent business strategies, plutocratic pseudo-markets are associated with the intrigue of business machinations. The natural inclination of pseudo-market firms is to use the cover provided by their characteristics (i.e., monopoly, multinational, plutocratic) to hide the true extent of activities they consider society will frown upon.

Business corruption, which has always been there on the sidelines, seems to have moved to centre stage, enabled by plutocratic pseudo-market conditions, where it cannot easily be seen, or proven if seen, as indicated by the European example just referred to. Raising the question of whether, on balance, pseudo-market firms are more trustworthy than untrustworthy, draws attention to the fact that they can be a force for good only if, among other things, the former feature is dominant. In less open circumstances, the performance of business becomes removed from matters such as efficiency, product innovation, and marketing, becoming dependent instead on hidden practices, the extent of which are unknowable by definition.

## 8.3 Pseudo-Market Dysfunction

As anti-social behavior is to the Mafia, anti-competitive behavior is to plutocratic pseudo-markets. Deregulation caused governments to cross the point of no return in their ability to regulate banks within the existing market setup (to be elaborated on shortly). This gave rise to difficult-to-reverse knock-on changes of an institutional, structural, and behavioral nature in the financial sector. These in turn gave an enormous boost to the rise of plutocratic pseudo-market conditions in key sectors of the economy, particularly in finance. As will be shown in the next chapter, although deregulation boosted the pseudo-market condition in the financial sector, the unholy surge has not been confined to that sector; the financial sector has a demonstrated disposition to spread the condition to other sectors of the economy, its ubiquity and ascendancy helping the diffusion. This means, like breeds like; new firms are fostered that are also semi-political entities wielding  hallmark market-cum-plutocratic powers capable of fashioning business environments in a way that benefits them to the exclusion of the general community (as financial deregulation was to banking) in areas such as grains, energy, insurance, media, mining, and pharmaceuticals. This produces behaviors in pseudo-market players that are secretive, manipulative, exclusive, and counterproductive. When in synergy they pack a potent anti-free-market punch. The upshot is widespread market dysfunction.

If a market exists to satisfy customer needs, can there be a proper market when many, if not most, businesses pursue strategies for preying on customers, instead of satisfying their needs? As stated earlier, keeping firms in line through the threat of customer loss is a crucial feature of functioning markets, a *sine qua non* of competitiveness. The widespread culture of corruption that was endemic to the financial sector would not have been possible under effectively competitive open market conditions. The pathology of pseudo-markets had traits and quirks that shrouded the market, denying it the transparency required for its proper functioning. Deep failings in the market mechanism enabled an institutionalized culture of corruption to exist, causing business practice to become, not working with the customer, but working the customer. In open competitive market conditions all customers and competitors are assumed to have full and accurate market information for efficient decision-making. Obviously, the absence of such transparency means the absence of information needed for markets to properly function; when markets prevent investment risk from being properly assessed, they would be only apologies for free markets. Hence, when anti-competitive practices are systematic there can be no free markets, only pseudo ones.

Who needs productivity when furtive manipulation can haul it in? When machinations are part and parcel of the business strategy of a pseudo-market firms, the performances of individual businesses are not determined solely, or even mainly, by operational factors (such as logistics, productivity, efficiency, technological innovation, and strategic marketing), within fixed and given business environments. Instead, in several industries operating in pseudo-market conditions, company performance is to some significant but unknowable extent determined by non-operational and non-market factors. Much of this would be behind the scenes, with cloak-and-dagger connotations.

215

The clear implication is that the performances of individual businesses in plutocratic pseudo-markets are at least partially the outcome of backroom negotiations, cutting secret hole-and-corner deals, backstairs understandings, unethical practices, illegal practices, and other more esoteric forms of "dirty work at the crossroads" (to use the title of Bill Johnson's melodrama). For all these sorts of covert dealing to be effective, they must necessarily take place behind closed doors, making their true extent unfathomable.

When orange-squeezing is the in thing to do, businesses are biased against productive investments. This means that in dysfunctional market conditions profits can be acquired by putting the squeeze on other market players, instead of being earned in the old fashioned way. Firms in plutocratic pseudo-markets can increase their profitability, not through pursuing operational and marketing visions outside the square, but by exerting undue pressure on their weaker competitors, clients, suppliers, employees, and politicians in a manner not obvious to others. These behind-the-scenes maneuvers enable them to acquire, rather than produce, profits. In the political arena, tactics include political arm-twisting, threats of adverse media campaigns against hostile politicians, and the carrot of campaign-funding. Market dominance from monopolization endows firms with strong-arm and stand-over capabilities for giving other market players the short end of the stick. For multinational firms, gains flow from exploiting inter-country environmental differences, and that includes taking advantage of jurisdictional ambiguity and complexity in international business environments. In addition, gains can be milked through questionable practices, such as transfer pricing and mis-invoicing, that take place stealthily in the cavernous bowels of international bureaucracies. The unseemly business behaviors referred to in chapter 4 can be added into the bargain for more than just effect.

The behavior of a cackle of hyenas fighting among themselves "seeking" a share of the lions' kill has a parallel in business behavior that has been given the following almost-respectable nomenclature by economists: "rent seeking." The hyena-type competition for spoils (formally called economic rent seeking) is another name for oligopolistic gamesmanship for profit-seeking in pseudo-market conditions. As economists know, rent seeking is a special sort of anti-social profit-seeking that is camouflaged in 'its-good-for-the economy' colors: firms make money by competing among themselves for a larger slice of the pie made by others, rather than making the pie bigger through their own efforts. The golden calf of financial deregulation was a shining example. Chasing money for jam through non-operational and non-marketing means (monopolistic exploitation, global manipulation, political influence, improper business practices) is an endeavor that falls short of the proverbial "honest penny" of Judeo-Christian ethic fame, the thing that is earned through productive hard work. It is no secret that rent seeking sectors usually make higher profits than open sectors. This is conducive to making pseudo-market firms role models for competitive market firms and giving the former pride of place in the economic mainstream.

Manipulative maneuvering in pseudo-markets is often mistaken for true competition. When there is oligopolistic gamesmanship, a few market leaders call the shots in the industry, and then attempt to outmaneuver each other for the spoils that come from exerting their four pseudo-market strengths. For these reasons, the competition that firms in pseudo-markets engage in is not autonomous, independent, and individualistic. Instead, the decisions of oligopolistic firms depend on what other relevant firms and politicians do. Changing the rules of the game (by altering *ceteris paribus*, as with deregulation) becomes a font of profitability in the circumstances.

The incentive to ratchet-up a notch on the basis of purely operational factors is reduced, when the alternative (manipulation) is more profitable. This makes business success dependent on unbusinesslike tactics in pseudo-market conditions. In these conditions firms could choose when to show their hand and when not to do so, and that decision could move the market on account of their size in the industry. Magnitude enables mega-firms to shape their industries in a manner that enables them to consolidate their position within that industry, and thereby get the best of both worlds – the world of high profits and the world of large market share.

Firms in pseudo-markets are able to prosper in economies that suffer. A plutocratic pseudo-market condition causes corporate performance (profits earned) to diverge from national economic performance (GDP growth). Although corporate earnings and stock markets are breaking records, growth in the American and European economies is far from stellar. Europe is in poor shape even as the American economy is hitting air pockets for patchy growth, false dawns, and a narrow recovery. Transnational firms make profits in the West by exporting growth to the East, while the forward march of pseudo-market firms stymies or sidelines firms in open competitive sectors (elaborated on shortly). The broad feature of plutocratic pseudo-markets is that they replace the efficient "invisible hand" that advances social wellbeing through business profits, with a hidden hand of manipulation for business profits at the expense of social wellbeing. Skewed economic growth, when income soars at the top but is stagnant for the majority, makes the operation of the market unfriendly to most households. The system of spoils has signally failed to let the majority in the community taste the fruit, particularly since financial deregulation. Such bifurcation between company profitability and social prosperity characterizes both financial and non-financial industries where plutocratic pseudo-markets are dominant, including grains, energy, insurance, media, mining, and pharmaceuticals. Although several industries are saddled with plutocratic pseudo-market conditions, it is probably justified to turn the spotlight on the financial sector because its firms operate in market conditions that were shown to feature the alpha and omega of anti-competitive market attributes.

In conclusion, there are three general features that distinguish plutocratic pseudo-market segments from open competitive market segments. First, in pseudo-markets businesses do not operate within sociopolitical environments that they regard as being fixed and given (i.e., exogenous); instead they systemically control or influence their environment as a normal part of their business strategy. Second, increased profitability for pseudo-market firms does not inevitably deliver real economic growth in the Western economies in which the firms are headquartered; profits flow from economic growth, not in their own country, but in foreign low-cost, low-tax, countries. Third, there is no automatic harmony between business and community interests when pseudo-market conditions are dominant. In fact, conflict is likely when the behavior of firms is not governed by properly designed institutional frameworks that are capable of reconciling private profitability with community prosperity (as was explained in chapter 5). These factors combine to enable the pseudo-market condition to automatically grow by feeding on its own success (explained next).

## 8.4 Pseudo-Market Momentum

*Ingredients for Metamorphosis*

It is a safe bet that the changes to the real economy from financial deregulation are the thin edge of a massive wedge. Deregulation and plutocratic pseudo-markets go hand in hand, for mutual extension through mutual back-scratching between money-dependent politicians and plutocrats with money in hand. The changes from deregulation have been a slippery slope to plutocratic pseudo-markets, whose leaders show an inclination to want to transform the world economy in their own narrow image of it. While the boost to the pseudo-market condition in banking was the direct result of financial deregulation, it will be shown that this condition does in turn foster the expansion of pseudo-markets in other sectors, such as through lending preferences that favor acquisitions and mergers as well as the growth of multinational firms.

Plutocratic pseudo-markets tend to be more grotesque than grandiose. From what has been stated so far, there are good grounds for regarding plutocratic pseudo-markets as four-headed monsters, with the four disagreeable features examined above presenting a hydra of a problem. The four features pack a deadly dynamism when they happen in packaged synergy: monopolistic market power compounds transnational manipulation, together these compound political influence, and the three then combine to compound corrupt business practices, to create a condition of wheels within wheels.

The plutocratic pseudo-market status enables firms to butter their bread on both sides. The advantage of size would butter one side of their bread, while their advantage of wide strategy latitude would butter the other. The bread now buttered on both sides facilitates for such pseudo-market firms an easier prosperity than for less endowed firms fighting to survive in the pressurized conditions of open competitive markets. Plutocratic pseudo-markets have been shown to be the seamy side of the economy, where firms get to play by rules different from those in open competitive markets; pseudo-market firms can break rules that firms in open competitive markets have to obey. This should not be surprising when such firms hold the whip hand in relation to their lesser counterparts and clients in open competitive markets. It is in the nature of the beast to be both a cut above and a breed apart.

It can be said that the four traits of pseudo-market firms combine like malignant cells in a cancer, to be both a cause and a consequence of plutocratic pseudo-markets. What has been stated above explains the nature of the causality (why and how monopolization, globalization, politicization and corruption combine in synergy to throw up the condition of plutocratic pseudo-markets). The four constituent elements are also a consequence of plutocratic pseudo-markets, because plutocratic pseudo-markets, once sufficiently in place, foster and nurture them. This enables plutocratic pseudo-markets to perpetuate themselves by feeding upon their own output. For this reason, nothing succeeds like success for pseudo-market firms, current success being a basis for further success, and so on *ad infinitum*. The pseudo-market road is downhill all the way, with a slippery slope that means the more of it there is, the easier it becomes.

Conditions are conducive to the steady drift of plutocratic pseudo-market conditions throughout the world economy, as the dice gets increasingly loaded in favor of pseudo-market firms and against firms operating with entrepreneurial spirit in effectively competitive open market conditions. This implies the existence of a cumulative momentum for the relentless progress of plutocratic pseudo-markets and the attendant continuing atrophy of economies – an unstoppable process within the existing scheme of things. The argument that pseudo-markets are sources of inequality in the economy is consistent with the central theme in Thomas Piketty's best-selling tome *Capital in the Twenty-First Century* (Piketty 2014). Piketty argues that the free-market system has a natural tendency toward a concentration of power and wealth. This is exactly what automatically results from the inexorable onward march of anti-free-market and anti-social plutocratic pseudo-market forces.

*Transformation Drivers*

Open competitive market conditions cannot realistically be quarantined from the relentless spread of plutocratic pseudo-market forces. Once in place, plutocratic pseudo-markets have a built-in tendency to set wheels in motion that unabatedly and forcibly spread the condition in the body of real economies everywhere. As markets seamlessly transform from decreasingly competitive open markets to increasingly plutocratic pseudo-markets, they increasingly envelope or influence wider sociopolitical processes (*a la*, "corporate universities")–thereby insidiously degenerating the health of economies. The advance of pseudo-markets will be shown to be unstoppable within the existing scheme of things, because the existing scheme of things provides fertile grounds for the mushrooming of pseudo-market firms. Conditions are in place for the escalation of market dysfunction due to an upward spiral of pseudo-market expansion.

The market pits the brawny against the scrawny, and gives rise to a marketplace featuring a debilitating dualism. Firms in plutocratic pseudo-markets, by holding the whip hand, cause entrepreneurial firms in open competitive markets to lose their grip. The former routinely use disproportionate market and political power to chip away at exposed competitive sectors denied pseudo-market protectionism. The advance of pseudo-markets through the unrestrained enlargement of firms with ever growing plutocratic influence spreads uncontrollably like a creeping cancer to devitalize or snuff out firms in competitive sectors and prevent new ones from entering. This has the effect of downgrading the overall level of competitiveness within the economy and metastasizing – that is, incentivizing competitive sector firms to mutate into pseudo-markets firms as an alternative to giving up the ghost. Just as cancer destroys cells, then uses their resources to damage the body, plutocratic pseudo-markets hinder firms in open competitive markets, and then expropriates their space to degenerate the economy. Like cancer cells, pseudo-market firms have defenses that prevent normal processes from stopping them, such as being out of reach of the legal system, having the inside track in gaining political benefits, engaging in transnational manipulation like transfer pricing, and having recourse to other more esoteric business strategies for avoiding taxes and regulations.

The damage to society happens when firms change from being creatures of their environment in open competitive markets into being designers of their environment in plutocratic pseudo markets. This means they go from being governed by community-fashioned institutional frameworks that are part of an environment that is external to the firm (i.e., exogenous and, therefore, fixed and given), into routinely manipulating their environment as a normal extension of business strategy. Just as cancer re-programs the body so its cells can feed upon it, plutocratic pseudo-markets re-program the economy so its firms can feed upon it through rent seeking – that is, taking possession of spoils unrelated to their contribution to production, as previously explained. This causes private profitability increases to be at cross-purposes with improving social prosperity.

The dynamism inherent in plutocratic pseudo-markets causes their frontier to move onward in different ways. The momentum of metastasis in its more direct form can be through the money that flows through the channels of larger banks and discriminates in favor of larger borrowers and squeezes smaller banking competitors. Both these tendencies are prevalent as will be subsequently shown (vide chapter 9). Their effect is to reward larger and more established firms already sitting pretty in pseudo-market conditions, while discouraging more dynamic and newer firms exposed to feisty competitive conditions in the more open sectors – thereby entrenching and growing the former at the expense of the latter. The onward momentum of plutocratic pseudo-markets is fuelled, not necessarily by greater efficiencies in their gigantic firms, but more likely by the ability of their firms to manipulate the system for self-aggrandizement, given the opportunities afforded by their monopolistic, plutocratic, licentious-prone, and transnational statuses.

This is not an exclusive avenue of advancement for plutocratic pseudo-markets. Firms in pseudo-markets give a rough ride to all open market firms they happen to interact with. Negotiations between powerful larger firms and ones exposed to more competitive conditions automatically place the former in the box seat and holding most of the cards, while the latter find themselves in the wrong box with a perpetually weaker hand. The cat-and-mouse type relationship implied in direct dealings between pseudo-market firms wielding market power and ones in open competitive sectors with cap-in-hand, creates a need for countervailing power on the part of the latter – specifically, the need to become bigger and more powerful in order to correct the lopsidedness that disadvantages them.

Wanting a larger market share is an aspiration for survival, success, and status; disadvantaged firms, fed-up of playing second fiddle have strong motivation to follow suit and become large, so they can level up. This is particularly so when they see cash cows on the other side of the fence in plutocratic pseudo-markets, where the grass always looks greener. Over six decades ago iconic economist John Kenneth Galbraith called this a "countervailing response" that is an "active restraint" (Galbraith 1952, 119-121), although it is doubtful that he foresaw the creeping destructiveness to markets from the relentless emergence of multinational plutocratic leviathans that pass for firms.

The conclusion seems hard to avoid that bigness begets bigness, with an automatic tendency for plutocratic pseudo-markets to spread destructively – implying that the further downgrading of remaining open competitive markets is in the cards. The very operations of plutocratic pseudo-market firms tend to push effectively competitive open-market firms into a twilight zone of uncertainty where the investment needed for their sustenance is discouraged. As a result, the growing pressures from the onward march of plutocratic pseudo-markets will bring down the curtain on an increasing number of firms in competitive sectors, causing their numbers to dwindle. Therefore, the dynamics of the marketplace make firms in open competitive markets a dying breed, something that would cause such markets to gradually slide into oblivion. It is an educated guess that most firms in open competitive markets would become an extinct species within a decade or three, as plutocratic pseudo-market firms compulsively snuff-out firms in open competitive sectors, and take over everywhere.

The condition is aggravated when Western pseudo-market titans have an unwitting hand in encouraging the rise of non-Western state-owned behemoths of the Chinese and Russian sorts. The increase in the number of pseudo-market mega-firms in the West justifies the growth of non-Western enterprises wanting countervailing market power. Their spunk to stare down Western pseudo-market titans comes from the prowess of state ownership (their government provides them with a rock-solid backstop). By intertwining political and market power, state-owned enterprises occupy commanding heights in their domestic economies. Thus Western pseudo-market firms have the effect of vindicating and encouraging state-owned enterprises in countries such as China, Russia, and Brazil. In fact, there are signs that South American countries like Brazil and Argentina are taking the wrong lesson from China in embracing state capitalism. Such organizations are, of course, a far cry from the idea of free enterprise based on individualism (the Judeo-Christian rationale for free market capitalism). Further, they have a bad reputation as money pits. For example, the Chinese government is famed for blowing huge sums on inefficient industries; their state-owned enterprises have grown lazy in their dependence on ever more credit. Besides, state-owned enterprises are hotbeds of nepotism and graft; when enterprises are shielded from market transparency, there is an open invitation to steal, as came to light in Brazil's Petrobus, a government-controlled oil enterprise. Also, state-owned enterprises are prone to operating outside market parameters, given that that their deal-making lacks market transparency, usually taking the form of backstairs bilateral bargaining. Swaggering outfits, like the Russian oil giant Rosneft, are alter egos of their governments, and can be dragged into being used as vehicles for pursuing political objectives, like preserving jobs and exerting geopolitical influence. These factors at least partly explain why state-owned enterprises among the world's top five hundred firms lost over a fifth of their value and experienced fallen earnings over the five years to 2014.

## Transformation through Consolidation

There are other structural developments taking place that are gathering pace. Adding to the drama referred to before is the current acquisition frenzy that is driven by a merger mania, about half of it in the form of foreign takeovers. This swells the ranks of pseudo market firms and feeds the innate tendency toward gigantism in pseudo-markets – thereby entrenching and growing the condition. It is a phenomenon that manifests a chain reaction for consolidation, with acquisitions and mergers begetting acquisitions and mergers for the unfettered enlargement of corporations. As there is no maximum size for a corporation that keeps making sufficient profits, the frightening reality is that there is no limit to corporate growth – raising the specter of "Franken-firms," some of which may already be here.

At some time in the future, there could be a throwback to the age of imperialism when mega-firms with quasi-government powers, like the British East India Company and the Dutch East India Company (VOC), carved monopolistic enclaves. The proposed free trade pacts contribute to such a possibility in the longer term, the basis for which may already exist in industries such as oil, banking, mining, and pharmaceuticals.

Corporate managers are not sitting on their hands because conditions are depressed; in fact, they are full of beans because of it. The evidence is that the pressures of the current crisis, far from throwing deterring cold water on the process of industry consolidation, seem, instead, to egg it on. The impetus for consolidation caused the global value of takeovers to be at least a third higher in 2014 than it was the year before. Acquisitions and mergers were valued at over $3 trillion in 2014, with cross-border mergers accounting for almost half of it – and becoming increasingly popular. The appetite for acquisitions and mergers keeps growing, whetted by cheap credit, easy money, and strong company balance sheets. Besides, an acquisition or merger comes in handy for hiding poor business performance in depressed times, especially when money is readily available for oiling the wheels of the process. In this sense, what is happening now is a throwback to the large-scale consolidation that occurred during the economic downturn following the "panic" of 1873 in the United States, when companies sought comfort in marriages of convenience. By encouraging acquisitions and mergers the economic crisis has seriously weakened openness and competitiveness in markets, pseudo-market consolidation adding another verse to the requiem hymn for firms in open competitive market sectors.

Although it is bad news for open competitive markets, company consolidation through acquisitions and mergers brings the blessings of togetherness to the parties concerned. One such boon is the avoidance of unreasonable corporate tax laws – a major incentive for US firms to fly the coop by finding foreign partners in lower tax countries for expedient unions. Running away also enables easier access to havens of secrecy for squirreling away cash. Another benefit is that a merger enables one or both partners to hide embarrassments, like managerial incompetence or internal inefficiency. Acquisitions and mergers are often a sign of businesses desiring greater strength by riding on coattails of better-performing companies in an attempt to offset their weaknesses, often at cost to their dignity; what is glamour and gratification for the predator is usually misery for the prey. Buying another company to get something it has is different from doing it yourself through your own innovative research and development (R&D) efforts or marketing brilliance. In fact, choosing a merger in preference to expanding your own company is often a sign that the company is running out of options within its present setup; the partners, although ostensibly seeking synergy, could really want to hide flaws. For companies needing wrenching reform, an acquisition or merger can be a wily tactic to dodge the emergency room. Consolidation is a means of escape from pricing pressure and for coping with the downturn. Ragbag conglomerates can improve their profitability performances by flexing their market and political muscles as a substitute for greater operational efficiency.

Getting together is a pathway to short-term gains for the involved companies that can pull the wool over the eyes of investors and governments with regard to their true condition. Seeing the writing on the wall is motivation for a mutual propping-up by merging partners that is reminiscent of two Friday night drunks who shore each other up to prevent concussion from a meeting between skull and ground, with no benefit for the underlying disease of alcoholism. Generating media hype that heralds improved prospective profitability for the newly consolidated company – that is now a bigger and more powerful player in the marketplace – would not necessarily do much for correcting the operational flaws and failings that were the motivation for the enlargement in the first place.

Recent events show that to avoid snafus and successfully conclude mergers, the predator must be strong enough – or the prey weak enough. Attempts at corporate unions will end in tears if a fundamental principle is ignored: the merger of equals is a practical impossibility. Conspicuous among the several examples of failed merger attempts are American Pfizer's fruitless courtship of British Astra-Zeneca, and 21st Century Fox's unrequited moves toward Time Warner. The necessity for an asymmetrical "predator versus prey" condition means that when the going gets tough, the tough go hunting.

Why bother with dynamism when plodding is better? Acquisition-and-merger merchants are after easy gains that make the newly consolidated firms even bigger hitters in the helpful conditions of plutocratic pseudo-markets. The consolidated and enlarged firms are now qualified to find their places in the sun, by joining the privileged ranks of pseudo-market moguls as members of the club. The transient shot-in-the-arm for profits from the acquisition or merger can be prolonged by milking the benefits on offer in pampering pseudo-market conditions. In other words, the easy pickings from the consolidation can be perpetuated by ambling down the easy streets of pseudo-markets where firms are insulated from the heat of feisty competition. There they can coast on easy profits acquired through political influence, monopolistic market power, international manipulation, corrupt practice, and other non-operational and non-market ways of making quick mega-bucks (in other words, through rent seeking).

The sobering reality is that the apparently soothing solution through company consolidation often masks an insidious implication for market functionality. On the surface, company consolidation is comfortingly associated with company endurance. Looking beneath the surface often reveals company amalgamation as a business strategy designed to get companies out of trouble by giving them access to the pseudo-market gravy train. This implies that the amalgamation can be a calculated move meant to make up for poor company performance by shifting to a higher ratio of *taken* profits (from increased monopolization, transnational manipulation, political arm-twisting, and licentiousness) to *earned* profits (from increased productivity, product innovation, clever marketing strategy etc.). This makes profitability increases for the consolidated firm compatible with efficiency decreases. Being sucked into the vortex of plutocratic pseudo-markets through acquisitions and mergers may be a desirable strategic option for inefficient or threatened businesses in quest of long-term survival in difficult times.

Further, every acquisition or merger also entrenches the market position of heavy-hitting incumbents in relation to potential new entrants i.e., would-be competitors. It is a reasonable presumption that dynamic firms that want to enter the industry are discouraged by the possibility of a plutocratic muscle being flexed by a consolidated incumbent. Reduced market contestability boosts the pseudo-market condition by denying wannabe competitors the confidence to break in – enabling incumbent pseudo-market firms to be less hindered in their quest for greater market and political power. Potential new entrants can expect to come up against other less subtle obstacles – barriers that have been made less surmountable by the consolidation. The barriers to entry get raised for reasons such as the higher up-front capital costs needed for entry and the absolute cost advantages of the consolidated incumbent from proprietary product technology and brand names. Capturing consumer preferences means that outsiders' hoped-for gain from entering fall. Wannabe competitors would often find that desired suppliers have been tied-up by incumbents, or that the incumbents' market position is strengthened by cozy relationships with politicians.

The crowding out of potential new entrants makes conditions more congenial for incumbents in the flashy, easy-profit, conditions that plutocratic pseudo-markets offer. The reduced threat to incumbents from the deterrence of would-be competitors through blunted market contestability can be expected to reduce the pressure on incumbent firms to get their act together – thereby discouraging dynamism and encouraging zombiism. When the enlarged firm has its market position safeguarded through an enhanced plutocratic influence over government, political manipulation can become even more a logical extension of business strategy.

Pseudo-markets continue to emerge by installments through acquisitions and mergers; several striking examples show a shopping mood for take-overs in the grand tradition of big firms that have already supersized themselves. Oil and gas companies are merger-happy; driven by size-lust, acquisition and merger deals in America and Japan reached an all-time high in 2012-13. When Devon Energy's purchase of shale oil assets heralded a wave of consolidation, nobody could foresee the tsunami from Halliburton's purchase of Baker Hughes. Pharmaceutical companies are in a deal-making frenzy, continuing their succession of mergers, like Pfizer and Merck have done, to gain control of promising drugs, spread their overheads, and escape onerous taxation laws. American Airlines and US Airways merged even as Australia's struggling national carrier, Qantas, sought comfort in the arms of Middle-Eastern giant, Emirates, because of suffering caused by union greed and company mismanagement. Even unromantic shipping company hulks are getting that certain feeling (the urge to merge), so they could cure corporate ill-health caused by the overcapacity of a swollen global fleet – a somewhat rusted symbol of globalization associated with the sinking of shipping firms like America's Genco and Danish Copenship. The possibility of content control arises from the cable tie-up between the Comcast and Time Warner Cable. The likely merger worth $60 billion between the cement giants Lafarge of France and Holcim of Switzerland promises to create an enormous unglamorous pile sufficient to meet some 20 percent of world demand. Moving from the inedible to food and drink, Tim Hortons, a Canadian restaurant chain, will merge with Burger King to shackle the fast-food market. Suntory, a Japanese drinks company, is buying the US firm Beam of "Jim Beam" bourbon fame for a cocktail merger, whereas the marriage between the Brazilian "orange king" Cutrale and the American "banana queen" Chiquita promises a fruit salad merger. But craving gigantism is not the only motivation for acquisitions and mergers. Excellence can also matter, as illustrated by the gobbling up of startup small fish "Nest Labs" (that makes internet connected thermostats) and "DeepMind" (into artificial intelligence) by big fish Google, and the glad eye given to quaint biotech firm Idenix by macho drug maker Merck.

There are more acquisitions and mergers in the pipeline, particularly in banking and professional services, which are poised to consolidate, on top of the wholesale consolidations referred to earlier. It should not be difficult to imagine that the deal-making frenzy driving the raft of giant mergers would shake up markets – the extra edge capable of precipitating the last gasp for many rivals in open competitive sectors.

Banking consolidation has continued with a vengeance in the post-crisis period. A small number of mighty banks are increasingly becoming cocks of the walk on the world economic stage, as banking increasingly consolidates in an ascendant financial sector. As troubled European banks withdraw into their shell, reinvigorated American banks have come to the fore, marching forward toward world domination in finance. European banks, in bad shape, are withdrawing to husband their precious capital, and are consequently losing market share. Despite the City of London being the center of global finance, even British banking champions are retreating from international markets, suggestive of tails between legs. It is natural that global banks would take up the space left by retreating second-tier banks.

This means that American banks' grip on global finance will tighten: a few mighty banks, mainly, but not exclusively, American, including JPMorgan Chase, Goldman Sachs, and Citigroup, will come to increasingly rule the roost in the international financial system. Dominating global finance will enable them to influence policy parameters of countries worldwide that are sufficiently linked to the world economy through collateral, trade, and capital. Because global finance is ascendant over real economies, one conspicuous means of influence is the threat of a ratings downgrade by agencies that have a symbiotic relationship with banks. The ratings agencies have an "attack dog" role whenever increased debt-servicing risks are a threat to the relevant banks' bottom line. The mere threat of a rating downgrade becomes a disciplinary cane for the purpose of keeping in line (blackmailing, to some) any government with international links, especially in the form of foreign borrowing. There has been a disposition on the part of global finance to ram austerity that is excessive and ill-timed down the throats of governments, thereby inhibiting or reversing recovery. Chronically low demand caused the eurozone price surface to sink by 0.7 percent in 2014, threatening a spiral of deflation into the abyss of depression – a perilous possibility that would cut enough ground from under the ambivalent American recovery to make the clued-up anxious (explained in chapter 10).

The global ascendancy of a myopic financial culture is in the cards, given that banking continues to be delinked from the real economy just as before the crisis. This happens when a few mighty banks and allied firms in the financial sector win the battle to fashion the economic world in their own narrow, balance-sheet-blinkered, image of it. In such a world the big banks and allied firms would rule the roost with a distinct world view, using the big stick of a standardized economic policy that is sharpened by narrow balance sheet considerations. Such an outcome will have the effect of embedding real economies in global finance – enabling the financial sector to circumscribe the economic policy choices of sovereign nations. It would usually exclude stimulatory spending as a practical option for governments fearful of treading on financiers' toes. If so, the end result will be that one set of policy options becomes dominant worldwide. Most Keynesian macroeconomists, wedded to the notion of government spending for pump priming, would probably blanch at the nightmare of a financialized economic future.

Looking ahead and extrapolating, it could come to pass that within a decade the diktats of a few colossal banks and allied firms in finance will establish monochromatic economic policies worldwide. This would make financiers standard bearers of progress at the cost of limiting national budgetary autonomy, contrary to the Westphalian norms of national sovereignty of 1678. The encroachment on national sovereignty seems to have been already accepted as inescapable. The more cynical would be inclined to argue that such resignation to be pushed around has taken hold, with countries like Spain, Portugal, Greece, Italy, Cyprus (and several other countries to a lesser degree), acquiescing to being under the thumb of financiers. Financiers have shown no coyness in lecturing sovereign nations, justifying fear in the minds of the timorous that financiers are on a mission to dehumanize the economic policy formulation process in a debt-weakened West. The logical implication is that the straitjacketing of the world economy from a domineering financiers' ethos would put economies on course to a new world order, possibly one featuring the weeping wound of a myopic financial imperialism sometime in the future.

When firms consolidate within plutocratic pseudo-markets, conflict arises between private and social interests: good business opportunities are associated with bad social outcomes. This is because, what is good for the amalgamating firm is bad for the general public; the acquisition or merger, while consolidating companies for private benefit, imposes an unwelcome social cost, as economies around the word come to be increasingly controlled by a stable of transnational mega firms basking in salubrious plutocratic pseudo-markets. More specifically, the private act of company consolidation has the socially deleterious effect of fostering, entrenching, and growing the plutocratic pseudo-market condition through greater monopolization, globalization, politicization, and corruption. Such an outcome may suggest a distressingly fatalistic view of the long-term picture, but it is a possibility that may need to be faced if current trends are allowed to continue unabated (see chapters 12 and 13).

*Transformation through Inertia*
The worrisome conclusion is that plutocratic pseudo-markets are changing economies in pernicious ways that seem out of control within the existing scheme of things. The weakness of market discipline, due to a lack of competitive pressures in pseudo-market conditions, is conducive to fostering companies with zombie quirks and twists, spoiled plodders that thrive in the short-term on the easy pickings on offer in salutary plutocratic pseudo-market conditions. It follows that these conditions can camouflage "dead wood" firms, and this implies inefficiency in the use of a country's resources. Such an inconsistency between company performance and market performance is, of course, the exact opposite of what is supposed to automatically happen in capitalist competitive free markets – *a la* Adam Smith's singular concept of the revered "invisible hand." As any economist knows, the concept of an "invisible hand" embodies as its

central notion the foregone conclusion of allocative efficiency (that the autonomous operation of market forces will mechanically bring about the efficient use of a country's resources). This shows that plutocratic pseudo-markets are likely to be bereft of a market's much-vaunted reason for existence: maximizing social prosperity through allocative efficiency enabled by private sector activity.

Plutocratic pseudo-markets pack forces that fuel a vicious circle for expansionism. Plutocratic pseudo-markets can have a two-pronged thrust for expansionism: one prong is primary and direct, and the other prong secondary and indirect.

Primarily, deregulation that enhances the market and political power of plutocratic forces in pseudo-markets, creates additional force for still more deregulation. Politicians who nurture pseudo-market mega firms tend to sow the seeds for the long-term weakening of their own ability to protect competitive open markets – implying that the plutocratic forces that politicians unleash could come back to haunt them. A hard-to-miss case in point is financial deregulation: bankers turned the tables on deregulators by transforming the big carrot deregulators held out to them into a big stick to beat the deregulators with. Plutocratic pseudo-markets are able to ensure that captains of industry continue to be ensconced in the driver's seat, enabling them to throw their ample weight behind measures needed to entrench their position, as well as nurture the condition to which they owe their strength.

Feeling fed up of being always the bridesmaid is another strong motivation for pseudo-market expansionism. The rise of larger firms in plutocratic pseudo-markets provokes pressures for countervailing structural changes; smaller firms, discontented with their second-rate position from living in the shadow of Goliaths, want to become Goliaths themselves. This refers to the emergence of more large firms through acquisitions and mergers to redress structural imbalances in the industry. The escalation of consolidation implies a proliferation of plutocrats and the amplification of plutocratic influence for protecting and advancing the pseudo-market condition.

The forces for pseudo-market expansionism engender a doom loop that causes market malfunction and economic degeneration to feed upon themselves. If the swelling plutocratic influence from continually expanding pseudo-markets has the effect of forcing politicians' hand for still more deregulation of the sort that further spreads the pseudo-market condition, there emerges the specter of a process that is *ad infinitum*. Consequently, deregulation can beget deregulation and aggravate the original pseudo-market condition. This gives rise to a vicious circle of deregulation and concomitant relentlessness in pseudo-market expansion that increasingly tightens the noose around firms in more open competitive sectors.

Exerting influence is useful when there is treasure to protect. As stated earlier, the ascendance of plutocratic pseudo-markets in several sectors, including in the financial heart of the economy, has unleashed insidious plutocratic forces that tend to be pervasive, hard to challenge, and are incessantly expanding. The longer such conditions are in place, the greater the strides plutocratic leaders can make in ensuring pseudo-market expansionism. The plutocratic forces in pseudo-markets enable business interests to weaken, if not neutralize, the very mechanisms needed to regulate them for the public good. Politicians showing opposition to plutocratic forces in pseudo-markets would tend to make a rod for their own back by antagonizing forces to which they are beholden. All these operate to secure the position of plutocratic forces, make them enamored of the status quo, and establish a socially deleterious vested interest. Consequently, pseudo-market firms become fiefdoms where, imperious barons of industry, standing on self-created pedestals become, like the larger-than-life merchants of Venice of old, swaggering figures of their age.

## 8.5 Pseudo-Market Re-regulation
*Backtrack*

The new financial regulations in the West manifest an unspoken admission of error, if not guilt. Re-regulation is an attempt to mend fences by turning the clock back, and keep the peace with a public that was let down by deregulation. The injustice has been brought home to them in no uncertain terms by the pinch of hard times that has become a test of endurance. The flurry of re-regulation means that the wisdom of hindsight has caused haphazard financial deregulation to fall from grace, at least for the less ideologically enchained. Examining the details of the copious information on regulatory suggestions and measures afoot is daunting and, mercifully for the reader, will be left to academics and others in the interest of minimizing mind-numbing boredom.

To express the matter simply and starkly: in America the focus is on the Dodd-Frank law designed to get Wall Street to toe the line, while in London the focus is on Libor-preventing and other measures designed to get the City of London to toe the line. The setting up of Britain's new financial regulatory authorities (Prudential Regulatory Authority and Financial Conduct Authority) could be regarded as belated measures for getting the genie back in the bottle – developments that deserve more skepticism than optimism for the reasons previously explained.

The tacit admission by more enlightened policy pundits is that bulldozing deregulation based on dogmatism was not such a good idea after all. Corrective legislation aimed at making up leeway and making things right can be seen as "Acts" of remorse – repentant deregulators seeking to make their peace with a hoodwinked public. The need for re-regulation draws attention to farcical machinations of the supposedly responsible. Specifically, it points to the pathetic failure of leaders to discriminate between deregulation that was medicine and deregulation that was poison, on the basis of research-based identification of critical inflection points (as was explained in section 5.4). Most of the culprits who did the damage have left the scene or done some sort of a disappearing act, thereby avoiding having to face the music.

Nevertheless, the dogma-driven financial deregulators of yesteryear have many worthy successors. Members of the new generation do not exhibit qualms about wearing the dubious mantle of *'deregulation champion'* as a badge of honor. Oblivious to matters such as institutional frameworks and pseudo-markets, they continue to be fervently wedded to the noxious cause of wholesale deregulation. Their inherited deregulation passion makes them ideologically driven to keep chasing the rainbow of free market utopia through the abolition of remaining regulation, with no regard for their effects on market functionality.

Does the promised salvation of re-regulation in America and Europe deserve joyous "hallelujah" chants from a cheesed-off public yearning for real resurgence? After all, it would be reasonable to suppose that the wheeling out of a spanking new regulatory architecture to replace that which was so clumsily discarded, should fix the underlying cause of the current suffering, by restoring proper institutional frameworks that can reconcile business and community interests (as described in chapter 5). Arguably, the massive rewrite can be supposed to compensate for the loss of the hallowed Glass-Steagall Act and other regulatory measures that were irreverently stripped away since the 1960s, and thereby restore the status quo ante in banking. The measures would put the cop back on the beat in Wall Street and in the City of London, and reestablish the lost respectability and responsibility of Western banking. Or so it may be hoped.

Hardly anyone is likely to disagree that the Dodd-Frank law is well intentioned and meant to achieve a goal that can be simply stated as: never again. It is supposed to strengthen prudential regulation, overhaul the derivatives market, and increase transparency. Its high-light is the so-called "Volker Rule" that seeks to limit proprietary trading. This loosely refers to banks gambling with other people's money, thereby infusing a streak of Las Vegas into supposedly staid, high-street, banks. The "Volker Rule" is supposed to bar banks from betting tax-payer guaranteed deposits and other assets on the markets for the banks' own profit. With Dodd-Frank in place, everything should be hunky-dory. Or so the theory goes.

It is a safe bet that the new Dodd-Frank law will find the old Glass-Steagall shoes too big to fill. In terms of being up to the job of adequately regulating banks, the present legal architecture for Wall Street regulation is but a shadow of its former New Deal self – and that despite a situation where the need for regulation is greater because of the growing pseudo-market condition. Yet banks, not sparing a thought for a public that was hurt by their previous misadventures, viewed the Dodd-Frank bill as a stick meant to beat them with rather than as an olive branch for making amends. Despite having being battered by the "Great Financial Crisis," and imposing community suffering of indeterminate duration, the banks failed to regard regulation like a law-abiding motorist would regard the speed limit – as something that is accepted because it is for the common good.

It was a difficult birth; there was no easy passage for the Dodd-Frank bill through the US legislative process. Banks, fearing regulatory torment from a deluge of new requirements, took up battle stations, using their lobbyists as hired guns to put the screws on politicians and riddle the Dodd-Frank bill with loopholes, the idea being to make it as lightweight as possible through exemptions and dilutions. For example, the statute allows the recently-created Consumer Financial Protection Bureau (CFPB) to define a category of loans known as "qualified mortgages" that are presumed to meet the "ability-to-pay" standard, thus reducing the lender's risk of being sued in the event of a foreclosure from an unsound loan. This exemption could become a loophole for the return to a devil-may-care attitude to lending. Also, the bill was designed to control the over $700 trillion derivatives industry, the opaque nature of which was blamed for making a disagreeable contribution to the current crisis. But last minute changes to the bill may have carved out self-serving loopholes large enough to drive a coach and horses through. Circumstantial evidence supports this supposition: ambiguity and complexity seem to have made the law unintelligible to the extent of making enforcement possible only behind closed doors and not in open court (see later).

Although still a work in progress (at a glacial pace due to banking-cum-political resistance at every turn), the current indications are that the Dodd-Frank law is doomed to be a voluminous weakling. It has been watered down and is likely to be an apology for the countless regulatory measures repealed since 1960 (including the legendary Glass-Steagall Act). It is a thicket of verbiage, with hundreds of pages of script requiring over two hundred financial rules of an allegedly byzantine nature, across an alphabet soup of at least eleven Federal agencies. Its door-stopper volume ironically reflects its lightness of effect from the numerous caveats that bought off opponents. According to Acharya, Cooley, Richardson, and Ingo, even at its best the Dodd-Frank law falls flat on at least three important counts: the perpetuation of government guarantees (an implicit subsidy); the failure to address systemic risk (i.e., the ability of banks to externalize costs to others in the system); and omissions in regulating parts of the shadow banking system (Acharya et al. 2010). These authors state that the net effect of these flaws is to potentially sow the seeds of the next significant crisis. Dodd-Frank reportedly fails to offer regulators a light that is bright enough to penetrate the shadows of the shadow banking system, given that the targets of regulation would naturally know more about their business than the regulators (that is, information is asymmetrical).

The deceptively innocuous money-market funds in the shadow banking system are a little-regarded lurking threat to the whole banking system. Going by its shabby record, the migration of activity to the complex and unseen world of shadow banking brings risk, but the magnitude of the danger from it is only known when things go wrong.

*Dead Duck*

Although the Dodd-Frank law is not yet a dead letter, there are some signs that it could end up close to being a dead duck when it comes to implementation. Its most worrying feature is the devil in the (labyrinthine) detail; it could have enough ambiguity to befuddle almost everyone and make a mockery of both observance and enforcement.

Looking at the Dodd-Frank law from a practical standpoint it is apparent that, apart from the theoretical weaknesses identified earlier, the law has many a slip in relation to effectiveness. Volume and intricacy are logical reasons for slippage; the exceptions and limitations put in to placate combative and hostile vested interests have made it a thicket of verbiage of byzantine complexity. It stands to reason that laws that are straightforward are more easily observable and enforceable than those that are cumbersome. For the thousands of small banks that have to wade through what is, for them, a swamp of gobbledygook, the Dodd-Frank law can be a fiddly compliance nightmare. In the end, the reportedly contradictory demands of the Dodd-Frank law's jungle of regulations could be too complex for *observance* on the one hand and too difficult to legally interpret for *enforcement* on the other. This could be the explanation for the spate of secret settlements, outside the open-courts system, between regulators and the blameworthy within banks.

The circumventing of normal legal processes raises two questions. First, is it the case that because no one knows what the law really is (because it is gibberish), it is necessary for the law to be inter-preted behind closed doors through backstairs wheeling and dealing between bankers and regulators? Second, is there in place an institu-tionalized system of in-camera trial for alleged violators that paral-lels the formal open courts system, where amateur procedures have kangaroo-court connotations?

Invisible chains shackle government regulators. Whether and to what extent the enforcement of regulations is plagued by incompe-tence is not known, but it is a fairly sure bet that the system makes a mockery of diligence in enforcement. Under the US constitution, banks have the same privacy rights as persons (*a la* the case of *Marshall v. Barlow*, 1979). This gives the coercive advantage to the target of regulation, while putting regulators on the back foot. It stands to rea-son that regulators have to tread warily, nimble pussyfooting being required to avoid stepping on bankers' ample toes. The evidence sug-gests that the constitutional ground rules deny regulator-Davids the sling in their confrontation with Goliath banks, and leave regulators no choice but to make consultation with prudence and discretion the natural order of things. To further undermine regulator enthu-siasm, hordes of lawyers gird their loins to tell their banking clients how to keep regulators on the hop, by suggesting ways and means to spike regulators' guns. Lawyers can make a drama out of a particular enforcement move at the drop of a hat. In addition, lobbyists are ever-ready to come down on government regulators like a ton of bricks. All these pressures can be expected to have a discouraging influence on regulators, to say the least.

When legal might is buttressed with public relations muscle and political opposition, the call to regulatory duty can be drowned by howling winds of hostility – rendering a healthy skepticism toward regulatory efficacy a pardonable inclination. The regula-tory arena can become a battlefield at any time, where banks and their political supporters go gunning for government regulators, peppering them with threats and demonizing them as meddlesome enemies of liberty. In such circumstances, ducking for cover by regulators will be at cross-purposes with the ramrod uprightness required for diligent enforcement. If there is "regulatory capture" as in the past by banks that are now much more powerful than in the past, the question arises whether any serious regulatory investigation can take place without hush-hush backstairs negotiations between regulators and banks to cut deals that most likely, in the end, must have the consent of the bank being investigated. In these circumstances, fines that appear to be shakedowns of banks by prosecutors may in fact camouflage bonanzas for banks. This seemingly bizarre paradox is shown to make eminent good sense in the analysis that follows because the method of enforcement can make a mockery of the letter of the law that lies behind the regulations being enforced.

There would be understandable reluctance about trying to discipline someone holding a pistol to your head. The question is whether government regulators, who are required to fish in muddy waters for a living, can pluck up courage to walk the talk and not be cowed by people too dangerous to displease. It seems a fair bet that *preemptive* enforcement of the Dodd-Frank law on *major* banking matters is not within the bounds of a noble calling for regulators. The information previously examined on enforcement (see section 4.4) signals that the Dodd-Frank law can be expected to provide only weak deterrence, by treating criminal acts as civil offences, with penalties taking the form of fines on innocent shareholders, rather than jail time for convicted law-breakers. When serious enforcement on a major matter threatens a bruising confrontation, dragging one's feet would be preferable to putting one's foot down. Regulators need to be seen to be doing *something* (if only to keep the public off their back), even as they keep an eye on the revolving door (in case a bank makes them an offer that is too good to refuse). In such circumstances, marking time by finding minor fish to fry and loudly trumpeting deceptively large penalties from secret settlements outside the rule of law, become survival techniques for cowed regulators in thorny circumstances. For example, in 2013, Fabrice Tourre was found guilty of "aiding and abetting" his former employer, Goldman Sachs, by misleading investors in a scam that caused three financial firms to lose a hefty $1 billion. No action was brought against the employer, the world's most successful investment bank.

In instances of enforcement, regulators have made a big show of fines on leading banks with no admission of wrongdoing on the part of the latter. Despite the fanfare associated with these announcements, it cannot be known whether the fines are too much, too little, or just right. For the reasons explained subsequently, there is good reason to suspect that there is a mismatch between penalties that are slaps on the wrist and violations that are on the scale of highway robbery. This is because regulators and prosecutors are in effect conducting secret trials without recourse to the process of the open courts system. Graver still, because the negotiations between regulators and the major banks have the predictable outcome of a fine without any necessary admission of wrongdoing, the whole arrangement smacks of a regulatory cop-out from failing to squarely face up to the wider implications of  the procedures being  adopted by regulators and prosecutors.  These refer to subtle matters that go well beyond the obvious matters of exemption from criminal action and the abnormal enforcement method being adopted. To see the hidden pitfalls, consider the following lines of reasoning.

There has to be a point beyond which the Dodd-Frank tiger becomes effectively toothless. Since information is power, the backroom negotiations between government regulators and the accused bank become a golden opportunity for the affected bankers to study the mindset of the government watchdogs. Identifying friendly loopholes and bendable rules means: "Bob's your uncle"! In other words, it is "all systems are go" for regulation violations in lucrative niches beneath the radar. Should such violations become routine they could be expected to have the effect of knocking out several teeth in the Dodd-Frank tiger.

This phenomenon could be of increasing significance because of the growing reliance on private sector regulators to oversee the US banking system. Since these private regulators are paid by the very banks they regulate, the farcical situation makes compromised independence more than just a possibility. Put kindly, the coziness is conducive to enabling regulation violations in tussle-free comfort. This is besides the damage to Dodd-Frank from the possibility of a blind eye being turned to selected requirements by bank-friendly private overseers, when a quizzically beady one would be the more appropriate.

Turning a Nelsonian eye to banking sins by regulators is not a possibility but a reality. According to an article by Edward Wyatt in the *New York Times* (February 3, 2012), the Securities and Exchange Commission (SEC) is said to have not proceeded with action for fraud against major banks in at least twenty-two instances (Stiglitz 2013, 149).

The news goes from bad to worse. The regulators' approach to implementation can be much more serious when it has the effect of knocking out most of the remaining teeth in the Dodd-Frank tiger. This happens when the adept manipulation of regulations and regulators by banks becomes a line of business that opens up an avenue of profitability for them. A rational response by banks to the expedient tactics of regulators (namely, closed-door deals outside the open courts system) enables calculated regulation-management to parallel money-management as a banking business strategy. Settlements become business decisions, not confessions. It would be perfectly rational for banks to regard the anticipated fines for regulation violations as simply additional banking operating costs that could be more than offset by additional revenue from business practices such as rule-bending, loop-hole seeking, own-account-trading, rate fiddling, and shadow banking.

In such circumstances, fines that have shock value for mollifying the public could be a no big deal for the allegedly errant bank. When banks are able to regard predictable fines as business operational costs, the observance or otherwise of regulations could come to be seen as business management strategies for profit-making – something that could evolve to give shenanigans the status of routine business practice. For example, paying a fine of $10 billion for breaching the "Volker Rule" would be chickenfeed if it were the result of covert trading that hauled in a stealthy $20 billion – with the fanfare accompanying the fine having the effect of keeping the public and politicians assuaged to boot. This is why what may seem like extortionist fines by prosecutors can still leave a nice enough profit for banks. The absence of a transparent judicial process in the behind-the-scenes deal-making between regulators and the accused banks could mean that the prosecutor's interest based in expediency is divorced from the public's interest in the need for justice. Such an outcome would have the effect of condemning the Dodd-Frank law, if not to a toothless tiger status, then to a condition featuring very loose dentures – a state of being that would be hilarious if it were not dreadfully serious.

There is every indication that the Dodd-Frank law, even if impeccably enforced, would be no more than an apology for its New Deal predecessors. That means, even if the Dodd-Frank law was a clone of the legendary Glass-Steagall law in its testosterone-charged prime, it would still lack the oomph to keep current banks in line. This is because of the major structural and related behavioral changes that have taken place since deregulation. These have drastically reposi-tioned the banking industry in relation to the economy in particular and society in general. The big banks are now effectively transna-tional fiefdoms, having many of their intricate operations take place in a variety of jurisdictions in far-flung operations. The resulting opaqueness is as favorable to global manipulation as it is unfavor-able to regulatory scrutiny. In addition, the big banks are now much more powerful than before in their lobbying strengths and influence over the domestic policy processes of Western countries, particularly in the United States. In any event, it is common knowledge that the agencies charged with enforcement, including the Securities and Exchange Commission (SEC), have not been adequately funded to properly undertake the job – thereby adding to the already fading hopes for credible and proper enforcement of the Dodd-Frank law through the open courts system.

## 8.6 Conclusions and Implications

*The Changing Big Picture*

For starry-eyed financial deregulation fans in search of a grand free market dream, the tragic reality is that the chickens have come home to roost in much-less-free plutocratic pseudo-markets. Putting a brave face on things cannot alter the fact that less-free plutocratic pseudo-markets are a different kettle of fish from the freer markets that the stripping away of financial regulations was supposed to uncover.

Going down the deregulation road seemed a good idea at the time (deregulators were unaware of the minefield ahead). They did not bother about the knock-on effect, namely, the boost to the pseudo-market condition – a ballooning monstrosity that has caused deregulation to blow up in the faces of its perpetrators. To expect orderly free markets to result from business license was prepos-terous. The fiasco of financial deregulation caused deregulators to reap the whirlwind with relentlessly expanding plutocratic pseudo-markets; they are placed in the unflattering position of a sorcerer's apprentice because of a process that they are unable to control.

The effect of deregulation on expediting the natural evolutionary process of free market capitalism is examined in section 12.2. The impetus is shown to hasten the demise of competitive open markets as they progress through their life-cycle stages. Should the evolution of the capitalist market system be allowed to follow its logical chronological sequence, undisturbed by fundamental reforms, the final stage would be a natural end for open competitive markets. The competitive spirit could become as good as irrelevant, and the unimaginable the norm.

Plutocracy goes hand in hand with pseudo-markets, with the proliferation of plutocrats being symptomatic of pseudo-market expansion. Plutocratic pseudo-markets have caused capitalism to lose its magic of being able to deliver community prosperity. Treading in the footsteps of the "father of *laissez faire* economics," Adam Smith, as laid down in his epic *Wealth of Nations* (1776), is not possible because the manipulative hand in plutocratic pseudo-markets has the automatic effect of erasing his footprints. Narrow corporate interests have come to systemically supersede wider community interests, leaving the bypassed majority disenchanted on the rack. Adam Smith, "the father of free market capitalism," would probably have found astounding the current widespread pseudo-market condition, with its anti-competitive and anti-social features. Those who support plutocratic pseudo-markets in his name could expect to cause him to turn over in his grave.

### Present Anxieties

By throwing light on the frightful reality of plutocratic pseudo-markets, we can better explain how critical parts of the world economy do actually function, as against how they ought to theoretically function, as claimed in increasingly obsolete standard textbooks on economics still believed by many. Pseudo-markets have made much of economics seem quaintly dated; the duality in the economy exposes an economics of limited relevance, one that is decreasingly germane to the prevalent and emerging market condition. Minds that are brainwashed by theories of the past can be slow to come around to the realization that once-valid beliefs have been overtaken by sneakily evolving events underfoot.

Today's economic battle does not pit communism against capitalism, but is a contest between open competitive markets and plutocratic pseudo-markets. It is an unacknowledged economic tension, which some might perceive as one between hope and despair. Hence, plutocratic pseudo-markets involve considerations that go well beyond the immediate problem of bubble creation – a problem that pales in comparison with the underlying difficulty of market malfunction. Pseudo-market expansionism implies a drift to plutocracy that casts an ever-darkening shadow over the health of economies. The vulnerability of the global real economy on account of plutocratic pseudo-markets, particularly in finance, makes such markets the Achilles' heel of the world economy. The leaders of pseudo-market firms in the financial sector, specifically those controlling colossal banks and ancillary firms like credit-ratings agencies, are riding ever higher on the international financial stage because of their growing ability to extend their reach into far corners of a global economy in increasing need of loans – creditors gaining power ceded by borrowers. Financiers are backed by fellow plutocrats in pseudo-market firms in other sectors, like media, energy and pharmaceuticals, singing from the same plutocratic song sheet. This means that the plutocratic leaders of a few mighty banks, together with fellow plutocrats in other pseudo-markets, could carve out a matrix of relationships based on the new sociopolitical reality, to increasingly rule the roost that is the world economy, national sovereignty notwithstanding. The more pessimistic may argue that a fearsome era of myopic plutocratic imperialism has already begun to take hold in the West, with a manifestation that can range from subtle pressure to intervention of the heavy-handed sort.

Now is not the time to kill the fatted calf in celebration of re-regulation measures, nor should the red carpet be rolled out for regulators. Re-regulation of the banking system is not all it is cracked up to be; its lack of regulatory remarkableness gives little to write home about. The need to accommodate powerful vested interests in formulation and implementation, has complicated and compromised the regulatory measures to a point where one could be excused for seeing in them the messiness of a pig's dinner. The success of bringing mighty banks under social control through re-regulation is far from assured because, apart from weaknesses in the letter of the law, diligence in implementation is questionable when regulators are unlikely to be cruising for a bruising. In fact, bankers seem to be already calling the government regulators' bluff, even as they nurture cozy relationships with private regulators they paid. Perhaps, they also use the cover of seemingly hefty fines to hide healthy gains.

It does not seem likely that the recently redesigned financial regulatory measures can ever to hold a candle to the numerous financial regulations that were ditched since the 1960s, because of the emergence of pseudo-market conditions. Those laboring under the illusion that re-regulation will restore the status of banks to their respected pre-deregulation days, can count on being disappointed. The re-regulatory apparatus and process seem a three-ring circus comprising regulators, politicians, and lobbyists. Regulators are keeping up appearances by making moves sufficient to keep the gallery in good humor for now, but such a period of contentment could turn out to be only a farcical interlude in the program of the circus, before the tent caves in.

Deregulators wanting to learn from their mistakes and do better the next time round would have as much chance of doing so as someone who has caused grievous bodily harm to innocent bystanders by shooting wildly. Re-regulation is suggestive of a situation where the stable door is being locked after the horse has bolted. If the Dodd-Frank law and similar measures in Europe are designed to put things right, being able to do so will depend on the extent to which the condition is reversible. Reversal must go well beyond ensuring regulatory effectiveness to eliminating the albatross of a dysfunctional plutocratic pseudo-market condition – boosted by bad deregulation – that weighs on the health of economies. For the many reasons adduced, the Dodd-Frank law seems too feeble an instrument to lift repentant deregulatory politicians off the hook. Eventually the truth will out about the mythical nature of financial reform. This could take until the next financial collapse, which many experts believe is in the cards (see section12.3). It is likely to be a while off, however, because of the various palliative measures taken (lots of printed and borrowed money) that can have the effect of buying time to postpone the inevitable (see chapter 12).

*Unnerving Questions*

It is now clear that there is no easy way of getting off lightly from the catalytic spin-off effects of deregulation. To all appearances the point of no return for market functionality has been passed, and the flowering of pseudo-market firms is hardly about to dry up in the current policy climate. The four ingredients of plutocratic pseudo-markets, namely monopolization, globalization, politicization and corruption, conspire to impair markets by eroding competitive sectors. Market malfunction from conflicting markets that tear the economy apart is the symptom of a market disease afflicting the economy that has come to be accepted as the natural order of things. But further collapse can be fortuitous if it jolts policymakers into recognizing the real problem: the dysfunctional plutocratic pseudo-market condition that warps the market fabric and distorts the economy into degeneration.

A healthy skepticism causes the following unnerving questions to define the overarching framework of the menace in Socratic manner. Are the enlarged banks and other pseudo-market firms, now *much* too big (*and* too numerous) to fail? Are the plutocratic leaders of pseudo-market firms too big to jail (i.e., beyond the reach of the criminal law)? Are pseudo-market firms too big to control, being laws unto themselves. Are Dodd-Frank and other similar types of measures just facades to mollify the trusting? Are banks and other pseudo-market firms so powerful that they do not need to be concerned about the niceties of ethical behavior? Are the enhanced powers and myopic vision of leaders in the financial sector sources of irritation to governments i.e., thorns in the flesh of sovereign nations that desire budgetary autonomy to decide their destinies? Are bankers and other captains of industry, like the merchants of Venice of old, a lionized plutocracy reigning over the realm of economic policy formulation for narrow private advantage at the costs of social wellbeing and economic recovery?

If the answers to the foregoing questions are in the affirmative, it would explain why industry tycoons act as if they own the place. It is because they do.

**

253

# Chapter 9

## PSEUDO-MARKET FALLOUT: STYMIED RECOVERY

### 9.1 "Butterfly Effect"

If the stymied recovery needs an address, it will likely be found down the easy streets of plutocratic pseudo-markets. Looking at the deregulatory fallout in the cold light of day reveals the hefty price that has been paid for bad policy, with more sizable installments to come. This chapter will attempt to show why deregulation marked the turning of the tide toward a market dysfunction that was behind the downturn and now impedes recovery. While the enlargement of firms was the proximate cause of the boost to the dysfunctional plutocratic pseudo-market condition, the resultant secondary changes in the behavior of such enlarged firms enables them to consolidate and grow by feeding on their own success – making the growing market dysfunction an insidiously spreading normality.

The damaging effects of deregulation on the wider market system can be ascribed to the "butterfly effect." (The concept is attributed to Edward N. Lorenz's paper presented at the American Association for the Advancement of Science in 1979; a butterfly flapping its wings in Rio de Janeiro might change the weather in Chicago.) The "butterfly effect" crops up when a relatively small change, such as a change in banking regulations, has wider ramifications, like bringing about a stubborn worldwide economic downturn. This explains why the party in the financial sector has produced a universal hangover. The "butterfly effect" is attributed to the complexity of the system in which the initial action occurred. Deregulation in the financial sector brought danger to Western economies by causing flawed market structures and plutocratic influences to be boosted. This means that what started as a banking crisis has decayed into a growth crisis – a development that can be attributed to the "butterfly effect."

The combination of ideas presented earlier has been probative in pointing the finger of blame at the single-most important flaw: the dysfunction that prevents markets from delivering a recovery that is sturdy and across-the-board. The plutocratic pseudo-market condition continues to change the balance of power between firms and governments. New phenomena are in play when the inexorable advance of plutocratic pseudo-markets causes the market arena to change in jerry-built fashion due to expedient couplings called mergers and the haphazard shrinking of open competitive sectors. Deregulation opened a can of worms by its boost to the plutocratic pseudo-market condition, the effects of which have been unanticipated, widespread, entrenched, and counterproductive. Governments, through acts of commission and omission, are responsible for bestowing on pseudo market firms the almost divine rights to monopolization, globalization, politicization, and corruption. Each such pseudo-market trait has been shown to be a barometer of market malfunction.

The condition is portentous because the pseudo-market road is downhill all the way. It involves a cumulative process with a steamroller momentum for global expansion. Such unremitting advances have the effect of edging out firms in open competitive sectors and causing free markets to die by inches. Small changes can add up to a huge loss of competitiveness in economies within even a decade from now. As a result, the majority in the community can be expected to languish, the middle class shrink, and economies fall into the groove of a degenerative process that forebodes an "unending recovery."

It follows that worries about genuine recovery in the real economy are amply justified. Pseudo-market conditions cause economies to be mired in trouble because of monopolization, globalization, politicization, and corruption. In other words, instead of being able to deliver an economic resurgence that is robust, across-the-board, and sustainable, the plutocratic pseudo-market condition gives every indication of being a formidable obstacle to it. The several ball-and-chain hindrances to a genuine recovery examined next are meant to throw light on inhibiting factors that are as insidious as they are intricate. Supposed achievements, like high corporate profits, mergers, bank lending, and globalization, will be shown to be camouflaged threats, because they mask impediments to economic recovery. Shown next is how hindrances to recovery, that may seem minor in isolation, synergize to become major in aggregate.

## 9.2 Obstacles to Recovery

*Market Hindrance*

There can be no authentic economic recovery without a market mechanism that is capable of delivering it. Such a market would have the key features of openness and competitiveness, and be governed by institutional frameworks capable of reconciling private profitability with community prosperity (explained in chapter 5). Since feisty competitiveness in markets is the elixir of economic activity, a weak recovery is a corollary of lackluster competitiveness. A solid economic resurgence that is robust and inclusive depends on the dynamism of markets from initiative, drive, and vibrancy, and these are features associated with effectively competitive open markets boasting lean and mean firms. The theory is that when markets are contestable, competitive pressure from the actual or potential entry of new firms to the industry will force incumbent firms to be alive and kicking to keep from going under.

Startup firms, as engines of economic growth, are at the cutting edge of recovery. These firms are wellsprings of innovation, where starry-eyed dreamers and hard-nosed business persons come together in the one individual called an entrepreneur, as someone said. Since entrepreneurs in startups are go-getter types who are also hotshot developers with commercial acumen for energizing growth, startups are the hotbed of new employment opportunities in the real economy. Startup kindergartners can be trailblazers when they buzz with ideas for solutions that target market segments experiencing unmet needs. Even startups that are one-man-bands can become impressively entrepreneurial, while wannabe startups may have star potential from spotting beckoning market opportunities. For reasons to be explained shortly, these bright lights of pioneering dynamism have drastically reduced in numbers, a phenomenon that explains at least some of the lack of energy sorely needed to fuel a durable recovery spurt in the real economy.

Deregulation confounded predictions of freer competitive markets and delivered less-free plutocratic pseudo-markets, where a historical proneness to "cardiac arrest" in the financial sector continues to threaten healthy recovery prospects in the real economy. Plutocratic pseudo-markets, where a manipulative hand holds sway, create conditions where market players with the potential for competitive dynamism have strong incentive to give up their search for efficiency and become ponderously elephantine. The protection afforded by plutocratic pseudo-markets enables buttoned-down executives to have fewer reasons for quaking in their boots due to market threats; there is comfort from the prospect of easy profits on a platter from non-operational and non-market business practices in plutocratic pseudo-markets. Pseudo-market imperatives give firms the incentive to eschew an entrepreneurial spirit in favor of heavy-footed and heavy-handed business approaches – dispositions associated with nest-feathering business strategies and enabled by plutocratic prowess. Uncompetitive market structures and institutional weaknesses provide opportunities to engage in international manipulation, political arm twisting, and corrupt business practices like rate rigging. Such profitability strategies tend to be anti-recovery because they sap the incentive and ability of competitive firms to succeed through creative innovation and operational acumen.

Therefore, in an age of lumbering mega-firms basking in the laidback conditions of plutocratic pseudo-markets, competitiveness in markets is becoming ever less relevant, even as entrepreneurial dynamism is becoming ever less prevalent. The conditions enable plutocrats to thrive without necessarily lifting a finger to promote economic growth for genuine recovery, causing pseudo-market firms, held up by concealed economic rents, to look ever less like the community-friendly national champions of yore. Unsurprisingly, to the extent that the moves and countermoves of such firms aim to get a larger slice of the existing pie, there is not much prospect of value being added to the cause of genuine recovery.

## Company Hindrance

Myopia reigns; durable economic recovery is undermined by short-term planning horizons featuring blocked foresight. A truncated perspective, that denies long-term strategic vision in business leaders, can be attributed to incentives that disproportionately reward those with the bird in the hand. Short-termism is the order of the day, with many companies living from quarter-to-quarter, or from year-to-year on what are arguably quick fixes. In order to placate valued institutional investors demanding short-term payoff, short-term performance has become the most powerful expression of business performance, and is, for managers, the surest path to career success. As a result, making a fast buck is in fashion; spikes in short-term profit get for top executives congratulatory slaps on the back, which usually translate into annual bonuses that can be generous to a fault. In other words, bouquets for top executives are more assured from business strategies that, although short on long-term vision, are big on short-term profitability that is showy.

Micro business practices give expression to the short-term business culture in vogue. Giving executives shares in their company has had the effect of causing executives to focus on the short-term performance of their shares. This they do by massaging short-term profits to make the most of it, given that the average period in the job for bosses in America is less than eight years. This means that the policy options for fostering the long-term health of the business, through expenditures for purposes such as R&D, plant expansion, and factory construction, tend to get short shrift.

The short-term management mindset is justified by the short-term horizons of activist shareholders who, by definition, refuse to see beyond the end of their nose. Shareholders burned by the recession and lacking confidence in the longer term future, have come out of the woodwork to pick fights with managers who resist their demands for quick returns – a post-crisis phenomenon that is becoming a universal problem. True, shareholders who take an interest in company operations can have a good influence by filling a void in governance and keeping company bosses on their toes. But they can harm companies when dispositions that are rowdy, opportunistic, or scavenging, trigger an activist attack against visionary managers pursing long-term strategies for sustainable competitive advantage.

Durable recovery depends on business strategies based on long-term strategic vision, a long-term investment offensive being needed for a recovery that is sustainable. That would require business goals to be forward-looking and be set in decades rather than quarters. A long-term perspective is regarded as a business virtue because it enables corporations to be "built to last" (to use the title of the book by management experts Jim Collins and Jerry Porras). The lack of strategic vision prevents managers from placing bold bets on the long-term innovative solutions needed for a recovery that has a future. There is every chance that the limited business vision in vogue, by precluding visionary projects, preempts company growth that is sustainable – and that cannot be good for a recovery that needs to be durable.

Promising to make a quick mega-buck more assuredly wins for borrowers the hearts of bankers; the evidence is that banks in America and Europe make a solid contribution to the culture of short-termism in business, thereby reinforcing anti-recovery forces. The pro-short-term disposition of banks makes business sense. Long-term loans require banks to hold more capital against them and to fund them with more expensive long-term borrowing – giving short-term loans a clear profitability edge over long-term loans. The disinclination on the part of banks to underwrite the long-term strategic vision of business leaders promotes a bias toward swift gratification on the part of myopic firms. It consequently diminishes incentives for investments of the strategic sort, such as in R&D, product innovation, and productivity that are associated with longer-term profitability. This means firms are being forced to make short-term profits at the cost of forgoing long-term strategic competitive advantage – implying that the banks' preferred business strategy encourages business practices in firms that can hinder a recovery that is sustainable.

The bankers' step-motherly approach to lending to firms in the real economy is characteristically cruel to durable recovery. When it comes to bank lending, the real economy (think factories) is the discriminated-against Cinderella reduced to unloved maidservant status, and the financial economy (think stocks) is the favored ugly sister. It seems that the real economy is a relatively less attractive proposition for banks than ever before, because Western economies are finacialized as never before. The sloshing about of cheap and easy money and the allure of veritable casinos in forms such as proprietary trading, stock market trading and rate rigging, mean that there are more fast bucks to be made in exciting finance than in the less glamorous real economy. The boost to mortgages from tax subsidies can also be expected to divert lending away from the real economy, especially from businesses in open competitive sectors. This is significant because over half of all bank lending is for mortgages. The prospects in the lackluster real economy pale in comparison with those in the financial sector, causing the investment action to naturally gravitate toward the brighter lights in finance. So it is little wonder that lending to firms in the real economy for employment-generating purposes, like factory expansion, suffer Cinderella-like discrimination and neglect. Unsurprisingly, the recovery is unbalanced, leaning more toward the bubbly mirage of dicey finance and away from manufacturing and the nonfinancial service sectors – the robust alternatives crying out for opportunities that are more than just incidental to the main game in finance.

What is more, banks play favorites – a behavior that happens to be antagonistic to recovery. Just as gigolos target old ladies with money, banks are apparently more enamored of old and established firms with greater financial assets than with new and unsettled ones. Such a preference does, of course, make eminent good sense when making money, not the romance of entrepreneurship, is the dominant motive. For banks, age and experience can be a better bet than startups with Keynesian animal spirits; staid established firms that are focused on preserving the old world that made them are usually less risky than feisty new firms that chance innovation in search of market gaps from unmet needs. The bigger banks are biased in their lending, funneling money to fellow plutocrats in pseudo-market conditions, mostly comprising jobs-cum-recovery exporting multinationals basking in the security that comes from monopolization, globalization, politicization, and corruption. This makes lending banks the powerful allies of borrowing non-financial pseudo-market firms in their quest for unearned and surplus profits – and an incidental party to their anti-recovery activities. In fact, rumblings from the direction of regulators suggest that banks are allowing such big corporate borrowers to lever themselves up to levels that smack of recklessness. Besides the risk to recovery from such large companies being allowed to load up on debt, bankers' indifference to the charms of the smaller and newer firms leaves the latter stranded, and robs the economy of their audacious talents for employment generation and dynamism. The privation suffered by newer and smaller business entrepreneurs who are deprived of the means of their livelihood would be especially rankling because of their reliance more on banks than capital markets for funding.

What this partially adds up to is that banks' lending practices take a toll on recovery by starving startup firms of funds and deterring entrepreneurial new firms from entering the industry. Because a major motivation for the enlargement of firms is the easier access to capital that bigness brings, the onward march of pseudo-markets is helped by the competitive disadvantage of smaller and newer firms in relation to funding, and their consequent readiness to being swallowed by pseudo-market giants. It is a fair bet that the subsumed firms would count themselves lucky: being gobbled up can be a merciful alternative to shutting up shop. In the circumstances, the prey plumps for survival at the cost of dignity.

The facts back the argument. The available evidence shows a drastic fall in the number of new businesses in the United States, particularly smaller firms. In fact, smaller firms keep losing ground to bigger firms because more are dying than are being born – implying space-filling pseudo-market expansionism. Startup firms are at the heart of America's economy, and they account for most of the net jobs created. According to an article titled "Not Open for Business" by Schumpeter in *The Economist* (October 12, 2013), the number of new jobs created by startups are said to have fallen by nearly half over the thirteen years to 2012.

When these startups are regarded as upstarts by incumbent firms and are an attraction or threat to them, the new firms can be subsumed by the established firms, disappearing into the vortex of the pseudo-market system. Just one example is the purchase of startup firm Nest Labs by giant Google. Banks facilitate the process when they deny capital to the startup prey and offer capital to the incumbent predator. When today's difficult times require R&D cutbacks in businesses, vibrant startups become irresistible to larger firms looking for easy R&D pickings. Denied capital backing, startups submit to reality and fall into the arms of larger firms attracted to (or threatened by) the innovative solutions they offer. In general terms, such takeovers, although offering smaller or newer firms a more attractive alternative to keeling over, could have negative effects if the subsumed prey is constrained by the culture, practices, and policies of the predator. If so, the consolidation could have the effect of smothering innovativeness from entrepreneurship and discouraging the development of technological blockbusters.

Smaller and newer firms lack the opportunity and the ability to engage in political and international manipulation like pseudo-market firms do. The latter are not only past masters at it, but also have deep-enough pockets to cope with it. Consequently, a lopsided playing field denies smaller and newer firms the ability to match pseudo-market firms' ducking-and-weaving skills for avoiding crippling regulations and onerous taxes. While equal rules for all firms fall harder on smaller firms, big firms can, in addition, benefit from lobbying. Smaller and newer firms could find regulations too difficult to deal with unless they succumb to being merged, as the smaller drug companies are finding when they have to cope with regulatory requirements for getting their drugs to market. Furthermore, relatively newer and smaller firms can be overwhelmed by the hurdles of foreign entry. Being unable to launch into new foreign markets is a matter of particular significance when they lose out on the opportunities from free trade pacts. As borders get ever less bothersome, pseudo-markets get ever more prevalent, occupying space taken over from retreating competitive markets (see later). Considering all these reasons, it is not surprising that the empirical evidence shows that smaller firms are more likely to go bust than large ones (Ibbotson and Idzorek, 2014). By disadvantaging the dynamic job-creating firms in more competitive sectors, the unlevel playing field adds to the stack of hindrances to a genuine turnaround in the real economy.

Adding to the bad news is the risk to sustainable and genuine recovery due to banks falling short of being the exemplars of recovery-friendly business practices. Suspicions have not been allayed that unreformed banks are a lurking threat to the real economy on account of their growing plutocratic pseudo-market status in conditions of global financial ascendancy. The banking scandals referred to earlier suggest that there are ongoing risks to the fragile world economy from a financial sector that cannot be adequately reformed or controlled, irrespective of whether the improprieties are due to gaffes or conspiracies. Judging by what has come out of the closet (see section 8.1), there is no plausible evidence that banks have cleaned up their act sufficiently to wash away the stains of the banking sins referred to before. As was pointed out in section 8.4, the rational response by banks to the expedient tactics of regulators (i.e., closed-door deals outside the open courts system) enables calculated regulation-management to parallel money-management as a banking business strategy. This enables regulation-breaking to be perceived by banks as business opportunities to be grasped – a mindset that dilutes the incentive to toe the regulatory line and is cavalier toward financial risk.

Because of its strong position, the financial sector is, paradoxically, the weakest link in the chain. It is hardly comforting that lofty out-of-control banks, ensconced in plutocratic pseudo-markets ruling the roost in global finance, are not only a chilling impediment to durable recovery (for the potent amalgam of reasons adduced earlier), but are also capable of precipitating a collapse of the real economy at any time (by being architects of scanty equity buffers in huge companies etc, as elaborated on in section 12.2).

Mutual suspicion has weakened the international finance system and spoiled the international trading environment like rarely or never before. Because financial institutions had cross-exposure to each other, the toxic bonds that were distributed throughout the international banking system poisoned the international business atmosphere by creating distrust among financial institutions. Mutual suspicion dissolved the glue of trust that was needed to hold the global system together. The lack of trust damaged international trading relationships, and continues to make an insidious contribution to the ongoing downturn.

These sorts of predilections can be expected to contribute to a doom loop: they make the downturn self-perpetuating by causing it to feed upon itself. This phenomenon is recognized in section 10.6 as being of an undoubtedly anti-recovery nature because of its innate tendency to make impediments to recovery mount rather than recede.

In spite of all this, it does not seem fitting to blame banks for doing what is best for their bottom line. Banks have a business responsibility to home in on policies that maximize profits for their shareholders; in fact, they have a legal obligation to do so (*a la*, the case of *Dodge v. Ford* in 1919). Market signals fashion banking strategy for risk management (risk being the font of profits for banks for those who know), and the fact that the signals emanate from dysfunctional pseudo-markets is unlikely to worry bank mangers when profitability is pleasing. Banks seek quick gratification simply because the market signals that is what does most for their profitability, for the reasons explained. They cannot be expected to worry about the possibility that encouraging short-termism might truncate the strategic vision of business leaders (essential for sustained recovery). Lending to the finance sector is more attractive and profitable in circumstances of cheap and easy money than is lending for less glamorous and riskier investments in the real economy for purposes such as R&D and factory construction. It should not matter to bankers that their bias against productive investments would result in forgone employment. Because lending to more established firms can be expected to reduce the chances of non-performing loans, bankers are not likely to lose sleep over the possibility that such a preference may deny the economy entrepreneurship from startups. It is understandable that banks would shy away from startups because the path from startup to success is littered with failures. In any case, the evidence shows that smaller firms are the bigger risk (Ibbotson and Idzorek, 2014), just as are longer term loans. Fellow plutocrats in other pseudo-markets have the edge when it comes to winning the hearts of bankers, and the likelihood that such infatuation entrenches and grows the pseudo-market condition at the expense of open competitive sectors could be regarded as a desirable side-effect by banks. The same attitude could be said to influence lending decisions that foster corporate gigantism and pseudo-market expansion through mergers and acquisitions. Furthermore, it is understandable that banks may not be prepared to forgo handsome returns from exciting practices such as own-account trading and rate-rigging, especially in circumstances where returns from humdrum mainstream activities are falling. There is an increased incentive to engage in such esoteric activities because banks' revenue from staples (bonds, commodities, currencies, and derivatives) has fallen by more than a third since the collapse. In addition, banks are forced to safeguard their position because less regulated non-banking credit sources (e.g., microfinance companies, "originators" in Wall Street's shadow) are giving them a rough time. For all these reasons, market circumstances make seemingly bad banking behavior eminently appropriate.

This draws attention to other factors that can work to stymie recovery: machinations in that shady place called shadow banking (whose history falls well short of admirable). The perils of shadow banking continue because its competitive advantage against mainstream banking comes from cutting regulatory corners. This means, the more regulations that shadow banking can circumvent compared to its brighter counterpart, the more it can undercut the latter to win over borrowers with better terms. The competitive strategy to drum up business has an element of "who dares wins" and can turn out to be not too far removed from games of dare like "chicken" and "Russian roulette" (as the last collapse so palpably demonstrated).

In sum, all of the foregoing banking behaviors involve picking fruitful strategy options for bountiful profits. This means that if what makes eminent good sense for banks is bad for society, it is not likely to be because of wickedness or bad taste on the part of bankers. It is true that pseudo-market firms have powerful allies in banks in their quest for unearned and surplus profits, thereby making banks willing parties to anti-recovery activities. But the considerable and crucial contribution of banking strategy to thwarting a robust and inclusive recovery is just an unintended by-product of what banks are there to do: maximize profits for their shareholders.

There is good reason for bank managers to want to do their damnedest for shareholders: shareholders are in no mood to be nice. For one thing, shareholders, scarred by the bitter experience of the collapse may still be licking their wounds. For another, they are smarting because of what they perceive as shakedowns by regulators and prosecutors in America. The huge fines, totaling some $50 billion within a year, that banks paid have not come out of the pockets of bank managers, but were charged to hapless shareholders who played no direct part in either the bad management decisions or the closed-door deals between banks and regulators. The hush-hush backroom negotiations usually keep shareholders in the dark about culprits and circumstances. Because bank managers atone for their alleged sins by lightening the wallets and handbags of shareholders (while leaving theirs untouched), it is understandable that the managers' priority would be to mollify shareholders with sufficient profits so they do not kick up too much of a fuss (and not worry about market dysfunction). If banks are not doing the right thing for recovery, the blame should fall squarely on the bad signals that the dysfunctional pseudo-market condition gives, and not on the banks that cannot help responding to them. Banks should not be blamed for rational responses to distorted incentives from a market system that is not like a market system is supposed to be. Anti-recovery business behavior is only a symptom of a deeper cause: system failure due to market malfunction.

*Momentum Hindrance*

Besides the anti-recovery disposition of pseudo-market firms in general and banks in particular, there are other forces driving pseudo-market expansionism for perpetuation of the downturn. The downturn, far from discouraging the growth of mega-firms is actually boosting the process, and is thereby entrenching and spreading the anti-recovery pseudo-market traits of monopolization, globalization, politicization and corruption. The progress of the pseudo-market condition gets considerable added momentum from acquisitions and mergers that keep feeding corporate gigantism and swelling the ranks of pseudo-market firms. As previously explained, what gives pride to predators can cause headaches for entrepreneurs. When expanding pseudo-markets inhibit small-to-medium sized businesses, the real economy is badly affected because they employ most of the work-force. This means that the expansion of plutocratic pseudo-markets can be associated with a net loss of employment in the economy sim-ply because pseudo-markets destroy more jobs than they create, the "Luddite Fallacy" notwithstanding.

The Luddites are likely to have the last laugh, their hilarity being justified by the likelihood that the shenanigans of globalization ren-der the "Luddite Fallacy" fallacious, as was explained in the previous chapter. The spate of consolidations is associated with widespread "rationalization," whereby businesses seek savings from restructur-ing by discarding overlapping functions – something usually syn-onymous with layoffs. Such labor-shedding adds to unemployment in depressed and immobile times. As was previously stated, even accepting that labor-displacement through technological progress does, in terms of the "Luddite Fallacy," result in greater capital for-mation, investment, and an overall increase in employment, most of this seems to happen in non-Western countries that benefit from the foreign direct investments of Western multinationals. This would explain much of the inconsistency in the real economy between healthy company profitability and lethargic economic recovery.

The consolidation of incumbents in salubrious pseudo-market conditions understandably makes the now toughened market con-ditions less attractive to firms mulling entry into the industry. The discouraging effect emanates from reduced market contestability. As explained earlier, this means that would-be competitors wanting to enter the industry now face barriers to entry that are less surmountable because of the consolidation of incumbents in protective and empowering pseudo-market conditions. Consequently, incumbent firms donning the pseudo-market mantle, by having an automatic discouraging effect on potential new entrants, give themselves a more relaxed existence. Such contentment adds to the pile of hindrances to recovery, because it is not a disposition that is conducive to the heavy lifting associated with genuine recovery (elaborated on in chapter 12).

*Inequality Hindrance*

Inequality of the virtuous sort is conducive to economic growth and recovery, as was explained (see section 5.3). This was said to happen in properly functioning markets where community-based institutional frameworks govern the profit-maximizing operations of businesses. As implied, not all inequality is antithetical to recovery, and some forms of inequality are necessary for it. Necessary inequality rewards productivity associated with technology, hard work, and initiative, implying that when it comes to entrepreneurship, even profits of obscene proportions can have social respectability.

Yet inequality can be another factor that is a drag on recovery. There is dissonance between economic growth and genuine recovery when growth benefits consistently bypass the majority. Inequality has widened because of technological change that has caused mechanization to dry up work opportunities, as well as globalization that has caused work to be shifted to low-wage countries. But this is not the full story.

The distribution of income reflects the distribution of political power. The exclusion of the majority of the population from growth benefits is explained by the disproportionate plutocratic control over the levers of power in the economies of America and Europe that gives rise to an "arrogation effect." This makes growth a necessary but insufficient condition for genuine recovery, one that is widely felt. The emergence of plutocratic pseudo-markets has caused the balance of power in the economy to tilt in favor of big business. This enables such markets to suck up most of the fruits of growth to the exclusion of the majority. The deprived majority comprises both *individuals* constituting the so-called "99 percent," as well as *firms* in open competitive sectors that lack a level playing field. The evidence shows that pseudo-market profitability has been synonymous with stark inequality for the majority of both individuals (e.g., Stiglitz 2013; Stockman 2013) and firms.

If much of the middle class, who are the backbone of the economy, joins the ranks of the underclass, as seems to be happening, it would be bad news for recovery. An emaciated middle class is emblematic of system failure, with an aggravation of the condition signaling that the worst is yet to come. Recognizing that a vibrant middle class is indispensable for economic prosperity puts a dent in the credibility of those waxing lyrical about the current economic recovery. In elementary macroeconomic terms, when the benefits of economic growth get confined to the so-called "1 percent," it means that increases in national income bypass the high-spending middle class. Consequently, consumers with a high propensity to spend additional income are denied the purchasing power for increasing business sales. Because consumer spending accounts for some two-thirds of overall demand in rich countries, and is therefore the *sine qua non* for powering economic growth, increased income inequality of the sort that exists can make a large contribution to fading recovery hopes. Apart from the fact that impecunious people buy less from businesses, such deprivation is also associated with poor health and limited skills, both of which weaken labor productivity. Also, when inequality ferments social discontent and unrest, the investment climate is spoiled, as in Greece in particular and the rest of Europe in general. Inequality that weakens the middle class backbone of the economy denies the economy the effervescence associated with good times. For these and other reasons inequality is bad for business – and economic growth. This is besides the fact that joblessness due to the absence of opportunity can constitute a waste of human capital resources. As many know, lengthy jobless periods depreciate human capital and make employment prospects more distant.

In addition, the inequality of *markets* is an impediment to recovery. As stated earlier, there is a growing market schism of the David-versus-Goliath type. Since the crisis, banks everywhere in the West have had a noticeable inclination to be friendlier in their lending to larger firms in pseudo-markets ("Goliaths," many with a multinational dimension) than to the "Davids" exposed to the howling winds of competition in open markets. Smaller companies, strapped for cash, rarely have a chance when flush pseudo-market plutocrats come knocking – a major explanation for acquisitions, as previously explained. This has the effect of benefiting the destiny of pseudo-market firms at the expense of firms operating in more open and competitive conditions. Consequently, borrowing handicaps can limit the potential contribution of smaller companies to recovery and jobs creation – something that probably goes a significant way toward explaining a recovery that exhibits anemia and exclusiveness.

The looming presence of plutocratic pseudo-market firms can be expected to cast a discouraging shadow on firms in open competitive sectors. This comes from the market leadership position and inside track status of the former and the consequent vulnerability of firms in open competitive sectors to buckling. The viability of firms in open competitive conditions depends on operational and marketing acumen, whereas the prowess of pseudo-market firms comes from the strengths of monopolization, globalization, politicization and corruption – sources of natural and strategic competitive advantage. Such forces can automatically spook the investment climate in open competitive sectors. As previously reported, such a superior position for pseudo-market firms must mean, and does mean, forgone investment in open sectors (Samuel and Ratnatunge 1993). The firms badly affected are mostly the relatively smaller ones and potential new entrants that are the major sources of entrepreneurial dynamism and employment in the economy. For example, Germany, which has the strongest small-to-medium sized company sector in the West, has also by far the lowest youth unemployment rate in the West.

*Perception Hindrance*

Acknowledgement of a problem is the first step to dealing with it; unless there is insight by policymakers of the real causes for a stymied recovery, hopes for recovery would be justifiably forlorn. Deregulators are divided in the assessment of their handiwork. Those wanting re-regulation have obviously done some soul searching that has ended their romance with indiscriminate deregulation. For deceived and disappointed deregulators who are true believers in truly competitive markets, their free market dreams can be presumed to have gone up in smoke with the emergence of plutocratic pseudo-markets. They would surely know that their ill-considered decisions caused the public to be put upon by anti-competitive, oligopolistic, and plutocratic firms that have been handed the advantage, mainly by their thoughtless "Acts" of deregulation. Some deregulators would probably feel a sense of betrayal by bankers and their supporters, who fooled them into catching a Tartar. Plutocratic pseudo-markets are every deregulator's skeleton in the closet, and is a huge item of cost sitting on the negative side of the ledger that must be counted when the net benefits of deregulation are assessed. To the extent that deregulation has backfired and hurt its perpetrators, deregulation would have for repentant deregulators an element of poetic justice that gives them something to worry about besides death.

In instances where catharsis has caused the scales to fall from the hitherto starry eyes of deregulators, it bodes well for the massive challenges for economic recovery that lie ahead. Penitent lamentations on past errors by repentant deregulators, and return by way of the "weeping cross," would be necessary for undertaking the fundamental reforms that are needed to get out of the current mess attributable to ill-considered financial deregulation. The necessary reforms demand transformed and vision-driven leaders who are prepared to reach for stars (see chapter 12) in search of an improbable dream (see chapter 13). Being a sheepish Monday morning quarterback, wise after the event, would on balance seem better than not letting the collapse have the enlightening effect that it should, as seems to be the case with some diehard unrepentant elements (the incorrigible pseudo-market deniers).

Such unrepentant policymakers are not known to be a particularly open-minded bunch; unsurprisingly, they fail to see the sham of a Potemkin village in plutocratic pseudo-markets. Importantly, they are in denial about lumbering plutocratic pseudo-market firms being a drag on recovery. Such hidebound deregulators, who made a pig's ear of deregulatory policy, and whose freer market dreams have consequently come to nothing, are unable to face hard facts. Blinded in one eye by their faith in the mythical merits of pseudo-markets and in the other by their conviction that they are the custodians of the beloved free market, they are unable to see that their grand dream of free-market utopia is a pseudo-market nightmare. Such diehard deregulators salve their conscience by being dismissive of the import of deregulation in the emergence of plutocratic pseudo-markets and continue to cheer them on, convinced that they are the real sort (i.e., free and competitive markets)–and that despite glaringly obvious attributes to the contrary. Exalted banks continue to claim the affection of such policymakers, who persist in making light of their unholy traits, namely, monopolization, licentiousness, global manipulation, and plutocratic influence. Seeing does not mean believing, the poignant lesson of the crisis being lost on them.

Why spoil the fantasy with the facts? Clearly these pseudo-market deniers are a long way from accepting that deregulation has brought nothing but trouble. It appears that such policymakers, who had a manic belief in financial deregulation then, cannot help themselves when it comes to believing in pseudo-markets now, even though the free market has gone kaput. They seek to rewrite history by regarding the crisis as happening, not because of deregulation, but in spite of it. For some, the long arm of coincidence, having spun a revolving wheel of fortune, brought bad luck in the form of the current economic crisis. These "bad-luck" believers include elements that, despite the obvious damage staring them in the face, are drawn like a moth to the flame of further unselective extirpation of regulation. They believe they can reach the promised land of capitalist utopia by handing the keys back to the very people who wrecked the train. For others, the crisis is due to government intervention through the mortgage agencies in the United States. They are oblivious to finer points like the nature of intervention, the notion of institutional frameworks, and have little eye for the big picture that encompasses impaired market structures, globalization, and market dysfunction. Hope must spring eternal for those finding comfort in denial.

Are politicians studiously ignoring plutocratic pseudo-markets in terms of "know little and care less"– that is, practicing ostrichism? Astonishingly, governments do not seem to have woken up to the danger from plutocratic pseudo-market firms edging out competitive markets firms. The obliviousness exists despite the several reasons why politicians should be rattled by the dire potential of the phenomenon – a startling complacency despite the cloven hoof of plutocracy being visible to those bothering to look.

It is a puzzling oddity that where politicians really deserve blame (about their apparent ease with the plutocratic pseudo-market condition), there is deafening silence from key analysts on this cardinal sin of omission. Politicians subscribing to the romanticism of free markets cannot be blamed for not looking out for something they are blissfully unaware of, especially when it is out of the ordinary. Some may wonder, though, whether politicians are soft-pedaling the problem by simply going with the flow, because of the awesome challenge that plutocratic pseudo-markets pose. There may be a strong incentive to shirk responsibility when the problem is daunting; disillusion can beget inaction when the intimidating state of affairs causes the thorny problem to be expediently relegated to the back burner. This means that even when politicians see and notice, they loathe being involved, being defeated by the complexity of the task.

Politicians are in the happy position of being able to serve two masters under competitive open market conditions, but not under plutocratic pseudo-market conditions. Specifically, under competitive open market conditions politicians are able to serve both the "business master" and the "public master" at the same time. This is enabled by a coincidence of interests: when politicians take up the cause of businesses operating in competitive open market conditions, they automatically advance the overall public interest. This is explained by the fact that when firms compete within community-designed institutional frameworks that are fixed and given, greater business profitability can be associated with greater social prosperity (an automatic harmony explained in chapter 5).

This is not usually so in plutocratic pseudo-market conditions, where greater business profitability has not translated into greater community prosperity, as explained earlier. In fact, in a broader sense, greater business profitability in pseudo-market conditions can be associated with an automatic *loss* of social wellbeing due to companies thriving on societal freebies (i.e., economic rent). This refers to profits being acquired (rather than being earned) through means such as monopolistic exploitation, international manipulation, political influence, and corrupt business practices (of the sort reported in chapter 4). All these probably imply an arrogation that explains why the household incomes and wages of the majority are largely excluded from the benefits of economic growth. In practical terms, judging by what is taking place on the ground, there is distinct disconnect between the profitability of firms and the prosperity of the majority, with firms able to thrive within real economies that wilt.

The bifurcation poses a dilemma for politicians and explains why some, if not most, politicians can be expected to be slow on the uptake when it comes to facing down plutocrats in pseudo-markets. Expecting anybody compromised by their dependence on big business for campaign contributions to look sharp in relation to plutocratic pseudo-market shenanigans, could be expecting too much. Politicians are in a cleft stick in pseudo-market conditions, having to serve two masters with conflicting interests, namely, the "business interest" and the "public interest." And because of the way in which the system works, trying to get rid of plutocratic pseudo-markets will likely require politicians to bite the beefy hand that feeds them. Therefore, even though the spirit may be willing (politicians have good intentions), the flesh could be weak (because of the temptation of benefits from business).

For this reason, there is strong incentive for affected politicians to regard gccsc as swans and glorify plutocratic pseudo-markets as open competitive markets – a convenient catechism for getting them off the hook. Being unfazed by plutocratic pseudo-markets gives them the rationale to sit on their hands and let things ride in relation to such markets. The long and the short of it is that it makes sense for politicians dependent on pseudo-market funding to fight shy of acknowledging a problem, since taking on pseudo-market tycoons is not likely to result in a pleasant experience. Such a mindset naturally leads to the "policy hindrance," examined next.

*Policy Hindrance*

The relationship between conventional economic policies and the plutocratic pseudo-market condition is fraught with difficulties. A tension simmers when the plutocratic pseudo-market condition undermines the capability of conventional policies to deliver recovery. The tension assumes menacing proportions when conventional policies actually nourish the recovery-inhibiting traits of the plutocratic pseudo-market condition. Hence, what leaves the pseudo-market condition in the pink is unwholesome for recovery.

There is good reason to think that the plutocratic pseudo-market condition foils the capacity of conventional policy measures to live up to expectations. If the conventional polices of austerity, public stimulus spending and others of the monetary type have flunked their targets for delivering a recovery that is adequate, it is unlikely to be for want of trying. Despite feisty attempts over several years, conventional policies have, instead of giving the world a recovery that is robust and inclusive, thrown up outcomes that are unexpected, deviant, and even perverse. Several oddities, that confound even seasoned experts, are embarrassingly visible for all to see. Take the deluge of money printing: it has defied economic logic by failing to generate inflationary pressures, and perplexes many by being associated with falling inflation rates. These rates are disquietingly low at below one percent in America and Britain, although the money pumped into their economies is in the region of a quarter of their GDPs. The stock market breaks a score of record highs, but the proclaimed recovery has signally failed to make most householders' hearts glow with hope, as gathered from Joseph Stiglitz's *The Price of Inequality* (2013). Below-zero nominal interest rates that offer investors dirt cheap money, does not attract a rash of borrowing and spending as might be expected, but is associated with the opposite, namely investor hoarding. Those who pinned their reputation on the winning policy of belt-tightening austerity must feel let down, not only because of its failure to galvanize private sector investment (the expected upliftment in investor confidence due to austerity has failed to materialize), but also because of the insult it added to injury by giving off a whiff of deflation in Europe. Then there is the bad memory of government stimulus spending that failed to benefit the majority in the real economy or firms in open competitive sectors, but is reported instead to have delivered record income and wealth rises to pseudo-market firms and the so-called "one percent" upper crust stratum (Stiglitz 2013).

To the extent that conventional policies do work, the plutocratic pseudo-market condition seems to automatically take the edge off them, to render them mere palliatives. If so, such policies could have the effect of swapping immediate problems for later chronic ones. That could prove detrimental to a recovery that is sustainable if the long-term deferred costs of the policies adopted end up outweighing their short-term soothing benefits. It is laughable that measures undertaken to enable recovery can have the effect of actually preventing it, however unintentional that may be. Plutocratic pseudo-markets are able to imitate a constellation of conventional symptoms associated with lethargic business behavior in functional markets (i.e. in markets that are effectively competitive and open); mimicking the trappings of such markets serves to sanctify their position with policymakers. Because of the daydream that what works in open competitive market conditions will also work in plutocratic pseudo-market conditions, the sluggish symptoms attract standard policy measures like austerity, public stimulus spending, and money printing. It will be explained in chapter 11 why these measures are mostly sideshows to the real action needed for genuine recovery.

Graver still, these unimaginative measures can hurt more than they help when pseudo-market conditions are present. This happens when conventional policies for economic recovery are anomalous – that is, when what seems a solution is in effect a bungle. This would happen when such polices do the opposite of what is intended and inhibit recovery by nurturing plutocratic pseudo-market conditions. The factors disconnecting company profitability and social prosperity (which enable companies to prosper within countries that flounder) have been explained. Policy measures meant to enrich pseudo-market firms in the hope that one can bribe them into delivering recovery peddle an illusion, and can make policymakers victims of their own success. Monetary policy that makes cheap and easy money available empowers banks to engage in the several practices just mentioned that are pervasively and significantly ill-disposed to recovery. Public spending enables pseudo-market firms to use their plutocratic strong-arm tactics to arrogate to themselves a disproportionate share of the benefits, leaving the majority of householders and firms in open markets in the lurch. Cheap and easy money, increased government spending, company tax concessions, production subsidies and the like, would have self-defeating (i.e., anti-recovery) effects to the extent that they beef up pseudo-market firms, particularly banks, through increased monopolization, globalization, politicization, and corruption.

Potentially facilitating and boosting pseudo-market momentum are the policy moves toward free trade pacts. Of particular significance is the Trans-Pacific Partnership (TPP), which includes America, Japan, Australia and twelve other countries that together account for some 40 percent of global GDP. These arrangements could be presented as a *fait accompli* to domestic open competitive sectors and foster a corporate gigantism that puts today's titans in the shade. Benefits to the majority of the American population in the real economy come into question when such trade pacts shift investment abroad and fuel the expansion of transnational pseudo-market sectors at the expense of domestic open competitive sectors. Jubilant cheers in pseudo-markets are probably heard as warning fog horns in competitive sectors. The rosiest scenario sees the domestic open competitive sectors unequally sharing in the gains from the expanded trading opportunities engendered by the trade pacts in the short term, but succumbing to the competition-suppressing expansion of plutocratic pseudo-markets in the long term, on the lines previously described (vide section 8.4).

Failure to recognize that the romantic harmony between the business and public interest is passé and outmoded in plutocratic pseudo-market conditions bodes ill for recovery. This misconception enables politicians to extol the virtues of free markets while inadvertently undertaking measures that undermine them – oblivious to an economy rent asunder and the need to harness entrepreneurial energy if recovery is to succeed. Enough has been stated to show that the warm embracing of plutocrats by politicians dazzled by the apparent star power of pseudo-market firms is likely to bring disappointment – and that the objects of their affection could come back to bite them. Pandering to pseudo-market interests by benefactor-politicians (such as with state subsidies, tax breaks, and market access), while capable of generating private sector activity for genuine recovery under competitive open market conditions, are unlikely to do so under plutocratic pseudo-market conditions. Rewarding pseudo-market firms with incentives plays into the hands of plutocrats, benefits foreigners, and makes for fretful times in domestic open competitive sectors whose firms are the engines of recovery. Empowering pseudo-market firms and invoking the blessings of plutocrats have been shown to have the spin-off effect of casting a discouraging shadow over investment by firms in open competitive sectors – thereby discouraging initiative, dynamism and growth, and even putting pressure on them to transform into pseudo-market firms via mergers to dodge having to pack it in. A doctrinaire commitment to frazzled conventional policies can, instead of galvanizing real recovery, have the opposite effect of subverting it (see chapter 11).

Central banks can be associated with an aura of fading relevance when their policies have the effect of diminishing market functionality. They dig a hole even as they try to dig themselves out of it. Central banks prevent recovery when they foster the several unwanted effects described by flooding the economy with cheap money to feed anti-recovery traits in pseudo-market firms, notably banks, and fuel pseudo-market expansion through acquisitions and mergers. Further explained in section 11.2 is why history is likely to show that central banks had a hand in future misery by their undermining of entrepreneurship in open competitive sectors and their denial of opportunity for the majority (that includes the middle class backbone of the economy).

## 9.3 The Mountain to Climb

From what has been delineated it is clear that dreaming wistfully about the capability of markets to rise to the occasion and deliver recovery is to ignore the complex and insidious barriers that forestall it. Hindrances that are cumulative and synergistic explain its protraction. Distorted incentives from broken markets give rise to pseudo-market profitability that is *not* yoked to widespread public prosperity. In fact, the plutocratic pseudo-market condition combines ingredients that tighten the noose around economies to circumscribe benefits, curb dynamism, and stifle recovery.

Genuine recovery requires from banks and other pseudo-market firms practices that tend to fall outside their preferred business model. What is good for pseudo-market firms is often bad for recovery; market dysfunction induces penchants in banks and other firms that are incidentally antagonistic to a durable economic resurgence that is sturdy and overarching. Ironically, consolidation due to acquisitions and mergers further divides an already polarized economy to impede recovery. The lopsided growth that emanates from dysfunctional market conditions gives rise to a type of inequality in individuals and firms that is not of the virtuous sort, because it excludes the majority in the real economy from opportunity and weakens the middle class backbone. This means that inequality is unhelpful when markets are dysfunctional. This is a pragmatic argument that prudently skirts value-loaded ideological notions of class warfare and is straightforward in concept: inequality is favorable to recovery when markets can operate properly. Consequently, because of plutocratic pseudo-market conditions, inequality is greater than it should be and recovery is weaker than it could be.

At the centre of the problem are banks, but banks are not the real problem. Although bankers are the public's favorite bogeyman, they cannot be validly blamed for remaining true to the life-giving cause of profit maximization. Because banks are doing nicely in terms of profits, they must be doing something right, and central to this would be making rational choices in relation to market incentives; what appear to be bad habits are really proper responses to market signals. If banks are not doing the right thing for recovery, logic suggests that it is the dysfunctional market and not the banks that should be in the public's crosshairs. It is a broken market system that creates incentives for banks to unintentionally throw wrenches in the recovery works, like favoring short-termism, the bigger companies, the more established companies, acquisitions and mergers, corporate gigantism, and the financial sector. This includes the facilitation through funding of the natural and rational motivation on the part of big incumbent firms to stifle or subsume smaller and newer firms in "big-fish, little-fish" terms. As a result, a genuinely sustainable recovery has come to depend on practices that the big banks and other pseudo-market firms are disinclined to favor because of the dysfunctional circumstances in which they are required to operate. All of the foregoing factors would explain some of the lack of vibrancy in the recovery, but the blame for the lost oomph in the economy must ultimately fall, not on firms or central banks, but on the flawed market system that engenders anti-recovery incentives.

Enough has been said to show that the plutocratic pseudo-market condition is a bad thing for recovery: it brings about a parting of the ways between business performance and economic performance – specifically, between company profitability and durable recovery. The business strategies in vogue, by fostering a pseudo-market condition and causing competitive dynamism to hemorrhage, have the effect of pervasively numbing the authentic recovery process, weakening the investment climate in competitive sectors, and enfeebling living standards. The pillars on which future social prosperity must rest continue to crumble because a winner-takes-all pseudo market system gains ground, and that is because policymakers' awareness of the problem is in short supply.

Plutocratic pseudo-markets are a protected species, but not just because they are nourished by conventional monetary and fiscal policies or accorded star status by kowtowing politicians. Their idiosyncrasies of monopolization, globalization, politicization, and corruption equip them well to protect themselves. For this reason, trusting in pseudo-markets firms to provide the heavy lifting required for real recovery should be more a hope than an expectation. By damaging the beating heart that is the competitive open market, ill-considered deregulation has through insidious knock-on effects seriously hurt the vital organ needed for sustainable economic health. As for prosperity for the groaning majority, that will have to wait.

The key to genuine recovery requires getting one's head around the problem posed by the plutocratic pseudo-market condition, the recovery-inhibiting fallout from which knows no end within the existing scheme of things. Shown in chapter 11 is that the forward momentum of pseudo-markets outstrips the ability of conventional policies to effectively respond. Although market reform is a major consideration in any strategy for real recovery it is, like gun control or tax reform in the United States, a hot potato for politicians daunted by the tall order. By standing back politicians are distanced from being able to halt the slide to decay caused by pseudo-markets spinning out of control and placing economies on the slippery slope to degeneration. Although it may be the last thing on their minds, unless politicians are jolted into sitting up and taking serious notice of the increasing degradation of market foundations, a growing number of entrepreneurs in competitive open sectors will find the ground disappearing beneath their feet. In the absence of a credible deterrent, it would be only a matter of time before a shift in the center of gravity away from competitive sectors gives rise to the day of reckoning that causes the atrophied economies in the West to crumble about their ears. As to when this will happen is in the lap of the gods – similar to the difficulty of knowing when someone who smokes will have a heart attack. The reasons for this will become better known when more is said in chapters 12 and 13 on the vital matter of coming to terms with the monstrous miscreation that is the plutocratic pseudo-market condition, if a durable recovery is to have a better chance of happening than a summer snowfall.

**

# Chapter 10

# THE LONG HAUL: ON BORROWED TIME

## 10.1 The West or Bust

The 2008-09 collapse is an unsettling memory. Its scale and lingering fallout make it hard to forget, especially if you are among the forgotten majority. Because the current piece of theatre fails to follow a familiar script, there is not much prospect of an end to unhappy anniversaries of the collapse. The crisis lurches on to condemn a large component of the Western workforce to stay at home to await the ending of interminable soap operas like "The Young and the Restless." The downturn has already lasted for a month of Sundays, taking over three times longer than the average period for past recessions and counting, making good times a distant memory. There are no bright lights to be seen on the economic horizon, giving rise to the fearful prospect that a durable revival to previous prosperity could take until the cows come home. The lights have dimmed in the West, with the ever-present risk of a blackout; proper recovery demands a level of investment in places that few are willing to risk. When the prolonged duration of the downturn is combined with its expansiveness, the large scale of the downturn is staggering and unprecedented except for the Great Depression, which was uniquely devastating.

The West holds the key to world recovery. Despite its woes, America is still a colossus on the world economic stage, its top dog status causing its national fate to make an international difference. Although no longer quite accurate because of the emergence of the Asian powerhouse, the 1950s' adage on knock-on effects (that when America catches a cold, Europe gets the 'flu, and the rest of the world goes down with pneumonia) nevertheless has an element of validity. (It can be argued that it is America that has the 'flu and Europe the pneumonia.)

The protraction stems from the fact that the problem needs to end where it started. Because the mighty American economy is the major source of the current economic problem, it will also have to be the major source of the solution, together with Europe's economies, many of which were sucked in by contagion. In no other postwar recession were American and European governments faced with having to lift such deadweight of collapsed economies. The weary world has every interest in seeing a quick American-cum-European recovery because these Western economies are the only engines capable of developing enough steam to pull the world economy out of the ditch it finds itself in.

Is there any hope of a Chinese savior with a quick fix in the event of further collapse? The question arises whether the apparently invincible China, with its growing geopolitical punch, can be the savior of the America-cum-European conglomerate (presumably, a less-than welcome one). After all, the Chinese economy is a proven shock absorber that is humming along despite a worldwide downturn, accounting for nearly half of world economic growth (GDP). What if the current economic problem drags on until China, the factory of the world, overtakes America to become the largest economy on earth, while at the same time undertaking overdue market reforms (such as freely floating the presently pegged yuan, reducing protectionism, and getting rid of government subsidies to flabby industry)? The Chinese economy has already overtaken the American economy in the areas of manufacturing output, energy use, gas sales, and shipbuilding, and is close to leading the world in international trade. The size of the Chinese economy is expected to overtake the American economy well within a decade, according to the International Monetary Fund (Gardner 2011). So can China spearhead a world recovery?

The parodic vision of a handsome Chinese knight in shining armor riding in on a white dragon to save Snow White West is unrealistic. Why would China want to suddenly become altruistic and dip into its bloated national piggybank to prop up resentful adversaries? It is not likely that China would be able to play the role of savior even if was willing to do so. Although the world's "China luck" is by no means over, what is most likely to happen is that the world's second-largest economy will not be able to ride to the rescue of the West because it will have its hands full coping with its own serious problems.

China's stunning advances conceal deep problems. The boats to China are slowing as foreign companies become less eager; the Chinese bowl of cherries has become less desirable than before. China is losing its allure as a profitable business destination because business conditions are becoming less congenial relative to alternatives elsewhere. Conflicts with joint-venture partners mount and government requirements (remittance control, enforced partnerships, technology transfer, among others) become onerous when profitability diminishes. The golden age for multinationals is losing its luster, even as Chinese charm offensives contain less of the charm and more of the offensive; more expatriates than before are getting cold feet because welcome mats are becoming scantier.

Having spent its pent-up energy, the Chinese dragon is tiring with growth down to a crawl by historical standards; the heady double-digit tempo of yesteryear is gone, perhaps for good. Growth decelerated to around 7.4 percent in 2014 (the slowest growth in twenty-four years), and will slouch even more says the IMF. The squeeze from market loss and cost blowouts means that Chinese factories are no longer humming. Chinese export demand is faltering as the worldwide downturn saps demand in China's top export destinations and shrinks its export volume. At the same time, China's hold on low cost manufacturing is loosening, with the Chinese export sector experiencing steeply rising wages and rents for factory floor space. China's labor force is aging, shrinking, and getting more expensive. In addition, an appreciating Chinese currency puts a dampener on its international competitiveness. As exports slide and costs mount, Chinese export sector firms must feel a punishing profitability pinch.

Worries about China loom large because China is a house of cards built on a foundation of cronyism and indebtedness. The imbalances that have built up to massive proportions could cause the economy to come crashing down at any time. All the pre-conditions for a messy banking crisis of incalculable proportions are in place, and include suspect horrors lurking in the dark corner of Chinese shadow banking. From what is apparent, the Chinese have sown dragon's teeth in the form of too many bad loans. Many of the loans have caused over-investment in real estate, the glut precipitating a rapid cooling of housing and office-space markets. A hidden property bubble is the unsurprising upshot of a frenetic pace of building (just as it was in Spain, where it gave rise to ghost towns). Also, there has been excessive lending by state-owned banks to cronies in state-owned enterprises and local governments, where defaults loom. Government subsidy-induced industrial overcapacity is increasing even as export markets are shrinking. The anecdotal evidence is more compelling than official Chinese statistics in suggesting that China is struggling to contain bad loans and investment bubbles. Credit growth in the Middle Kingdom is suspected to have swelled to some 250 percent of GDP – a macro-risk from financial fragility that is suggestive of a collapse waiting to happen. This view is backed by the International

Monetary Fund (IMF). Noting the roughly one-third drop in previously burgeoning Chinese growth rates, the IMF reports the possibility of a hard landing because of a fissure in China's armor from exceptional credit growth (IMF 2012).

Nevertheless, despite its sharply decelerated economy, China is not likely to have a Japan moment (explained in section 10.5). It must be remembered that Chinese banks are effectively an extension of the fiscally robust Chinese Treasury and, hence, comfortably centrally cosseted. This makes blanket guarantees a near certainty. Consequently, a banking collapse could be expected to trigger an automatic bailout from China's healthy stockpile of reserves. The ample headroom makes it uncertain how hard a landing can be expected for the Chinese economy from a Chinese banking collapse. On balance it seems that the odds of a Chinese banking collapse are low and one with global ramifications negligible.

Be that as it may, the overall situation is worse than what the Chinese government is letting on, bad news encouraging obfuscation of the truth. On the face of it, China's investment rate is unlikely to be sustainable, even though China has a vise-like grip on its financial sector and ample capital reserves to protect its investment mojo. Further economic collapse in America and Europe would drag the Chinese economy down and, by transforming a slowdown into a slump, limit China's ability to step into the breach for any significant rescue role (even if it was willing). All things considered, there is not much chance of a Chinese savior, a deliverer on the lines of a *deus ex machina* who saves the day.

Facing reality reveals that the only engines capable of powering resurgence in the world economy are the American and European economies acting in concert; these economies will continue to be the world's chief theatre of events into the foreseeable future. Their poor shape does not detract from their brawn and continuing vital status as the economic powerhouse of the world. America has the world's largest national economy, with a GDP of $17 trillion, about the same as that of the EU countries put together. The combined output of America and Europe accounts for about half of all economic activity around the world. Only a sustained take-off in the economy of the still-mighty America, backed by the driving force of a properly recovered Europe, would provide enough impulsion for the world economy to be off and running.

## 10.2 Weakness in Unity

*America's Condition*

For most of those bothering to take a close enough look at vital signs, the American economy would seem like death warmed up. The economy lumbers along ambivalently and at an underwhelming pace despite plucky monetary measures to get things going. Stimulated upticks in the financial economy are accompanied by a level of hyperbole that developments in most of the real economy have been unable to match. Superficially, the US economy is showing signs of a rebound with a GDP growth rate of around 2 to 3 percent, fuelled by cheap oil and gas as well as help from the fracking bonanza. Beneath the artificial exterior is a less appealing scenario of underlying atrophy. The current economic performance, even if accepted at face value, is more slothful than stellar. It is in any case patchy, with vast swaths of the economy left behind. National averages do not paint an accurate picture; they obscure a reality featuring extensive pockets of regional disparity, lopsidedness between financial and non-financial sectors, market malfunction, and fundamental macroeconomic imbalances.

The sort of recovery that is apparently happening masks underlying strains in the real economy of the United States. Despite induced perkiness in the house and stock markets and some apparent improvement in employment, the US Census Bureau reports some fifty million people were in poverty and on food stamps in 2014. The number on food stamps increased 50 percent in the six-year period to that time (although much of the increase is probably attributable to demographic changes and food stamps being easier to get). In any event, middle-income jobs are being replaced with low wage jobs. This is associated with a loss of purchasing power in the economy, cutbacks in consumer spending and, most troubling, the weakening of the middle class backbone of the economy.

Asset prices could be bubbling up because institutional and structural flaws that gave rise to the recession in the first place remain uncorrected – something that should become clearer from the analysis that follows. Much of the apparent buoyancy, artificially induced through unsustainable monetary policies, provide a reassuring veneer for public appeasement. Because the entire world economy is held up by the fragile mainstay of human psychology, it is vulnerable to unbalanced behavior. This makes belief in what comes next to matter greatly and gives rise to an ongoing need for good-news stories, however hollow. But singing the praises of a recovery that the majority does not feel must eventually lose credibility. In fact, the hollow ring has apparently caused most normal people to tune out. This would explain much of the tightfistedness being exhibited by investors and consumers.

For the foregoing reasons, there is some basis for believing that, despite the familiar upbeat refrain of hope in headlines, the apparent rebound smacks of fakery. A disposition exists for creating a buzz about trivia by using hyperbole to inflate grains of truth – perhaps in the hope of making overblown claims self-fulfilling prophesies. If all the hype that growth was afoot translated into genuine recovery, the events of 2007-08 would have reversed by now and the economy booming with pre-crisis Eldorado fervor. Analysts responsible for headlines, especially the more excitable types who stick it on in their role as professional spin doctors, could have a vested interest in using pretty talk to trumpet a "dead cat bounce" as real buoyancy, not allowing the negatives in the fundamentals to tone down the optimism.

Self-service cognitive bias could be the unwitting stock-in-trade of relevant news media; for the print media, today's headlines are tomorrow's waste-paper. Given that the economy is upheld by the brittle mainstay of psychology, talking up markets serves the purpose of infusing oomph into the economy through a contrived spike in investor expectations. As previously reported, drawing the long-bow to put a spin on deceptively hopeful signs, or being economical with the truth, is not alien to Wall Street analysts, as alleged by former Wall Street insider Mike Mayo (Mayo 2011) and later by former senior analyst at Moody's, William Harrington (*Market Watch* 2012). Lest we forget: it was the same media that served as blunt propaganda instruments for portraying the pre-crisis financial bubble as the real thing. It was analysts' skills at planting fairy tales in the media that caused the 2007-08 implosion to be a bolt from the blue, catching almost everyone off-guard. Cruising down the river does not mean there is no waterfall around the corner; a collapse that is a distant memory can suddenly become frighteningly present.

There is a good chance that the trumpeted recovery is a false dawn because it lacks robustness and inclusiveness. A sustainable sprint to previous opportunity is in the wild blue yonder for the excluded majority. Authentic recuperative upswings in business cycles take place at a much faster rate, and are more widely felt, than what are being experienced in the United States; the momentum of a durable recovery is simply not there, and what little there is could easily be lost through adverse external developments or faulty domestic policy. It is a recovery that is not what anyone has ever known a recessionary recovery to be. What it justifies is closer to sobriety than jubilant tap-dancing; the exclusive, brittle, and lopsided American rebound does not deserve extravagant faith.

Solace is discouraged for other reasons as well. The ability of the United States to pull itself up by its own bootstraps is largely a fantasy. Despite its economic dominance, and domestic demand accounting for some 75 percent of growth, mighty America is hardly the master of its own destiny. Globalization in an intertwined world means that no one country, not even the largest economy on earth, can recover by itself, something which most people find hard to come to terms with. Globalization has diminished the ability of America to manage its economy by its own efforts for several reasons, the likes of which have never before been known. For one thing, the rise of stateless, multinational, corporate titans has caused America's control over its own economy to wane and its ability to ward off foreign dangers to be undermined. Corporations that are global behemoths are not renowned for feelings of gratitude and cannot be relied upon to patri-otically serve the interests of the country that created them. In any case, their multinational sprawl tends to make them less controllable for home governments. Corporate titans have the reputation of being a nuisance to their creators, and this can take the form of unfriendly, and even illegal, behaviors. Money laundering would hardly qualify as an act of patriotism, and neither would other similar practices, such as the sale of toxic bonds in the past and tax avoidance in the present. As explained in the previous chapter, transnational mega-firms, par-ticularly banks, are significantly outside the jurisdictions of national governments and can influence the fate of nations in a "tail wags dog" manner. A related point is the unprecedented disconnect between company profitability and national prosperity, with companies able to thrive in the West by exporting recovery to the East.

Let us not forget the European wild card: the ever-present dan-ger that further major economic collapse in a shaky Europe and its attendant effects would put the skids under the incipient American recovery. Although the American economy is primarily driven by domestic demand (foreign trade accounts for about only 25 percent of GDP), precariousness stems from an economic relationship between America and Europe that is both large and close. It is by far the largest bilateral relationship on earth, with the interdependency implying an integrated transatlantic relationship for a mutually hobbling potential. It seems farfetched to think that America can keep growing while Europe is shrinking, especially when a European nosedive can trigger a hard landing in China, transform the Japanese recession into depression, and stymie growth in the rest of the world. Together America and Europe account for a hard-to-miss 30 to 40 percent of global trade in goods and services. So what affects them jointly is not likely to go unnoticed in other countries around the world. In fact, it can be expected to give rise to kickbacks of an unwelcome nature. Other countries trading with Europe, including emergent China, Brazil, and India, will find their export industries battered by shrunken European markets – crimping their growth and forcing them to cut back on trade and investment with America. It is therefore unlikely that a European collapse which spreads international gloom will leave the investment climate in America unaffected. There has to be a limit to the divergence of American and European fortunes; it is unlikely that America can be an island of prosperity in a sea of torpidity.

Ring fences cannot be high enough to prevent contagion; America cannot hope to escape unscathed from a very possible European collapse and its knock-on effects. Although the obnoxious fallout from such a eurozone bust would settle most heavily in its own backyard, enough of it would waft across the Atlantic to reverse the American recovery – and then together sweep through to bruise most other economies worldwide. It stands to reason that an American recovery worthy of the name would require Europe to more than level out and pull its weight. History has a lesson: following Europe's devastation in the Second World War, America gave massive aid to help European recovery under the Marshall Plan of 1948 (with ample kickback to itself). It seems reasonable to think that Europe's plight puts America on notice that any recovery it can have will be limited without Europe playing its commensurate part in the same recovery boat.

Mutual damage for the American and European economies can stem from several factors. Firstly, America is dependent on Europe for about a fifth of its exports and Europe exports a fifth more in goods and services to America than vice versa. The European export dependence on the US market is expected to increase due to the recently introduced policy of money printing by the ECB. Secondly, direct capital investment in each other's economies is several times greater than anywhere outside their economies. Thirdly, the gravest worry is the threat from the exposure of American banks to the financial crisis in Europe. The third point is a likely Achilles' heel of the trans-atlantic relationship – a lurking threat of uncertain dimension. The America-caused European crisis could come back to bite American banks that made bad European bets in the reckless pre-crisis period. It is true that American banks are rebounding, having got rid of the excess debt and righted many of the imbalances (their risk-weighted capital ratio is far above the new global norms). But the full extent of the exposure of American banks to Europe's financial mess is not known, as evidenced by the Securities and Exchange Commission's (SEC's) unheeded request to American banks to disclose the full extent of their exposure to Europe. What is known is that billions of dollars in "credit default swaps" have been written on sovereign debt by American banks. ("Credit default swaps" refer to an arrangement in which the seller agrees to compensate the buyer if a third party defaults on a loan.) This means that American banks have guaranteed that those who bought insurance will be paid if Greece or other countries default. *The Wall Street Journal* cited a US Congressional Paper to report that the direct exposure of American banks to Europe could be $640 billion (Eavis 2012), but this is likely to be only the tip of the iceberg; indirect and overall risks are most likely to be very much greater. America can expect an unfriendly migrant from across the pond if the very possible European financial cave-in takes place, the collapse weighing heavily on US banks in particular and on the American economy in general.

Because the destinies of America and Europe are inextricably intertwined, America must accept the grim reality that: what is there is over here. The cynical would regard this as tit-for-tat payback for all the toxic bonds exported from America that so damaged Europe's financial system. It must be recognized that Europe already had self-inflicted wounds from excessive credit creation and euro free-riding by economically scrawny eurozone members. For them the euro was something between an opiate and a magic carpet, because its strength addicted them into borrowing well beyond their means for a trip to dreamland. Much of Europe's continuing plight is because of its non-sensical (mis)creation of a common currency, the euro, without fiscal coordination within the eurozone. The euro saga has given rise to a two-speed Europe that pitches northern creditors (the responsible sort) against southern debtors (the profligate sort). Divergent economic performances makes nonsense of the notion of a single currency, as illustrated by the following poignant example: creditor-Germans have to keep working until age sixty-seven, so that debtor-Greeks can retire at fifty-nine. This example caricatures the absurdity of imposing an imaginary currency on the world economy.

## Europe's Condition

Europe is in a sorry state; it is a grandma on feeding tubes. The loss of economic puff in the old world is indicative of a Europe that is on a sick bed and, like America, suffering the after-effects of unhealthy living: the painful malady from over-indulgence in toxic bonds, resulting in the eurozone debt exceeding a staggering $11 trillion. Europe has over 26 million unemployed, real wages are lower than seven years ago, and industrial production is falling. In 2014, output in the eurozone was still 3 percent lower than its 2008 pre-crisis peak. Darkening the picture is an ominous mix of debt and deflation that appears to dog the wobbling eurozone; with prices for food and industrial materials heading south, there is a deflationary chill in the air. The price surface has sunk in eight European countries and by 0.7 percent in the eurozone. That markets consider the deflation threat to be real is shown in investors' willingness to invest in bonds at negative yields. (It also means that savers have somewhere to park wads of banknotes too bulky to fit under the mattress.) If deflation is allowed to take hold, the grim scenario will feature withheld consumption, wiped out jobs, an increased debt burden, discouraged investment, and throttled growth. Since the status quo threatens the future, money printing has become the straw to grasp (see later).

Europe was not an innocent victim of American excesses as it also engaged in rash borrowing from American banks to buy dodgy American securities. Underpinning much was indiscipline in dealing with the euro opiate and indulgence in welfare lunches by high-living members, the latter mistakenly thought to be free. European banks, battered by losses from financing billions of euro's worth of dud assets, have yet to properly recover from their wounds. Any growth at all in the eurozone would be welcomed as blue skies, considering that prices and growth signs for the majority are heading south, while the youth unemployment rate is heading north (with help from job-killing taxes).

The poverty of debt has forced many in the once-great Britain to move down market and live in Queer Street, with artificial and ephemeral growth being causes for cheer. Although the British economy is showing surprising growth (there is joyousness from low expectations being exceeded), Keynesians are likely to be withholding grudging admiration. This is because it is not known how much of the growth is bubble-based because of massive money printing (amounting to over 25 percent of GDP). The British economy could be hallucinating due to a housing bubble; with the housing market rebounding with worrying speed there is a justifiable sense of déjà-vu that the British recovery is based on the same toxic mantra that caused the last crash – measures that have a troubling resemblance to those behind the previous housing bubble. Even if the signs of a turnaround are really due to austerity (they could be happening *despite* austerity, due to measures such as massive money printing), the question not being asked is: at what permanent cost to the community at large? Productivity fell even as unemployment ran at a high 7.2 percent in 2014. The manufacturing and construction sectors are undershooting at more than 10 percent below their 2008 peaks. Moreover, Britons are poorer in 2014 than they were seven years back – a condition at least partly attributable to wages tracking falling productivity. Lacking a sturdy manufacturing sector, brittle finance spearheads the British recovery. This recovery could well be a house of cards, given the banking fragility reported in chapter 8 (including the alleged machinations at HSBC, that look suspiciously like the tip of an iceberg), and the possible housing bubble. Britain is among nine debt-laden European countries that have had their credit-ratings downgraded. This means that despite Britain's prestigious status as the center of global finance, it was compelled to take a few steps down to be lumped in with financially "sick men of Europe" who epitomize Europe's embarrassing economic mismanagement: Italy, Spain, Iceland, Greece, Portugal, and Cyprus.

Because Europe's sick banks have not been put out of their misery, their continuing impairment is a source of vulnerability (*a la* the slow-motion collapse of Banco Espirito Santo some seven years after the body blow of the financial crisis). Many of Europe's banks are sitting on a pile of bad debts caused by pathetic debt-to-equity ratios. The International Monetary Fund has warned that as the European banks impose a credit crunch to fix their balance sheets, there would be shockwaves around the world. European banks have to prune back between 20-40 percent on their loans – a deleveraging of over $3 trillion. Hopes are pinned on money printing (i.e. quantitative easing or QE) to counter deflation and save the day. This is optimistic because the causal link between money printing and price increases is uncertain; the adventure of massive money printing in America and Britain, some three times greater in relation to GDP than is proposed for the eurozone, failed to generate inflationary pressures in those countries. In fact, the inflation rate in both countries, at less than one percent, is worryingly low. If the eurozone's pernicious descent into deflation is not halted by the ECB's money printing (QE) escapade, the European debt would become unsustainable, and that would likely be the coup de grâce to the eurozone.

Joyous tap-dancing at prospects for a QE-induced recovery in the eurozone would likely be an undignified over-reaction. The growth benefits for the majority in the real economy, from the bolstering of capital markets by the ECB's foray into QE, will hinge on two main factors. One is the extent to which an induced exchange rate fall will spur exports, so that businesses can reap greater sales volumes or fatter margins. This is bound to be an uphill battle for exporters due to torpidity in international markets that have their own problems with consumer and investor tightfistedness in relation to the types of European products on offer (e.g., consumer goods, cars, and chemicals). The other is the extent to which there will emerge within the eurozone enough investment opportunities (including from import substitution) that competitive businesses can get hot on. This is an unpromising prospect due to the pseudo-market damper on entrepreneurship in open market sectors within the eurozone, as well as the leakage of investment to salubrious foreign climes through multinational activity. For similar reasons, the proposed solutions of labor and budgetary reforms, generally seen as the be-all and end-all of economic reform, stir a healthy skepticism; they involve trying to get out of the morass using measures that fail to address the underpinning causes of it: the plutocratic pseudo-market condition. It follows that such reforms would be mostly self-defeating as far as economic resurgence for the majority in the economy is concerned. This is because their biggest impact would be to confer benefits on, and thereby entrench, the recovery-inhibiting pseudo-market condition at the expense of the open competitive sectors (explained in chapter 9).

The clock is ticking in Europe; the absence of enough green recovery shoots means there is no blossoming optimism with regard to Europe's economic condition. Obstinate European fragility justifies at least some anxiety. After over seven can-kicking years of crisis and austerity, and the threat of deflation looming, the scale of uncertainty is staggering, as Europe's faltering economies, some of which are falling apart at the seams, limp from one Band-Aid financial fix to another. These superficial measures are designed to soften the situation by tempering alarm among myopic investors looking for straws to grasp. But incremental responses will prove to be ineffectual, especially when time is not on Europe's side, with each response sliding Europe into an ever-deeper debt hole where, if QE fails to provide the necessary lift, the vortex of a deflation spiral waits.

Europe's chronically straitened condition is the world's soft underbelly; Europe is ground zero for the collision of economic and political forces. The frightening specters of sovereign debt default and eurozone dissolution are swords of Damocles overhanging the American economy in particular and the world economy in general.

The eurozone-dissolution ball would start rolling if one floundering country (e.g., Greece) decides that the pain of adjustment outweighs the risks of leaving – that is, that the suffering within is greater than suffering without. Such a possibility is increased by anti-establishment feelings finding political expression; what seem like sounds of fury emanating from upstart anti-EU parties (Greece's Syriza, Spain's Podemos, France's National Front, and Italy's Five Star Movement) may really be requiem hymns for the eurozone.

How protective are Europe's firewalls? The so-called firewalls are meant to be solid enough to protect weaklings on the periphery from contagion. They are meant to provide a guarantee of adequate liquidity from the European Central Bank (ECB) that is credible enough to placate markets and prevent panic in normal circumstances. But are they thick enough to withstand unusual threats? If there is a serious loss of market confidence because of sovereign defaults in the larger economies like Italy and France, or if the eurozone starts to unravel, the firewalls could turn out to be like cardboard once the bank runs start.

The bank runs will make Montezuma's revenge seem mild. If that should happen, adversity can be expected to unfold in a cumulative manner. First, financial markets and credit availability will freeze, and cross-border capital flows will dry up. These will trigger a spate of defaults and spending cuts. Trade will slow to a trickle. Money printing could be cranked up to reach wantonly extravagant proportions. Corporate bankruptcies would be commonplace. If some countries leave the eurozone, the problem will exacerbate, with possible killer blows to companies holding foreign debts in newly depreciated currencies. There would be terrifying uncertainty from a flurry of evasive action, as the vast edifice of cross-border finance gets rearranged. The eurozone itself could collapse as the public debt of the more prosperous creditor countries assumed unbearable proportions, especially in the present climate of anti-EU feeling. The current debt pit pales beside the chasm that waits. Such a European catastrophe would have wrenching reverberations across the Atlantic for the blue-on-blue of friendly fire, and then cascade to wreak havoc on the world economy.

The current fragile circumstances are likely early signs of such future misery. Lurching from one crisis to another involves marking time by buying time with borrowed or printed money, to postpone the evil day of denouement. Cheap and easy money through QE is expected to defy gravity and lift investment in markets weighed down by the albatross of dysfunctional plutocratic pseudo-market conditions. In addition, debts are expected to be repaid from a real recovery that is nowhere in sight. Current low-to-negative growth rates would be a cause for celebration when compared to the abysmal negative growth rates that would result if the nightmare of sovereign debt default by a major country or eurozone breakup triggers a nosedive of European economies into the abyss of deep and indefinite depression.

## The World's Condition

World market uncertainty is tied to Western economic volatility. The economic condition in America and Europe casts a pall over most of the world's economies. This is not your typical recessionary business cycle, as the wheels have come off as never before. There is a sense of ongoing gloom for some and doom for others, as realization grows that a full American recovery cannot happen without Europe rising from the ashes and pulling its weight. Till such time, the rest of the world's battered economies will have no choice but to keep staggering forward against buffeting headwinds from the West. The West is seen as a hindrance to global growth, international multilateralism heightening the mutuality of fates. A collapse in Europe would derail any nascent recovery in America and tank growth in the rest of the world. It is a comforting but vain hope to think that there can be a proper American recovery without a proper European recovery, and that there can be a proper world recovery without a recovery in both Europe and America that is not a financial mirage.

Although an abhorrent prospect, wholesale collapse cannot be ruled out. The formidable foursome (America, Europe, China, and Japan), are the four legs of the table that is the world economy. Not surprisingly, despite the ramshackle nature of their economies, they set the pace for the world economy by virtue of their commanding economic position. In pseudo-market circumstances it is unrealistic to expect that the table, already rickety, would not collapse if one shaky leg that is a mainstay breaks. Containment of reverberations from the cave-in of the formidable foursome would be out of the question in a globalized world where the fates of most countries are mutually hitched. Consequently, individual performances would tumble together for a spectacular and deadly ensemble.

Those in the same boat would sink together. There is not strength, but weakness, in unity, as declining international sales track a shrinking world economy. Around the world, bustling docks would be replaced by vacant quays, as exports and imports fell away. This dispiriting condition would be aggravated by the simultaneity of austerity-induced cutbacks in major Western markets. Such cutbacks would dash hopes of coveting exports as a means of making up for slack domestic demand. Although dwindling domestic consumption would make it a case of export or die for many firms, exporting one's way out of trouble would not be easy because of the lack of market opportunity caused by demand-sapping austerity in markets that matter. Most countries would be in hot water, scalded in a world linked by collateral, capital, and trade. Asian and Latin American growth would take a tumble because of subdued global demand. A synchronized global slowdown seems inescapable, as the ill winds from the

West blow no good for anybody – and leave the economies of several innocent countries in tatters. It would certainly blow away the hopes of several economies struggling to emerge from poverty. Therefore, a world helplessly exposed to the West would need to accept the dismal reality that: what is there is everywhere.

Not quite everywhere, though; not in several, mainly Asian, countries that managed to weather the financial crisis relatively unscathed. The maverick banks in these countries were protected by previously deplored regulatory walls and, happily for them, suffered very little contagion from the West's financial toxicity. Resilience will be shown by the erstwhile poor that escaped the worst of the financial maelstrom and, as a result, have protective self-insurance from stashes of foreign currency reserves. Although their heady double-digit growth days are over, and they show signs of faltering growth, these countries, sand-bagged by reserves, will provide to the world a bulwark against the slowdown in the West and a cushion in the event of the West's further collapse.

Although the glow is fading in China, it will still have the capacity to soften the worst effects of a collapse in the West by transitioning to a more domestic-demand driven economy to avert the threat of a Japan moment. The signs are that it will not be too long before China, as the world's second biggest consumer economy, takes over from America as the consumption superpower. On the production side, China is taking over from the West; an up-scaling Chinese economy will move manufacturing up the value chain and enable its firms to push upmarket and away from being low-tech sweatshops. This would create factory space for emerging new-comers like India and Indonesia, whose firms are next in line to be low-tech sweatshops. Other ascendant non-Western countries, like South Korea and Vietnam, will seek protection by turning away from deflating opportunities in the West toward ballooning opportunities among themselves. Almost 55 percent of Asian trade is now intra-regional and growing. Asian countries will proceed under their own steam to find trade and investment opportunities based on economic complementarity and a proliferating middle class. The swelling middle class in these countries (currently well over twice as large as in the West), will be increasingly well-heeled, with fists full of discretionary renminbi to spend. The Chinese market will be the high-end lynchpin, with the rest of Asia snapping up low-end opportunities. China is expected to be restored to its pre-1840 eminence as the largest national economy on earth in the not-too-distant future (Gardner 2011).

As the geopolitical calculus alters, the meek could inherit the earth. Roles will be reversed, as debtor banana republics of the past become the relatively richer creditor nations of the future. Asia is emerging as the world's piggybank, as shifting fortunes from wealth changing hands enable *nouveau-riche* countries to ratchet up their status in the world. The Philippines, despite its shocking pockets of poverty, have become a net creditor to the rest of the world, and South Korea has changed from aid recipient to donor. Indonesia illustrates the reversal of international roles; Indonesia's central bank has shown a readiness to buy $1 billion of International Monetary Fund (IMF) notes, so that it could lend to needy governments. The world's formerly poor are now lending to the world's formerly rich. Despite India's repeated capacity to disappoint on account of its slothful economy and suffocating bureaucracy, it will be too big to ignore in this emerging Asian century, especially with a seemingly better government in place. It must be conceded that, due to the scourge of bureaucracy, the lumbering Indian elephant will be no match for the wily Chinese dragon, for at least the next decade or two. The reality is that India's importance relative to China will grow in the future, as it cashes in its demographic dividend: India's working age population is increasing by twelve million a year, while China's is shrinking by three million a year, the latter hoisted by the petard of its one-child policy. India's much younger population than China's will buy it time to get richer before it gets grayer, as others have pointed out.

After an era in which the West carried all before it in the world, a new world order is in prospect, one involving a significant shift in fortune. As the economic interests of the once-poor nations crank up and converge, they will replace the West to become the future engines of world economic growth. Non-Western countries are now responsible for over 80 percent of global growth, with China accounting for over half of that. In the foreseeable future, the meek will be led by the now not-so-meek China with its ever-growing geopolitical clout – a development that will be make it less of an adorable panda and more of a swaggering dragon, as someone said. The grass will no longer be greener on the Western side of the fence as the darkness of depression settles in the West and the sun of recovery rises in the East. Western economies once held up as showcases for the world have lost their relevance; Western banking has ceased to be everyone's idea of a financial template. There is a distinct possibility that the once-admired image of the West will count for little and the tarnished Western economic model shunned in shared disillusionment.

## 10.3 The Ordeal of Debt

On the face of it, debt means poverty. The bailouts spared the private sector the unpleasant after-effect of the financial crisis, namely debt, by shifting it to the public sector, where the burden painfully lingers. Public debt is a lead weight on real recovery, so countries hobbled by hefty government debt are unlikely to be going anywhere fast. In fact, the albatross of government debt in America and Europe, when combined with timorous, mistaken, and rather useless policy measures (see chapter 11), threatens to deepen the economic trough and extend it into the indefinite future.

It should not be surprising that blue skies are not visible from the depths of the debt hole. With the gross US national debt amounting to some $18 trillion ($56,380 per person), about equal to the size of its economy (GDP), the US government could be described as being at risk of drowning in red ink (being broke, in stark terms). It is a whole lot of debt by any standard. According to US Republican senator Coburn in his book *The Debt Bomb*, America is effectively bankrupt (Coburn 2012), although this is a matter of opinion (see chapter 11). In Europe, the government debt amounts to nearly 90 percent of its combined output (GDP). Paying off the European-cum-American debt is a herculean task for the obvious reason that the debts are mountainous. Research findings reveal that when a country's gross government debt rises above 90 percent of its GDP, median growth rates fall by one percent and average growth rates by more (Rogoff and Reinhart 2011). Besides the suffocating effect on growth of the *level* of debt, a condition where debt keeps *rising* aggravates the menace. At worst, the combination of high and rising debt could bring about a total economic collapse.

The public is periodically treated to the process of budgetary policy formulation for debt reduction that is rarely an edifying spectacle. It usually involves the locking of horns for a battle of the giants, each fiercely defending its supposedly infallible corner with unmistakable hubris for a testy ideological slugfest. The hardliners on the opposing sides become unfriendly bedfellows in the common cause of a stalemate that benefits entrenched interests that love the status quo. Although the need to get debt levels down is as strong as ever, the mechanisms for the purpose are as weak as ever; political institutions enable political dithering that causes the policies that finally get through to promise little and deliver less, the latter due to market dysfunction – implying economic drag.

Contributing to the bad news is a fractured economics that offers fiscal policy alternatives that are diametrically opposed. The absurdly contradictory solutions flummox policymakers and blur the distinction between the doctrinaire and the rational. Budgetary policy disagreements are hardly distinguishable from ideological scraps because of the unholy entanglement of science and prejudice; the conflation of weak science and strong beliefs makes it difficult to know when economics crosses into ideology (more fully explained in the next chapter).

As is well known, in the United States debt repayments are at the mercy of stymied political processes that are, moreover, associated with shambolic maneuvering. Seen from afar the system seems decidedly odd: there is predictable deadlock that makes getting money bills passed seem almost as hopeless an endeavor as trying to milk a bull – with a similar lack of accommodation for those who try. This explains budgets that seem forever in the red. Paralyzing partisan combat is not bemoaned by everyone; a gridlocked government is good news for vested interests because it locks in the status quo for the continuation of gravy trains.

The Europeans are no paragons of virtue with regard to public debt and the service of it, decisiveness not being a strong point (understandably, though, because it takes too many to tango). Despite feeble attempts at a common budget, the eurozone countries are too divided for coordinated and effective action on sovereign debt reduction, their promise of fiscal integration seeming a hollow pledge; their policy to reduce debt falls well short of deft.

The eurozone's recovery process is also undermined by the shackling effect of a common currency. This refers to the inability of freeloading and undisciplined member countries to walk away (or be shown the door), so they can treat their economic wounds by recourse to the individual exchange rate devaluations necessary for the healing-adjustment of their economies. The pain being experienced by Greece from having to bear the albatross of debt is an obvious example. Greece, the cradle of Western civilization, has allowed inebriation by the euro to diminish its economy through large-scale corruption, cronyism, and incompetence. This made the Greek economy a laughing stock; an incredibly bad situation that is all Greek to responsible societies baffled by the irresponsibility of its massive profligacy. Greece cannot be given the heave-ho from the eurozone so it could revert to its own currency and sort out its problems, without disastrous consequences for it and other countries. A Greek exit from the eurozone would be bad news for Western banks – although the risk of contagion is lower than before because more than three-quarters of Greek debt was shifted to "official" hands circa 2011. But it would still expose several economies to financial loss and encourage copycat responses from other debt-ridden countries that threaten the eurozone itself. Greece's case illustrates Europe's dilemma, with the implication that it could take decades, if not forever, for the European economy to pay off its debts.

Don't hold your breath. Attaining the supposed virtue of debt-free living is impossibly distant, the West facing decades of pain to eliminate the massive debt overhang (think 2040, perhaps 2060, or even 2080), within the existing scheme of things. No amount of austerity, no matter how suffocating or how it is sliced, will enable the political perpetrators of austerity to personally reap the benefit of their sacrifice within a meaningful planning horizon. And this assumes that nominal interest rates, currently near zero in America, Europe, and Japan, will not rise above their historical equilibrium of around three percent. In Europe, countries on the ropes due to high debt and deficit levels, including Spain and Italy, are paying punishing interest rates that average over six percent – usurious by historical standards (although only if risk factors are ignored). If America and other countries in the West have to pay the same exorbitant interest rates as Spain and Italy at some time in the future, it would dash hopes of debt-free nirvana for several generations; debt will cause money to travel through time and inflict pain on future generations (but only if the currently impaired sociopolitical system remains unchanged – see chapter 12).

## 10.4 Financial Intransigence

Recovery would be more assured if it can be confidently reported that banks have turned over a new leaf. This may happen through better enforcement of regulations or, less likely, because bankers have suffered pangs of conscience.

There is more convincing evidence that the practices of the big banks have *not* changed, than evidence that they *have* changed. The absence of mended ways was starkly revealed when, for example, the banks took up battle stations and used their lobbyists as hired guns to riddle the Dodd-Frank bill with holes to make it as lightweight as possible. Bankers' rediscovery of the taste for aggressive lobbying in relation to attempts at re-regulating their domain shows that loosening their grip is not among their aspirations. Their reaction to attempts at remedying the situation through regulation for the benefit of all (including them), had connotations of a red rag to a bull and clearly showed them up as unprepared to pull in their horns, even when measures are taken for the general good. Their sledgehammer reaction was more than a slight hint that they did not spare a thought for the public and raises continuing concern about their renunciation of bad behavior. Sanguinity can come only by blandly ignoring their proneness to committing the sins identified in the preceding analysis (section 8.1), proprietary trading and rates fixing being cardinal ones among them. Living dangerously seems irresistible, as the JP Morgan Chase "London Whale" and HSBC activities showed.

The question arises whether much has changed since the collapse. Cloak-and-dagger practices were allegedly in vogue before the collapse, and this took the form of plotting and scheming for rule bending and loophole seeking, according to Yves Smith (Smith 2010). Assuming that the enormous fines totaling some $50 billion coughed up over a twelve-month period by banks (Bank of America, JP Morgan Chase, Citigroup, Goldman Sachs, Credit Suisse, Barclays, and BNP Paribas, among others) were not for nothing, it is hard to banish suspicion that something is rotten in the state of finance.

The Rubicon appears to have been crossed in relation to governments' abilities to preemptively control big banks on major matters. The reality must be faced that financial deregulation has irreversibly weakened governments' ability to make banks toe the line of propriety. The identified scandals provide evidence of the ongoing risks to the fragile world economy of an unreformed financial sector, which is the weakest link in the chain. As explained earlier, the task of bringing banks under social control through re-regulation seems largely a lost cause; re-regulation measures involve going through the motions to make a show of regulations that are likely to be much ado about nothing much. The stark reality is that financial sector firms have become too big and too powerful to allow effective regulation of them, particularly in preemptive terms and on major matters. Their size and complexity imply a murkiness that enables them to keep crossing the line in secret, the opaqueness from size and complexity making at least some temptations too great to resist.

When it comes to banks' relationship with the community, the setbacks threaten to be more painful than victories can hope to be sweet. Regulation is at best a barely visible punctuation mark in a long saga of banking practices that are unlikely to end within the present sociopolitical setup. The seemingly anti-social culture of banks is forced upon them by markets, market signals and competitive pressures combining to make it a matter more of necessity than choice, as previously explained. This provides justification for dismay about the inescapable nature of the drag from the financial system on the process of durable recovery. It is hardly comforting that mighty banks, ensconced in plutocratic pseudo-market conditions holding sway in global finance, are not only an impediment to real recovery (see chapter 9), but are also a lurking threat capable of precipitating a collapse of the real economy at any time (see chapter 12).

## 10.5 Self Perpetuation

*The Doom Loop*

A doom loop threatens an interminable recovery. A doom loop arises because this downturn shows signs of self-perpetuation by feeding upon itself. A piling up of negatives contributes to the downturn's self-renewal – thereby foreshadowing a long haul to genuine recovery in the real economy. The ingredients that can potentially trap the economy in a downward spiral are unmistakable, and have their basis in investment. Given the gloomy outlook, reduction in investment now could mean less investment later: if cutbacks in capital spending lower business productivity and product innovation, it would mean less competitiveness and profitability – fallen profitability reducing the willingness and ability of affected business to invest. As implied, a loss of competitiveness could lead to a downward spiral of investment in firms.

For those who know, progress in the West has always been driven by its propensity for technological leadership – a traditional strength of America in particular and the West in general. The technological achievements of Western firms have long-excited imaginations around the world. The application of engineering technology through invention and improvement is a hallmark of Western progress and prosperity. New ideas bear fruit through technological innovation;

when scientific knowledge, in the form of the newest ideas and up-to-date features, gets embodied in capital and consumer goods, technology can be expected to propel upward both private profits and economic growth (in Schumpeterian "creative-destruction" terms). Technological innovativeness provides opportunities for competitiveness and profits that businesses can grasp, because today's civilization reflexively looks to ever-evolving technology to deliver it from yesterday's condition. Technological innovation has distinguished America and Europe from the rest of the world ever since trailblazers like Henry Ford and Thomas Edison in America, and John Baird of television fame in Britain, worked their magic.

The West's inventive glory is at risk if its technological acumen slacks. The age when the hands were Asian but the brains were Western is approaching its end. The numbers tell you why. The evidence reveals a significant downturn-induced decline in research and development (R&D) spending in America, both in absolute terms and relative to the rest of the world. According to the National Science Foundation (NSF), R&D spending in all US companies fell 13.1 percent between 2007 and 2008 (from $269 to $233 billion). During the recession of 2001, R&D expenditures fell much less, by a mere 0.5 percent. Weissberger (2011) reports that a R&D crisis is brewing in America, with huge cutbacks in pure research at companies like IBM, GE, AT&T, Verizon and others. The lending practices of banks do not help the situation, given their inclination to favor the funding of projects delivering quick returns, rather than dreamier and riskier R&D investments. Furthermore, the US Federal government has cutback R&D funding due to budgetary reasons. Shockingly, America is a straggler, having fallen behind seven other countries in R&D spending as a percentage of GDP. McKendrick (2012) reports that, over a period of ten years, the American share of global R&D expenditure decreased from 38 to 31 percent. According to the US National Science

Foundation (NSF), America is quickly losing ground in research to increasingly assertive China, whose share of global R&D is said to now exceed America's. In fact, archrival China, although still lagging the world, is well on its way to becoming an innovative powerhouse. While in America the rate of patent filings have tended to stall, in China they are increasing with gusto.

The poor economic outlook has caused governments and companies in many countries, including America, to drastically scale back on R&D, education, and training. Anemic human capital growth due to poor training and education is associated with low labor productivity and weak product innovation. As economists know, weak productivity will raise production costs and reduce cost competitiveness, while weak product innovation will stymie development of new-fangled "must have" inventive products vital for competitive advantage in strategic marketing. The cutting edge of state-of-the-art technology is often also the cutting edge needed for strategic competitive advantage – implying that in today's business world it is a matter of mostly innovate or perish. Moreover, businesses will buy less machinery and equipment (i.e. cut back on investment) when they have fewer technological breakthroughs to exploit. In addition, skills are needed for coping with global technological advance as reflected in global productivity rises, which took place at an average of rate of 1.7 percent a year over the 50 years to the crisis in 2007. When domestic skills are lacking for coping with global technological progress, technology is disadvantageous: it undermines rather than enhances domestic productivity. It is not known to what extent falling middle class wages in America tracks weakening productivity.

Government policies have been penny-wise and pound-foolish. Government cutbacks for basic research harm businesses and reduce their strategic competitive advantage – thereby dampening growth and lessening public revenue. The government's role is indispensable because basic research will not by definition be funded by the private sector because of the factor of externalities: the inability of the private sector investors to capture enough of the benefits to make the investment worthwhile to themselves. Because basic research is a public good and not a private good, government cutbacks to basic research dry up the well of knowledge that businesses need to draw upon to create innovative products of commercial value. As just three examples: government investments in the Internet and human genome projects delivered enormous benefits to business, as did the pouring of public money into anti-cancer research in the 1970s. These considerations show that government funding cutbacks to R&D can be counterproductive when they close a gateway to sustainable competitiveness for Western firms.

Alas, for all its impressive inventive record, the West can still find its leading light status in R&D losing its radiance under the dark cloud of this downturn – implying that its technological edge is at risk of blunting. With Western economic recovery in the balance, the American and European economies risk losing productivity and international product competitiveness to their chief rival, China, as well as to other countries like South Korea. Any withering of America's and Europe's innovative capacity must be recognized as a factor that will contribute to prolongation of the current downturn – and is suggestive of a reason for its self-perpetuation.

To make matters worse, cutbacks in consumer spending now could result in still less consumer spending later – a development that could further fuel the doom loop. As most analysts know, consumer spending accounts for about two-thirds of demand in Western countries and its escalation is imperative for powering valid recovery. This makes a downward spiral in consumer spending very bad news indeed. Such a phenomenon can result from the "paradox of thrift." If consumers feeling the pinch collectively save more, the resulting cutback in spending would mean less retail sales, production cut-backs in factories, job losses, less income in the community due to unemployment, more cutbacks in consumer spending, further falls in retail sales, and so on. The typical American family has yet to make up the income lost to the recession. Low incomes and high levels of household debt (10 percent above household income in America and 40 percent in Britain in 2014) discourage consumer spending and leave the economy at risk to a sort of "death spiral." According to Paul Krugman in his *End this Depression Now* (Krugman 2012, 44, 52), that is because my spending is your income and your spending is my income; so if both you and I spend less, we both suffer. Such an outcome, by debilitating demand, is obviously capable of aggravating and perpetuating the downturn. In fact, it may be contributing to the deflation of 0.7 percent in the eurozone and the worryingly low infla-tion rate of less than one percent in America and Britain in 2014.

Even monetary policy can make an unwelcome contribution to the doom loop; current palliatives threaten future trouble. As will be explained in section 11.2, the money-creating policy of quantitative easing (QE) has done wonders for the stock and housing markets but not done nearly as much for the majority in the real economy. For the various reasons to be identified, the monetary policy that is soothing today could be toxic for future generations in the absence of a real recovery that is soon enough, pervasive enough, and robust enough. Central bankers are putting off the evil day by ignoring the cloven hoof, namely, the grotesquely warped fundamentals of asset markets that can be a foreboding of future misery without a proper recovery.

The doom loop is further reinforced by the condition of eco-nomic stagnation. Stagnancy has given rise to dog-in-the-manger type behavior by business managers (reminiscent of the dog in *Aesop's Fables* that kept the hungry ox from the hay even though it could not eat the hay itself). Businesses in the West are holding on

317

to precious capital amounting to some $3 trillion, not investing it or returning it to shareholders – a negativism that denies the economy desperately needed growth from investment. This means the very condition of depressed times, creates conditions for perpetuation of such depressed times. An explanation can be found in Stephen King's *When the Money Runs Out: The End of Western Affluence*, where he states that stagnancy destroys positive entrepreneurial spirit and replaces it with a negative strategy; pessimistic businesses and consumers tend to hang on to what they have when the outlook is bleak (King 2013). This must discourage the formulation of business strategic thrusts required for fulfilling long-term strategic vision. It seems that pessimistic managers, still shell-shocked by the collapse, are hanging on to piles of money as their security blanket in troubled times – thereby perpetuating the condition that caused their behavior in the first place.

*Japan Inc.: Sobering Example*

Japan's experience shows that distant futures have limited present relevance. The experience provides a sobering reminder that economic downturns can last so long as to be outside the strategic planning horizons of all but diehard optimists. The Japanese downturn has lasted well over two straight decades (the "lost decades"), with more to come because of the protracted downturn in Western economies. The Japanese experience provides an unpleasant foretaste of difficulties for the West.

The features were as nasty as they are familiar. Japan's sudden economic collapse in the late 1980s was precipitated by factors broadly similar to those that set off the current Western unpleasantness. In both the Japanese experience and the current joint American-cum-European experience, there were common reprehensible characteristics: cheap and easy money that fuelled speculative asset bubbles that burst; a massive stock market crash; battered banks that received rescue money motivated by a "too big to fail" philosophy (that was also a moral hazard); a resultant massive debt crisis; and a persistent liquidity trap. To top it all off, a stifling corporate culture of cronyism has frustrated progress in Japan, a condition that has an arguable counterpart in the plutocratic influences that stymie economic performance in the West (shown in chapter 9).

Hobbled by the gangrene of crippling debt, Japan already belongs to the club of the walking wounded. Consequently, it is in no position to march to the rescue of the club's new members, namely America and Europe. Its anemic economic performance has persisted for over two decades despite being beneficially buttressed by the boom times in the West. In the five prosperous years preceding the recession (to 2008), the Japanese GDP growth rate averaged 1.28 percent, only about half that of Britain (2.52 percent) and less than 40 percent that of America (3.34 percent). The Western economies cannot hope to receive similar reciprocal support in this their time of need, even though Japan has the third largest economy in the world. This is because Japan is in an even greater debt mess than the West. Although the Japanese debt level is about half the total combined debt level of America and Europe, Japan's gross national debt stood at 240 percent of GDP in 2014, putting Greece's debt (at 175 percent of GDP) in the shade. Japan's debt causes the average Japanese person to be head over heels in debt; the debt level per person is over 2.5 times higher in Japan than that in the West, and is increasing because of population decline.

Further collapse in America and Europe is bound to take Japan down. As Japan staggers under the increasing weight of public debt, it will have little chance of being able to keep away from joining America and Europe in the dreaded abyss, in the event of their further collapse from present depressed levels.

## 10.6 Conclusion: Dark Horizon

The above explanation gives less reason to wonder why there are no bright lights to be seen on the economic horizon. Although the downturn has dragged on for much longer than any previous recession, the end of the crisis has still not marked the beginning of prosperity. The interwoven strands responsible for the drawn-out nature of the downturn unravel to indicate a long haul to a recovery that may never happen. The protraction is fuelled by factors that are so incorrigible that it would not be surprising if it turns out to be as long as that proverbial piece of string.

What seem like signs of recovery may well be camouflaged threats of collapse. The song and dance about America's and Britain's recoveries enables many to find in the triumphalism a distraction from their froth and bubble. A persistent lack of puff in the eurozone has condemned it to an indeterminate future in Queer Street. This is bad news because the fates of America and Europe are inextricably intertwined. The American recovery cannot be fully-fledged without Europe rising from the ashes and pulling its weight, especially when poor European performance has a dampening effect on China, Japan and the rest of the world that causes them to go from being beacons of hope to places of gloom. The prospects for mutual support are far from encouraging. The sluggish, patchy, and unsustainable American recovery, the dubious British recovery, and the almost-imperceptible European recovery, are explained by several factors: the near-exhaustion of a monetary policy that is being done to death; political policy drag in America and Europe; and the fact the conventional fiscal policy remedies are mostly predictable duds because of plutocratic pseudo-market conditions. The ineffectiveness of repeated tries with conventional policies causes nagging doubts to eat away at recovery hopes; each used-up shot in sluggish circumstances limits the future shots available in the locker. As will be shown in the following chapter, the effect on recovery of the conventional policy measures taken have, at best, been palliative, not curative. This is because usual policy measures cannot work to deliver a recovery that is inclusive and robust when markets are dysfunctional and pseudo.

Even the present hollow recovery is shown to be at risk from perceived wild cards, both domestic and foreign, that sap confidence with a cold dose of reality. Domestic policy is in uncharted waters due to market dysfunction. External perils take the form of collapses waiting to happen in Europe and China, while Japan plays the role of albatross on Western recovery. The financial sector, because of its strength is, paradoxically, the weak link in the economic chain. The continuing bad practices by banks stymie recovery in the present and are a lurking threat for the future (no one can know what further horrors lie in wait in the mustier corners of their vaults). Central banking practices warp fundamentals and threaten long-term damage in the absence of a soon-enough recovery that is robust and inclusive (that is, one that is genuine and not a farcical financial mirage).

The self-perpetuation of the downturn is fed by the several negative factors unsurprisingly thrown up by the downturn itself. Less investment now means still less investment later; the weakened strategic competitive advantage of Western firms because of falling R&D, productivity, efficiency, and deficiencies in human skills, means lower profits and diminished investment – for the possible trap of a downward spiral. Not being up to speed due to a lack of relevant skills relating to the latest manufacturing methods, would make global technological advance more a minus than a plus for domestic productivity. Consumer spending cutbacks could accelerate the downward spiral. Moreover, the conjunction of economic doldrums and dysfunctional market conditions weakens the entrepreneurial spirit needed for recovery – the invaluable loss aggravating the conditions that gave rise to it in the first place. The scale and type of the policy effort have not proven equal to the recovery task, and Europe is banking on a money printing exercise that has fallen short of being a model of success in America and Britain.

By taking the wind out of the recovery sails, these debilitating elements condemn the journey back to prosperity in the West to an indeterminate duration: to a long haul on borrowed time. The disconcerting reality is that the outlook is cloudy; uncertainty beckons.

**

# Chapter 11

## POLICY OPTIONS: LET US PRAY

### 11.1 Tired Tools

Flunking targets for growth raises questions about the quality of the measures taken to rekindle the economy. Despite repeated tries in a high-stakes environment, what policymakers have to show for their efforts is strikingly modest. Expecting that today's policy options for recovery will replicate successes of times past despite the bugbear of the pseudo-market phenomenon, requires a lot of faith – and, perhaps, some prayer. If the sorry experience of the last seven years of downturn teaches anything, it is that, despite plucky efforts, the contentious conventional policies have fallen short of being a big hit with the general public, being more palliative than curative. Are conventional policy tools on their way to becoming relics in mutating market conditions? This chapter will address the question.

There is no silver bullet available to vaporize the problem. The current policy measures are synonymous with disarray; they have involved clumsily muddling through a complex phenomenon on a wing and a prayer (and a lot of wishful thinking)–hardly a ready solution. Although economists do not have a grand innovative solution that they are keeping a secret, a friendly view is that genuine, mainstream, economists, do nevertheless have a threadbare policy option or two in their anemic and shabby bundle of policy tools that offer better than nothing within the confines of the existing scheme of things. The overall question is simply this: which of the dim policy options on the table offers the relatively brighter prospect of igniting growth in subdued economies, given the reality of current and growing market dysfunction from plutocratic pseudo-market conditions?

There are four policy options for examination. The tiresome choices that supposedly promise economic growth are simplified to bring them into sharp relief, their finer points being outside the scope of this non-academic book. The two sides of the budgetary question (the fiscal policy options) condense to the choice between "fiscal austerity" (i.e., government program cutbacks) and "fiscal stimulus" (i.e., increased government spending on programs). These fiscal measures are obviously conflicting (i.e., they are competitive). The budgetary policy options are rooted in competing visions and reflect a fractured economics that is at war with itself, something on which more will be stated shortly. The much-loved monetary options are "quantitative easing" (i.e., money printing) and "interest rate policy." These instruments work together (i.e., they are complementary – increased money supply supposedly having the effect of reducing interest rates). Besides being more hackneyed tools than magic wands, these policy options are sources of discord. They are bedeviled by serious controversy about their short-term validity and long-term viability.

The analysis that follows is expected to throw light on whether past bad decisions have disabled the policy options presently on the table. This could mean that blunders of the past have undermined the ability of conventional polices to work because changed market fundamentals have cut the ground from under them. A bulldozing approach to deregulation, less than fully effective government stimulus spending, crippling public and private debt, monetary policy options that have been worked to exhaustion, and the mollycoddling of recovery-impeding plutocratic pseudo-markets, could well have combined to emaciate policy efficacy – causing the current underwhelming policy options to condemn the future to suffer for decisional errors of the past.

## 11.2 The Monetary Defense

*Unfamiliar Territory*

Western governments, disinclined toward the fiscal options of austerity and public spending, have bet the farm on monetary policy. Having painted themselves into a corner, they have come to expect monetary alchemy from central bankers. They have gained for themselves the option of putting desperately needed policy reforms on the back burner, buying time by booting the problem to central bankers who, in tough-guy manner, placed a brick on the money printing accelerator. Shown later is why, although the pressure has eased, the damage may already be done.

Breaking ground with unprecedented monetary policy in misunderstood economic conditions must involve living dangerously. Since gambles can misfire, the measures taken would fall somewhere between dicey and deadly. Trusting in hope, central bankers kept moving beyond past boundaries to unknown territory to coax resurgence by being recklessly accommodative toward monetary policy. True, monetary stopgaps have kept things bubbling along and enabled governments to stay one jump ahead of the threat. But policymakers must surely know that the measures taken were experimental and that experiments often fail.

In any event, excessive money printing comes at the cost of losing effective currency in the form of credibility, especially with the outcast majority in the real economy for whom monetary policy has been mostly beside the point. The below-par effectiveness of monetary policy in current circumstances makes it plain that monetary policy has known better days. This is particularly so for the excluded majority for whom it could prove irksome by signaling that conventional solutions are unsuited to atypical conditions.

*Monetary Munificence*

Here comes the money. The unfettered ease of pushing monetary policy is seductive in giving the green light to red ink, much of it grotesquely warping market fundamentals without too many crying foul (explained later). The recently discovered tool of money printing by central bankers (counterfeiting, if done by others), is given public respectability by the camouflaging label of "quantitative easing" (QE) in America and Britain. As analysts know, quantitative easing refers to open market transactions to buy up government bonds aimed at increasing the money supply. This effectively means creating money out of thin air – something that the Federal Reserve Board and the Bank of England have shown they are clever at doing. Over a twelve-month period, the Federal Reserve pumped well over four trillion greenbacks into the US economy (some 23 percent of American GDP), at about the same time as the Bank of England pumped newly minted sterling worth over $690 billion into the British economy (over 27 percent of Britain's GDP). The scale of money printing is unprecedented, and the gargantuan stockpile of bonds ($4.5 trillion in the US in 2014) would be grossly distorting in the absence of a soon-enough and sufficient recovery in the real economy to mop it up.

The European Central Bank (ECB) bought time by resorting to Long Term Refinancing Operations (LTRO), which involved a huge injection of cash into the beleaguered eurozone banking system. But belatedly joining the QE club constitutes a tacit admission by the ECB that LTRO, despite its unprecedented scale, was not up the job of getting things going – thereby baring for those who might have missed it, the scary dimensions of the European problem. Hence, hope springs eternal as the ECB desperately reaches for the last tool in the box (QE valued at over $1.5 trillion for quenching deflationary pressures), to the chagrin of the Germans and delight of the rest, particularly France and Italy, characteristically looking for an easy way out of their plight. It was explained in section 10.2 why the ECB's foray into QE is likely to, despite banks brimming with money, fall short of making the eurozone an investors' paradise or engendering enough benefits that are widely felt. This raises the chilling question: what's left?

One point of view bluntly portrays QE and LTRO as ploys that deliver worldwide hallucinatory trips – that is, induced temporary highs in eager international markets ahead of themselves and looking for straws to grasp. The uncharted bursts of US money creation from QE, have pumped up stock and housing markets worldwide (referred to as a "global gravy train" by the more cynical), because the international monetary system is US-dollar based. Everywhere investors craving decent yields and having nowhere else to turn, flood the stock and housing markets with capital. The highs from the shots in the arm can provide illusory signs of recovery for the more romantically inclined, even though short-term traders have shown they can be nothing but trouble. The reason why the signs of a turnaround are misleading can easily be pinpointed: stock market investors are more optimistic than the fundamentals warrant. The artificial buoyancy is not backed by hard data in telltale fundamentals like employment, wages, productivity, and the household incomes of the majority of the population – implying a disturbing bifurcation between the simulated economy and the real thing. If more proof is needed, it is to be found in the following anomaly: there is an odd three trillion dollars hanging around in the back pockets of company executives in America and Europe, the huge amount of cash being hoarded rather than invested by companies lacking faith in the future. This makes the splurges from QE and

LTRO incongruous: more money is being injected into a situation where less ought to be necessary.

Unlike before, the current reality is that stock markets operate like casinos, to a large extent independently of what is happening in the real economy. Stock markets' buoyancy reflects investor confidence, but it is a confidence more in the unconventional practices of central banks than in the real economy. Stock markets have been driven more by psychology than fundamentals. When bonds are sold to activate money printing presses in America ($85 billion per month at its zenith in 2013, but since ended, probably more out of diffidence than self-assurance), they push US government bond prices up and push yields down. This induces income-hungry investors to dump cash and bonds, pile into equities, and inflate stock markets. When the rallies are predicated on debt, their propulsion reflects punter manias that cause bull markets to conceal bear traps. The Dow Jones Global Index more than doubled in the seven years since its nadir in 2008, breaking a score of record highs in the process. The absence of an equally attractive "cash cow" alternative probably makes many frustrated investors reluctant bulls.

Because of the allure of debt, stock markets no longer provide companies with equity capital to the extent that they are believed to. Most company capital is raised though debt or own funds, thereby weakening the nexus between stock market signals and the business outlook in the real economy. Borrowing is the most profitable option for businesses in the United States; recent research findings confirm that, because of tax-deductibility for the borrowings of companies, debt capital is cheaper than equity capital (Admati and Hellwig 2013). It is not just the stock market that is affected by the gambling disposition; speculation (and likely rigging) in the commodities and foreign exchange markets are collateral consequences of cheap and easy money, as is the house price inflation across the globe.

Monetary policy is associated with several mollifying effects that enable things to keep bubbling along, as seems to be presently happening. Most importantly, it has done the job of quelling fears that previously stalked stock and housing markets by instilling investor confidence (albeit more in central bank policies than in the economy). Induced frothiness in those markets has served the purpose of allaying public anxiety by keeping good news stories coming, with declarations of recovery buying time to avert any imminent threat from psychopathic market behavior. Monetary policy is helpful for believers in austerity because its proclaimed benefits to the financial economy can be used to justify cutbacks in the real economy. Money printing in America helped to increase exports through its effects on devaluing the dollar and increasing their price competitiveness – but only until competitor countries, mainly Britain and Japan, made countervailing devaluations to offset the benefit. Money printing has kept dud companies afloat that would otherwise go under by giving them artificial buoyancy with cheap and easy money. Monetary policy has a favorable cosmetic effect on the labor market despite a zero increase in hiring because cheap money enables businesses to shelve layoffs. At best, monetary policy cushions hardship and buys time, with no assurance of being able to present a lasting solution like it used to do under less dysfunctional market conditions. At worst, it is mostly smoke-and-mirrors in the short-term and undermines recovery for the non-shareholding majority in the long-term (see chapter 9).

Leading a horse to water does not mean you can make it drink. As most people know, the effect of quantitative easing depends on the extent to which people want to borrow the additional money made available to the banks. Conversely, it depends on whether banks can lend out the additional money. The problem is that nervous consumers and investors, spooked by gloom, are not rushing to borrow and spend; scarred businesses and households are not showing enough inclination to move future investment and consumption forward to the present through borrowings. As a result of such negative group-think, the hoped-for surge in the presently subdued demand for loans has failed to materialize. Since the 2008 high, bank lending to American firms is down by over 6 percent and to European firms by some 11 percent. This means the horse can refuse to drink even when the water is sugared with low interest rates and served in the victory cup of generous borrowing terms. So where do financial markets stand? You've guessed it: on a mountainous stockpile of bonds.

If money printing should resume in a big way, the "almighty dollar" could develop feet of clay. For those who know, the integrity of the dollar has come to depend on faith rather than on gold (as was the case until 1971); trust imbues value. Because America has the privilege of issuing the world's reserve currency, over-egging the monetary pudding through quantitative easing has the incidental potential to undermine the integrity of the US dollar. This would reduce its robustness as a "safe haven" currency to which investors flock when they are worried about the future. Depending on market perceptions, the increase in money supply that a profligate bout of quantitative easing brings could make that currency worth less to other people and cause a tumbling dollar to lower the American exchange rate. It is true that America as an issuer of reserve currency has greater scope to raise debt, but how far the Federal Reserve can go before it fuels a damaging across-the-board decline in the value of the US dollar is something left to be seen.

The Chinese renminbi is a distant but increasing threat to the US dollar. China is starting to promote its currency beyond its borders, with dire signs of eagerness on the part of foreigners to hold renminbi in preference to US dollars. The renminbi is now the second-most used currency in trade finance, having overtaken the yen and the euro (although the United States is well ahead, backing over 80 percent of trade finance). The evidence is that international trading in the renminbi has tripled in three years to 2014, to reach $120 trillion a day. These must seem like early warnings that you can push monetary policy only so far, and that QE policy thrusts are shots in the dark that can yet boomerang on the shooter in the long run.

Most analysts know that America and Europe have joined Japan to be caught in that non-mechanical device called a "liquidity trap." It happens when money is hoarded rather than spent, even when low interest rates make the spending of borrowed money cheap to do. Interest rates reflect the time value of money and the interest earned is the reward for parting with liquidity for a specified period, as John Maynard Keynes wrote in his epic *General Theory*. As a policy tool, interest rate policy is a blunt instrument that is associated with a wide bandwidth of uncertainty when wielded.

It is not nitpicking to complain that the disease of economic lethargy in the real economy has, despite the deluge of money printing, ceased to be sufficiently responsive to the medicine of low interest rates. The allure of loan money for jam has not stirred the interest of enough consumers and investors, because their feelings of gloom continue to outweigh the charm of cheap money – causing them to be stingy when it comes to chipping in with their contribution to the worthy cause of economic growth. The impotence of monetary policy in a recession was likened to pushing on a string by legendary economist John Maynard Keynes. For the non-shareholding public and businesses in open competitive sectors, money for old rope is an empty promise, whereas for savers it must feel like robbery. For savers who have earned next to nothing and seen their nest eggs shrink because of inflation, a zero interest rate may well denote a zero mark for monetary performance – a clear fail.

By defying accepted wisdom, interest rate policy has central bankers whistling in the wind. With interest rates nailed to the floor at near-zero nominal in America, Europe and Japan, central bankers have pushed the policy to its limits. Any lower would make under-the-mattress an attractive alternative to a bank account (if there were enough mattresses, that is). They have done so on the dicey presumptions that neither further collapses nor deflation will happen. And this even though American inflation is worryingly low at less than one percent and slipping, and deflation is actually occurring at 0.7 percent in the eurozone due to chronically low demand. It is true that low interest rates have made life easier for high-end consumers and big companies. It had enabled large firms to swap debt for equity by buying back their own shares (although share buybacks are a bad sign for society that companies have run out of good ideas for investment, such as in R&D , factory expansion, and foreign entry). Also, the close-to-zero nominal interest rate has the effect of giving less creditworthy borrowers a break. Most important of all, inflating stock and housing markets engenders an aura of recovery to preempt frenzied behavior by market players who have amply demonstrated a proneness to wild excitement.

For central bankers, sitting on the horns of a dilemma is an occupational hazard associated with understandable discomfiture. The unfavorable alternatives confronting central banks in downturn-affected advanced countries must be understood to be appreciated: they are "damned if they do and damned if they don't." True, money printing has not been pointless; it has achieved the goal of loosening monetary conditions at a time when nominal interest rates are close to zero, making further rate cuts impossible. In this it has provided a breath of fresh air for buoyancy, although not the hoped-for breath of life needed for authentic recovery.

Central bankers are putting a brave face on things by trying to make a virtue out of necessity. For them tiresome policies are not as yet exhausted policies, as they push their luck with known and expedient policies from within the familiar box to stay within their comfort zone. It is perhaps true that for the bypassed majority these policies may seem irrelevant replays that keep going round in circles with drearily predictable inefficacy. Moreover, economies biased toward debt are prone to crises. But the policies, however unromantic, cannot be avoided; they are driven by the belief that it is better to be safe than sorry and are, therefore, regarded as essential for staying ahead of the threat. For central bankers wedded to easy money policy, now is not the time for hesitation, or to give pause for thought; there is just no alternative to keeping things bubbling along, even though such behavior would make a rod for their own back should bubbles burst in stocks and housing.

It would be wrong to suspect central bankers of taking measures they know are bad just to make the public the butt of some cruel joke. The crack hands in central banks surely know what they are doing and, no doubt, dutifully have their eyes on the ball. They must surely know that easy money without enough new investment will create bubbles (how can they forget Iceland, Argentina, and subprime debt?). But these experts cannot help themselves and do not know how to stop as they go through the motions. Several examples spring to mind. Can central banks wean the suckling financial system from the expectation of further money printing that is already a frightful glut? Can central banks raise interest rates to their historical equilibrium of 2.5 to 3 percent without causing widespread bankruptcies? Can central banks stop buying second rate assets such as mortgage-backed securities and stop subsidizing risky commercial loans without causing companies to go belly-up – and converting poor business confidence into unbridled business panic? With economies hanging by a thread, the answers to the foregoing questions are obviously in the negative. There is not much hope that the day will come when these measures will be found as unacceptable as making fun of obese people.

Central bankers have come to be accepted as stimulators of last resort, even though they can bring forth a lot of froth in the process. When fiscal options are a no-no, the monetary option becomes a welcome straw to grasp if recovery, however hollow, is not to be aborted. In an age when the fiscal options of public spending and government program cutbacks are regarded as damp squibs, politically repugnant, or both, central banks have provided an indispensable policy prop to beleaguered Western governments. This they have been able to do in their role beyond monetary policy of being "financial supervisor"– standing between present torpor and future cave-in. Governments have tended to paint themselves into the corner of monetary policy to be carried out through central banks as it offers an easy solution in a difficult situation, expedient palliative measures that buy time until the next election. In his book *When the Money Runs Out: The End of Western Affluence*, Stephen King makes the point that, while monetary policy may have prevented the recession from turning into a repeat of the Great Depression, it has made central banks political instruments (King 2013), perhaps convenient ones that enable politic politicians to dodge real solutions to difficult problems from hard decisions (see chapter 12).

### Living Dangerously

For central bankers and governments wedded to monetary policy, reheated pizzas are good enough when one is hungry enough. But stale or expedient tools may be unsuited to fixing unusual problems, especially when a freak recession is happening in unprecedented plutocratic pseudo-market conditions. Perseverance in their use manifest a hope against hope that monetary policies, that have served economies adequately in the past, will work their charm and do the needful in the future – and this even though the market mechanism on which recovery banks on has changed for the worse.

There is policy comfort in regarding the current economic downturn as a larger-scale version of previous ones, which can therefore be treated with larger and bolder versions of previous policy solutions – a belief associated with the comfort zone paradigm described in section 2.1. In the absence of a spontaneously recuperative upswing in the business cycle, central banks' bubble-creating shots in the arm for hallucinatory highs may be crucial to prevent economies from going cold turkey. Although they may only be postponing the evil day, it would be better to have froth than blood in the meantime. When conditions are not properly understood, the measures taken provide a margin of safety against the unknown, on the basis that it is better to be safe than sorry. Central bankers may not have much choice if they are to stay one jump ahead of a catastrophic plunge into depression.

Because their actions are fraught with long-term uncertainties of unknowable dimensions, chance would be a fine thing if it happens. The longer-term future of economies could be threatened by opportunistic monetary tools being used in misunderstood market circumstances that are a whole new ball game. Although monetary policy offers a path of least resistance and suits the limited planning horizons of expedient politicians, most of the measures taken seem more in hope than in expectation. While printing money provides the means to paper over the cracks in the economy, it is not exactly benign. Cheap and easy money tends to incidentally kill jobs, implying that any resulting growth would be weak in its ability to increase employment. One way in which cheap money reduces jobs is by encouraging the substitution of capital for labor, such as by the use of self-check-ins at airports and self-check-outs at supermarkets. While many unskilled jobs have already been lost to mechanization, machinery is starting to crowd out even middle class positions. The facts are that middle class real wages are falling in America and Europe, at least partly due to automation. In addition, as explained in chapter 9, monetary policy harms employment generation when it causes bank lending to favor short-termism over strategic vision, investments in stocks over investment in factories, larger firms over smaller ones, plodding established firms over dynamic startups, and firms in pseudo-markets over firms in open competitive markets.

Furthermore, there is the distinct possibility that too much money from monetary stimulus continues to be a dangerous glut that sloshes about to irreversibly distort, rather than transform, market fundamentals. Printing money has the effect of encouraging excessive risk taking by pushing investors into riskier assets; investors' consciousness of risk becomes disorientated, and that must cause risk to be mispriced and capital to be misallocated. The value of junk bonds, for example, is uncomfortably close to that of investment grade bonds, evidencing risk distortions in the economy. Moreover, housing and other hidden bubbles around the world will be inflated if currency relativities are distorted. Playing the stock, commodities, and foreign exchange markets by banks must be regarded as a temptation that is a collateral consequence of cheap and easy money. Generally, fundamental imbalances are created between saving and investment for an unsustainable condition that sets the stage for another, still worse, collapse.

Although the inflation specter is missing, winning current battles with money printing and other measures does not necessarily win the war on future poverty; future generations are condemned to bear the burden of present excess. Monetary stimulus involves living today at the expense of tomorrow by lowering returns for future generations that must carry the can despite having no current voice. The breath of fresh air from money printing in the short term, could transform into toxic fumes in the longer term because of the fundamental imbalances mentioned. Even though ceased, it is probable that enough damage has already been done.

This highlights a worrisome reality: central bankers have placed all their eggs in the "inevitable-recovery" basket; their whole strategy rests on the rosy expectation that the recovery will assuredly happen within a finite time frame (i.e., soon). Central bankers seem to have upped the ante in the hope that a durable recovery in the real economy will make the dicey policy all right in the end. This it would do by having resurgent economic activity in the real economy validate simulated prices. The expectation is that a genuinely expanding economy would put things right by developing the ability to pay back the loans and absorb all the excess money that is still out there. But what if the present condition is not temporary as is supposed?

Hope springs eternal in central bankers' breasts (with apologies to Alexander Pope, 1688-1744). It is hard to square with central bankers' notion of returning the economy to genuine recovery, let alone previous prosperity. The central bankers' rationale implies confidence in previous patterns of recovery, but they could be waiting for a level of recovery in the real economy that may never come. Their policies ignore the bugbear of the pseudo-market phenomenon. Consequently, measures that worked in the past may not work in circumstances that are different from those of the past. The problem is that a robust and inclusive recovery in America and Europe (whose economic fates are inextricably intertwined for reasons previously explained), is nowhere in sight. To expect that America can rise to its previous heights while Europe is sinking to new depths is probably wishful thinking. Moreover, monetary policies are subject to diminishing returns: each shot at money printing in stagnant circumstances limits the future shots available in the locker. The continuing skittish response from investors in the real economy suggests that the money printing escapade could turn out to be a bad bet. This reality must undermine confidence in the future. The logical implication is that investor and consumer betting against a replay of financial tragedy will inevitably weaken over time. .

Elastic deadlines enable the stretching of a veneer of normality by central bankers playing for time. But there has to be an inevitable breaking point somewhere along the line. Their period of grace cannot be expected to last indefinitely; in the absence of a soon enough and genuine recovery, it seems only a matter of time before the sand runs out and the QE opiated chickens come home to roost. Given the diminishing returns from monetary policy in sluggish circumstances (that is, in the absence of a sprint to authentic recovery for the majority in the real economy), persistent European dysfunction, and the threat of deflation in conditions of near-zero nominal interest rates, the question is: at what point would central bankers have shot their bolt and run out of options?

Protraction aggravates the problem; the longer it takes for recovery in the real economy, the harder it will get to keep turning a blind eye to the money glut and growing indebtedness. If the expected self-correcting upswing in the supposed business cycle, that high-roller central bankers have pinned their hopes on, does not soon come to pass, they could be in more than a bit of bother. By gambling on an unlikely outcome, central bankers' policies arguably amount to a gigantic lottery, one where the odds are stacked against them because of a system malfunction due to the plutocratic pseudo-market condition. If the recovery is not robust and rapid enough, central bankers' great promise will turn out to be a grave peril. Their current actions would then amount to kicking a can of red ink along the road to fend off of the moment of truth: a catastrophic finance-sector induced economic collapse, this one much worse than the one before that leaves future generations saddled with a frightful bill for current palliatives.

More will be said on the likelihood of the crisis to come in subsequent chapters. It will be shown that central bank measures taken condense to a strategy for living, not just on borrowed money, but also on borrowed time. Central bankers are trying to slip in a few extra years before the tipping point of a recovery spurt or, much more likely, a plunging collapse. It is hard not to suspect that the seeds of the next financial collapse are probably already sown. This view is shared by a range of experts who are united in their belief that the next collapse is more a question of when, not if. They are all agreed that what is around the corner is something that it would be nice to steer clear of. Section 12.2 will present an assemblage of expert views on the possible nightmare.

## 11.3 The Austerity Path

*The Personal-Debt Monomania*

Living a life free of debt is important to most responsible people in the Western world. Being debt-free is a virtue that is firmly embedded in the Judeo-Christian ethic as is, for example, expressed in the following quote: "...the man of God...said 'go, sell the oil and pay your debts.'" (2 Kings 4:7 NIV). But is the halo for politicians paying off government debt as luminous as it is for individuals paying off personal debt? The short answer is: not necessarily. Shown next is why the parallel is inexact.

To regard a country's budget as being different from a personal budget is counter-intuitive to the many people who regard living debt-free a virtue. In terms of this value-loaded belief that regards indebtedness as a vice, it is good and necessary that countries, like persons, balance budgets; it is simply the right and proper thing to do – even a religious duty in terms of Judeo-Christian ethics. Although at first blush this view ticks every box, it could have counterproductive results if allowed to blindly drive policy on the basis of ideological enchantment. For this reason it is questionable. And who better to question it than Jacob Viner of the early Chicago

School of Economics? He wrote, "There is nothing as unsound as hoary doctrines that have acquired the support of authority simply because they are traditional...One of these moldy fallacies is that regardless of the circumstances the government must balance its budget each year...Why not in each month, or week, or hour?" (James 1981, 93).

For those who know, an individual's budget is different from a country's budget for several reasons. For one thing, persons have much shorter planning horizons than do countries, whose planning horizon can span generations. For another, because countries have coercive taxing and money-creating powers that individuals do not have, countries have a wider range of debt-management options that are economically rational and legal than do individuals. Moreover, many people believe that governments have a broader responsibility than persons, one that extends from support for frail members of society (like the old, the poor, and the ill) to ensuring that the free enterprise system is free to get on with its wealth-creating function. (It was laboriously argued in chapter 5 that it was the government's responsibility to proactively ensure that markets are able to freely operate, and that such responsibility was not one-off but ongoing.) Some believe that when the government spends more than its revenue through borrowing, it could get the economy going through multiplier effects that generate enough additional revenue to more than service the debt – implying a net benefit or profit (no different than what a business might seek from borrowing to invest). In addition, countries' economies grow over time due to technological progress, making the next generation richer than the present generation and, hence, better able to service previous debt –something far less certain for individuals. A related reality, and perhaps the most important of all, is that public debt need never be repaid as in the case of personal debt. This is because sufficient growth of the economy would automatically reduce the size of the debt in relation to GDP when certain conditions are met (explained shortly).

This means, all debt is not the same; some debt is chalk and other debt is cheese. So regarding national debt policy as needing to be treated the same as personal debt policy may seem like common sense to many, but can be a dangerous policy misconception. This is because it may erroneously reject the policy option of using public debt as an instrument of growth and development, as would a business. Borrowing is a perfectly legitimate strategy for businesses development, and farmers need loans to smooth the seasonality of their income. To contemptuously reject the public spending policy option out of hand could be regarded by the Keynesian school of thought as exhibiting the monomania of a "personal-debt mentality"–a prejudice that tends to get in the way of keeping an open mind on public policy choices. Those favoring fiscal stimulus as a valid policy option would be inclined to regard a belief in austerity that is based on the personal-debt monomania as being, in the words of Sir Francis Bacon, the "idol of the tribe" (i.e., a deep-rooted false notion).

Consequently, the way that government debt is handled can be cruel rather than virtuous. Wrong decisions in relation to government debt can deny politicians the righteousness they associate with matters of personal debt – the false parallel depriving politicians hellbent on debt repayment at any cost the hoped-for aura of nobility. If company managers and other investors eschewed debt for the same moral reason as myopic politicians do, banks would be out of business and the economy in tatters.

Despite these considerations, the deeply ingrained and widely held personal-debt monomania is not something likely to be discarded in conditions dominated by the narrow balance-sheet values of an ascendant financial sector. It is not recognized that the virtue of living debt-free could convert to being a vice when it becomes a pathological obsession that truncates policy options – and pushes economies from the frying pan of lethargy into the fire of depression. According to philosopher Albert Camus (1913-60), "Virtue cannot separate itself from reality without becoming a principle of evil" (Dingle 2008). Many people around the world are being murdered on supposedly virtuous religious grounds by extremists – one person's act of religious virtue being another person's barbaric bomb blast. A sobering view of virtue was expressed by Bernard Mandeville who, in his *Fable of the Bees* (1705), stated that virtue was hypocrisy for keeping people in line – a motivation that most of those favoring government spending as a means to economic resurgence would gladly attribute to austerity devotees. The point is that there is nothing absolute about virtuous beliefs, including the belief that it is a virtue to be debt-free under *all* circumstances, no matter what, as any honest business person will readily concede. Where would business development be if businesses did not shun the virtue of living debt-free and resort to commercial borrowing as part of normal business strategy?

*The Love of Austerity*
Ardent support for austerity seems a fashionable stance; it is seen by devotees as a means of balancing the books, delivering economic growth, and projecting a virtuous persona to boot. How can opposing indebtedness, like supporting motherhood, not deserve brownie points? Deep-seated cultural values enable fetish to trump diffidence in politicians giving austerity the thumbs up; they steal the show by advocating the virtue of drawing in the government's horns in today's difficult times. The grip on economic policy of trendy austerity advocates has been tightening in both America and Europe, implying a strong inclination to cut back on government programs and, conversely, a corresponding antagonism toward spending money on government programs.

Achieving austerity and achieving smaller government are two sides of the same saved coin. The two go together, since believers in small government are on their own ground when it comes to supporting austerity; shutting the door on public spending through austerity measures goes down big with small government believers. This means that belief in austerity is allied with the belief that government is a self-serving Leviathan bulging with bureaucrats who hatch schemes to follow people around and run their lives. For these reasons, arguments in favor of austerity strike responsive chords among small government believers, who intuitively warm with affection to public program cutbacks. Such buttressed belief makes the castor oil of austerity a panacea for the ills of the economy; it may be hard to take but its remedial benefits are believed to be surer. By eliminating needless government, it clears the way to economic health.

Austerity supporters claim that current government intervention is crowding out private sector activity, thereby preempting it. Hence, retreating into smaller government would lift spirits in the private sector – thereby spurring business confidence for a surge of investment that would kick-start recovery. Authoritative naysayers to greater government spending, like John Taylor, a professor of economics at Stanford University, believe that austerity policies, through the narrow path of financial rectitude, will bring about investor confidence for economic growth, which would far outweigh the immediate negative effects of the program cutbacks. It is a matter of "first principles" that retreating into smaller government would give companies the confidence to invest and get the economy going (Taylor 2013). This means there are no "ifs", "ands", or "buts" to it; recovery will follow government cutbacks as certainly as day follows night. In his book *The Debt Bomb* (2012), US Republican senator, Thomas Coburn, in similar vein advocates public spending cutbacks and smaller government as ways to get the private sector going and prevent, among other things, "unimaginable social unrest." Coburn, Taylor and others of their ilk believe that smaller government is better government; growing government limits freedom, including the freedom of enterprise. These considerations inspire affection for cuts to America's entitlement programs (Medicare, Social Security, and Medicaid), as is being done to welfare programs in Britain, Greece, Spain, Italy and other European countries. For the more devoted supporters of reduced government spending, cutbacks to welfare will, apart from denying pork to society's alleged layabouts, deliver growth for a winning trifecta comprising the virtue of debt-free living, the Shangri-la of smaller government, and the joy of economic recovery.

Underpinning the reigning public policy option of austerity is a mix of psychological, sociological, ideological, and religious elements. Evidence that rushing to balance the books is a deep-seated cultural value is found in the view expressed by founding father, Benjamin Franklin, whose image is befittingly depicted on US one hundred dollar bills He is reported to have said that he would rather go to bed without supper than rise in debt.

The lead factors for the belief in austerity are easily identified. Foremost among them is the personal-debt monomania (a mental state that succumbs to intuition by equating personal and government debt) and the allied belief that smaller government is better for the economy. Underpinning the faith in austerity is the trite cliché "no-pain, no-gain" which stems from the biblical exhortation, "Let the righteous smite me; it shall be a kindness" (Psalms 141:5). This means that the moral life is the ascetic life, as was so palpably demonstrated by Italian Saint Francis of Assisi (1181-1226). Accordingly, even a teeth-gritting level of suffering for austerity is worthwhile, if the associated crushing squeeze in the present can make amends for the sin of loose profligacy in the past; the more the pain, the quicker the recovery – self-flagellation being supposedly good for atonement.

Hence, belt-tightening austerity has a sort of religious redemptive quality to it because purification through austerity-caused suffering can bring about the salvation of economic recovery – for a happy ending. This notion automatically renders the idea of greater government spending to get the economy going insufficiently divine – even wickedly Satanic. It gives austerity supporters the status of holy warriors fighting the sinfulness of budget deficits in pursuit of the noble cause of debt-reduction (debt being considered an addictive feel-good drug). In addition, austerity is seen as a means of avoiding visitation by a resented Chinese Santa Clause, whose sleigh is envisaged to be laden with piles of renminbi on the way in, and with stacks of the family silver on the way out.

The combination of these captivating ingredients makes austerity policy the closest thing to a religion for some, engendering in believers a messianic zeal tinged with righteousness. This makes the policy vulnerable to ideology-driven overreach. Fiscal stimulus has to play second fiddle to the more glamorous alternative of fiscal austerity, because fiscal stimulus is perceived to be a lazy and even immoral solution to a difficult problem. Passionate devotion to austerity could consequently make austerity supporters see red at the heresy of government stimulus spending for economic growth, particularly when it causes red ink from government borrowing. While austerity supporters may be disdainfully regarded as myopic ideologues by their critics, the critics can be expected to be contemptuously dismissed as lefty hacks and closet socialists by austerity supporters.

### Austerity: Misplaced Affection

The feverish pursuit of excessive and untimely austerity can make the cure worse than the disease. Supporters of fiscal stimulus would tend to regard austerity slashers as architects of bloodletting who miss the Keynesian macroeconomic big picture; the enchantment of ideology is seen to triumph over the logic of rationality, to cause more harm than good. Narrow policy perspectives that seek to force the pace of recovery through painful austerity could exacerbate the problem and be counterproductive if pushed too far, claim its opponents. One hard lesson from the Great Depression, some assert, is not to jump the gun by trying to get the government budget back into balance too quickly. Ignoring the lesson from the parable of the Great Depression means that the seed sowed has fallen on hard ground.

If the austerity cutbacks fail to trigger the investment surge on which hopes have been pinned, both safety nets and business sales will sag – throwing the economy into reverse. Reining in government spending too fast undermines the working of automatic stabilizers in the economy, like unemployment relief and subsidized housing; they are prevented from performing their intended function of cushioning the effect of the downturn on the private sector by holding-up consumer spending for business sales. In the United States, some two-thirds of the growth in government spending in recent years is attributable to sharply increased welfare measures. In their absence business sales would have fallen, causing pain to economic growth. Automatic stabilizers also reduce reliance on monetary policy, which has a noticeable disposition to let the side down. For these reasons, it is understandable if believers in resurgence through increased government spending regard ill-timed and excessive austerity cutbacks as being tantamount to cutting one's own throat.

Simultaneous austerity in several relevant countries means a loss of salvation from increased export sales – that is, a denial of opportunity to export one's way out of trouble. In other words, revenue from increased foreign sales cannot come to the rescue of firms and people by compensating them for domestic sales lost to austerity cutbacks. Logically, because the recession is worldwide, austerity everywhere would choke off exports; exporters everywhere will suffer and world production fall if the expected investment surge fails to materialize. Even though this possibility is bad, things can, in fact, get worse. Hopes for turnaround will be dashed if the adversity associated with austerity causes market sentiment to slide from gloom toward doom – the precipitated downward spiral in consumer and business confidence propelling economies out of the frying pan of recession and into the fire of depression.

Those seeking recovery through government spending programs would view austerity with a sinking feeling because it is fuller of dreamy hope than proven success. According to critics of the austerity approach, confidence in the austerity policy option is misplaced because blind faith has trumped cold reality. For example, Paul Krugman calls the austerity option "The Confidence Fairy" hoopla (Krugman 2012, 199) because of the allegedly illusory belief that reduced government spending will automatically result in increased business confidence. The belief that reduced government spending through program cutbacks will arouse business confidence sufficient to engender a surge of investment for a spurt of growth is, arguably, only just that – belief in a dogma that may be true in some circumstances but not in others.

On the basis of what is happening on the ground, it seems that what the economy stands to gain from austerity is less obvious than what it stands to lose – the pain is plain and immediate, while the gain is veiled and distant. Doubting Thomases cannot be that far off-beam in their skepticism that austerity as a solution can be fine and dandy, because factual evidence shows it has been cheap and nasty. In other words, the belief that austerity measures will, by reining in government programs, automatically lift business spirits and engender business confidence for galvanizing business investment, can be questioned on the basis of facts that are staring everybody in the face.

The International Monetary Fund (IMF) has raised doubts whether austerity is worth the candle in particular circumstances, and has warned that austerity can sap, rather than invigorate, demand. Although diehard ideologues of all hues have an inclination to rail against the International Monetary Fund (IMF),when they are not laughing at it, they do both at their peril. The IMF reckons that a one dollar cutback in public spending cuts two dollars from total output (GDP), on the assumption that other things remain equal. Additional evidence reported by Paul Krugman bolsters this information: in 173 cases of fiscal austerity studied between 1978 and 2009, IMF researchers found that austerity policies were followed, not by economic growth, but by economic contraction and higher unemployment (Krugman 2012, 199). Hence, the evidence is that austerity, far from engendering growth, actually shrinks the economy. The IMF has warned America against excessive tax increases that would deny the economy steam and advised both the American and British governments to slow down the deficit reduction process (IMF 2012). The same IMF report expressed concern about Spain and other embattled European countries slashing government spending too quickly, stating that prematurely deep cuts would be self-defeating when they deny the economy desperately needed growth for paying off the loans. In Japan, a rise in the consumption tax in 2014 choked demand and precipitated a recession.

In fact, the clammy grip of austerity is noticeably deepening Europe's plight, as some of Europe's economies grow achingly slowly, others grind to a halt, and the rest go into reverse. Over-zealous austerity imposed by lenders on borrowers has several eurozone countries on the ropes, including Greece, Spain, Portugal, Italy and France. Deficit overshoots may be difficult to avoid when deficit-cutting has to be done in the teeth of deepening recession or fierce opposition. Stumbling politicians have engendered rumbling unrest. Deflation, due to chronically weak demand in relation to goods produced in the economy, is a real threat, with prices falling in eight European counties, and the eurozone price surface sinking by 0.7 percent in 2014. It seems that ill-timed and excessive austerity can push wounded eurozone economies into deflationary spirals that lead to the depths of depression (unless money printing amazingly comes to the rescue). This implies that insistence on excessive and untimely fiscal austerity will make flagging economies needlessly weaker, fuel downward price spirals, and increase the chances of default on loans – implying that insistence on austerity could be self-defeating to lenders, as seems to be the case in some European countries.

Politicians prepared to accommodate intemperate financial interests are driven by ideological bias, or play to the gallery out of necessity, often engaging in political histrionics in the process. Dramatic representations from dancing to financiers' tunes are necessitated by the reality that the loans forthcoming will not be large enough unless the austerity accepted is painful enough. It is clear and understandable that financiers would use ceded dignity to influence the budgetary policies of countries that are broke and "in hock." Beggars cannot be choosers, even when the beggars are sovereign nations; several borrowing European governments are arm-twisted by lenders into taking drastic and untimely belt-tightening measures at high social cost, their knuckling under seemingly reflecting an element of bondage. Countries are required to slash their way to recovery, even though onerous loan conditions to debt-laden countries could cause economies to founder, threaten deflation, and foment social unrest, as it is doing in Greece and other European countries.

Financiers can even influence the budgetary policies of sovereign countries that do not have serious debt problems because of the ubiquitous big stick called "credit-rating." The threat of a ratings downgrade is cause for consternation, triggering obsequious responses in worried governments. This curbs the budgetary discretion of all governments sufficiently linked to the international economy through trade and collateral. No doubt economies in trouble have benefited from having lenders of last resort, but it is question of *how* this recently enhanced financial power is used by the modern day merchants of Venice who hold the purse strings.

Because the evidence shows that the belief in austerity can, in some circumstances, fly in the face of reality, it would be over the top to dismiss IMF red-flag waving with scorn. The cold reality is that the IMF warnings are occasioned by a paucity of reasonable arguments in favor of austerity, given the weak record of recovery despite the ballyhoo for austerity (*a la* the eurozone). Ignoring the warning signs risks a situation where the several dangers of austerity mentioned earlier converge synergistically to send affected economies up the proverbial creek.

Timing is everything; like alcohol-drinking for most people, austerity is not for anytime. Austerity is for times of sufficient growth, not stagnation or contraction: first reach escape velocity, only then impose austerity. For austerity to work, austerity cutbacks must strike only when the iron is hot: that is, adopted when economies are heated enough at the upper end of the recovery cycle of growth. An austerity approach enabled Sweden to climb out of a debt hole by pulling itself up by its own bootstraps, but only once growth had reached full swing; synchronization was the secret. According to the opponents of austerity, program cutbacks are unwise when ill-timed and excessive, as it would heap Pelion on Ossa; it would compound the problem by enfeebling already emaciated demand and further undermine the confidence of investors and consumers. And the slide in confidence could precipitate a downward spiral in the economy.

Here is the fiscal stimulus advocates' sermon in a nutshell: One should not bet one's bottom dollar on the expectation that belt-tightening will get the economy going, unless an adequate growth spurt to recovery is already happening; to persist with austerity measures despite signs of worsening conditions, cuts the ground from under the measures. For this reason, austerity before escape velocity involves the anachronistic illogic of putting the cart before the horse.

## 11.4 The Government Spending Path

*The Love of Government Spending*

If austerity supporters are fiscal hawks, then public spending supporters are fiscal doves. As analysts know, government stimulus spending is the other side of the coin and means in essence: Spend your way out of trouble, even if you have to borrow to do so. To the skepticism of austerity supporters, such a view holds that government debt can actually be a solution to a problem caused by debt. Those wanting big government to lavish cash on public programs would regard the candy of fiscal stimulus to be better for the economy's health than the castor oil of austerity. It is believed that the deep pockets of big government will, by means of the stimulus spending injected into the economy, restore luster to a faded economy. This it would do by galvanizing listless demand, lifting business spirits, eliciting investment, creating jobs, sparking off multiplier effects for growth, and keeping deflation at bay. It is believed that pursuing such an expansionary fiscal stimulus option would provide breathing space for the private sector to repair its impaired balance sheets. The brisk demand actuated by the fiscal stimulus option can also be seen as a way of lubricating a cranky credit market for secondary benefit.

Hence, government stimulus spending for reigniting growth is a soft option. It places politicians in the happy position of being able to walk and chew gum at the same time, by reconciling succor (welfare) with prosperity (recovery). Fans of the fiscal stimulus option are inclined to throw out as balderdash the moralistic Judeo-Christian belief that there can be no gain without pain; after all, one person's debt is another person's asset. Not suffering pangs of conscience from the blasphemy of rejecting the concept of necessary pain believed in by allegedly heartless austerity supporters, public spending supporters point out that the fiscal stimulus option can be self-financing. That would be so when the government expenditures for stimulus spending come from money saved through cutbacks to programs such as unemployment and poverty relief, the need for which falls as growth rises.

Like manna from heaven, the ramped-up government spending is expected by its supporters to be capable of providing benefits for everyone. According to public spending supporters, with the economy weak and borrowing cheap, it makes sense to boost America's public infrastructure spending that is at a twenty-year low. Private sector activity is not likely to pick up the slack because banks have shied away from lengthy lending (because of Basel 3 rules). Targeting the government's money at those in the general community who will spend most of what they get (that is, those with a high marginal propensity to consume), enables pump priming for down-to-earth measures that are close and personal. Improvements to schools, more college aid, better highways, restored parks, more police officers etc would be a different kettle of fish to the previous large-scale pump-priming exercise with a bad reputation called "bailouts." Such expenditures could restore what has been lost, given that the US Bureau of Labor Statistics reports that over seven hundred thousand teachers, fire fighters, and other public officers have been laid off since the crisis hit. The process is believed to be associated with key triumphs in terms of increased business activity, reduced unemployment, improvements to human capital, and the diminished threat of deflation. The expectation by supporters is that the spending by these immediate beneficiaries of government stimulus money will engender spin-off multiplier effects that enable the revitalized growth in the economy to produce enough revenue to pay-off the government debt. Or so it is hoped.

One way of inducing recovery in current circumstances is by the government spending cash that businesses have hoarded. The stash of cash is preventing today's saving from funding tomorrow's growth – the stinginess implying wasted capital, forfeited earning for savers, and a stymied recovery. The evidence is that businesses in America and Europe are holding on to a mountainous cash stock-pile estimated to be in the region of $3 trillion, because they are spooked by a gloomy future. Nobel Prize-winning economist Paul Krugman has a suggestion about what to do with all the money that is being squirreled away under bulging mattresses instead of being used to rev up GDP. In his *End This Depression Now* (2012), Krugman argues that government should put the wasted capital to good use by borrowing and spending it; he says it won't be a tragedy if the government debt continues to grow from spending idle money, as long as it grows more slowly than the sum of inflation and economic growth; "we won't ever have to pay off the debt" (Krugman 2012, 141-2). Since cajoling companies into making their own investments has not worked, borrowing and spending the stockpile to stimulate economic growth is expected to do the trick. Such action, instead of causing public debt to hit the roof as many suppose, is said to auto-matically dissipate the debt problem – get enough growth going and, "Abracadabra," no debt problem. This position is consistent with the view of another Nobel-prize winner, Joseph Stiglitz, who says that modern macroeconomics calls for expansionary monetary and fis-cal policies in the face of an economic downturn (Stiglitz 2010, xvi). Such expert supporters of public spending are looking for a proper second bite at the fiscal stimulus cherry, one that is large enough to shock an inert economy into reaching escape velocity, this time by directly bailing out the public, rather than firms.

Lending color to the argument is that government-spending stimulus can buy time for additional opportunities to be harnessed – an alleged spin-off feature that further justifies a relaxed attitude toward the urge to splurge. When the opportunities for structural and institutional reform are grasped as the economy takes off, it is believed the ensuing improvements will provide the traction needed to sustain the initial growth spurt through an ongoing business cycle upswing. In principle, all types of reform are very much easier to introduce when the economy is growing rapidly than when it is stagnant or in the teeth of crises, and that raises hopes for reforming even the absurdly labyrinthine US tax system. Mexico is a recent case in point. A slug of deficit spending has finally begun to register there, shoring up support for ambitious reforms. For supporters of public spending, the above package of potential benefits makes the case for fiscal stimulus persuasive and pressing, offering hope to the cheesed-off "99 percent."

Cutting taxes provides a means of stimulating the economy into growth, but for those in the know it is a raggedly poor relation when it comes to igniting weak demand. Tax cuts are intuitively appealing to those who dislike big government. They ensure a taxpayer-determined pattern of growth: the taxpaying public with more money in its pockets from the tax cuts will get to decide which sectors will expand, not the allegedly repulsive hand of government. The tax-cut option is obviously not relevant to people like the underemployed and pensioners, whose incomes are too low to be taxed. Because the higher the income the greater the benefit from tax cuts, it would be bad news for growth prospects if those with more discretionary income from tax cuts, tuck most of it away as savings instead of buying things. Lower-income people getting smaller tax cuts would be inclined to spend every penny that came their way because of their strapped circumstances, whereas high-income people getting the larger tax cuts and already sitting pretty would be more inclined to save most of it. Empirical studies show that the well-off people (who get the greater tax cuts), will spend the least of it and save the most of it. Tax cuts imposed by George W. Bush are reported to have provided only limited stimulus to the US economy (Stiglitz 2013, 110). The paucity of benefits to overall demand from tax cuts compared with direct public spending dilutes the raison d'être of the exercise: to boost demand. Obviously, government choices for stimulation through public spending would engender a different pattern of growth than if the stimulation were left to the beneficiaries of tax cuts. For example, the government focus might be on spending money on infrastructure like school buildings and roads, while if the stimulation was made through tax cuts, luxury car production might be the sector stimulated instead.

### Government Spending: Misplaced Affection

Looking closer, the fiscal stimulus option is no magic bullet. Although it provides hope, its seemingly virtuous cycle does not deserve unbridled optimism for the reason that it comes in a bundle accommodating both joy and risk. It seems a case of "you spends your money and you takes your chances."

An immediate difficulty is that advocates of the government spending option see cabbage as cauliflower and optimistically seek a free-market solution from a pseudo-market condition. This means faith is being placed in a dysfunctional market mechanism for the delivery of recovery that requires a properly functioning market mechanism. The question arises as to the extent to which the plutocratic titans of pseudo-markets are the jokers in the pack. They are likely to be a source of unpredictability for the success of the stimulatory exercise since it would be out of character for plutocrats to be cheerful about threats to their gravy trains. It appears that Keynesian macroeconomists generally fail to consider the inhibiting effects of structural factors (e.g., monopolies and multinationals) and institutional factors (e.g., political arm-twisting by big business and business corruption), when making conventional policy prescriptions, like stimulatory public spending. They focus on the whole economy but strangely neglect its component parts and underpinning aspects. Can the expected market solutions emerge from plutocratic pseudo-markets with their anti-competitive and anti-social traits? The information in chapter 9 explained why the answer to this question is firmly in the negative.

When public spending stimulates economic growth, the question that jumps out is: growth for whom? What prevents the loaf of stimulus-induced growth from landing on the dining table of plutocrats in pseudo-markets, leaving only the crumbs that fall off the table for the benefit of dynamic firms that operate in open competitive sectors that are the bigger job creators? But the perils go beyond a lack of effectiveness to counter productiveness: what will prevent the new government spending from growing and entrenching the very plutocratic pseudo-market condition that is a major impediment to recovery? The explanation in chapter 9 is that it is not farfetched or scaremongering to claim that stimulus money spent to achieve recovery can end up preventing it. It was shown why and how the growth of the plutocratic pseudo-market condition tightens the noose around firms in open competitive sectors, causing such sectors to be shrinking pools. By fostering the pseudo-market condition, fiscal stimulus can be expected to have a pervasively numbing effect on the authentic recovery process, spoil the investment climate in competitive sectors, and entrench fallen living standard. That means it can be tragically self-defeating.

Moreover, there is sobering evidence of a bifurcation between the performance of private businesses and the performance of national economies, with businesses able to prosper within countries that flounder. To what extent will policy measures meant to increase business profitability translate into national prosperity in the home country, if the increased investment attributable to the stimulus spending takes place in a foreign country? That means, of course, the investment is lost to the domestic economy because capital takes flight to salubrious foreign climes. This happens when it is pushed by high taxes, cramping regulations, anemic domestic demand, and the chill of deflation on the one hand, and lured by warm foreign welcomes and bright prospects, on the other. A company doing better as a result of the stimulus might have greater motivation to shift its base abroad by merging with a foreign partner in a lower tax country, as is actually happening (reported in chapter 8)–the hightailing being associated with a leakage of capital, growth, and tax revenue.

The more ideologically inclined may ask what the benefits of growth would be for the so-called "99 percent." What is to prevent well-off people from getting better off because the lion's share of stimulus spending benefits fall into the laps of the lucky "one percent," as in the past? Lest we forget, there is a record of habitual arrogation: in the five years preceding the collapse, 90 percent of income gain in the US flowed to 1 percent of households and the household incomes of the majority barely moved. The stimulus-induced investment enables Western companies to prosper, but the cars, televisions, and vacations are purchased by *nouveau-riche* foreigners or affluent locals, as growth benefits flow to foreign countries, the well-off local minority, and into the pockets of shareholders, many of them foreigners. In the post crisis period, the distribution of the benefits of recovery continues to be skewed. In fact, inequality between the "haves" and "have-nots" is said to be increasing (e.g., Stiglitz 2013; Stockman 2013). In Portugal attempts at igniting flagging demand through increased consumer spending produced little growth and few benefits for its citizens (although there may be special reasons for the disappointment).

These considerations deny the public spending option the infallibility it might seem to have at first glance, especially because plutocrats in pseudo-markets are not known to be a particularly altruistic bunch. Hence, the overarching question is whether the pseudo nature of markets would seriously undermine or dilute the efficacy of the fiscal stimulus option, because of the ability of dominant firms in plutocratic pseudo-markets to suck profits away from open competitive sectors, engage in rent seeking, and generally inhibit recovery in the various ways identified in chapter 9. While accepting that, for the most part, definite answers to these overlapping questions are not known, the questions may be disturbing enough to put an *a priori* damper on the government stimulus spending option.

A whole lot of eggs are being placed in the "sustainable recovery" basket. The critics of fiscal stimulus see in it, besides the sin of debt, a deceptive primrose path, proceeding along which provides initial pleasure from worldly ease but leads to pain further down the track. This is because those advocating stimulus spending are, apart from advocating bigger government that is offensive to many, counting on a resurgence that is large and long enough to cope with a future where debt is up and hoardings down. In other words, stimulus based on debt is a contingent solution; it mortgages the future on the assumption that it fuels rapid and sustained recovery, while downplaying the risks of ephemeral growth based on the mushiness of debt in dysfunctional plutocratic pseudo-market circumstances. And that is besides the bothersome unknowns that threaten from across the pond, European precariousness being a wild card. If matters do not work out as expected, the economic problem could end up being bigger than before. Although a government never needs default in a currency that it prints, being more in the red could make the public debt burden harder to bear if growth falls short of expectations. That said, these killjoy considerations should not be regarded as vindicating manna from heaven by austerity supporters. The pitfalls along the austerity path are no less deep, as previously explained and elaborated on in the analysis that follows.

## 11.5 Loggerheads and Conundrums

It would be understandable if the crowded canvas of arguments presented gives the impression that economic policy is unfathomable – "an enigma wrapped up in a riddle" (to borrow an expression from British historian and politician, Winston Churchill). Is business waiting for opportunity (from fiscal stimulus), or is opportunity waiting for business (denied by big government)? Shockingly, for each side of the policy divide, the solution is the problem: government spending is the problem for austerity supporters whereas austerity is the problem for stimulus spending supporters. As a result, what is reprehensible for one side is laudable for the other. Clearly, the dichotomy embodies both a moral and economic dilemma. Fiscal stimulus is seen as the "idol of the tribe" of Keynesian macroeconomists by austerity supporters, and *vice versa*, each regarding the other as fixated on insane or deceptive beliefs and wanting to knock the others' allegedly ignorant delusions on the head.

Although the difference of opinion between those touting public spending cutbacks and those touting public spending increases are poles apart, the gap is more than just a chasm. This is because, although the conflicting views seek the common ends of generating private sector activity for recovery and getting the country's finances on the path of financial rectitude, they are contradictory to the point of being mutually exclusive. Consequently, trying to impose a coherent structure on a policy package containing both options does not make sense because of a cancelling-out effect. It is impossible to reconcile the contending flanks of economic opinion; one or the other must prevail completely for rationality to triumph over nonsense.

Understandably, there is a struggle for policy ascendency, with hardball being the only game in town. Each side sees a beam in the other's eye, resulting in inevitable confrontation, each defending their supposedly impeccable stance with a cocksureness that leaves little room for compromise. The perpetual squabbling by politicians at loggerheads is caused at least partly by the need to go to the mat for their secret corporate sponsors in plutocratic pseudo-markets. Debate becomes useless in a situation where conflicting wavelengths give rise to a dialogue of the deaf.

In a world where austerity values are dominant, the policy option of government stimulus spending tends to get strangled at birth. Those on the influential austerity bandwagon presently ruling the roost cause the policy option of further government borrowing to cure a problem caused by government borrowing to be rejected out of hand because, apart from being immoral (debt is sinful) it appears to compound the problem (debt begets debt). The counter-intuitive nature of the public spending option based on debt, makes it easy for austerity supporters to poke holes in it, especially when debt is likened to a feel-good drug. It is understandable that austerity supporters would look down their noses at fiscal stimulus support-ers, seeing them as debt addicts unable to kick the borrowing habit. Antagonism based on these intuitively appealing arguments makes the fiscal stimulus option a heretical non-starter – a lost cause with pariah status.

We might ask: "which way madness lies?" (to quote Shakespeare in *King Lear*). The ironic, even laughable, situation arises of two sides crossing swords with adversarial vim, working at cross purposes, yet desiring the same sacrosanct end of stimulating business activity. If one believes that the *losing* solution that supports *increased* public spending will likely *win* the recovery, it must logically follow that the *winning* solution that supports *reduced* public spending will likely *lose* the recovery (especially because of looming deflation). Perplexed observers should be excused for fearing they might be going mad.

Okay, let's unravel the conundrum. Although the reason for such antithetical solutions to the same problem may be hard to understand, it is not too hard to pinpoint: is the evidently weak private sector activity due *primarily* to too much *government* or too little *demand*? The answer to the "government versus demand" bone of contention lies in the different beliefs that underpin the respective views. On the one hand, supporters of increased public spending want the government to galvanize collapsed demand and stimulate subdued economic growth. This means that there is a lack of private sector activity and government must take up the slack. On the other hand, supporters of reduced public spending want the government to intervene less so that the private sector could gain the confidence to undertake activity that is crowded out by too much government intervention. This means, obstructive government should get out of the way, stop hampering and harassing business, and let the private sector get on with its essential task of investment for economic growth.

What side do the facts support? The answer will determine which policy, if any, is better able to place the economy on the road to sustainable recovery. Since the choice requires choosing one option over the other, do the available facts take the shine off a winning policy position of austerity by buttressing the losing position of fiscal stimulus? If so, it means that the medicine of austerity is being poured down the throats of sick economies allergic to austerity that need, instead, the therapy of fiscal stimulus for revival. This condemns the patient to a gloomy prognosis for recovery. If the fiscal stimulus medicine turns out to be inappropriate, a similar fate awaits the hapless patient. On way out is to recognize the hopes and risks in each of the policy options and reach the cowardly conclusion that neither policy should be completely reassuring to its supporters or alarming to its opponents. Understandably, this position is neither here nor there and smacks of copout. But this need not be the case if the difficulty is squarely faced i.e., there is thinking outside the box. This is what the rest of the book is about.

## 11.6 Policy Caricature: Sink or Swim

*Taking Stock*

Ranging one's gaze over the disconcerting macroeconomic policy scene reveals a choice between sinking and swimming, but only in familiar waters that are badly polluted. (The options in fresh, unfamiliar, waters are examined in the following section.) The sink-or-swim choices for the public are examined in the context of implementing the two fiscal policy options for getting business activity going within the existing scheme of things, assuming that monetary policy has been done to death. The effect of the fiscal policy measures in battling the recession will depend, on the one hand, on the components comprising the domestic policy package adopted (i.e., endogenous factors) and, on the other, on policy omissions and commissions in other countries (i.e., exogenous factors).

A misstep on the macroeconomic tightrope from adopting the wrong option is presumed to precipitate a headlong fall into the abyss of severe depression. The following caricatured scenarios in relation to the US economy are designed to throw light on the large element of uncertainty associated with both sets of policies. They expose the vulnerability of the policies to brittle assumptions that can easily make them go from the sublime to the ridiculous.

*The Sink Scenarios*

The economy could abruptly sink because the particular fiscal macroeconomic policy option pursued (austerity or stimulus) has the opposite effect to that intended, and the threats from several wild cards (domestic and foreign) actually come to pass.

How might austerity sink the economy? The dogged pursuit of austerity (featuring major public spending cutbacks and tax hikes) is ill-timed. It clobbers demand in an economy already on the ropes (the monetary options assumed to be ineffectual), to sink the economy through choice. The large government spending cutbacks cause already flagging demand to sink still lower, in turn dragging down business sales, profits, jobs, public revenue – and aggravating the problem it is meant to alleviate. The supremacy of plutocratic pseudo-markets in key sectors of the economy causes most of the adversity from austerity cutbacks to fall on the more competitive sectors of the economy, with successive bouts of austerity drastically shrinking that sector. This smothers competitiveness in those dynamic parts of the economy associated with vibrancy, productivity, and employment, and expands the rent seeking pseudo-market sectors associated with plodding listlessness.

From the standpoint of austerity opponents, austerity devotees, by ignoring the mistakes of history, are condemned to repeat them; the austerity option is doomed to fail for the reason that it clings to hope based on the enchantment of ideology. It flies in the face of macroeconomic theory fashioned by the reality of the Great Depression, recent empirical evidence from the IMF, and chilling deflationary signs. Therefore, proceeding down the path of excessive-cum-untimely austerity leads to a deep hole into which the economy proceeds to sink.

How might fiscal stimulus sink the economy? The public spending for priming the pump is huge. The debt-funded stimulus injection induces an initial boost in demand that triggers an economic growth sprint. But the stimulus effect soon fizzles out, causing economic growth to taper off and fall below expectations. The induced boost to economic growth is not as sustained as expected for several reasons. For one thing, most of the stimulus benefits flow to the parts of the economy dominated by behemoth mega-firms showing distinct signs of a zombie from pseudo-market disincentives to vibrancy, initiative, and drive. The plutocrats in pseudo-market firms that are global giants flex their rent seeking muscles to pocket most of the stimulus benefits as they are so used to doing, leaving only the residual crumbs for stimulating the vast majority of the economy where the "99 percent" live. For another, most of the stimulus benefits go to India, Indonesia, China and other developing countries where prospects are brighter, enriching societies in those countries at the expense of domestic societies in the West. Moreover, the absence of badly needed structural and institutional reforms (blocked by plutocratic vested interests), denies the stimulated short-term growth the traction needed for long-term sustainability, leaving a debt burden greater than before. These factors will cause the economy to sink into the abyss of a double-dip depression, this one much deeper than the previous one because of the deadweight of greater government debt.

The concluding assessment on the "sink scenario" is this: it will happen if the policy option adopted is the wrong one i.e., if austerity is adopted when it should have been government spending, or if government spending is adopted when it should have been austerity. A wrong choice will mean that the economy's number is up and that the collapse that was waiting to happen will actually happen. When it does it will be no accident, because the hard lessons of economics and experience would have been ignored; the disastrous outcome will be the cumulative result of more bad decisions on top of previous blunders. This is besides the European wild card, a European economic collapse being the deathblow to hopes of a genuine US recovery, irrespective of the policy choice.

*The Swim Scenarios*

How might things go swimmingly with austerity? A policy of austerity cuts a swath through government programs and peps-up the economy for a virtuous circle. Because of the now smaller government,
business confidence gets a joyous boost and the lifted business spirits
motivate a surge in business investment for galvanizing growth. The
boosted buying and hiring by revitalized businesses puts money in the
pockets of the public, for a surge in consumer spending. The oomph
to overall demand from the combined investment and consumption
pizzazz sees everyone enthused and animal spirits racing. Bingo:
there is a brisk clip to the nirvana of economic recovery. As implied,
the suffocating effects of austerity are far outweighed by the vibrancy,
drive, and initiative in the private sector, whose reinvigorated activity
powers the economy into creating jobs, increasing company earnings,
and enhancing community wellbeing.

How might things go swimmingly with fiscal stimulus? Fiscal stimulus involves taking the plunge to swim with the current of Keynesian
macroeconomic policy in the belief that the virtuous circle is not a
whirlpool. This approach generates a burst of government spending
to get the economy going great guns. In current circumstances, this
means borrowing and spending idle money on infrastructure programs
like roads and social capital programs like education. This approach, a
pump-priming shot in the arm for a listless economy, cures the lethargy
by boosting investor and consumer spirits. Such exuberance by market
players perks up subdued demand, which boosts the overall economy
through spin-off multiplier effects. Bingo: there is a brisk clip to the
nirvana of economic recovery. The fiscal stimulus is self-financing to
the extent that it saves government expenditure on unemployment
and poverty relief, which would be less needed. This option gets the
economy back into the swing of things.

Is the swim scenario a cure or snare? The secret to valid recovery depends on choosing the winning policy solution. Picking the correct option is assumed to make things go swimmingly – thereby enabling the public to revel in Eldorado conditions they thought had gone for good. Economic growth at escape velocity from either policy will make much-needed structural and institutional reforms easier. The icing on the cake would be if Europe, by copycatting the same smart policy option and associated reforms, rebounds astonishingly, for spiraling mutual benefits in America and Europe. Pseudo-market firms with zombie quirks reform themselves: they go from being rent-seeking, plodding, free-riders to paragons of dynamic efficiency, exuding a new-found effervescence for powering the economy onward based on marvelous technological advances in every field of human endeavor.

*Conclusion on Both Scenarios*
It is time to wake up, smell the coffee – and get real.

## 11.7 The Devil and the Deep Blue Sea
*Underwhelming Choices*
In the light of the above mind-boggling policy scenarios it would be understandable if bewildered policymakers have been put on the spot, being caught between the devil and the deep blue sea. Being of two minds is an understandably nervous predicament for policymakers faced with having to take the plunge while tied up in knots by the vexing issues posed by confusing policy choices. With fiscal policy alternatives that are as broad as they are long, many thinking policymakers could be at their wits end not being able to make heads or tails of the complex situation. The ambiguity of the economic problem, which makes solutions as clear as mud, have put many pragmatic policymakers at sea, looking for a port in the storm. Such a port is not to be found because they have been looking in the wrong places, as will

soon become apparent. The more astute policymakers would understandably be reluctant to bet the farm on policies that have repeatedly sent them on wild goose chases in search of real recovery. The ideological types, unwittingly caught in the cobweb of misconception from fixed beliefs, have confidence from blind spots that make complex issues crystal clear. This enables a manic approach to policy formulation that can make big mistakes seem like patriotic brownie points (*a la*, financial deregulation). For all types of policymakers there is ample food for thought, as they mull over the mismatch between the weakness of the policy tools available and the hardness of the nut needing to be cracked.

There are reasons to worry because the proof of the policy pudding is in the eating. Predictability, although crucial, is alarmingly scanty; the winning policy is a toss-up in *ex-ante* terms, because the policies do not come with clever algorithms that define their effects prior to implementation. It cannot be known in advance which side will win the argument and which policy will succeed, as each policy requires the test of experience to enable wisdom from hindsight. This means that the acid test of policy success (a robust and inclusive recovery in the American-cum-European conglomerate) can be known only in retrospect after waiting to see which way the cat jumps, given that austerity and public spending are united in aim but at cross purposes in implementation. Moreover, each is supposed to work despite the existence of dysfunctional pseudo-markets run by plutocrats, who are the unacknowledged jokers in the pack. Consequently, for policymakers facing contradictory options in unprecedented circumstances, there is no way of knowing in advance whether austerity or public spending is the real McCoy. Moreover, such uncertainty comes with a high penalty for error: backing the wrong option will send economies up the proverbial creek, where waits the grim reaper for big-time national misery.

If neither treatment suits the ailment, the convalescent economy could sicken again, and even slip into an incurable coma. Conventional policy options have proven too crude to make the current disease of economic lethargy properly succumb to usual treatment. Given that monetary policy is a disappointment because of its feeble record in improving the real economy, the question arises as to what else can be done if both budgetary options of austerity and public spending are doomed to fail. Although both sides assure the public that their policy approach holds the solution, it is likely that the economy is being torn by disagreements that are irrelevant to the main game (analogous in Aristotelian terms to children fighting over toys). It takes a lot of faith to believe that damp squib policies of the past can fire up lethargic real economies into resurgence in the future. The policy question is a "Riddle of the Sphinx"–the wrong policy answer will destroy the perpetrator in the ruthless fashion of Greek mythology.

It is understandable if things seem up in the air within the square to which current policy is confined. Conventional policy measures of whatever type (the devils we know), come from decrepit play-books of times past. Although they enable policymakers to stay within their comfort zones and avoid rocking the socioeconomic boat, the evidence shows that their effects in bringing about a turnaround in the real economy are dismayingly underwhelming; a string of disappointing statistics on economic fundamentals, the weak resurgence in open competitive sectors, a shrinking middle class, and the plight of the lagging majority in the real economy, combine to stir a healthy skepticism. It seems time to accept the reality that for achieving a robust and inclusive recovery, the conventional policy pathway is a blind alley.

Where's the beef? It does not seem to be found within the existing policy space; it seems the solution is something else entirely. A polarized economic policy means that the science of economics is not at ease with itself. For all their expertise, even seasoned economists are scratching their heads in bafflement at what is happening, and they are diametrically opposed on solutions.

Could it be that the answer to this stubborn problem lies outside the bounds of orthodox economics (and out of reach of conventional macroeconomic policy)? After all, if central banks can print large amounts of money without generating inflation, something is happening that seems incompletely understood. The stock market breaks a score of record highs, but the trumpeted recovery bypasses the majority. Then there is suffocating austerity that, instead of instilling much vaunted investor confidence, threatens deflation. Let us not overlook the impotence of a zero nominal interest rate that confounds economic logic by failing to adequately bolster investor borrowing. And to draw attention to something not remembered fondly, the public stimulus spending benefits were arrogated by plutocratic pseudo-market interests to the exclusion of firms in open competitive sectors and the majority in the real economy. Adding to policy progress studded with such deviancy is the failure of markets to behave true to form and enforce the penalty of customer loss on businesses that deceived customers. Generally, things seem out of whack when, despite repeated feisty attempts over more than seven years to galvanize the real economy into durable recovery using conventional policy options, economic performance falls well short of being a resounding success. If policymakers have not made the grade, it will not be for want of trying.

Granted the failure of the market mechanism to deliver to expectations due to the convergence of reasons cited, the crucial question, then, is this: for how long more can one bank on an economics that has lost much of its explanatory power? Logic suggests that the scope of the current problem could well transcend economic orthodoxy. It could mean that Mother Hubbard's economic policy cupboard for dealing with this crisis is bare, and that policymakers have precious little room for maneuver within the existing scheme of things. Because there is not much else on the runway, it means the public must grin and bear the hit-or-miss approach to compulsive economic policy practice based on shaky principles and flawed assumptions. An economics blinkered by (*ceteris paribus*) assumptions ignores dysfunctional plutocratic pseudo-market conditions and impaired sociopolitical institutions. In other words, the signs are that the West's fate seems sealed irrespective of the known macroeconomic policy option implemented within the existing scheme of things.

Textbook solutions cannot work when much of what they assume have been overtaken by underpinning events and given rise to a seemingly unbridgeable rift between principle and practice. Within the current setup, which accepts market structures and institutions as given, all conventional policy options seem capable of surprising its practitioners by having the opposite of the desired effect – and sooner or later pushing Western economies into the abyss of indefinite depression. This means, rather than offering policymakers a way out of their troubles, economics presents new ones all its own. If true, it means that a backfiring economics is in credibility-sapping shambles. The pathetic plight of economics is explained by the discipline becoming undisciplined for the reasons stated in chapter 7.

Fresh thinking is, therefore, required; the retribution from past bad decisions has hobbled future action, and "fresh fields and pastures new" (John Milton 1608-1674) are not visible from within the policy box to which policymakers are confined. A markedly different structural-cum-institutional situation cries out for new perspectives with regard to policy. It is hard to see how even with the best will in the world, conventional policies that assume properly functioning markets (i.e., markets that are effectively open and competitive) can work well, or at all, when what exists are dysfunctional markets of the plutocratic and phony sort. Expecting conventional policies to work in the mare's nest of pseudo-market conditions is illusory of sustainable recovery; shifting between conventional policies in such conditions would seem like rearranging the deck chairs on the Titanic.

Escaping the tight situation tests policymakers' mettle, as it requires breaking with policy orthodoxy to think outside the box. Such thinking is expected to open the eyes of policymakers to the elephant in the room that needs to be tamed. If policymakers are not to be in a fix, their attitude would need to change from regarding the pseudo-market matter as something that is beside the point to something that is central to the issue. There is an urgent need for the standard mold used for shaping current economic policy to be radically recast if policymakers are to avoid continuing to put their foot in it (as they are presently doing). When looked at in the cold light of day, it becomes obvious that breaking the overworked mold cannot happen without shattering policy insight that comes from thinking outside the box – thereby hitting on the stark reality that hope for salvation lies in fixing broken capitalist market foundations.

### Breaking the Mold

As implied, getting nowhere with the present unimaginative policy options should not come as a surprise. If the problem seems as confounding as a Greek crossword puzzle, it is because policymakers are looking for solutions in the wrong places. The unresponsiveness of the problem to conventional policy measures for the majority in the real economy speaks volumes on this. The clear message is that policymakers should stop trying to get blood out of a turnip or stone.

To avoid being stuck for ideas, policymakers need to look for answers in places where they have not looked before. With some luck, the present practice of repeatedly trying the same hackneyed measures will phase out, as the still-small voice of reason gains increasing audibility. A loud-enough voice of reason could, by concentrating minds, bring about a change of heart in relation to policy. Then, policymakers inspired by insight could think outside the box to bring new wisdom to bear on the stubborn economic problem. Wiser policymakers, realizing the limitations of current policy options, would want to look deeper at underlying factors – specifically, at the foundations of the market. It may finally dawn on the now perspicacious policymakers that what they considered were swans (i.e., effectively competitive open markets) are really geese (i.e., recovery-inhibiting plutocratic pseudo-markets). This dichotomy means they are not spoiled for choice; there is only one way to skin the cat.

The only way out of the impasse is for policymakers to go back to the drawing board, hark back to times past, and make no bones about a return to basics through fundamental reforms. This would enable clear thinking for a bold solution beyond muttered disapproval, the odd flourish in favor of the free market, or half-hearted tinkering at the edges. The "big ask," currently in cold storage, would require policymakers to take up courage in both hands and reach with a will for the key to true recovery: the expansion of effectively competitive open markets and the concurrent curtailment of plutocratic pseudo-markets. The radical revamping from the paradigm shift in policy can be expected to give backbone to the limp recovery process. Only once policymakers confront the reality that what is required is nothing less than major renovations to dilapidated capitalist market foundations, would it be possible to save capitalism from the capitalists. As a result, the rent seeking languid sorts lose pride of place and opportunity would be created for durable recovery through entrepreneurial drive in the real economy. The logical deduction: finding a way out of the woods of recession and into the sunlight of recovery will take visionary leadership with nerves of steel to fit the bill.

That would require politicians who can lead change, not just respond to it. Without policymakers taking the bit between their teeth for fundamental reforms (to curtail plutocratic pseudo-markets and expand effectively competitive open markets), there can be no projected end to the current problem – implying that the current condition would then be like eczema: it can only be managed, never cured. The goal of knocking the malformed market mechanism into shape to get open competitive markets has hope because belief in free markets is political glue; it is a universal common ground that plays well across the political spectrum and transcends the bitter divergence of opinion on policy options.

Alas, while broad agreement on the policy goal suggests easy adoption, it will not be like pushing at an open door. The task of dismantling pseudo-markets is unlikely to be on the "to-do" list of plutocrats, and asking nicely will not do. For plutocratic pseudo-market firms accustomed to plenty, cutbacks will be a hard sell; resistance from such vested interests is a sure thing, as oligarchs are not likely to take the threat to their fiefdoms lying down. The prospects for a new dawn are assessed in the final chapters that follow, while recognizing that even the doughtiest of policymakers is not likely to jump for joy at the prospect of facing down plutocrats.

## 11.8 Conclusion: Policy Obsolescence

It would be naïve to expect policies to be relevant forever – that is, not have "use by" (expiration) dates. Recovery in the West stumbles but faith in conventional policy does not wane; there are no strong signs of recognition that all conventional policy options (austerity, public spending, and monetary policy) arc incapable of having more than scant impact in novel conditions. Policy fatigue has yet to kick in even though current policies have not succeeded in doing more than nibble at the problem, the weight of evidence from low-end results not evincing admission of defeat. Dogged commitment to usual policy is based on the questionable assumption that the problem to be dealt with is a mechanical one, and that using past templates for recovery by numbers will work in new misunderstood conditions – making faith in more of the same seem curiously arcane. In fact, the usual measures bespeak ineffectiveness; they seem more a distraction than a solution. The obliviousness is arguably attributable to insidious market conditions never before experienced in either degree or kind.

Contrary to accepted wisdom, it seems that all conventional policy measures, of whatever type, are associated with outcomes where success is a surprise. The pillars holding up the current set of economic policy measures have been exposed as being dangerously decrepit. One crumbling pillar is the assumption that markets, being open competitive markets, will work like before to deliver real recovery as a result of an inevitable upswing in the business cycle. This seems a pipe dream because of the absence of a run-of-the-mill recession; the upswing in the business cycle would need to defy gravity because of the albatross of the plutocratic pseudo-market condition. The second pillar, also rather shaky, is the assumption that policy measures that bring about increased profitability in pseudo-market firms will automatically result in increased social prosperity. This would be about half right; the theoretical and empirical evidence available indicates that while the former expectation of increased company profitability may be true, the latter expectation that greater social prosperity automatically follows is boldly presumptuous. The third tottering pillar is the assumption that conventional policy measures (austerity, public spending, and monetary policy), are capable of engendering a turnaround in the real economy despite the dysfunction of markets in key sectors, particularly in the financial sector. This assumption has been shown to be highly questionable.

The success of conventional policies depends on the heroic assumption that investor and consumer confidence, now down in the dumps, will rise to the occasion despite being weighed down by the albatross of dysfunctional plutocratic pseudo-markets in America and Europe. These conditions underpin several uncontrollable wild cards, both domestic and foreign, that are already sapping confidence by simply revealing their ominous existence. The tightfistedness of consumers and investors is irrefutable proof of uncertainty, if not fear of the future. As manipulative pseudo-markets increasingly take center stage in economies, and open competitive sectors get increasingly marginalized, markets will experience less transparency and, therefore, more uncertainty. The greater uncertainty due to the increased stealth and opaqueness in markets (from practices associated with monopolization, globalization, politicization, and corruption), would likely further reduce confidence in the future. Apart from these confidence-sapping considerations, the pressures for short-termism – including from the lending preferences of banks – will truncate corporate planning horizons and add to longer term uncertainty.

What is more, uncertainty and opaqueness could increase because conventional macroeconomic policies were shown to be capable of giving a fillip to mergers and acquisitions (see chapter 9). A drastically changed market landscape, due to the proliferation of transnational mega-firms through acquisitions and mergers, would enable anti-recovery pseudo-market firms to gather strength and make the outlook cloudier still. Because profits would more assuredly come from orange-squeezing than from efficiency, productivity, and innovation, conventional government policy measures are fraught with danger. The policies, by toughening the rent seeking hand of plutocrats in pseudo-markets, could become recipes for oligopolistic gamesmanship, not economic growth. If so, they would cast a discouraging shadow over firms in open competitive markets and bring little comfort for the majority in the real economy. Also, because investors currently favor the brighter lights in finance over the dimmer options in the real economy, investment that is spurred by conventional economic policies would end up ramping up stock and house prices more than job numbers and household incomes for the majority.

The believers in conventional policy daringly assume that the trenchant uncertainty from Rumsfeldian "known unknowns" will turn out to be nothing but good news, despite current indications to the contrary. On the US domestic front, public confidence is plagued by the uncertainty of the annual budgetary process and other political unknowns (in particular, whether adequate structural and institutional reforms are possible). To top it off, there is the European wild card. A proper, genuine, and sustainable American recovery would be pie-in-the-sky if Europe fails to rise up and pull its weight. The present indications are that Europe's anemic economies will be a drag on American economic recovery irrespective of the conventional policy option adopted. The specters of sovereign debt default and a euro-zone breakup were previously recognized as swords of Damocles overhanging the American economy in particular and the world economy in general. These threats can in the end be traced to confidence-subverting pseudo-market traits that are capable of administering the coup de grâce to the viability of all policies in vogue.

Chasing tails by keeping faith with failed policies proves that old habits die hard. While conceding full marks for trying, even a pathetic record of repeated failure over seven grinding years has failed to put conventional policymakers off their unflinching strides. Money printing is arguably only a sop to the real economy. As there are no signs of a requiem chorus for failed policy, more of the same has an air of inevitability about it. If policy ineffectiveness is chronic, there is every reason to worry. Some may wonder whether these realities speak of deep failings in economic policy formulation, with policymakers unable to rescue their country's fortunes because of a cavalier or blinkered disposition that prevents them from thinking outside the box. It seems that dissatisfaction with the sustained failure of conventional policies will need to build until foot-dragging policymakers finally cross the line to belatedly get to grips with the real problem in the novel situation.

It follows that the West drifts due to the absence of fresh vision from a failure to concentrate the mind on real solutions for real recovery. Conventional economic policy is of limited use because economics is fractured, riven by fault lines and at war with itself. What has been stated underscores the message that it might be time for policymakers to face up to the reality that expecting any of the standard macroeconomic policy measures to work like clockwork is a forlorn hope; they fall lamentably short on effectiveness. "The past no longer illuminates the future, the spirit walks in darkness" (to quote Alexis de Tocqueville, 1805-1859). At best, the conventional policies in vogue are likely to be only stopgaps (temporary expedients) and not capable of providing lasting solutions (means to a durable recovery). In fact, it seems arguable that they have become habitual palliatives that swap immediate problems for later chronic ones that will perpetuate the downturn. If the present public is paying a high price for mistakes of the past, a future public will likely pay a still higher price for mistakes of the present. Consequently, there are good reasons for believing that advocates of conventional policy options are being optimistic to a fault. In the end, if, as is likely, all current options are more peripheral than central to the problem, all the hot air generated by the dust-up among buttoned-down policy antagonists contesting control over policy could prove to be much ado about nothing very much.

**

# Chapter 12

# FUTURE PROSPECTS: NIGHTMARES AND DREAMS

## 12.1 The Heart of the Matter

In order to set the scene for the solutions that are to be subsequently presented, the monumental conclusion that lies at the heart of the matter will be identified and the arguments leading to it duly delineated. As a precursor, relevant background highlights are recollected thus: the capitalist free-market mechanism is the beating heart of the economic system in the West; it is the vital mechanism upon which hopes for the longed-for recovery have been pinned; it has been the engine for unprecedented prosperity since the Industrial Revolution and enshrines the hope of good times in the future.

Be that as it may, the market seems to have shaken the faith of its true believers by letting them down with a serious and stubborn economic downturn. At first blush, the intensified criticism of the capitalist market system appears to be with good reason. The market is allegedly to blame, not only for the *degree* of recovery, but also for the *kind* of recovery. The market lacks responsiveness despite repeated plucky policy attempts to kick-start it into delivering genuine recovery. It is not for want of trying that the recovery is feeble; like the fabled mountain, the market has labored and brought forth a mouse.

Not only has the market been criticized for delivering a recovery that lacks robustness, it is also accused of short-changing society. Evidence exists that companies are thriving in economies that are wilting – for a perilous bifurcation that enables company profitability to peel away from social prosperity. The cleaving of common economic interests was shown to be a sign of the times. Markets treat society shabbily when the majority of people and firms in the economy do not sufficiently benefit from the growth that they generate. The numbers show that markets are weakening the middle class backbone of the economy by reducing its wages and limiting its opportunities. Competitive sectors are shrinking, causing a loss of dynamism from entrepreneurship. Consequently, despite the capitalist market mechanism being the only realistic hope for authentic recovery, its veracity is under a cloud. With the unfolding reality of global financial ascendancy, and plutocrats from pseudo-markets riding high in several sectors, it would be understandable if market capitalism looks ever less a rainbow worth chasing for the disgruntled majority left behind.

Yet for all that, doubts about the market are unjustified. Market-bashing seems a frame-up for victimization of the innocent. Tarring and feathering a cherished mechanism that is, in any case, indispensable for recovery, misses the point by the proverbial mile. Making the free-market mechanism take the rap for the current crisis is a lazy option for those who are not responsible for coming up with a proven and workable alternative that can deliver its ample good works. For the cogent reasons adduced in chapter 5, the capitalist free market system does not deserve to be in the public's crosshairs. The releasing of commercial zeal through the vents of opportunity offered by the capitalist market system has always been the secret to wealth creation; no other system in history has been able to foster human ingenuity and creativity on such a scale. It is a grave mistake for those discomfited by the market's current performance to attribute the fading sheen of capitalism to the failure of the free-market mechanism.

The system of free-market capitalism oddly requires government support for its existence; it needs proactive and ongoing government intervention and protection to properly function, as was previously explained and validated by the dictums of expert scholars Hubert Henderson and John Gray (see section 5.2). And institutional frameworks, capable of reconciling business and public interests, were shown to do very nicely for the purpose. The free market was undermined by the withdrawal of government support through unselective deregulatory measures that were unmindful of social outcomes, and it continues to be hobbled, if not crippled, by business practices and government policies that are as dubious as they are usual. By a process of evolution, plutocratic pseudo-markets have come to occupy front and center in economies. They were shown to undermine the operation of the free-market mechanism because of practices associated with monopolization, globalization, politicization and corruption. This includes the denuding of open competitive markets that are wellsprings of growth. Governments have failed to assiduously protect the institutions and structures essential for the viable operation of free markets. As a result, the socially friendly "invisible hand" has been ousted and come to be replaced by a hidden manipulative hand that suppresses much of the vital bourgeois, and prevents the majority of the people from partaking in the goodness that functional markets have shown they are capable of.

For those wondering, an apparent paradox challenges conventional wisdom. By and large, the economic woes of the West are caused, not by a failure of the free-market mechanism, but by a failure of *government* to prevent open competitive markets from mutating into dysfunctional plutocratic pseudo-markets. The necessary legislative and administrative safeguards for protecting open competitive markets are conspicuous by their absence – implying system failure. Hence, to call into question the free-market mechanism is to miss the point. The economic crisis is due to the failure of fundamental sociopolitical institutions resulting from license being mistaken for freedom, because ideology was mistaken for pragmatism. A properly functioning free market no longer existed to fail and trigger the current crisis. A breakdown in law and order in business had caused the market to become dysfunctional, and the market that crashed was a mutation that had only the semblance of a proper market – an imposter that was a free market in name but not substance. The markets dominant in Western economies today are dysfunctional mutants that are able to successfully masquerade as free markets and attract polices that nourish and foster them. Accepting these points leads to this crucial conclusion: the economic collapse happened and the downturn continues not *because* of the competitive free-market mechanism, but because of its *absence*.

## 12.2 The Ravage of Age

Waxing nostalgic about pre-deregulation banking respectability will not make it rise from the ashes. Setting about regulatory reforms amounts to closing the stable door after the horse has bolted. Even if there is full implementation of the banking and other economic reforms that are in place or intended the world over, it will do little, if anything, to get the horse back into the stable. In other words, even if all the intended economic regulations everywhere are somehow implemented and miraculously made fully effective, they will not breathe new life into the current deflated economic condition in the West. The economy's troubles run deeper still.

Could it be that after some two hundred years of spectacular travel, the gilded engine of free-market capitalism is not far from reaching the end of the line in the West, given the absence of facilitating tracks over the chasm that lies ahead? The speed of this engine was tremendously accelerated by unwise financial deregulation that poured on the coal to ball the jack, and doomed its journey to premature termination sometime in the not-too-distant future – but only in the absence of radical measures to yank it back on track (along the lines described earlier in section 11.8, and elaborated on below).

A different angle points to this same conclusion. The capitalist market system has evolved over a period of some two hundred years, and can be assumed to have gone through, or is going through, the usual stages of its life cycle. These are: an initial stage of slow economic growth prior to take-off; a second stage of exponential growth; a third stage of maturity when waning momentum causes growth to slow and plateau; and a fourth and final stage of decline exhibiting negative growth (the stage of its natural end, *ceteris paribus*). By this final stage, pseudo-markets would have evolved to end up being front and center in economies. The excessive progression of gigantism in firms would have by then caused the market to mutate into incongruous deformity, meaning that it would have ceased to be a mechanism that is vibrant, efficient, and effective from being open, competitive, and entrepreneurial. The hallmark of this stage is the excessive political influence of plutocratic forces. It would signal that the free-market system has run its course and is on its last legs.

Plutocratic pseudo-markets then become a new frontier for the capitalist market system. Some may see the new frontier as threatening, if not also wild. This is particularly so in the ascendant financial sector, which is enlarging its footprint on the global stage, to financialize economies everywhere. The relentless march forward of pseudo-market firms across a tilted playing field that features lopsided competition, eats away at the edges of effectively competitive open markets – causing them to gradually grind to a halt in increasing areas of the economy. This pushes mutating economies into a new chapter of economic history where "markets ain't markets."

Large areas of the market of today display symptoms of premature aging. Important parts of the market system have quickly grown to be big and fat, exhibiting an unhealthy appetite (rent seeking), lethargy (plodding), and coronary blockages (uncompetitiveness). The premature aging is attributable to the malfunction of capitalist markets caused by the ballooning knock-on effects of gung-ho deregulation. This has brought about the debilitating age-related disease of the plutocratic pseudo-market condition in economies exhibiting the symptoms described. This means deregulation has expedited the arrival of the future, the "future shock" (Toffler, 1965) prematurely causing the capitalist free-market system to leapfrog toward or into its final stage of decline. Crossing the Rubicon into pseudo-market territory can be a one-way street if nothing is done. The question is: for how long can the current form of top-heavy capitalism in plutocratic pseudo-markets continue to weaken the middle class backbone of the economy without collapsing under its own weight?

It is a vain hope to think that the milk-and-honey exponential growth stage of the capitalist market system's life cycle could have gone on forever. The peak of prosperity in recorded human history was reached by the capitalist market system in the Eldorado period preceding the crash of 2007-08. That there had indeed been an exponential growth trend over many decades is convincingly documented in the sobering book *Limits to Growth* (2004) by Donella Meadows, Jorgen Randers, and Dennis Meadows. The information in this book reinforces the previously reported empirical evidence that world economic growth surged seventy times more in the some two hundred years since the Industrial Revolution than it did in the two thousand years before then (Madison 2010).

At the risk of seeming ridiculous, the following question is posed: can there be perpetual growth? The belief in it is received wisdom, a common belief presumably based on the rationalist notion of linear progression. Notwithstanding its popular appeal, it involves trite extrapolation with perturbing implications. Although it is underpinned by an assumption that embodies more than a touch of the absurd, it nevertheless sits squarely within the domain of civilization; belief in it is quite respectable and not at all outlandish. As incredible as it is, faith in perpetual growth is a pervasively fashionable belief that underpins everything that is happening in relation to economies everywhere today. Every policy measure contemplated or taken is based on the assumption that restoring previous growth rates is something to aspire to as a feasible and attainable objective. Joining the fray against recession with conventional policy tools makes policymakers complicit in the belief that exponential growth is realistically achievable, at least for now. Policymakers look to past prosperity as a guarantee of future success. Such policies as quantitative easing, government spending stimulus programs, and austerity cutbacks, are underpinned by a belief that historical trend rates of growth can resume, and that economies will be able to carry on as before. Underpinning such sanguine policy perseverance in the midst of crumbling free markets is the following unmistakably placid belief: the end is *not* nigh.

If we posit that an exponential rate of growth cannot go on forever, it follows that the concept of infinite growth is a nonsensical absurdity, and belief in it is an irrational fantasy. Acknowledging that the economic policies being pursued are driven by a belief in perpetual growth uncovers the uncanny assumption underpinning prospects for future happiness in the Western world. Those who refuse to ease up on fantasies about unending growth need to come to terms with the incontrovertible truth that the Egyptian,

Mayan, Greek, and Roman civilizations – times of great achievement – have definitely ceased to exist. They might find it useful
to note the informed views of Donella Meadows, Jorgen Randers,
and Denis Meadows who establish that wanting sustained growth
is nothing but "wishful thinking" (Meadows et al. 2004, xix). The
finite nature of any process of growth was succinctly explained by
MIT professor, Jay Forrester, of Club of Rome fame, who shocked
people back in 1972 with his insightful but unpopular view that
growth is an inherently temporary process. He stated, "...in every
growth situation growth runs its course, be it in seconds, or cen-
turies." Rejecting the view that growth can go on for all eternity
implies acceptance of the position that the capitalist market system will go the way of all flesh, and that the end could be now,
although not necessarily.

When all factors are considered, it is arguable that the recession of 2007-08 is a turning point in the economic history of the
West. The landmark measures taken to deregulate economies have
expedited momentum toward a new world order, where plutocratic
pseudo-markets firms, led by banks, take over key sectors of economies for overall influence. The new world economic order is thus
diminished by a beguiling and insidious plutocracy. This drastically
redraws the economic landscape and signals a quantum change in
the fate of Western society. The pseudo-market features of globalization, monopolization, politicization, and corruption synergistically
combine to mark a pivotal change in the way economic-cum-political
systems work. This makes the increasing domination of economies
by plutocratic pseudo-markets a ground-breaking development
that causes the present post-crisis period to be a watershed in the
economic history of the West. This makes the present generation a
witness to momentous developments in economic history that are
capable of changing things forever.

Yet, it can be argued that, although in bad shape, the capitalist market system is not necessarily done for. The final stage of free market capitalism's natural life cycle can be justifiably portrayed as the beginning of the end, only if the life-cycle curve is not shifted upward through rejuvenating market reforms of a fundamental sort (which involves taking a quantum leap to save the situation through non-marginal life-cycle change). This means that much will hinge on make-or-break reform measures that enable policymakers, driven by the realization that there is only one way to skin the cat, to stay ahead of the curve. This dire prognosis makes the case for structural reform of the market decidedly persuasive. As noted by German philosopher Georg Hegel (1770-1831), it is only at dusk, when the shades of night are falling, does the owl of Minerva (symbolizing wisdom) spread its wings and take flight. The redeeming reforms required for deliverance involve reaching for the stars identified later (see section 12.4). In order to better appreciate the hope in the solutions, next laid on the line are the sobering perils in the problem.

## 12.3 The Possible Nightmare

*A Dire Unanimity*

Who is bold enough to laugh at wise men in agreement? Informed opinion from a range of analysts shows an alarming lack of confidence in all solutions for this crisis, although not for the same reasons. They are all agreed that the current crisis has yet to hit rock bottom and are waiting for the other shoe to drop; for them, the next collapse is more a question of "when" than "if."

It would have been good if the frightening consensus on throwing in the towel could be dismissed on the ground that it amounts to nothing more than the ravings of superstitious soothsayers. Unfortunately, the amply documented views are too much in agreement for comfort and too respectable to treat with contempt. The body of opinion, by not euphemistically calling a spade an agricultural implement, brings home to the more open-minded the dire prediction of catastrophe. There is agreement by the cited experts that what the world can have, at best, is only a temporary appearance of recovery (happening now), and they make no bones about their fears that further indefinite collapse into the abyss of depression is more likely than not. It is not expected that this range of thinking people would express belief in a doom scenario with confidence, without at least some of their predictions being founded in scientific knowledge. Moreover, given their professional stature, they are not likely to lightly place themselves in a situation of having to eat their own words (some quoted below).

While ignorance is bliss, insight could be misery; some fearful analysts have broken cover by slipping their anxieties between the covers of books. Take the view of Tony Crescenzi (2012). He believes that nations are stuck with old playbooks and few choices left to revive the global economy. There is support for such a dejected conclusion from Wiedemer et al. (2011), who doubt that an upswing of the business cycle will ever take place because we have entered new territory where normal business-cycle behavior is a thing of the past.

The opinion of experts from the groves of academe or other intellectual think tanks is difficult to ignore, particularly when their foreboding of gloom and doom has credibility from scientific reasoning. Those of the no-nonsense Austrian School of Economics (like J.H. De Soto, a professor at Juan Carlos University in Spain and financial expert Detlev Schlichter of the Cobden Center in London), apply rigorous logic to demonstrate the terrifying likelihood of a monetary breakdown; they fear that the state of play in the financial sector will ultimately put the skids under limping economies (De Soto 2010; Schlichter 2011). Those of the Austrian school and others of similar ilk think that what we have now is not a setback but the final act (the "end game," according to Schlichter) in a saga of irresponsibility that will end in tears for the public. This can mean that the financial system is poised to fail beginning in Europe, where the IMF (2012) estimates that the deleveraging needed is a massive $2.6 trillion – making the current simulated uptick the economy's last hurrah for baby boomers.

Behind all the upbeat propaganda on recovery, America harbors precariousness that it can call its own (one that does not need any input from Europe). According to predictions by Acharya and Sundaram (2009), there is a lurking threat from a pattern of economic collapse that will inevitably repeat because of systemic economic fragility – the bailouts have sown the seeds of the next crisis. Joseph Stiglitz presents a bleak prognosis for the financial sector in America in his *Freefall* (2010, 296), and predicts recurrent crises. In his *Republic Lost*, Lawrence Lessig expects the unreformed financial system, which caused great harm once, to cause great harm again (Lessig 2011, 2). Paul Krugman, in his *End This Depression Now*, is in agreement when he says that the economy will remain sluggish for a very long time unless policymakers change course (Krugman 2012, xii)–something they have signally failed to do.

Not only ivory-tower intellectuals belong to the alliance of pessimistic prognosticators. A touch-and-go situation for the world economy has been recognized by the staid International Monetary Fund, when it refers to continuing fragility from a financial system under stress (IMF 2012). Such a grave conclusion from an organization not given to hyperbole adds enough weight to the aforementioned body of opinion to justify the running for the exit by thoughtful investors. This they seem to have already done; the fact that businesses in America and Europe are presently withholding some three-trillion dollars of investment capital is clear manifestation of investor trepidation.

The IMF's warnings, although dire, are mild compared with the doom predicted by other analysts who do not see a fighting chance of winning. Such sources do not fight shy of expressing their frightening belief that there would be a monetary-induced crash, characterized by bursting interactions among the "multiple bubbles" in the economy, with an "aftershock," when finally the dollar and the government debt "bubbles" burst (Wiedemer, D., Wiedemer, R., and Spitzer 2011). Others see in the American economy a powder keg of debt. For example, the Republican senator Thomas Coburn (2012) in his *The Debt Bomb* dolefully notes that Americans are sitting on a powder keg, which he calls a "debt bomb." The scenario he paints includes the collapse of the stock market, a further collapse in housing prices, runaway inflation, and "unimaginable social unrest." Although this scenario is a possibility, it is more likely to come about through austerity measures that he supports than through the refusal of investors to buy US debt. In the remote event that investors refuse to buy new American bonds, the Federal Reserve would simply step in and buy federal debt (that is, print money to meet government expenditures). A government never needs default in the currency that it prints. The view that America is skating on thin ice is shared by David Stockman, who darkens the gloom by fearing the worst. In his *The Great Deformation* Stockman foresees a situation where America runs out of balance sheets to leverage up because of serial bubble blowing by the bogeyman: the US Federal Reserve Board (Stockman 2013, 711). There are good reasons for believing that overreliance on central banks is a big reason behind the present sluggishness. And the fact that there is no room to lower interest rates further in the event of another collapse or deflation justifies a sinking feeling.

If the foregoing unanimity on gloom and doom has validity, as it probably does, those central bankers and politicians pinning their hopes on stale and overdone credit and borrowing policies for authentic recovery, are bound to be disappointed. The following narrative is meant to show why they may have missed the boat.

*Facing Reality*

In the light of the dismal prognostications it would be tempting to shoot the messengers who bring indigestible news. But prophets of doom are like weather forecasters in times past: they were not always wrong. The apocalyptic predictions of the grim day of reckoning are plausible for the reason that none of the persons whose views were cited is known to be an incense-burning hippie.

The cited views of those who qualify as experts clear away at least some of the cobwebs to arguably deserve the status of, as in the words of Alexander Pope (1688-1744), "feast of reason and the flow of soul"–and be acknowledged as having intellectual validity. Rebuffing unpleasant prophesies out of hand would be justified only if the logic of reason exposes their bases as hogwash, and that was not so in most of the views reported earlier. For this reason, the cited views, when taken collectively, deserve more than the *qui vive* when the penalty for letting things slide is so high. A realistic reading recognizes that the current condition stacks the cards against economic revival within the existing scheme of things; the status quo does not secure the future but jeopardizes it. This means, there is little prospect of a new prosperity rising from the ashes of the current crisis if nothing different is done. The message to policymakers is that wanting the usual medicines to cure an unusual disease amounts to a big ask and, if the experts cited are to be believed, would be tantamount to asking for the moon.

Should the unthinkable happen and the balloon goes up, economies will hit the skids. It seems a safe prediction that the 2007-08 collapse could feel like a church picnic compared to what would take place when the roof falls in. Because companies with the "too big to fail" status are larger or more numerous than before the crisis, they would be *"much* too *big* to save" and "too *many* to save." In circumstances where interest rates have hit rock bottom and governments are stone-broke, the option of finding solace in the arms of the state through bailouts does not appear to have bright prospects. As for saving countries with large economies like Italy or France that are teetering on the brink of collapse, it would be out of the question. If worst comes to worst, the peal of thunder heard will be the crack of doom, because governments, as the last bulwarks, will be helpless to prevent the cataclysm. The helplessness of affected governments will be sad to behold – their plight being like that of fire fighters rendered useless without water in their fire engines. When push comes to shove, their worn policy tools will prove mostly useless in dysfunctional conditions where plutocratic pseudo-markets can incapacitate them.

Given such a somber prognosis, fundamental reforms to fix the broken foundations of market capitalism are not to be sneered at if the door is not to be shut on hope for a turnaround in the real economy. Although no sane person would have an appetite for another crisis, in the absence of fundamental market reform everyone may get one all the same. Although headaches abound, it stands to reason that the economy cannot be set up for growth without the pre-requisite of proper foundations upon which to build the recovery. As stated earlier, support for such reforms would come in from the cold, as policymakers gradually wake-up to the reality that plutocratic pseudo-markets are a handbrake on durable recovery. When they do, the subterfuge of plutocratic pseudo-markets will wear thin and the public's consciousness of their harmfulness will increase. If realization of the real nature of the problem impels a do-or-die quest for authentic economic recovery, such bold aspiration will involve optimistically reaching with relish for the two stars identified in the analysis that follows.

## 12.4 The (Not) Impossible Dream

*Hope Springs Eternal*

For policymakers who have fought losing battles with worn policy instruments and wonder why things are not happening as expected, structural and institutional changes offer something different that might just do the job. This makes the establishment of effectively competitive open markets that embody entrepreneurial spirit a lifeline for capitalism; it is expected to resuscitate markets that are marred by plutocracy and scarred by dysfunction. Setting their sights on such a goal is an escape hatch for policymakers currently caught up in a situation that threatens an unpleasant ending.

How best to heal the worsening wound of market malfunction that torments the economy? The short answer is: mollycoddle open competitive markets while upending or expunging plutocratic pseudo-markets. But market reforms cannot be successful against a backdrop of plutocratic influence. As explained in the following pages, open competitive markets can be protected and fostered, and pseudo-market malfunction rectified, only if the political system is first reformed. Impaired markets and impaired political systems are joined at the hip. The plutocratic "lion in the way" of market reform is not imaginary when it exerts an influence that is real.

Because the impaired market system worsens the impaired political system, and vice versa, there results a spiral of dysfunction. Consequently, the process of getting there is hardly plain sailing, but "hope springs eternal in the human breast" (Alexander Pope, 1733). Hollow flourishes or tinkering around the edges will not do; drastic root-and-branch reforms seem unavoidable for a proper solution. Seeing the light could inspire the leadership vision required to go back to the drawing board with a never-say-die determination for the purpose of designing a plan that hitches one's wagon to two stars: the star of political reform and the star of market reform. Daunting though they be, the bold measures that reaching for these stars would require are precisely what the doctor ordered for curing the persisting debilitating disease of economic lethargy.

*The Free Market Star*
Restoring effectively competitive open markets involves reviving the golden egg-laying capability of a goose in poor shape. Durable economic recovery relies on the drive, initiative, and vibrancy, of effectively competitive open markets to autonomously power economies into recovery through productivity, efficiency, product innovation, and strategic marketing. Plutocratic pseudo-market conditions have crippled, if not destroyed, the open competitive market mechanism in key sectors of economies by their anti-competitive structural features and behavioral traits (described in chapter 8). As was pointed out, plutocratic pseudo-market conditions nurture firms with zombie-type idiosyncrasies in conditions conducive to such quirks, where easy profits come from sitting pretty (enabled by monopolistic power transnational manipulation, political influence, and licentious-prone business practices, all fountains of surplus profits, formally called economic rent). The lack of enough competitive pressure in pseudo-market conditions changes business incentives in a way that denies firms the disciplinary imperatives to be sufficiently alive and kicking.

Revitalizing an effectively competitive open market system involves reestablishing a juggernaut of firms capable of generating dynamic effervescence aroused by feisty competitive pressures. This is expected to revive the golden egg-laying capability of a once-sprightly goose now in poor health, and on its way to breathing its last. Establishing effectively competitive open markets would revive the spirit of the revered mechanism responsible for unprecedented human prosperity in the two hundred years since the Industrial Revolution (the achievements of which were recorded in section 5.1). Enabling an effectively competitive open market system to take center stage in economies would provide the bedrock to a recovery that restores the middle class backbone of the economy.

Moving toward open competitive markets involves swimming against the stream to undo the damage from past policy blunders – something easier said than done, but to which there does not seem to be an alternative. The global giants that banks and other firms have become contain hidden operations spanning several countries, which were shown to cast a dark shadow over economic recovery. These behemoths that pass for firms are not to be trifled with, their prowess being reflected in the size of their budgets which exceed the budgets of countries. As a result, the decisions of such firms have the ability to move markets, and even economies (as well as politicians). The mightiness of such pseudo-market firms finds expression in several anti-social ways. Their strengths threaten bruising confrontations with elected governments, particularly when gravy trains are at risk. Several key areas are crying out for remedial reform in relation to pseudo-market firms. These are: monopolistic market power over competitors in open sectors, clients, and employees; the ability to manipulate strategies across countries to the detriment of competitiveness; undue influence over elected politicians for socially unfriendly arrangements; and licentious business practices toward competitors, clients and customers.

Although not as impractical as unscrambling eggs, structural reforms go some way toward being as challenging and may not, in any case, provide the full answer. Like some dreadful joke, ponderous plutocratic pseudo-markets need to be dismantled and replaced by thriving open markets – implying the need to transform a sow's ear into a silk purse. "The wish is father to the thought" (to quote Shakespeare's *King Henry IV*); tackling what seems improbable does not mean it is impossible, particularly when it is essential. The reality is that while the buttoned-down policies of quantitative easing, interest rate reductions, austerity, and fiscal stimulus have been a disappointment, it must be conceded that not everything has been tried. Given the obstacles facing economies of the West within the existing scheme of things, there may be no alternative but to change the existing scheme of things. This will require sufficient redesign of the market architecture so that plutocratic pseudo-market conditions are minimized and competitive open market conditions are maximized. Without fundamental structural reform, persisting with usual measures would seem analogous to building walls without regard for the state of the foundations upon which they must rest. It is assumed that the transformation achieved by reining in pseudo-markets will be sufficient to erode the entrenched dominance of plutocratic influence; plutocratic obstacles can be expected to be blown away when oligarchs are transformed into ordinary business people. Logically, this should enable a sturdy and widely enjoyed recovery to take place without let or hindrance.

Visionary leaders of the strategic sort hold the key to success i.e., those who can stare plutocrats full in the face. Turning the clock back in relation to the market mechanism would be a counsel of perfection, hopelessly idealistic, unless policymakers have got what it takes to be up to the job. The leadership should be able to convert strategic vision (designing markets that reconcile business and community interests) into political mission (proceeding to bring such market functionality into fruition). Hence, proper leadership would transform the outlandishly possible into the challengingly doable by knocking plutocratic pseudo-markets on the head. This would require policymakers to face up to the challenging task of revamping dilapidated market foundations through both structural and institutional reforms – measures that, because they have happened before, are not offbeat. An example of the former is the break-up by US president Teddy Roosevelt of pioneer-philanthropist John D. Rockefeller's Standard Oil Company Inc. (the world's largest refiner) into thirty-three smaller companies back in 1911. An example of the latter is President Woodrow Wilson's (1913-21) attempt to achieve market functionality through the Federal Trade Commission, besides taking anti-trust measures by clarifying company guidelines (effectively, designing institutional frameworks of the sort described in chapter 5). Admittedly, it is not known the extent to which these precedents offer valid templates for the present; as the job of unscrambling contemporary pseudo-markets would be hellish, they may well be altogether irrelevant.

This suggests that "small is beautiful" (to use the title of E.F. Schumacher's 1973 book). This implies merit in the shift to a growth model based on entrepreneurship from competitiveness, in contrast to one based on the notion that bigger is better. Germany, which has the strongest small-to-medium sized company sector in the West, also has, by far, the lowest youth unemployment rate and, arguably, also the most vibrant economy in the West. Some observers will no doubt justifiably regard the breaking up massive banks and other similar firms wearing the "too big to fail" mantle a messy and harebrained fantasy. "Demergerfication" refers to the orderly carving up of gargantuan corporations for a Goldilocks solution: units large enough to be efficient, but small enough to feel competitive pressures within socially-designed institutional frameworks governing company operations. In this context it means that relatively smaller firms are more efficient and better able to deliver real recovery for social prosperity than ponderous transnational pseudo-market behemoths that pass for firms. Contrary to popular belief, they have been shown to be operationally inefficient semi-political entities that are inherently obstructive to recovery (as was explained in chapter 9).

Steps would be needed to limit the adverse consequences of demergerfication. For one thing, it could place firms in a strategic straitjacket in relation to acquisitions and mergers that may have operational merit in the future. Another difficulty is that defining "small" is awkward when operations and markets are global. A further complication is that demergerfication could weaken Western firms in relation to Asian corporate giants, like Samsung, Toyota, and Alibaba that have global scale. There is an ongoing drive to create Asian multinationals that can grow and adapt to match the corporate clout of Western titans. Government support may be needed when shrunken Western firms have to engage in bilateral bargaining with such foreign privately-owned and state-owned behemoths of the Chinese and Russian sort, described earlier.

Time is precious; it is a case of "the sooner the better" when it comes to stopping the progress of pseudo-markets. Because plutocratic pseudo-markets have automatic forward momentum that can be easily exploited, there is an inexorably growing problem. Consequently, early action cuts losses because delays will require ever-larger remedies due to ever-wider circles; the longer that market reform takes to get going, the harder it will be to make it succeed. For this reason, sweeping the problem of plutocratic pseudo-markets under the rug now (as seems to be happening) will make it more difficult to deal with later (because of further ossification).

In the absence of soon-enough fundamental reforms, full-blown plutocracy looks like the coming thing; pseudo-markets are on course to take over everywhere for an unholy mess that dashes free-market hopes. To allow the creeping cancer of the plutocratic pseudo-market condition to continue its unrelenting advance would likely result in a crisis of progress; the entire world economy could end up being engulfed by such impaired markets within a decade or three. If this should happen, plutocracy will take front and center within societies and pseudo-markets firms will be the pillars of a new finacialized civilization. In these circumstances plutocracy, often cross-dressed as democracy, would gradually become the predominant political system everywhere. The implication is that such a development is likely to take place, not openly but craftily, behind a façade of democracy (democracies in form but not substance, like Russia and several third world countries are today). Arguably, such mutant democracy has already begun to take hold in woebegone parts of Western society, the camouflaged plutocracy gradually spreading to become the new normalcy. The prospect of reality catching up with such Orwellian conjecture would understandably make the next generation's blood run cold.

What other stars are there to reach for? For a start, do the obvious: have simple and straightforward industry laws and regulations that are strictly enforced i.e., laws that work. The Dodd-Frank re-regulatory reforms have been shown to give every indication of being the proverbial half a loaf of bread and, in addition, have the untidy connotation of a dog's breakfast when it comes to interpretation and enforcement. It would be helpful if there was less reliance on thickets of labyrinthine verbiage full of fiddly exemptions and limitations that are likely to deliver no more than gentle slaps on the wrists for those guilty of committing business sins on the scale of highway robbery. Less reliance on these pointless laws will not make much of a difference in any case, because they seem mostly window dressing put up to deceive the trusting into complacency (see section 8.5).

Since the debate about how to fix banks burns as fiercely as ever, the plain-spoken home truths presented next may help to give an impression of what is needed to overcome despair. As any analyst knows, good banking rests on the elementary principle of preventing mountains of debt from being piled on tiny foundations of equity. In America before the crisis, the big banks' capital bases were far too thin to protect them from the corrosive effect of toxic bonds. European banks have yet to recover from the same scantiness. Retail bankers should go dreary by sticking to their knitting (their traditional area of business activity). This implies that banks should be run like utilities, not casinos; the reforms would need to strictly quarantine retail banking from investment banking and control derivatives. For retail banking, this will involve going back to a future where cavalier, shareholder-focused, banking for selling exciting products is expunged and sedate, customer-focused, boring banking for selling sleepy products is reestablished. This would mean there is a different competitive dynamic for each type of banking. In relation to retail banking, there would need to be hard capitalization limits for capital buffers. At the risk of scaring finance industry boffins, Anat Admati and Martin Hellwig advocate a capital ratio of up to 30 percent (Admati and Hellwig 2013), something that would force banks to hold more capital than under "Basel 3" rules. (As analysts know, higher capital ratios force banks to fund their loans and investments more with equity and less with money borrowed from investors and depositors.) This idea of "the more capital the better" will understandably be regarded as draconian by vested interests, for whom slim-and-risky trumps fat-and-safe. The squeeze on profit margins from higher capital standards can be regarded as a worthwhile insurance premium to bear against the risk of a financial catastrophe, very likely much worse than the last one. All this supposes star-quality enforcement of free-market-supporting regulations that is better-enabled by their straightforwardness.

*The Democracy Star*

If there is a jungle out there called pseudo-markets, then plutocratic elements like banking fatcats would be the lions, the king of the beasts. They exercise a ruling influence over a domain where the law of the jungle (i.e., "might makes right"), unsurprisingly, prevails. The lions are not expected to relinquish their power and privilege without a game change in the game park. The game change would require changes to the laws of the jungle, with some changes to the structure of the jungle itself, for the benefit of all the species living there, on the lines previously explained. Here's the rub: *how* are the lions to be tamed or defanged, and *who* would have the intestinal fortitude to do so?

At the bottom of things is the need to achieve proper representative democracy in day-to-day policy-making. This would ensure the automatic supremacy of the public interest over the corporate interest when they happen to conflict. That is the secret for ending the economic ordeal arising from the scant compatibility between the interests of plutocratic pseudo-markets and those of the wider community. Otherwise the future will look like the present writ large; it will feature a multiplied number of pseudo-market firms with enhanced plutocratic power that continue to deplete open competitive markets and degrade economies at an accelerated pace, even as politicians are increasingly incentivized to forsake competitive sectors. True democrats confronting the disturbing reality of democracy further succumbing to plutocracy would need to watch their step: the onward momentum of pseudo-markets will cause the democratic levers needed to save open competitive sectors to increasingly slip from their grasp.

Desperately needed open competitive markets will emerge fairly automatically in the wake of proper political reforms, which are at the sharp end of the process – in practical terms, killing two birds with one stone. Belief in such symbiosis between the political and the economic has its basis in the information delineated in section 5.3; the idea is to rally politicians so they could recruit open markets to attack economic lethargy, with competitive forces weaponizing markets for the purpose. Social control through a properly representative democracy is the only effective antidote to the sort of lionization of plutocrats that was pungently illustrated by the humiliating spectacle at Davos and the apparent capitulation by European Union officials (referred to in relation to "politicization" in section 8.2). Political reform needs priority because plutocratic forces, that are integral to pseudo-markets, would operate to stay the hand of policymakers wanting to move in and establish open competitive markets. The good news is that open competitive markets have near-universal appeal from being the gratifying common ground behind the bitter differences of Western ideology. The bad news is that the potential winners are diffuse but the losers are concentrated and influential (the latter refers to the narrow pseudo-market interest – the so-called "one percent" – whose grain it would go against).

The deregulation-crazy political class that made an ungrudging contribution to the mess that is the plutocratic pseudo-market condition cannot be expected to make a serious effort to clean it up. For the reasons explained in section 6.4, politicians who are secretly beholden to plutocratic interests cannot help being drawn to the mess; they have come to depend upon it for their existence as never before, unable to resist plutocratic money like the biblical washed sow that could not help returning to the mud. Politicians sheltering behind the very barriers that require change, particularly the gilded fabric of lobbyist largesse, are not likely to step up to the plate with an appetite for fundamental reform. Because their style is cramped from being committed to the vested interest over the public interest, hamstrung politicians, as secret agents of plutocratic pseudo-markets, are unlikely to embrace public causes when they are busy embracing corporate causes antithetical to those of the public. The inherent processes of government make influence peddling, deal making, and campaign money doling stand in the way of genuine representativeness. This is the concept of "dependence corruption" developed by Lawrence Lessig and referred to in connection with the constitutional element in section 6.4 (Lessig 2011); it unsurprisingly explains why truly representative democracy has gone missing.

The implication is that politicians, shackled as stalwart allies of vested interests, are not likely to fervently embrace reform that requires them to reform themselves or, alternatively, be so overcome by the ignominy of their condition that they gladly chuck themselves out on their ear. Reforms are not likely within the present political set-up for at least two possible reasons: one reason is that most of the potential reformers, who have a gravy train going, will be inclined to welcome needed political reform like they would a hole in the head; another is that they may be riding a tiger and cannot dismount without being eaten.

It follows from the foregoing that the most basic solution of all requires putting heart and soul into reaching for the brightest star of all. This refers to the star of community insight that confines community support to tenacious political candidates who do not shy away from grand ambitions on behalf of the public. They would be driven by a vision of truly competitive markets and have ready a prospectus of market reform. Such aptitude would enable politicians to clean house by sweeping away plutocratic influences – thereby enabling the orchestration of reforms that give paramount status to the public interest over the corporate interest when they are in conflict. For movers and shakers to be able to move and shake in the public interest, the cords that bind them to plutocratic vested interests would obviously need to be cut. The resulting suppleness from casting off the shackles of dependency would see the rise of free-lance politicians, independent of entrenched interests, able to stand on their own legs, and, once again, call their souls their own.

Hence, it would take nothing less than a clean sweep for unchained "Mr. Cleans" of both sexes to emerge. This is better late than never, as Lawrence Lessig explains in his *Republic Lost* (Lessig 2011), where he calls for widespread mobilization for regaining control of a corrupted but redeemable representational system. David Stockman backs him up with a commonly espoused cause; in his *The Great Deformation*, Stockman makes the common sense and unoriginal suggestion that political campaigns should be exchequer funded, public money being presumed to purify the process (Stockman 2013, p. 708).

The West is experiencing political retrogression as manifested in a movement away from democracy (informed public control over public policy formulation) and toward plutocracy (where the vested interest triumphs over the public interest, as happened with financial deregulation, bailouts, European borrowing, and many other matters). This makes highly questionable the view that the exercise of political power without public consent ended with the shift from monarchy to democracy. The fact is that the failure of sociopolitical institutions is enabling a surreptitious plutocracy to overshadow and erode real democracy. Although the exercise of plutocratic influence is currently mostly nuanced, camouflaged by the trappings of an increasingly hollowed-out of democracy, it could, over time, escalate to become more open and brazen, as pseudo-markets advance to take over everywhere. Such a process would culminate in the emergence of a state-corporate capitalism with its hallmark chokehold on society from an amalgam of capital, market, and political power.

What is called for is the transformation of current nightmarish visions into dreams of the future. Such aspiration is achieved by ensuring conditions that the likes of John Locke, Thomas Jefferson, and Tom Paine took for granted. This refers to an informed general public, specifically the silent majority, ensconced in the driver's seat, driving leaders who are gluttons for punishment on its behalf, and who are prepared to go that extra mile for a labor of love. In the Western world, this requires a new generation of community leaders to come on deck, who do not allow narrow minds to bog down radical reform. They can expect to have their work cut out for them; they would need to know what they are about and be prepared to battle long odds to build a great future. Presumably, the invigorating force of new blood would instill in the fresh leadership the necessary gumption to bell the fatcats of big business. The ascendancy of the will of an informed public would tend to automatically seal the fate of plutocrats in relation to public policy formulation. This implies a shift from plutocracy to democracy that parallels the momentous historical shift from monarchy to democracy in Europe. It would, however, be whitewashing history to claim that the transformation in Europe was a cakewalk; sweeping away the fusty old order in the transition to Western liberalism featured setbacks (e.g., Metternich's Austrian empire) and upheavals (e.g., the ubiquitous revolutions of 1848). For this reason, optimism will need to trump defeatism if dysfunctional markets are to be reformed and plutocrats are to be transformed into ordinary business people who are more valued than feared.

## 12.5 Conclusion: Conquer Pessimism

Unless reforms can be undertaken for recalibrating the present, the door will shut on a hopeful future; for change to happen, the nostalgia for free market conditions must triumph over the cornucopia of pseudo-market forces. Wishing that the troublesome market dysfunction will just go away is a forlorn hope; simply hankering for genuine recovery from economies hamstrung by plutocratic pseudo-market conditions is a pipe dream that implies game over for the bypassed majority yearning for restored opportunity through economic recovery. The motivational drive for salvation comes from taking heart that economic resurgence is the logical result of a regenerated dynamism from giving primacy to effectively competitive open market conditions. The noble ambitions embodied in the policy goals previously addressed will need to come in from the cold and hold sway by overriding biased hunches about the adequacy of current market circumstances.

It would take the right political leadership to save the capitalist free-market ship from sinking due to the weight of a corrupted form of top-heavy capitalism that weakens competitiveness, enfeebles the middle class backbone of the economy, and diminishes opportunity for the majority. Although no mean feat, it would be nice if fundamental reforms can fix dysfunctional markets and forge a hitherto absent link between public policy and real economic recovery. Having the right stuff would enable the new generation of leaders to go the whole nine yards and get cracking on the essential task of sidelining ponderous plutocratic pseudo-markets. The path to success, although rocky, is expected to enable vibrant competitive open market conditions to occupy front and center in economies. It would revive something that up to now has proven to be frustratingly elusive: reviving the beating heart for a recovery that is not farcical financial mirage, one that opens the way to a future featuring widespread prosperity. As clearly implied, for such an outcome the leadership will have to muster a level of resolve that will enable those given to skepticism to yield to optimism. The importance of seeing the glass as half full, not half empty, is explained in the following, final, chapter.

\*\*

# Chapter 13

## SUMMARY AND CONCLUSIONS:

## REACHING FOR THE STARS

### 13.1 Something Different

Finally, the pieces of the jigsaw puzzle scattered among the preceding chapters can be drawn together and fitted to form the big picture. It portrays the current economic crisis as an interwoven phenomenon, one that is broader than the central feature on the canvas, namely economics. The range of aspects spelled out shows that a multidimensional approach is useful for making perception better click into place for clearer focus on causes and solutions, vulnerabilities and opportunities. Going beyond orthodox economics has enabled reaching deep to get to the bottom of the problem, while preserving the far-ranging scope of the story – thereby enabling both a worm's eye view as well as a bird's eye view, for an integrated perspective. Such a vantage position has provided a fuller understanding for setting the record straight, and revealed a line of reasoning to pursue to see where things might head in the future. Accordingly, in this chapter a venturesome attempt is made to envisage that future.

By and large, visiting the past throws daylight on the future. The lingering economic downturn is no normal phenomenon, although symptoms that mimic the past can make the lethargy seem familiar on the surface. Those looking for the predictability of a comfort zone would tend to attach exaggerated importance to the superficial parallels between this and past recessionary downturns. Enough has probably been said to show why people would be deluding themselves by regarding the current downturn as just a larger version of a run-of-the-mill business cycle downswing, one that is different in size but not type, and subscribing to the romantic belief that a recuperative upswing is only a matter of time.

The world had an American recession with a European twist. Central bankers were asleep at the wheel, ignoring telltale fundamentals and being unmindful of the ability of markets to behave in a mentally disturbed fashion. The high quotient of sheer excess ensured a drawn-out field day for the grim reaper of the real economy. The tempest has passed but dark clouds remain; the crisis is gone but a robust and inclusive recovery is nowhere to be seen. Looking behind the curtain of spin reveals a condition that is wretched for the weary majority in the West. A public that has known better days is required to roll with the punches, trim its sails to suit the ill winds, and play make-believe that a recovery is happening. For the majority yearning for a better tomorrow from the proclaimed recovery there is a perpetually disappointing condition that must make pronouncements of recovery sound bleakly comical.

Although the recession looks like a duck and quacks like a duck, it is a turkey. Despite superficial similarities between this and past recessions, it is really a freak recession when an awful lot went wrong at once. This makes it thoroughly distinct from post-industrial antecedents. What took place puts previous recessions in the shade with a magnitude that dwarfs them, a persistence that tries the patience of Job, a level of corruption that was a game changer and, crucially, camouflaged causes that enable policymakers to be in a state of denial about the true state of play in economies. The bizarre scale of the pre-crisis credit expansion made asset price bubbles inflate to dimensions unprecedented for a recession. Their bursting caused Western markets to drop like ninepins, with a shattering that reverberated to rattle economies worldwide to this day. The wrenching scale has an economic recovery in its wake that is as dodgy as belief in the market is stodgy. The protracted absence of buoyancy suggests there is no knowing when the downturn will end; it is impossible to turn the corner when things are stuck in the rut of market malfunction. The best guess, in the absence of fundamental reforms to correct the corrupted market system, is when the cows come home.

Ingloriously distinguishing this crisis were countless scandals, although not of the sexy sort. A game change attributable to the scandalous scale of corruption means that the current economic downturn is not only quantitatively different from previous recession-induced slumps (i.e., different in degree), but also qualitatively so (i.e., different in kind). The synergy from the mutually reinforcing convergence of degree and kind makes this downturn an economic weirdo. Activities that were illegal were as creative as those that were unethical. These had the effect of pulling the wool over the eyes of investors who, because of the absence of accurate risk assessment, were denied knowledge of lurking horrors. Such business practices epitomize the excesses of the crisis, with the credit-ratings agencies being in the vanguard of things that went bad. Consequently, even smart investors, unable to weigh up the risks, were reduced to being not much better than dart-throwing monkeys when it came to picking winners.

Because management-driven strategic thrusts in business took the form of concealment and deception, a befitting business mission statement might have been: "Take the money and run." The lurking presence in the economy of those with impunity from past corrupt practices is a nagging concern for future market functionality. Can corruption that goes unpunished be forever contained? The possibility of a deeper economic downturn from a replay of financial misdeeds makes holding the line on stagnation an achievement to be grateful for. The current state of abeyance would then qualify as a cause for celebration.

Finance economists were a part of the problem when they should have been a part of its prevention. Economics was the secular religion of the West and the finance economists, as the high priests of economics, became the darlings of corporate world. This new tribe of cowboy economists and fellow travelers galloped to the forefront of the profession from a murky intellectual backwater, sporting borrowed plumes and brandishing mathematical weapons. The results from their mathematical models rationalized and encouraged the process of bubble-creation, causing mathematical tools to become anti-social weapons when used for financial gamesmanship. Statistical models were regarded as spouting gospel, God's gifts to banks and credit-ratings agencies, even though separating statistical signals from contrived noise was impractical (especially when information manipulation was integral to business strategy in markets that were stealthy, phony, and dysfunctional). The intellectual dignity from perceptual depth in the science of economics was overridden by a narrow vocationalism on the mistaken presumption that information was knowledge. This had the inevitable effect of causing mathematical nicety to be achieved at the expense of social relevance, and supposed social scientists to be laughably alienated from considerations of social welfare.

The mathematical models based on superstition introduced a dash of voodooism into the field of economics, and caused it to drift away from its social science moorings. They delivered results that had the perverse and diabolical effect of increasing business profitability at the expense of social wellbeing – thereby denying the raison d'être of the science of economics. The results from these models, which predicted the opposite of what happened, worsened the problem by throwing dust in the eyes of investors and snakeoil rather than water on the speculation fire. The collapse was a painful rebuke for the finance economists' models based on their beloved culprit theory, the "efficient market hypothesis," which says that the current market price always reflects all relevant information about asset values. Although the resulting devastation shows that their beliefs and methods were clearly out of whack, all is not necessarily lost; the mistaken economists can have some consolation from knowing that the beauty of their mathematical formulations enabled them to be wrong in an elegant manner.

Taking stock gives us less need to wonder how we got here. Enough has been said to show that something is rotten in the state of Western economies. What we have now, besides a recession featuring a scale change and a game change, is one that exhibits system failure in key sectors. This means that the foundations upon which to build the recovery are impaired like never before. Hence, the current downturn, as bad as it seems, is worse than it looks. Having presented a synopsis of why we are here, the question of where we might be going is examined next.

## 13.2 Facets Fashioning Prediction

*Big Picture Components*

Playing the role of seer without the benefit of a crystal ball is hazardous for obvious reasons; prediction is difficult, especially about the future, as Neil Bohr famously observed. Trepidation from sticking one's neck out is unavoidable, and this despite the laborious investigation that reached to some depth to get to the bottom of things in the preceding analysis. While there are no pretensions to prophecy, the predictions wrung out will have some basis in the logic of reason, and be more in the nature of educated guesses than wild ones. It is hoped that the sifted material from the preceding analysis will, when synthesized, join the dots for a better-than-ballpark perspective of what the future might hold. In other words, it is hoped that the factors identified next will help to craft a conjectural prognosis for the longed-for economic recovery.

Numerous flies in the ointment cause the economy's woes to have several edges to it. The criterion applied for identifying each of the several facets of the problem in the economy is straightforward in concept: simply size up the extent to which each element drives a wedge between where economies are at and where we would like them to be. The gap between the actual and desired positions will then identify the drawbacks plaguing the economy. Excerpted information from the preceding analysis is gathered to profile sets of factors that bedevil the economy and shape its future within the existing dysfunctional pseudo-market setup. The facets fashioning prognosis are examined under these five labels: Institutional, Market, Business, Economic, and Policy. Take each in turn.

*Institutional Facet*

Financial deregulation made propriety optional. It opened a Pandora's box that set financial plumbers called bankers on their way to becoming masters of the economic universe, besides redefining the rules of the marketplace for a whole new ball game in banking and beyond. Western governments surrendered control of finance, not to the market, but to bankers who thereby gained a pervasive influence over it. Because financial deregulation exuded a hypnotic charm on politicians, there was remarkable sang-froid about giving near carte blanche to powerful and aggressive big banks on a roll. There was tragic policy failure to differentiate between regulations that weaken business performance and those vital for open competitive markets to properly function. Although Western policymakers gave the world the Greek gift of financial deregulation, their lasting legacy is the boost given to the plutocratic pseudo-market condition. The spin-off "butterfly effects" of financial deregulation continue to reverberate disturbingly in the relentless forward momentum of pseudo-markets. Such ongoing fallout has the incidental effect of foiling recovery. As a result, what was hailed as a victory looks a lot like defeat.

Indiscriminate financial deregulation based on slash-and-burn dogmatism gave enlightened deregulation a bad name. The crucial message is that when laws vital for the orderly functioning of open competitive markets are absent, the regulatory architecture governing the operation of businesses is weakened, thereby causing systemic conflict between business and public interests. Increases in company profitability, which are expected to engender social prosperity, have become as antithetic to public wellbeing as joy is to despair. Financial deregulation with a mild and kindly touch showed all the hallmarks of a blithe overconfidence in the haughty assumption by deluded policymakers that license was freedom and unfettered markets the pathway to free-market heaven (when the opposite destination is the likelier prospect). A stunning coup for bankers was a massive gaffe for politicians.

There was amazing obliviousness to the tectonic significance of the flawed calculus from these mistaken perceptions. Pseudo-market expansionism has shifted the tectonic plates in world markets, putting downward pressure on competitive forces, and thrusting up the pseudo-market forces of monopolization, globalization, politicization, and corruption. Consequently, the deregulation process undermined effectively competitive free markets in the name of freedom, and facilitated a slippery slope to less competitive plutocratic pseudo-market conditions in all sectors of the economy, but most dangerously in the financial heart. A hazard arises from the financial sector's use of its pseudo-market prowess to foster pseudo-market expansionism in all other sectors – thereby draining the entrepreneurial dynamism in open competitive sectors of economies just about everywhere. The plutocratic pseudo-market condition, with its concomitant hydra traits, was shown to be as anti-social as it is anti-competitive. Financial deregulation, celebrated as a triumphant culmination of political achievement – the finest hour of free market believers and the crowning glory of policy advisors – is more appropriately mourned as the nadir of policy failure, an act of gross ineptitude and something to be to be ashamed of. It has led to anti-social shots being called by plutocrats in the spreading wild frontier of pseudo-markets. For this reason, financial deregulation could go down in economic history as an embarrassing artifact from capitalism's misspent past.

The attempt to re-regulate the finance industry constitutes an unspoken admission of error by the previously duped. The difficulties of re-regulation suggest that most enforcement attempts that begin with hope will end as farce. The need to buyoff powerful opponents with caveats, exceptions, limitations, preferential carve outs, and loopholes, has given re-regulatory measures the raggedness of something the cat brought in. Besides, the much larger size of banks after the deregulation means that bankers not only pack a much greater market-cum-political punch, but also have wider latitude for covert action in the dungeons of internationalized bureaucracies that operate across opaque and confounding foreign jurisdictions. This is besides the murkiness of shadow banking whose history casts a shadow over the future of financial stability.

The fusion of colossal size and attendant operational mysteriousness – including from the mistiness of transnational vastness – provides titanic firms with a sizable shield against meddlesome regulatory intrusions. Regulators are easy punch bags because of the hostile attitude of banks, bank-paid solicitors spoiling for action, the unfriendly disposition of politicians, and human rights laws protecting allegedly inhumane banks. In the circumstances, it would be understandable if regulators run for cover when bankers bare their teeth, taking refuge in backrooms for closed-door deals outside the open courts system. Such action could smack of cop-out when negotiated fines that seem extortionist to the public leave ample net gain from stealthy practice for banks. The nature of the regulation-enforcement process gives predictable fines the status of business operational costs for banks. For this reason it would make good business sense for regulation-management to parallel money-management as a business strategy in pursuance of profit. In these circumstances, there should be nothing surprising about an institutional inclination on the part of financial firms to furtively cross the line whenever opportunity knocks. If so, it would make a mockery of regulators' attempts to track infractions yielding payoffs to banks in magnitudes that give the seemingly hefty fines paid by banks chick-enfeed status.

For those who can see behind the scenes, the bloom is fast going off the rose of financial regulation. Consequently, there is not much justification for joyous chants at prospects for bringing banks into line through re-regulation, the setbacks in this regard promising to be more painful than victories can hope to be sweet. Because regulatory efficacy is a forlorn cause, it means that, for bankers, the nexus is weakened between regulation-breaking and fitful sleeping. The situation has been helped by the penchant of central bankers for perilous bubble-fostering behavior. For these less-than uplifting reasons, global finance seems a long way from safe.

*Market Facet*

Although the current economic downturn is not anywhere as deep as the Great Depression, it is probably more intractable due to plutocratic pseudo-market conditions in key sectors of the economy. This phenomenon of the plutocratic pseudo-market condition, particularly in the financial heart of the economy, makes this crisis an odd beast outside the bounds of standard economics. It has changed the face of economies and altered the balance between firms and governments, by pivoting real power toward firms and away from governments. The anti-free market effect of deregulation was a blow to those policymakers who poured their hopes into a policy for market freedom, but ended up catching a Tartar (the plutocrat in the not-so-free pseudo-market).

Plutocratic pseudo-markets are the misbegotten step-children of deregulation with traits shown to be big, bad, and ugly. Plutocratic pseudo-markets are plagued by an anti-competitive pathology of monopolistic strong-arm capability, global market manipulation, influence over political processes, and licentious-prone business practices. Each attribute is a nail in the coffin of entrepreneurs in open competitive market sectors.

The plutocratic pseudo-market condition gives rise to phony markets where firms can find funny business to be normal business. In such markets, the rent seeking manipulative hand gets the upper hand over the revered "invisible hand." This causes the "invisible hand" of efficiency for social wellbeing through private profits, to be superseded by the hidden hand of manipulation for private profits at the expense of social wellbeing. Such deviancy incidentally causes the manipulative hand to operate a handbrake on economic recovery. Furthermore, it is not possible to follow in the footsteps of the "father of *laissez faire* economics," Adam Smith, because the manipulative hand in plutocratic pseudo-market conditions has a natural tendency to erase his footprints.

Things look grim because plutocratic pseudo-market conditions are shown to have an inherent dynamism for cumulative momentum: a disposition to relentlessly spread their somewhat wild frontier in unfettered higgledy-piggledy ways. They tend to advance imperceptibly through a myriad of incremental steps that enable the spread of corporate gigantism to be, ironically, nimble-footed enough to outflank policymakers with a beguiling insidiousness. The gigantism characterizing the plutocratic pseudo-market condition is being fostered by a spate of acquisitions and mergers, many of them foreign takeovers. A merger can come in handy when corporate consolidation provides an opportunity to conceal embarrassments like a profit squeeze, operational inefficiency, or managerial incompetence. These structural developments toward corporate gigantism are radically reshaping the international market landscape – one featuring the image of a herd of woolly corporate mammoths ambling roughshod over the face of the earth.

The relentless forward momentum of plutocratic pseudo-market forces is associated with spreading atrophy in affected economies suffering the loss of precious competitive pressure. Conditions exist for a vicious circle of deregulation and a spiral of pseudo-market expansionism, causing firms in open competitive sectors to be routinely out-competed and out-bred by pseudo-market firms. The result is that plutocratic pseudo-market forces cut an insidious swath through the international economy, the silent encroachment causing effectively competitive open markets to die by inches as they lose ground to steamrolling anti-competitive forces.

In pseudo-market conditions, plutocratic influence comes with the territory – and plutocratic forces provide the wind at the back for pseudo-market advancement. The relationship between business and politics has mutated to a stage beyond informal cronyism to the institutionalized shaping of public policy by plutocrats behind a facade of democracy. This means that the leaders of pseudo-market firms are not ordinary business people because the supposedly governed are known to wield a behind-the-scenes governing influence for securing private benefit at social cost. Plutocratic influence tends to be invulnerable and growing, driven by a sense of entitlement to national resources.

Financiers are becoming the standard bearers of progress in the debt-obligated West. The diktats of global financiers can, with number-crunching acumen, fashion the economic world in their own narrow, balance-sheet-blinkered, image of it. In such a world, the gnomes of Zurich types get close and personal, causing the financiers' ethos to hold sway, and the financial sector to win the battle for supremacy in the global economy. The financial footprint on the world economy enlarges when countries cede sovereignty in relation to socioeconomic policy and budgetary autonomy to ascendant financiers contrary to the Westphalian (1648) notion of the nation state. It seems arguable that a straitjacketing financier's ethos has put Western economies on course to a new world order. Speculation centers on whether, given time, the evolving condition is susceptible to morphing into the running sore of a myopic plutocratic financial imperialism.

*Business Facet*

Gigantic firms are the hallmark of plutocratic pseudo-market conditions. In such conditions, business operations are a new ball game where unclear rules permit stealthy moves. There are several reasons why the present recovery is not a riot of business enterprise. It is because several dispiriting factors haunt the business environment. An overwhelming one is pseudo-market expansionism at the expense of competitive-market dynamism. With plutocrats in charge, opportunities for untoward practices increase, causing sensitivity to matters considered ethically delicate to decrease. Specifically, plutocrats are not known for shying away from non-operational strategies of a manipulative nature. These include strong-arm tactics against politicians, artful exploitation of jurisdictional differences and opaqueness in international environments, stand-over and strong-arm monopolistic practices, and recourse to licentious tactics like price fixing, customer hoodwinking, and rate fiddling.

Pseudo-markets are characterized by pseudo competition. What passes for free competition in such markets is mostly oligopolistic gamesmanship for a share of the spoils gained from exerting pseudo-market muscle. Pseudo-market firms earn profits not just through textbook means such as improved productivity, efficiency, and strategic marketing, but also acquire (not earn) profits through non-operational and non-marketing means (formally called rent seeking). In other words, a significant but unknown component of the profits of such firms comes from acquiring a share of what is made by others, rather than adding to the size of the pie by their own productive efforts. A few market leaders call the shots in the industry, and then attempt to outmaneuver each other for the spoils that come from monopolistic market power, plutocratic political influence, global manipulation, and newfangled corruption.

Plodding firms are fostered in plutocratic pseudo-market conditions, making zombiism fashionable when markets are dysfunctional. Hemorrhaging competitive pressures reduce the need for pizzazz associated with dynamism. Because pseudo-markets are graveyards for entrepreneurship, their firms tend to become "dead wood" in secret by using their pseudo-market traits to camouflage inefficiencies, at least in the short term. There is no reason to doubt the pseudo-market firms' ability to protect much of their mystery. In the period before the world economy turned turtle, the image of corporate prosperity was a facade for atrophy; the much-vaunted record company earnings turned out to be hollow shams – *a la* Freddie Mac, Fannie May, Lehman Brothers, bailout recipients, and all the rest.

All this is helped by the fillip given to gigantism by a spate of acquisitions and mergers. The wave of company consolidation keeps rolling on, driven, rather than impeded, by the current downturn. It is revolutionizing the international business structure by expanding and entrenching anti-recovery plutocratic pseudo-market conditions. The blessings of togetherness from corporate marriages of convenience include being able to hide internal embarrassment (like managerial inefficiency) and dodge the emergency room (for wrenching reforms). Besides, every acquisition and merger entrenches the market position of heavy-hitting incumbents in relation to potential new entrants. The weakened competitive pressure enables incumbent firms to sit pretty in salubrious pseudo-market conditions, pampered by the rent-providing comforts of monopolization, globalization, politicization, and corruption. Under these conditions, political strategy unsurprisingly becomes a normal extension of business strategy.

Ponderous Leviathan organizations that pass for firms can use their international presence to avoid dancing to national tunes. Such sidestepping means that government regulatory measures aimed at banks and other multinational firms are unlikely to achieve much domestically, when company operations take place globally. Squeezing the balloon in one place can result in its expansion in another, one country's tough measure becoming another country's golden opportunity. Additionally, the escape hatch called shadow banking has ample space for accommodating such bulges. Financial deregulators, by tremendously boosting the plutocratic pseudo-market condition in the financial sector, have set up a fiefdom more of mammon than of angels.

The business environment is not favorable to recovery because of the smothering effects of plutocratic pseudo-market conditions; hindrances that may seem minor in isolation synergize to become major in aggregate. The several pseudo-market caused impediments are these: excluding the majority of individuals and competitive firms in open markets from opportunity and income gain (resulting in forgone consumption and investment); truncating business planning horizons for quick pay-offs (fostering a short-termism in business culture that discourages bets on long-term visionary projects for strategic competitive advantage); favoring investment in finance in preference to the real economy (limiting job creation and confining the benefits of growth mostly to investors with bundles of shares); destroying more jobs than they create (through strategies like acquisitions and mergers and the export of jobs); discouraging investment by smaller and more entrepreneurial companies, including startups (suppressing dynamism and employment creation); and using their four anti-competitive traits for pursing profits through manipulation rather than through operational and marketing acumen (fostering inefficiencies by instilling a zombie-type disposition in rent seeking firms).

The banking business strategy in vogue inhibits recovery in the real economy, but not out of spite. It makes eminent good sense for banks to play favorites by biasing their lending toward their own kind wearing the pseudo-market mantle. This means, the blue-eyed companies attracting the more favorable loans are more likely than not to be the larger and more established multinational companies – the types that export jobs as well as recovery. As a result, the bankers' favorites can use their inside-track status with the banks to keep beefing up their plutocratic pseudo-market muscle and entrenching their anti-recovery disposition. This is obviously a sad state of affairs as far as genuine recovery is concerned, because the competitive firms in more open sectors create most of the jobs, while pioneering startup companies are the hotbed of employment opportunities and innovative dynamism. It can never be known how many startups were denied stardom because of financial-market-caused distortion. In addition, many of the loans go to those who favor investment in buoyant finance, where the bang for the buck is greater and faster in conditions of cheap-cum-easy money and stimulated stock-cum-housing markets, than in the lumbering real economy. Banks are driving stock and housing markets wild, while grinding factories and patents to a halt – thereby dulling recovery. Most loans have gone into purchasing existing financial assets (not into new factories, offices, equipment, etc), thereby denying job-creation and driving up the prices of existing assets to levels that look suspiciously like inflating bubbles with a reputation for grisly busts. In fact, the bubbles may already be hideously overblown.

Banks are at the centre of the problem, but banks are not the problem. If banks are not doing the right thing for recovery, logic suggests that it is the dysfunctional market – not the banks – that should be in the public's crosshairs. The broken system creates incentives for banks to unintentionally throw the aforementioned wrenches in the recovery works. Doing so is a rational response to distorted incentives; it is behavior with inadvertent side effects that happen to be of the anti-social and anti-recovery sort. Market circumstances make seemingly bad banking behavior eminently appropriate. Hence, there is good reason to question whether banking practices can be presented as a valid *casus belli*.

*Economic Facet*

Bleak is chic; confidence in the future is the key to recovery, but confidence has proven elusive in a West given to pessimism. True, optimism has trumped reality for the few speculator sorts with bullfighter nerves. But the evidence is that normal people in America and Europe are finding their confidence in the future eroded by wild cards, both domestic and foreign (as evidenced by the some $3 trillion in cash hoarded by firms as well as by the consumer inclination to tightfistedness). Western economies rank poorly on several measures, giving rise to low business and consumer confidence in the mainstream. European economies are in the dumps and the American economy is hitting air pockets for patchy growth and false dawns. A genuine upswing in the real economy is nowhere to be seen; what is regarded as just another run-of-the-mill business cycle downswing was shown to be dangerously exceptional, not reassuringly traditional.

Blooms of new investment cannot sprout when there is a drought in confidence. The economic obstacles to durable economic recovery are elusive, if only because they are shadowy: how can we turn on switches in people's heads for a behavioral shift from "frugal" to "spend"? The hangover persists for investors and consumers trying to sober up after the pre-crisis binge, the downbeat market players being in a funk about the future of the real economy and suffering from a "bad attack of pessimism" (to use Keynesian phraseology). In practice, because the intangibility of psychology holds the key to powering authentic recovery in the real economy, the unsettling effect of business uncertainty means: 'don't build, don't hire, don't buy, just wait and see.' Few firms are bullish enough to expand even when banks are happy to lend. It is clear that market players are not fooled by all the hype about good times around the corner; stinginess from downheartedness continues to enfeeble aggregate demand and foil recovery for the majority.

Threatening wild cards cast a shadow over both Europe and America. The trigger for the next economic collapse could come from either side of the pond, although Europe is the shakier end because of the deadly mixture comprising torpidity, debt, and deflation. Deflation will cut back consumption, dry up investment, and trigger loan defaults – for a pernicious negative spiral that will likely cause the wobbling eurozone to fall apart (unless money printing battles deflation and saves the day). The specters of European sovereign debt default and eurozone breakup are chronic swords of Damocles that loom over the American economy in particular and the world economy in general. Hope for a durable recovery in the West grows dimmer even as Europe's political and financial dysfunction gets deeper – and hopes for vital structural reforms become dreamier.

*Policy Facet*

The package of policy tools available is not anything like a box of tricks; it lacks the capability of amazing everyone by triggering a recovery spurt in the real economy. Past folly foils current success; conventional economic policies have been rendered anemic or useless by blunders that have boosted recovery-undermining plutocratic pseudo-market conditions to an unprecedented extent. Monetary policy, austerity, and government spending have seen good service as the devils we know, but their reliability and relevance are in doubt because these worn measures are required to work in novel market conditions. The focus on habitual policy prescriptions from moth-eaten playbooks promise nothing better than having to muddle through a rolling series of crises. What these overworked policies can offer, at best, is an expedient palliative, not a lasting solution. It is pardonable if the bypassed majority see the unimaginative policy measures as gimmicks promising drearily predictable disappointment.

Monetary policy gets you only so far, even when the candle is burned at both ends; at one end is immoderate money printing and at the other is a near-zero nominal interest rate. Despite the open-handedness with monetary policy, few in the real economy are applauding; paradoxically, large amounts of cheap money cannot by itself buy economic prosperity for the outcast majority. Because stock markets are driven more by confidence in central banks' supportive policies than in the economy, bad news is good news; bad news brings comforting central bank intervention for mispricing risk. Over-egging the monetary pudding makes it look good now, but taste awful later. Central banks are putting off the evil day by ignoring the cloven hoof: the grotesquely warped fundamentals of asset markets that are dire forebodings of future distress if the robust recovery they are counting on does not happen soon. In the absence of a recovery that is sturdy-enough and soon-enough, something will have to give. Near-zero interest rates, indicative of interest rate policy having run into the sand, can be interpreted as a zero mark for monetary performance, especially in deflationary circumstances – a clear fail.

Besides the overdone monetary policy, the budgetary policy scene is starkly split between two conflicting templates for economic growth that give rise to a bewildering tension. Contradictory advice from the proverbial two-handed economist probably makes economics seem like nonsense to non-economists (i.e., most people). On the one hand, there is "fiscal austerity" (cutbacks in government programs); on the other hand, there is "fiscal stimulus" (more spending on government programs). A polarized stalemate is assured because the options are mutually exclusive. One side vilifies the other and is cordially detested in return. From an *ex-ante* standpoint, the question of which policy is the real McCoy is a toss-up, since proof of the policy pudding is in the eating.

On the one hand, the austerity policy, dominant in the West, advocates cutting back government programs to cut deficits and repay loans. This involves tightening the purse strings for tightening belts, but not out of meanness. Harnessing austerity is seen as a virtuous means of overcoming the sin of debt and returning budgets to the holy grail of balance. There is, however, a question mark over the austerity policy approach based on the experience of the Great Depression, recent research findings by the International Monetary Fund (IMF), and the chill in the air from deflation caused by chronically weak demand. The stagnant plight of Europe may offer a case study on the perils of excessive and ill-timed austerity. Opponents of austerity claim that cutting back on government programs before the economy reaches escape velocity involves the anachronism of a cart before the horse. This means, jumping the gun with untimely and excessive austerity will make a bad situation worse by further weakening faltering demand, and have the opposite effect to that intended – drag down growth and increase the deficit. Austerity has not yet proven itself to be a groovy option. On the basis of the examined evidence it seems that what the economy stands to gain from austerity is less obvious than what it stands to lose, especially now that the specter of deflation looms. Austerity may well end up as just another name for a flop if undertaken excessively, before the economy is in full swing, and in malfunctioning plutocratic pseudo-market conditions that have the capability of subverting it.

On the other hand, the burst of government spending for fiscal stimulus is seen as a shot in the arm that is claimed to cure nervousness in spenders and perk up anemic demand to get the sick economy going, but not without the risk of side effects. This option enables governments to borrow wads of money from firms hoarding cash, and then shovel it toward roads, schools, police, parks, fire fighters, and the like. Besides handily reconciling succor with recovery, such expenditures for pump-priming are believed to spur the private sector into going great guns because of spin-off multiplier effects that are presumed will wash through the economy and generate revenue for debt service. Prudent borrowing for government expenditure cannot be such a bad idea when interest rates are at rock bottom, cash stockpiles lay idle under the mattresses of businesses, public goods like roads and schools are crying out for funding, and deflation is threatening. The best way to rapidly revive growth, it is claimed, is to plough money into infrastructure – the sound of jackhammers being music to the ears of business people wanting confidence from vitalized demand prospects.

Advocating community upliftment by a course of action that sinks indebted communities further into debt is a jittery prospect for many, and can be counter-intuitive to most policymakers. It does not make sense to many that the answer to the problem of government borrowing is to borrow more to pay it back. What is more, stimulus spending in dysfunctional pseudo-market conditions could result in the already-well-off arrogating to themselves the lion's share of the benefits, with only the crumbs being available for the majority in the community, as happened before and continues to happen today. Even more worrying is the likelihood of counterproductive outcomes. Plodding pseudo-market firms, enriched by the stimulus money, could use their added strength to weaken or eliminate firms in open competitive sectors that are the major sources of employment and dynamism in the economy – causing the open sectors to become shrinking pools. Consequently, it is understandable if the policy of fiscal stimulus based on borrowing is a lost cause – with a pariah status to boot.

The budgetary policy options, being mutually exclusive, make *rational* compromise impossible. Hammering out a compromise does not make sense; it must all be one way or the other because of their cancelling-out effect. Consequently, it is understandable that fiscal policy formulation is automatically stalemated when give-and-take is sought. A fractured economics is at war with itself, with budgetary policy disagreements being hardly distinguishable from ideological scraps because of the unholy entanglement of economics and prejudice. A befuddling economics understandably flummoxes policymakers – and just about everybody else.

Conventional economic policies have not proven to be up to par; the deficit in their credibility compounds the deficit in the budget. Dogged perseverance with expedient measures that are more of the same, by those finding comfort in policies that are "the better the devil you know," have failed to sufficiently resurrect real economies, where the majority continues to feel the pinch of hard times. If the sorry experience of the last seven years of downturn teaches anything, it is that even massive doses of conventional policy therapy have not succeeded in setting the economic world on fire. Pursing recovery with conventional policies is a wild goose chase when the policies are thwarted by impaired markets and tattered institutions. Advocates of conventional policies fail to recognize that the system is broken. Since a simulated recovery with shallow roots cannot be more than a farcical interlude, policymakers risk the charge of culpable complacency because of their reckless disdain for the truth.

If the fiscal austerity option is nicknamed "Tweedledum," the fiscal spending option becomes "Tweedledee" (with apologies to Lewis Carroll). There is not much difference between policy options that are equally guilty of ignoring the elephant in the room; both strangely neglect to expressly consider the dysfunction of the plutocratic pseudo-market condition and its propensity to undermine the effectiveness of whichever policy option is chosen. Both options blithely assume away the very condition that needs to be centrally addressed: the challenge posed for durable recovery by the hydra-headed plutocratic pseudo-market condition, with its distinctly anti-competitive, anti-social, and anti-recovery traits. Both policy avenues confine policymakers to comfort zones, sparing them the pressure needed to force them to think outside the box. As a result, policymakers fail to notice the feeble state of the beating heart needed for true recovery, namely the impaired free-market mechanism. This suggests that the two fiscal options may qualify for the following Shakespearean condemnation: "A pox on both your houses."

## 13.3 A Prognostication

The pulse remains weak in the ailing West; ongoing sputter is symptomatic of a dark horizon visible to business people and consumers not fooled by the everyday hype trumpeting recovery. The economy hangs in from day to day and policymakers are in public denial about a fragile and spurious economic recovery that can take a turn for the worse with narcoleptic predictability (i.e., at any time). Plausible signs of a recovery are not seen beyond the deceptively reassuring

immediate vicinity. There are no signs on the horizon that the economies of the West are capable of sprinting back to pre-crisis prosperity
any time soon; there can be no hope for a prolonged boom when even
a proper cyclical recovery is proving elusive.

Achieving previous levels of prosperity seems impossibly distant. This is because repeated plucky attempts with the usual policy
measures have mostly drawn a blank insofar as opportunity for the
majority of people in the West is concerned. The hype about recovery obscures in shadow a majority struggling with a lack of opportunity. If the majority is despairing of experiencing recovery, it is
because the flaunted GDP increases and falling jobless rates are
average measures that are only average in their capacity for con-
veying a true impression of the real situation; they cloud a skewed
reality featuring disparities and lopsidedness. That is besides the
element of smoke-and-mirrors in the statistical methodology used
for computing them. They camouflage the truth about the absent
recovery for the excluded majority that includes much of the middle
class, the backbone of the economy.

The feeling of exasperation at problems in the economy shows
up as a chronic breach between where things are at and where we
would like them to be. The somber gap between the actual and
desired positions is occupied by a multiplicity of issues. These are
classified within five sets of fiendishly challenging flaws that explain
how it came to this: broken institutions; worrying business practices;
sagging investor and consumer confidence; obstinate commitment to
ineffective economic policies; and, underpinning and overwhelming
everything, the monstrosity of the plutocratic pseudo-market condition in key sectors. When these failings in the economy are stacked
up, they form an unwieldy heap resembling the mangled complexity
of a train wreck. Dealing with the problem will involve the daunting
task of cutting through the tangle of intertwined aspects. If that does

not sound like much to cheer, that is because it is not. In terms of an old Austrian adage, "The situation is hopeless, but not serious," as will soon become apparent.

Even a cautious sense of triumph is unjustified because appearances can be deceiving. Despite happy talk to the contrary, Western economies are in water that is far deeper than most governments and analysts are letting on. Telltale fundamentals speak for themselves. There are enough unpleasant signs to keep knowledgeable people worried, and one such sign is the repeated failure of conventional policies to get things going in circumstances of looming deflation and lopsided growth benefits. Worn policies have been shown to be expedient palliatives that swap immediate problems for huge chronic ones, the latter hampering a recovery that is robust and inclusive. Monetary policy-induced hallucinatory zips are a poor substitute for the genuine spark of life capable of awakening the dormant potential in the real economy for deep-rooted growth.

The currently adopted policy measures enable, at best, death by slow motion, possibly lasting several years. Some options, like lavish money printing and public spending enable a slow death (like by strangulation in the coils of a python), whereas other options, like drastic and untimely austerity, are associated with a much quicker demise (like from the bite of a viper). The slower process would better suit the three-to-five year planning horizons of elected politicians looking for politic electoral pay-offs from holding the fort. Periodically elected politicians are locked into vision-destroying electoral cycles, where success can take the form of marking time by buying time and doing so with borrowed or printed money. The downturn has shown politicians to be masters of the dark art of the classic fudge enabled by short planning horizons. Because long-term choices do not sit well with short-term perspectives, the strategic vision needed for spearheading fundamental reforms for sustained gains tends to get sacrificed at the altar of political expediency.

Simulated upticks make extrapolations rash; upbeat expectations are unwarranted optimism when based on amorphous factors and unsustainable policies. Artificially induced upticks in housing and share markets are false dawns that are widely heralded as signs of true recovery to soothe the situation, given that the whole economic edifice rests on the fragile mainstay of volatile human psychology. Good news stories have to keep being churned out to prevent a replay of hysterical market behavior that precipitates another collapse. The periodic clutching at phantom straws by those with an inclination to put a brave face on things, or have a penchant to keep deluding themselves, is a predictable pattern in a short-term future that can only promise fake recoveries in fits and starts.

Can the current recovery be taken seriously when it depends on proclamations by the very people who mistook pre-crisis bubbles for real prosperity? Analysts responsible for headlines and others who qualify as professional spin doctors could have a vested interest in using pretty talk to proclaim a "dead cat bounce" as real buoyancy; they are probably hoping that truth will catch up with hype to make the latter a self-fulfilling prophesy. When there is skewed economic growth that excludes the majority of the population from benefit, and it is based on shallow confidence and brittle expectations, it cannot be more than an apology for a recovery. Overblown recovery claims betray a sense of insecurity permeating Western policymaking and justify any reluctance on the part of the bypassed majority to uncork champagne bottles in victory celebration.

There seems to be an element of cock-and-bull in the view that America can be an island of recovery in a sea of economic torpidity. Although the American economy is some seventy-five percent domestic-demand driven, how fast can America be growing while Europe is shrinking, if not collapsing – especially when its nosedive transforms beacons of hope into places of gloom by dragging down China, Japan and, in turn, the rest of the world? This is besides the direct threat to American exports, its foreign investments, as well as to its banking system from guarantees given by American banks to Europeans against loan defaults (billions of dollars in "credit default swaps" have been written on European sovereign debt by American banks). The investment climate in America is unlikely to be immune to such developments. Enough has been said to show that the fates of America and Europe are inextricably intertwined, as they were when they rose together with the Marshall Plan of 1948 and collapsed together in the recession of 2008. This must make a sustained and full-fledged American recovery to previous levels impractical without an attendant European recovery. Economic resurgence in both America and Europe is being held back by the unacknowledged albatross of a plutocratic pseudo-market condition. If nothing is done, it could be only a matter of time before economies buckle under the deadweight of a top-heavy form of corrupted capitalism that rests on market foundations that are treacherously misbegotten.

There is every indication that, in the end, the truth will out. After repeated false dawns and failed promises, people will come to realize that a robust and inclusive economic recovery is not in the bag after all. They will stop scratching their heads once it dawns on them that an "unending recovery" signals that something is rotten in the state of the market. Making pin-up boys and girls of plutocrats riding high in anti-social pseudo-markets and pandering to pseudo-market firms through means such as generous state subsidies, more tax breaks, and greater market access, is bound to disappoint policymakers in search of genuine recovery; they have the wrong targets for largesse. Adulations and benefits of this nature can be expected to stimulate private sector activity for genuine recovery in dynamic competitive open-market conditions, but are unlikely to do so in dysfunctional plutocratic pseudo-market conditions; for the most part they are boondoggles that play into the hands of pseudo-market oligarchs.

Faith in the idea that benefitting businesses inevitably benefits the community is quaintly dated when the business operates in pseudo-market conditions. By blundering into bribes for pseudo-market firms, politicians will only harm recovery by cultivating and rewarding the very forces that impede it. For this reason, the anti-recovery blowback from mollycoddling plutocrats of pseudo-market firms would make governments architects of their own misfortune. In the end, the current short-term and unimpressive recoveries will increasingly be recognized for what they really are: nothing more than transient upticks in terminally ailing economies on life support, that need nothing less than the equivalent of a heart transplant for any hope of a lasting recovery to previous health.

Pronouncements that ignore market fundamentals only beg questions; they are, by and large, trite explanations for a recovery unworthy of its name – "the solidified commonplaces of established wisdom" (to use the words of contemporary American literary critic, John Simon). The real reason for the absence of proper recovery is less obvious and less acknowledged, because it is to be found in broken and underlying fundamentals that are disavowed. The laughable effectiveness of current economic and regulatory policies is not what should be gnawing at the West's once boundless confidence. What should be nerve-racking is dysfunction in the very mechanism needed for powering durable recovery: the effectively competitive open capitalist market system that embodies entrepreneurial spirit. Because economies are weighed down by the plutocratic pseudo-market albatross, a business cycle upswing will need to defy gravity if it is to happen.

The growth-sapping features previously reported are the products of markets that have degenerated into farce. Unlocking the black box that is the plutocratic pseudo-market condition reveals it to be a mare's nest, incapable of delivering valid recovery. In fact, there is every indication that the plutocratic pseudo-market condition is a formidable impediment to genuine recovery in the real economy. Markets are debased when they delink company profitability from both operational efficiency and a recovery that is sturdy and widely felt. A recovery that is robust and inclusive depends on the dynamism of markets from initiative, drive, and vibrancy and these features are associated with entrepreneurial firms operating in effectively competitive open market conditions – and not with manipulative Leviathans operating in opaque plutocratic pseudo-market conditions. Consequently, the normal course of developments is increasingly circumscribing the fertile competitive market terrain essential for the sprouting of strong recovery shoots. It appears that the fallout from pseudo-markets in stymieing recovery knows no end within the existing scheme of things.

The chances for a durable recovery dwindle with protraction; the longer it takes to materialize the less likely is it to happen. Protraction causes a doom loop when the downturn feeds upon itself to be self-perpetuating. In current circumstances, less investment now could diminish the ability of the economy to grow later. This makes indeterminate the point in time when a genuine upswing would raise the economy far enough from the bottom to enable a deprived majority to see distant blue skies. Spending cutbacks for cost savings in education, research and development, and infrastructure investments are shown to smother productivity and blunt the cutting edge of technology. These in turn dull the cutting edge of competitiveness in companies. Less competitiveness means lower sales, less profit, less investment, still less competitiveness, further cutbacks, and so on – implying economic stagnation at best, and a spiral of decline at worst.

Adding to self-perpetuation is the "paradox of thrift" from greater household tightfistedness due to the uncertainty. When consumers penny-pinch together it means less buying, lower sales, and less

business profits, lower investment, and so on. For this reason consumer spending cutbacks can add to the downward spiral of investment and accelerate the doom loop. So can monetary policies that are
soothing in the short-term but toxic in the long-term. Consequently,
the longer the slump lasts, the harder recovery becomes.

Permanently shrunken economies in the West are not just
expected; they are already here. A permanently diminished condition
will result from a lower economic surface that has permanently shifted
downward due to wealth destruction. A troubling possibility must be
squarely faced: the majority of the population in America and Europe
is all too likely going to be poorer into the indefinite future, with future
income falling well short of pre-crisis levels. This means that limited
opportunity and a lost American dream are a new normality for large
swaths of the population in a situation where a significant component
of an increasingly hard-up middle class is forced to join the ranks of the
underclass. Such indefinite downtime and loss of status would mean
a Spartan future for those left behind. In the absence of just the thing,
namely fundamental market reform, there would need to be a quiet
sense of inevitability that the West would have to cut its coat according
to its shrunken cloth as it downsizes to reality and adapts to a lower
level of living in a time-warped future. Where the future meets the past
is where the new normality would exist. That would mean an enduring
reversion to an income level of many years back for the outcast majority – implying entrenched wretchedness i.e., misery sans a silver lining.

Confounding matters is that regardless of the economic policy
options chosen, authentic recovery seems to depend more on a stroke
of luck than on a stroke of genius. What this means is that durable
recovery depends largely on wild cards beyond the control of national
governments acting alone, however brilliant their policies. Conditions
are not propitious for a recovery that is robust and inclusive when
account is taken of the extraordinary nature of the current condition:

the lackluster, artificial, and patchy recovery in America; the back-sliding in Europe; and the black boxes with regard to Japan and China – these four economies being the four rickety legs of a table that is the world economy. All it would take for the tottering table to topple is for one leg that is a mainstay to break. Except for some former banana republics that have assumed *nouveau-riche* respectability because of ample foreign currency reserves, a collapse of the big four will cause most of the economies around the world to tumble together for a spectacular and deadly ensemble.

It goes without saying that visitations of disaster have the status of unwelcome guests, especially when the guests are of a cataclysmically unfriendly disposition. Whatever the exact source of vulnerability for the world economy may be, even a remote prospect of Armageddon is something that, arguably, should not be lightly dismissed – especially when it threatens to be of heart-breaking "buddy-can-you-spare-a-dime" proportions. Even assuming only half what is possible happens, it means "you ain't seen nothing yet."

The policy vacuum within the existing broken market system has set the scene for unhindered further decent into the abyss of depression. Marching down the current path is no cakewalk along a royal road. It involves soldiering along the beaten track of a long rocky road punctuated by twists and turns, humps and dips, persevering towards a distant recovery that could turn out to be a mirage. If a ghastly chasm should suddenly appear in the road ahead, the long march to recovery will become a death march to hopelessness in those Western countries that are transformed into basket cases by the further collapse. Although the casualties of such a cataclysm would be banana republics in denial, their reduced status from penury will likely be felt as wounded national pride all the same.

The wretched state of austerity-battered European economies like Greece and Spain, exhibiting stubbornly sky-high

435

unemployment, is a straw in the wind that foreshadows unpleasantness for the lost majority in America and Europe. Despite
massive financial assistance, and showing some incipient signs of
improvement, Greece and Spain still have unemployment rates of
US Great Depression proportions and a majority groaning on the
rack. The Greek economy went from feast to famine and shrank
by a quarter. If Greece was hypothetically stripped of its massive
financial life-support, a third-world bellwether would be uncovered. It would be an example suggestive of what conditions could
end up looking like throughout the West in the event of further
collapse – justifying any uneasy feeling on the part of the bypassed
majority in America and Europe.

The implied message for the bypassed majority in the West is
simply this: enjoy this slump while you can and hope that it lasts
forever. The present sluggishness is probably the closest thing to
success within the existing scheme of things; there may be no time
like the present because this is probably as good as it gets. That
means: stop craving prosperity, settle for torpidity. Consequently,
it appears that the chronic downturn in the economies of the West
is the blue skies of a new makeshift normality for the forgotten
majority. The present languorous economic condition, which has
made feeling the pinch of hard times a test of endurance for the
afflicted, would be cause for celebration when assessed against the
worse alternative; seizing the day to stay in the sizzling frying pan
of recession would be preferable to the proverbial alternative (the
dreaded fire of depression). Because close shaves from near-death
experiences are not prone to much repetition, gratitude for the
present languid economy is a justifiable feeling for those able to
read what is in the cards.

Cutting to the chase exposes inaccurate labeling. Describing this
downturn as a "Great Financial Crisis" or "Great Recession" can be

regarded as propagandist understatements that deserve the label: "The Big Lie." This refers to repeated, self-serving trivialization designed to mollify the public and hide the seriousness of the condition behind a curtain of humbug. It would not be surprising if many find it hard to accept the awful truth that the old order has gone forever and that economic growth can never reach previous levels (the fallacy of perpetual growth has been explained and revealed to be a nonsensical absurdity wrapped up in an irrational fantasy). It may be even more difficult to submit to the reality that what is needed to fix things properly is a quantum leap by way of fundamental market reform to reinvent the economy

## 13.4 The Glimmer of Hope

*The Needed Perception*

In the absence of fundamental market reforms to revamp the economy, there arises the disagreeable condition of Hobson's choice (meaning, a choice between taking what is there or nothing at all). The choice is between the following alternatives: indeterminate continuation of the current downturn (with an indefinitely lower quality of life for the majority of the population in America and Europe) or Armageddon (a catastrophic plunge into an unknown future). The dismaying implication is that there is no real choice because the choice is between the proverbial frying pan and fire. These unhappy alternatives serve to clear away the cobwebs and question rosy misconceptions rooted in ideology, leaving little room for putting a gloss on things. If things seem like misery to a sick-at-heart public, it is because they are. The experts cited have pronounced that the brink of collapse is now. The frustrating absence of "tidings of comfort and joy" should be enough to make grown men cry. The confluence of issues that have been laboriously delineated in this book has led to this cheerless conclusion. Nevertheless, there is no reason for anybody to slit their wrists

437

in despair, because it is possible to take heart from the ray of hope in the information that follows; the curtain has not been brought down because the fat lady has yet to sing "Kumbaya."

Omens need not be grim to the extent of becoming the handwriting on the wall; there has to be hope no matter how hopeless the situation may seem, and that cannot occur except by setting one's sight on lofty goals. As economic problems cumulatively multiply from an "unending recovery," there will be increasing realization that there is no future in the status quo. The current state of frustrated expectations would be a precursor to success if it is educational in pointing to the true cause of thwarted recovery: plutocratic pseudo-market dysfunction. The logical implication is that support for the present type of dabbling by policymakers would fade, as policymakers ease up on fantasies about markets, and recognition of the real problem finally dawns.

It should be clear by now that the nut needing to be cracked is a tough one. The difficulty stems from the fact that the basis for a durable recovery, the one that enabled recovery from the depths of the Great Depression over seventy years ago, is mostly gone. Although the present economic trough is nowhere as deep as it was then, climbing out will be much harder because of system failure – that is, market dysfunction. The unprecedented entrenchment of plutocratic pseudo-market conditions in key sectors of the economy means that what worked adequately then is less able to work now. This observation finds support in the fact that all conventional policy options have proven incapable of more than scant impact in current conditions. They have not been able to do more than scratch the surface of the problem for the simple reason that the problem is unprecedentedly underpinning. The situation marks a new departure from antecedent conditions. Maltreatment of the market mechanism through ill-considered deregulation has expedited and amplified a serious nuts-and-bolts failure in the form of broken down sociopolitical institutions (impaired political systems, plutocratic influences, bad laws, ineffectual regulations, and poor business ethics) and anti-competitive industry structures (comprising anti-social transnational behemoths that are semi-political entities but considered mere firms).

Fundamental reform refers to the commonsensical requirement that the disintegrating foundations of capitalist markets must be repaired before any real recovery can be built on them. So much for theory; practicalities are another matter. Despite the horse sense in the above argument, it is a suggestion that runs the risk of being snowed under by the implied tall order. The question is: who, having entered into the spirit of such fundamental reforms, are rolling up their sleeves and getting ready to rush to action stations for undertaking the task of fixing the busted foundations of capitalist markets? Vision-driven political stirrings, for the heavy lifting that would be required if radical market reforms to reinvent the economy are to take place, are conspicuous by their absence.

*The Needed Action*

There is a glimmer of hope for those inclined to optimism. If waiting until kingdom come is not an acceptable option, something must be done to put things right, preferably with a suggestion that cannot be easily mocked by ideologues of whatever hue. The erosion of open competitive sectors, or even economic collapse, will not be hard to achieve: a persistent refusal to confront reality and undertake fundamental reforms to overhaul dysfunctional markets, will likely do the job. Looming adversity can be a spur to radical change; the threat of a degenerated economy demands a preemptive solution driven by sense of urgency because delay can cause the growing thorny problem to become a veritable gorse bush. Although nothing like a blueprint, leaning on generalities will enable a general configuration of what needs to be done to suggest itself.

The solutions for true recovery require reaching for stars that lie beyond the hangman's noose. While acknowledging an improbable dream, the two "must reach" stars are the star of political reform (to ensure supremacy of the public interest over the business interest when they are in conflict) and the star of market reform (to eliminate plutocratic pseudo-markets and expand effectively competitive open markets). For this to happen it would be necessary to gain acceptance of the paradox that unfettered markets lead to the erosion of competitive free markets and a consequent loss of economic performance. Understanding that plutocratic pseudo-markets are a handbrake on recovery will enable realization that the lever to pull for getting the real economy going must shift from the heavy manipulative hand (in plutocratic pseudo-markets) to the efficient "invisible hand" (in effectively competitive open markets). This line of reasoning is based on the premise that enthroning effectively competitive open markets in economies will stir things up through the infusion of entrepreneurial spirit, and calm things down through the reconciliation of business and social interests.

Cleansing the Augean stables involves purifying corrupted capitalist markets that impede recovery. In mapping a future policy path, governments need to face up to the daunting obstacle to genuine recovery: the nasty business of plutocratic pseudo-markets, where monkey business is normal business. Although late in the day, there seems no alternative to clearing the decks with a clean sweep of plutocratic influence. And that will take a level of courage adequate for bearding the plutocratic lion in its den.

Plutocratic pseudo-markets need to be taken to task with the gloves off. That is needed because they are powerful, entrenched, and have the remarkable capacity to perpetuate their condition by feeding on their own success. They have an unstoppable momentum within the global economy, and this comes with an unkind inclination to tighten the noose around remaining firms in effectively competitive open markets. Such a threat makes protecting entrepreneurial competitive open markets cheap at any price. Courage comes from recognizing that supposed icons of the past that have bitten the dust, are not exactly missed. Take two striking examples: Enron was once revered for revolutionizing the energy business; Lehman Brothers was regarded as the smartest of the smart in business management. The demise of such hypocrites did not signal the end of the world, or even of the economy. Furthermore, battling anti-competitive practices of big business is nothing new. The American presidents Teddy Roosevelt and Woodrow Wilson did so in the early part of the last century as part of an overall effort to tame "robber barons" and improve competitiveness. The Mexican government is presently breaking up its telecoms and media cartels because they impede the efficient functioning of markets, and the Japanese government intends to break-up energy monopolies for the same reason.

The basic idea, then, is to save what is left and regain as much as possible of what is lost. It is crucial to hold the line on open competitive markets by containing pseudo-market forces so that the free market flag can be kept flying in the face of adversity. Protecting and even coddling firms in remaining open competitive markets has an obvious urgency if genuine recovery is the goal. Thereafter, taking bold steps to give open competitive markets pride of place in the economy is the be-all and end-all of measures that must define the shape of things to come. This means that a market overhaul of epic proportions is needed to save capitalism from the capitalists.

The sweep of reforms that are needed to give the economy the desired lift can be easily seen and is theoretically prosaic. Setting things straight is, however, more easily said than done considering the mismatch between the size of the task and the ambition needed to tackle it. This requires having the stomach of a Trojan to take the bull by both horns – political reform and market reform. In Gilbert and Sullivan terms, "faint heart never won fair lady"; a grave crisis calls for gutsy measures, even if it requires a lurch into dreamland. What may seem improbable does not mean that it is impossible, especially when it is essential. The daunting dimensions of the task means reformers have their work cut out for them if they are to blaze a trail.

This is where leadership comes in; leadership that is capable of putting a shoulder to the wheel with a herculean will to succeed seems the key to salvation. While recognizing that hopes for durable economic recovery rest on politically fanciful solutions, looking on the bright side reveals that great societies were built on the dreams of leaders who were are able to move mountains. This refers to leaders who are prime movers, capable of rising to the occasion by straining every nerve to pull out all the stops – then turn the improbable around to fulfill their strategic vision (like, perhaps, Abraham Lincoln and Winston Churchill). The current crisis requires leaders who can gird up their loins and go the distance to perform the class act: replace plutocratic pseudo-markets with effectively competitive open markets that embody entrepreneurial spirit, to accomplish a sturdy recovery for everybody.

When all is said and done, cutting the Gordian knot involves a paradoxical return to basics. We must reach back into history to get what is best for the future; it is an exercise in nostalgia that requires reincarnating the lost fundamentals of Western civilization as envisaged by founders such as John Locke, Thomas Paine, Thomas Jefferson, and Adam Smith. What is required to do the trick is simple in concept: hark back to better times when there was sufficient harmony between business and public interests. This goal is achieved by having an *informed* public, ensconced in the *driver's* seat, ride to a brave new world where the glittering opportunities of truly competitive capitalist open markets await. Replacing ersatz markets with the genuine kind would be a winning solution by virtue of its near-universal appeal from transcending the bitter differences of rigid partisan ideology.

In the light of all that has been written, being over the moon about the future is undoubtedly an over-reaction; the arduous reforms needed would take years to bear fruit. But then, nobody said it was easy. We now have some idea of what a happy ending would need to look like, and that makes what it takes for successful recovery to be less of a surprise. As French minister Charles de Calonne said circa 1783: "The difficult is done at once; the impossible takes a little longer." Hope springs eternal; Rome was not built in a day.

**

# REFERENCES

Acharya, Viral, Thomas F. Cooley, and Matthew P. Richardson (2010) *Regulating Wall Street: The Dodd-Frank Act and the New Architecture of Global Finance*, John Wiley & Sons, Hoboken, NJ.

Australian Associated Press (2012) 'Palmer, Abbot had fierce disagreement', *Sydney Morning Herald*, news.smh.com.au

Acharya, Viral, Matthew P. Richardson, Stijnvan Nieuwerburgh, and Lawrence J. White (2011) *Guaranteed to Fail: Fannie Mae, Freddie Mac and the Debacle of Mortgage Finance*, Princeton University Press, Princeton NJ.

Acharya, Viral, and Rangarajan Sundaram (2009) 'The Financial Sector "Bailout"; Sowing the Seeds of the Nest Crisis', *Financial Markets, Institutions & Instruments*, Vol.18 (May), 180-182.

Admati, Anat and Martin Hellwig (2013) *The Bankers' New Clothes: What's Wrong with Banking and What to Do about it,* Princeton University Press, Princeton NJ.

Arrow, K. (1951) 'Mathematical Models in the Social Sciences', in *The Policy Sciences*, D. Lerner and H.D. Tasswell (eds.) Stanford University Press, Stanford CA.

Barnes, John (2013) Personal communication, Surrey UK.

Boulding Kenneth E. (1973) 'After Samuelson Who Needs Adam Smith', in *Collected Papers, Volume 111*, Colorado Associated University Press, Boulder CO.

Boyer Peter J. and Peter Schweizer (2012) 'Why Can't Obama Bring Wall Street to Justice?'*Newsweek*, May 14.

Bryce Robert (2002) *Pipe Dreams: Greed, Ego, and the Death of Enron*, Perseus Books Group, New York.

Cialdini, Robert (2006) *Influence: The Psychology of Persuasion*, Harper Business, New York.

Coburn, Thomas A. (2012) *The Debt Bomb*, Thomas Nelson, Nashville TN.

Crescenzi, Tony (2012) *Beyond the Keynesian Endpoint*, Pearson Education, Upper Saddle River NJ.

De Soto, J.H. (2010)'Economic Recession, Banking Reform, and the Future of Capitalism', Hayek Memorial Lecture at the London school of Economics and Political Science, The Cobden Centre, UK.

Dingle, Carol A. (2008) *Memorable Quotations: Philosophers of Western Civilization*, Writers Club Books iuniverse, Lincoln NE.

Eavis, Peter (2012) 'US Banks Tally Their Exposure to Europe's Maelstrom', *Investment Banking*, January 29.

Farley, Richard (2012) *New York Times*, May 23, http://dealbook.nytimes.com.

Federal Bureau of Investigation (2012) 'Financial Crimes Report to the Public: Fiscal Years 2010-2011', FBI Reports and Publications, Washington DC.

Financial Crisis Inquiry Commission (2011) 'Conclusions', Report, US Government. Washington DC.

Friedman, Milton (1953) 'The Methodology of Positive Economics' in *Essays in Positive Economics*, University of Chicago Press, Chicago IL.

Fukuyama, Francis (2014) *Political Order and Political Decay: From the Industrial Revolution to Globalization of Democracy*, Farrow, Strauss & Giroux, New York.

Galbraith, J.K (1952) *American Capitalism: The Theory of Countervailing Power*, Houghton Mifflin, Boston MA.

Gardner, David (2011) 'The Age of America Ends in 2016: IMF Predicts the Year China's Economy Will Surpass the US', *The Daily Mail* April 26.

Garnaut, Ross and David Llewellyn-Smith (2009) *The Great Crash of 2008*, Melbourne University Publishing, Melbourne Vic.

Giles, Chris (2012) 'The Bank That Roared', *Financial Times*, July 14-15, 5.

Gray, John N. (1998) *The Delusion of Global Capitalism*, The New Press, 3, New York.

Ibbotson, Roger and Thomas Idzorek (2014) 'Dimensions of Popularity', *Journal of Portfolio Management,* Vol.40, No.5.

International Monetary Fund (2011) Report for Selected Countries, *World Economic Outlook Database*, Washington D.C.

International Monetary Fund (2012) *World Economic Outlook*, April, Washington DC.

James, Simon (1981) *A Dictionary of Economic Quotations*, Barnes and Noble Books, Totowa NJ.

Janicki, Herbert P. and Edward Simpson Prescott (2006) 'Changes in the Size Distribution of US Banks 1960-2005', *Economic Quarterly*, 92/4, Fall, 291-316.

Keen, Steve 2012. 'Economics in the Age of Deleveraging', *Viewpoint, Australian Christian Lobby*8, February.

Keltner, Dacher and Paul Piff (2012) 'Greed Prevents Good', *New York Times*, March 17.

King, Stephen (2013) *When the Money Runs Out: The End of Western Affluence*, Yale University Press, New Haven CT.

Krugman, Paul (2012) *End This Depression Now*, Norton, New York.

Lessig, Lawrence (2011) *Republic, Lost: How Money Corrupts Congress - and a Plan to Stop It*, Hachette Book Group, New York.

Maddison, Angus (2010) *Historical Statistics of the World Economy: 1-2008 AD*, Table 2 GDP Levels1AD2008AD.http://www.99dc.net/maddison/historical_statistics.

Market Watch (2012) 'Breaking News: Corruption and Greed on Wall Street', *Wall Street Journal*, April 26.

Mason, Rowena (2012) 'David Cameron Raises 1.3 Million Pounds from Donor Dinners', *The Telegraph Group*, 22 August.

Mayo, Mike (2011)*Exile on Wall Street: One Analyst's Fight to Save the Big Banks from Themselves*, John Wiley & Sons, Hoboken NJ.

McKendrick, J. (2012) 'The US needs more R&D Spending on Technical Graduates: Government Report', *SmartPlanet*, January 20.

Meadows Donella, Jorgen Randers, Dennis Meadows (2004) *Limits to Growth, The 30-Year Update* xix, Chelsea Green Publishing Company, White River Junction VT.

Morris, R.L., (1954) 'The Position of Economics and Economists in the Government Machine', *Economic Journal* (December) 759.

Muellor, Robert (2009) 'Back to Basics', June, F.B.I. website http//:www.fbi.gov.

Palazzolo, Joe (2011) 'An Ex-FBI Official Explains Lack of Convictions Tied to Financial Crisis', *Wall Street Journal* (December 6).

Piketty, Thomas (2014) *Capital in the Twenty-first Century* (Translated by Arthur Goldhammer), President and Fellows of Harvard College, Boston MS.

Reich, B. Robert (2012) *Beyond Outrage: What Has Gone Wrong With Our Economy and Our Democracy and How to Fix It*, Alfred A. Knopf, New York.

Richter, Franziska, and Peter Whal (2011) 'The Role of the European Central Bank in the Financial Crash and the Crisis in the Eurozone', *World Economy, Ecology & Development,* Berlin.

Rogoff, Kenneth and Carmen Reinhart (2011) 'A Decade of Debt', NBER *Working Paper 16827,* National Bureau of Economic Research, Cambridge MA.

Roubini, Nouriel (2006) 'The Unsustainability of the US Twin Deficits', *Cato Journal*26 (2).

Rowland, Wade (2012) *Greed, Inc: Why Corporations Rule the World and How We Let it Happen,* Arcade Publishing, New York.

Samuel, Nicholas and Janek Ratnatunga (1993) 'Structural Constraints on the Development of Food processing Industries: A New Research Agenda', *Australasian Agribusiness Review*, 1(1) 50-79.

Scheer, Robert (2010) *The Great American Stickup: How the Reagan Republican and Clinton Democrats Enriched Wall Street While Mugging Main Street*, Norton Books, New York.

Schlichter, Detlev (2011) *Paper Money Collapse: The Folly of Elastic Money and the Coming Monetary Breakdown,* John Wiley & Sons, Hoboken NJ.

Schlichter, Detlev (2012) 'What Gives Money Value and is Factional-Reserve Banking Fraud', The Cobden Centre, March 2.

Schmid A. Allan (1994) 'Institutional Law and Economics', *European Journal of Law and Economics*, 1(1) 35-51 doi: 10.1007/B F01540990.

Sester, Brad and Nouriel Roubini (2005) 'How Scary is the Deficit', *Foreign Affairs* (July /August).

Simkovic, Michael (2011) 'Bankruptcy Immunities, Transparency and Capital Structure', Presentation at the World Bank on January 11, *Seton Hall Public Law Research Paper* 1738539.

Smith, Elliot Blair (2008) 'Race to the Bottom...'*Bloomberg,* September 25.

Smith, Yves (2010) *Econned: How Unenlightened Self Interest Undermined Democracy and Corrupted Capitalism*, Palgrave Macmillan, Hampshire.

Stiglitz, Joseph (2010) *Freefall: America, Free Markets, and the Sinking of the World Economy*, W.W. Norton, New York.

Stiglitz, Joseph (2013) *The Price of Inequality: How Today's Divided Society Endangers Our Future*, W.W. Norton, New York.

Stockman, David A. (2013) *The Great Deformation: The Corruption of Capitalism in America,* Perseus Books Group, New York.

Taylor, John B. (2013) *First Principles: Five Keys to Restarting America's Prosperity*, W.W. Norton, New York.

Toffler, Alvin (1965) 'The Future as a Way of Life', *Horizon magazine* V11 (3).

Weissberger, A. (2011) 'Can US Reverse the Decline in R&D Spending: Global Competitiveness at Risk', *Viodi*, February 27.

White, Alasdair (2009) *From Comfort Zone to Performance Management*, ISBN 978-2-930583-01-3. White & Maclean Publishing, Hoeilaart, Belgium.

Wiedemer, Robert A., and Eric Janszen (2006)*America's Bubble Economy,* John Wiley & Sons, Hoboken NJ.

Wiedemer, David, Robert A. Wiedemer, and Cindy S. Spitzer (2011) *Aftershock: Protect Yourself and Profit in the Next Global Financial Meltdown* (2nd Edition), John Wiley & Sons, Hoboken NJ.

Williams Mark T. (2010) *Uncontrolled Risk: The Lessons of Lehman Brothers and How Systemic Risk Can Still Bring Down the Financial World*, McGraw Hill, New York.

\*\*

# Index

accountants: 52,53,72,91,201,213

acquisitions (see mergers)

auditors: 52,53,75,97,213

Australia: 59,112,143,144,153,154, 194,206,209,280

Austrian school of economics: 387


bailouts: 38-39,43,54-55,138,183, 307,352,388,391,403

Bank of England: 22,38,187,326

Barnes, John: 198

Basel: 50-51,352,399

behavioral: 90,181,184,214,247, 393,422

biblical: 54,114,160,344,401

Britain: 79,87,144,154,181,186,194, 198,202,278,298,299,300,314, 317,319,322,326,329,344

budget: 79,117,127,309,339- 340,345-346,426

business culture: 42,47,67,98,211, 259,419

business cycles: 13-15,293

business environment: 60,66-67, 102,116,173,197,417,419


campaign contributions: 139-140, 144-145,277

Canada: 153,206,208

capitalist free markets: 37,78,79, 81-82,96,99

central banks: 21-22,282,284,328, 333,334,335,369,389,423

ceteris paribus: 155, 157,159,177, 217,370,382

China: 79-80,209,225,287-290, 295,304,305-307,315-316, 320,321,330,431,435

City of London: 78,187,233, 238,239

Clinton administration: 118, 121-123,125,132

comfort zone: 12-13,25,333, 335,407

comparative advantage: 199,204

Congress: 29,55,61,105,129,145-146

consumer debt: 18

consumer spending: 31,43,271,
292,316-317,321,346,357,365,
434

contestability (see market
contestability)

credit ratings agencies: 60-65,67,
69,72,250,408,409

criminal: 48,58,63-66,69,70,77,86,
245,253

critical inflection points: 111-112,
127,152,239

culture (see business culture)

culture of corruption: 42,60,72,
211,212,215

deficit: 310,348,354,425,426

deflation: 233,279,298,300-301,
317,332,338,348-349,351,352,
357,361,369,422,424,425,429

democracy: 7,99,136,145,146,147,
192,207,209,398,400-404,416

derivatives: 50,61,73,121,126,186,
189,207,240-241,267,399

directors: 52

Dodd-Frank: 147,207,238-248,
252,253,311,398

dogmatism: 110,238,412

doom loop: 237,265,313-318,
433,434

economic rent: 20,217,223,229,
277,358,363,364,366,372,375,
383,393,415,418,419,420

Enlightenment: 23,97,150

Enron: 36,47,119,125,133,441

ethics: 29,46,48-56,84,88,
93,146,339,439

Europe: 297-303,404,421,422,424,
431,434,435

European Central Bank (ECB):
22,302,326-327

European Union (EU): 291,
302,303

Fannie Mae: 33-35,38,40,68,103,
138,197,418

Federal Bureau of Investigations
(FBI): 57

Federal Reserve Board: 8,18,21,
22,44,62,123,326,330,389

finance economists: 17,28,
149-179,409-410

Financial Crisis Inquiry
Commission (FCIC): 46,57,
61,105,128,140

financial institutions: 27,40-41,
43,54,105,207,265

Fitch Ratings: 60

Freddie Mac (see Fannie Mae)
free trade: 209,227,264,280
Friedman, Milton: 89,154
future shock: 191-192,383

gamesmanship (see oligopolistic
    gamesmanship)
Glass-Steagall: 119,121-124,
    238-248
government debt: 76,138,199,302,
    307-308,311,319,339,340-341,
    344,351,353,358,364,389
Great Depression: 4,14,27,29,30,
    46,49,90,100,108,119,123,125,1
    28,133,203,286,334,346,363,
    414,424,436,438,458
Great Financial Crisis: 7,44,
    240,436
Great Moderation: 8,14
Great Recession: 7,44,436
Greece: 15,79,203,271,296,299,
    302,310,344,348,349,435-436
Greenspan, Alan: 123

household debt (see private debt)
household income: 19,35,110,277,
    317,357,376

ideology: 77-84,105-106,113-115,
    122,135,140-141,309,345,363,
    381,401,437,443

illegal: 43,46,47,48,56-71,72,87,110,
    173,211-213,216,294,408
imperialism: 227,234,251,417
India: 79,80,83,90,153,200,227,295,
    305,306-307,364
inequality: 99-101,270-273,
    283,357
Industrial Revolution: 49,81-82,
    150,378,383,394
industry self-regulation: 67,89,92,
    104-107,115,123,128,129,133-135,
    187
inflation: 22,25,278,300,317,328,
    331-332,336,353,369,389
inflection points (see critical
    inflection points)
institutional economics: 109,153
institutional frameworks: 84-96,
    98-100,102-
    105,107,110,115,130,
    147,156,212,219,223,239,256,
    270,275-276,280,396
interest rates: 23,25,29,33,187,279,
    310,311,324,330,331-333,338,
    389,340,423-424,425
International Monetary fund
    (IMF):
    61,288,290,300,306,348,
    388,424
investment banking: 30,41,59,69,9
    2,124,180,182,183,185,245,399

investor behavior: 17

invisible hand: 58,80,82,83,128,
130,150,158,184,218,235,380,
415,440

Japan: 209,231,232,280,290,295,
304,305,310,318-319,321,329,
331,332,348,431,435,441

Jefferson, Thomas: 135,403,442

Judeo-Christian ethic: 17,32,77-78,
136,210,217,225,339,351

justice: 54,56-74,79,98,140,238,
247,274

Keynesian: 34,234,261,299,341,345,
355,359,365,422

Laissez faire: 82,87,249,415

law of the jungle: 102,115,400

Lehman Brothers: 36-37,38,39,53,
55,59-60,68,418,441

Leontief, Wasilly: 167,169

liberalization: 204

liberty: 39,54,88,97,119,134,135,
136,244

Libor: 106,107,186,187,188,197,212,
238

license: 21,67,101-107,114,127,212,
248,381,412

licentious: 66,102-104,113,114,122,
134,172,177,210,211,212,216,21
7,224,393,394,415,417

life cycle: 249,382,383,386

liquidity trap: 319,331

lobbying (see also lobbyist): 123,
124,139,142-145, 206,208,210,
248,264,311

lobbyist (see also lobbying): 120,
126,127,128,137,139, 147,174,
240,243,251,311,401

Locke, John: 97,98,99,100,103,402,
403,442

Luddite: 62,199-200,203,269

Maddison, Angus: 82

Madoff, Bernard: 66

Main Street: 39,96,124

manipulative hand (see also
market manipulation): 58,128,
130,249,257,380,415,440

market contestability: 149,179,
230-231,269,270

market fundamentalism: 90,
104-105

market manipulation (see also
manipulative hand): 163,
173-174,196

market sovereignty: 35

market structure: 44,84,156,
180-184,191,226-235,255,258,
275,370,380,393-399,415,416
Marshall, Alfred: 140,150,151,
160,167,173,177
Marshall Plan: 296, 431
Marx, Karl: 83
mathematical models (see also
quantitative models): 105,159,
160,162,164,166-171,409
mercantile system (mercantilism): 81,151,152
mergers and acquisitions: 31,181,
191,195,220,226-235,236,255,
256,266,269,272,282,283,284,
375,397,416,418,420
middle class: 4,8,101,200,202,256,
271,282,283,292,306,315,335,36
8,379,380,383,393,405,428,434
monarchy: 403,404
money printing (see quantitative
easing)
Moody's: 60
multinational firms: 90,174,195,
196,197,200,201,208-209,213,
216,220,224,272,294,301,366,
397,419,420

New Deal: 28,108,116,118,119,120,
121,213,190,240,247

new entrants: 186,230-231,250,
257,269,270,273,419

oligopolistic gamesmanship: 93-9
4,143,168,171,179,217,273,375,
409,418
orthodox economics (see standard economics)
own-account trading (see proprietary trading)

Paine, Thomas: 135,404,442
paradox of thrift: 316,433
Pecora Commission: 46
personal debt: 339-342, 344
Pigou, A.C.: 150,167,171
plodding: 130,183,222,229,336,
363,366,382,418,426
plutocracy: 7,129,135,146,147,
204-205,207,209,249,250,
253,276,385,392,397,398,
400,403-404
Political Action Committee
(PAC): 145
political economy: 150-151,165,
170,177,178,179
Ponzi scheme: 66
presidential system: 142,144
private debt: 18,31-32,317,324

private sector: 136,184,236,246,2
79,281,307,316,343,346,351,35
2,359,361,365,425,431
productivity: 77,99,101,149,173,202,
206,215,230,260,270,271,299,
313-316,321,327,363,375,393,
418,433
profit maximization: 6,78,84,
90-91,94,95,150,154,283
proprietary trading: 174,185,186,
240,247,261,267,311
prosecutions: 48,58,69,70
protectionism: 20,204,222,287

qualitative factors: 45,72,73,97,
152,408
quantitative easing: 21, 278,280,
296,298,299-300,302,317,
322,324,325-339,349, 350,351,
355,376,384,395,422,423,429
quantitative factors: 74,408
quantitative models (see
mathematical models)

Reagan administration: 116-118.
122
regulatory architecture: 88,91,97,
112,114,118,239,412
regulatory control: 138,185,207

re-regulation: 238-248,251-252,
273,312,413,414
research and development (R&D):
206,228,259,260,261,263,266,
313-316,321,332
risk management: 30,170,266
Russell, Bertrand: 48

Securities and Exchange
Commission (SEC): 66,71,
126,246,248
securitization bonds: 37,40,41,
50,63
self-regulation (see industry
self-regulation)
shadow banking: 39,49-50,180,
185,186,198,213,241-
242,247,267,289,413,419
share holders: 52,71,86,92,94,95,
201,213,244,259,266, 268,
318,357
small government: 37,136-137,343
Smith, Adam: 82-83,90,151-152,
249,415,442
social science: 150,165,170-171,
175,179,409
Spain: 15,79,100,203,234,289,299,
310-311,344,348,387,435-436
speculation: 17,18,19,24,28,32,
328,410

Standard & Poor's: 60,63-64

standard economics: 10,150,151,
153,155,156-157,161,203,369,
406,414

startups: 232,257,262-263,
266,420

stock markets: 15,19,24,25,28,29,
51,86,88,165,218,261,278,291,
319,327,328,369,389,423

structural change: 181

structural concentration: 181,182,
193,207

sub-prime: 41

teaser rates: 33,36

technology: 81,192,206,230,270,
288,313-316,433

transnational firms (see also
multinational firms): 51,143,
163,177,186,196,197,200,203,
205,218,220,223,224,230,235,
248,281,294,375,393,396,413,
439

underclass: 4,202,271,434

vicious circle: 236,237,416

virtue: 31,32,48,77,84,99,135,163,26
0,270,283,304,309,310,332,339,
341-342,355,365,424,443

Volker Rule: 186,240,247

welfare: 38,81,100,108,136,148,
150,157,167,171,178,298,344,
346,351,409

Westminster parliamentary
system: 140-145

Zombie: 231,235,364,366,393,
418,420

# AUTHOR INFORMATION

Nicholas Samuel is a professional writer, academic, researcher, former research manager and senior policy analyst in the Australian government's economics research bureau. He played a leadership role in the deregulation of Australia's primary industries. He has also held the position of chair professor of agribusiness at the prestigious University of Adelaide and served as the managing editor of a professional journal for several years.

Samuel holds degrees from the London School of Economics and Political Science and Michigan State University, and he has had more than one hundred articles published. His writing has appeared internationally in a variety of professional journals and has been recognized with awards for excellence, by the British Literati Club for published research and by the Chinese government for nationwide pioneering market research on behalf of foreign agribusiness.

Samuel is the author of four books, including a text on applied economics published by Macmillan. His most recent title, *Unending Recovery*, is simple without being superficial and scholarly without being academic; it is a breezy and sharp-witted take on the world's current economic crisis.

**

29017502R00263

Made in the USA
San Bernardino, CA
12 January 2016